PETER NORTON'S®
Essential Concepts

FOURTH EDITION

 Glencoe McGraw-Hill

New York, New York   Columbus, Ohio   Woodland Hills, California   Peoria, Illinois

Library of Congress Cataloging-in-Publication Data

Norton, Peter, 1943—
  [Essential concepts]
  Peter Norton's essential concepts.—4th ed.
    p. cm.
  Includes index.
  ISBN 0-07-822728-3
  1. Computers. 2. Computer software. I. Title.
QA76.3.N6818   2000
004—dc21   00-034101
                      CIP

Glencoe/McGraw-Hill

*A Division of The **McGraw·Hill** Companies*

Send all inquiries to:

Glencoe/McGraw-Hill
21600 Oxnard St. Suite 500
Woodland Hills, CA 91367-4906

ISBN: 0-07-822728-3

3 4 5 6 7 8 9   083   04 03 02

About Peter Norton

Acclaimed computer software entrepreneur Peter Norton is active in civic and philanthropic affairs. He serves on the boards of several scholastic and cultural institutions and currently devotes much of his time to philanthropy.

Raised in Seattle, Washington, Mr. Norton made his mark in the computer industry as a programmer and businessman. *Norton Utilities*™, *Norton AntiVirus*™, and other utility programs are installed on millions of computers worldwide. He is also a best-selling author of computer books.

Mr. Norton sold his PC-software business to Symantec Corporation in 1990 but continues to write and speak on computers, helping millions of people better understand information technology. He and his family currently reside in Santa Monica, California.

Editorial Consultant

Tim Huddleston

Academic Reviewers

Teresa Beatty
ECPI College of Technology

Bill Boroski
Trident Technical College

J. Timothy Dunigan
West Virginia University

Lynn Dee Eason
Sault College

Terry A. Felke
William Rainey Harper College

Mary Hanson
Northwest Technical College

Patrick A. T. Kelly
Mount Royal College

Ron Lenhart
Mohave Community College

Jan L. McDanolds
Hamilton College

Alex Morgan
West Valley College

Cindi A. Nadelman
Naugatuck Valley Community College

Mava F. Norton
Lee University

Ronny Richardson
Southern Polytechnic State University

Annette Sarrazine
College of Lake County

Melissa L. Stoneburner
Moraine Valley Community College
College of DuPage

Wilson E. "Bill" Stroud
Joliet Junior College

Jacqueline Wall
Chaffey College

Technical Reviewers

Barbara Bouton
Bill Brandon
Emmett Dulaney
Kurt Hampe
Molly E. Holzschlag
Steve Probst

Acknowledgments

Others who contributed to the content and development of this project: Sue Coons, Robert Goldhamer, Cynthia Karrasch, Marianne L'Abbate, Elliot Linzer, Purple Monkey Studios, Charles A. Schuler, and Tom White.

Special thanks goes to the individuals at Glencoe/McGraw-Hill whose dedication and hard work made this project possible.

Foreword to the Student

Why Study Computer Technology?

The computer is a truly amazing machine. Few tools can help you perform so many different tasks. Whether you want to track an investment, publish a newsletter, design a building, or practice landing an F14 on the deck of an aircraft carrier, you can use a computer to do it. Equally amazing is the fact that the computer has taken on a role in nearly every aspect of our lives, for example:

◆ Tiny embedded computers control our alarm clocks, entertainment centers, and home appliances.

◆ Today's automobiles could not even start, let alone run efficiently, without embedded computer systems.

◆ In the United States, more than half of all homes now have at least one personal computer, and the majority of those are connected to the Internet.

◆ An estimated ten million people now work from home instead of commuting to a traditional workplace, thanks to PC and networking technologies.

◆ People use e-mail for personal communications nearly ten times as often as ordinary mail, and nearly five times more often than the telephone.

◆ People do an ever-increasing amount of shopping online. During the Christmas season of 1999, an estimated seven billion dollars worth of retail business was conducted over the World Wide Web.

◆ Routine, daily tasks are affected by computer technologies such as banking at automated teller machines, talking over digital telephone networks, and paying for groceries with the help of computerized cashiers.

Here are just a few personal benefits you can enjoy by developing a mastery of computers:

◆ **Improved Employment Prospects.** Computer-related skills are essential in many careers. And this does not apply only to programmers. Whether you plan a career in automotive mechanics, nursing, journalism, or archaeology, computer skills will make you more attractive to prospective employers.

◆ **Skills That Span Different Aspects of Life.** Many people find their computer skills valuable regardless of the setting—at home, work, school, or play. Your computer education's usefulness will not be limited simply to your work.

◆ **Greater Self-Sufficiency.** Those who truly understand computers know that they are tools—nothing more or less. We do not give up control of our lives to computer systems; rather, we use them to suit our needs. By knowing how to use computers, you can actually be a more self-sufficient person, whether you use computers for research, communications, or time-management.

◆ **A Foundation of Knowledge for a Lifetime of Learning.** Basic computing principles have not changed over the past few years, and will be valid well into the future. By mastering fundamental concepts and terminology, you will develop a strong base that will support your learning for years to come.

Regardless of your reasons for taking this course, you are wise to do so. The knowledge and skills you gain should pay dividends in the future, as computers become even more common at home and at work.

VISUAL ESSAY: COMPUTERS IN OUR LIVES

A Millions of people use handheld computers to manage their schedules, send e-mail and faxes, create documents, and more.

B Using 3-D CAD tools, designers can create photorealistic three-dimensional renderings of a finished building's interior and exterior. These capabilities enable the designer and client to visualize the completed project before the first shovel of dirt has been turned.

C Factories use computerized robotic arms to do physical work that is hazardous or highly repetitive.

D Computers have become a creative tool for musicians. The Musical Instrument Digital Interface (MIDI) allows different electronic instruments to be connected to one another, as well as to computers.

E The military is often at the forefront of technology. This man is using an Airborne Warning and Aircraft Control (AWAC) system to track the in-flight progress of missiles and jets. The military also uses computers to keep track of one of the largest payroll and human-resource management systems in the world.

F Perhaps no area of science has benefited more from computer technology—or contributed more to its growth—than the space program.

G Many movies and television productions now use motion-capture technology to enable computer-generated characters to move realistically. Special sensors are attached to an actor, who moves in a tightly choreographed way. Movements are recorded by a computer. The data can then be assigned to the corresponding parts of a digital character's body, so that its movements exactly mimic the actor's movements.

Brief Table of Contents

Table of Contents

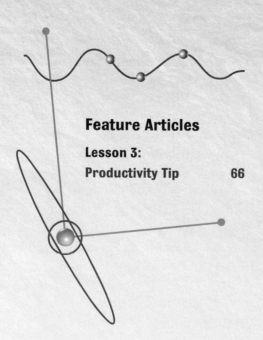

Feature Articles

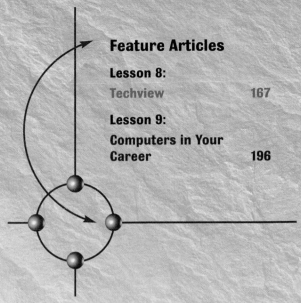

Unit 5: The Internet and Online Resources   182

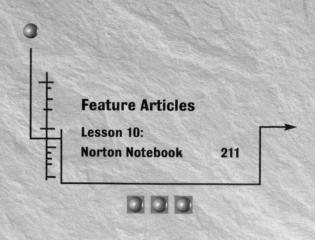

Feature Articles

Lesson 10:

Norton Notebook   211

Feature Articles

Prerequisites

What You Should Know Before Using This Book

This book assumes that you have never used a computer before, or that your computer experience has been very brief. If so, you may need to learn some basic computer skills before proceeding with this course. This section introduces basic skills, using illustrations to help you recognize and remember the hardware or software involved in each skill. Some of these skills are covered in greater detail in other units of this book. In such cases, you will find references that point you to more information.

Equipment Required for This Book's Exercises

- ◆ A personal computer
- ◆ A keyboard
- ◆ A two-button mouse
- ◆ Windows 95, 98, 2000, or NT
- ◆ An Internet connection
- ◆ A Web browser

TURNING THE COMPUTER ON AND OFF

As simple as it may sound, there is a right way to turn a computer's power on and off. If you perform either of these tasks incorrectly, you may damage its components or cause problems for the operating system, programs, or data files.

Turning On the Computer

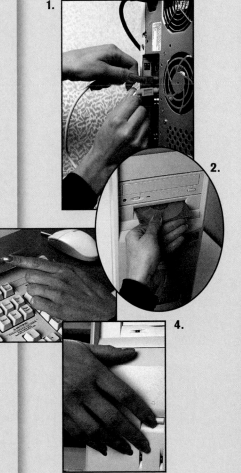

1. Before turning on your computer, make sure that all the necessary cables (such as the mouse, keyboard, printer, etc.) are connected to the system unit. Also make sure that the system's power cords are connected to an appropriate power source.

2. Make sure that there are no diskettes in the computer's diskette drive, unless you must boot the system from a diskette. (The term *booting* means starting the computer.) If you must boot the system from a diskette, ask your instructor for specific directions.

3. Find the On/Off switch on each attached device (the monitor, printer, etc.), and place it in the ON position. A device's power switch may not be on the front panel. If not, check the sides and back.

4. Find the On/Off switch on the computer's system unit—its main box, into which all other components are plugged—and place it in the ON position.

Most computers take a minute or two to start. Your computer may display messages during the start-up process. If one of these messages prompts you to perform an action (such as providing a network user ID and password), ask your instructor for directions. After the computer has started, the Windows desktop will appear on your screen. (See the sample desktop on the following page.)

Turning Off the Computer

For more information on Windows and other operating systems, see Lesson 5, "Operating Systems."

In Windows-based systems, it is critical that you shut down properly, as described here. Windows creates many temporary files on your computer's hard disk when running. By shutting down properly, you give Windows the chance to erase those temporary files and do other "housekeeping" tasks. If you simply turn off your computer while Windows or other programs are running, you can cause harm to your system.

1. Remove any disks from the diskette and CD-ROM drive, and make sure that all data is saved and all running programs are closed. (For help with saving data and closing programs, see your instructor.)

2. Using your mouse pointer, click the Start button, which is located on the taskbar. The Start menu will appear. On the Start menu, click Shut Down. The Shut Down Windows dialog box will appear.

3. In the Shut Down Windows dialog box, select the Shut Down option; then click the OK button.

1.

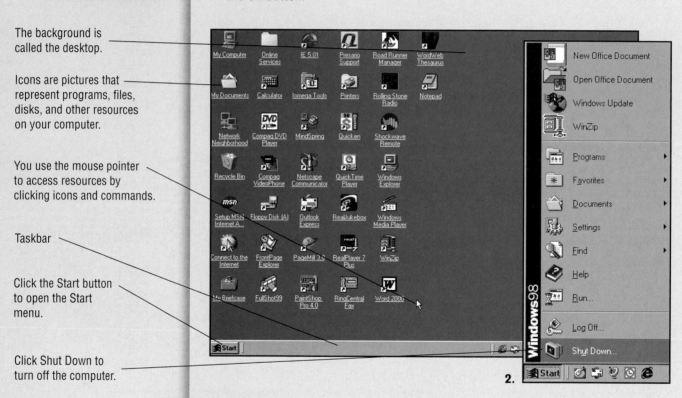

The background is called the desktop.

Icons are pictures that represent programs, files, disks, and other resources on your computer.

You use the mouse pointer to access resources by clicking icons and commands.

Taskbar

Click the Start button to open the Start menu.

Click Shut Down to turn off the computer.

2.

Windows will begin the shut-down process. Windows may display a message telling you that it is shutting down. Then it may display the message "It is now safe to turn off your computer." When this message appears, turn off the power to your system unit, monitor, and printer.

In some newer computers, the system unit will power down automatically after Windows shuts down. If your computer provides this feature, you need to turn off only your monitor and other devices.

3.

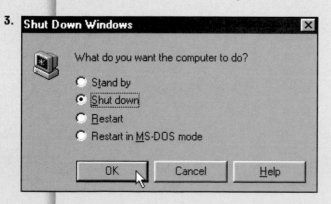

USING THE KEYBOARD

A.

For more information on the keyboard, see Lesson 2, "Interacting With the Computer."

A. If you know how to type, then you can easily use a computer keyboard. The keyboard contains all the alphanumeric keys found on a typewriter, plus some keys that perform special functions.

B. In Windows, the Enter key performs two primary functions. First, it lets you create paragraph ("hard") returns in application programs such as word processors. Second, when a dialog box is open, pressing Enter is like clicking the OK button. This accepts your input and closes the dialog box.

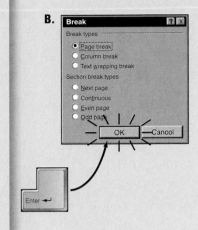

B.

C. The Shift, Ctrl (control), and Alt (alternate) keys are called modifier keys. You use them in combination with other keys to issue commands. In many programs, for example, pressing Ctrl+S (hold the Ctrl key down while pressing the S key) saves the open document to disk. Used with all the alphanumeric and function keys, the modifier keys let you issue hundreds of commands.

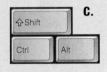

C.

D. In Windows programs, the Esc (escape) key performs one universal function. That is, you can use it to cancel a command before it executes. When a dialog box is open, pressing Esc is like clicking the Cancel button. This closes the dialog box and ignores any changes you made in the dialog box.

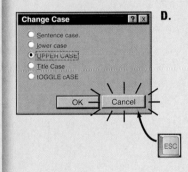

D.

E.

E. Depending on the program you are using, the function keys may serve a variety of purposes or none at all. Function keys generally provide shortcuts to program features or commands. In many Windows programs, for example, you can press F1 to launch the online help system.

F. In any Windows application, a blinking bar—called the cursor, or the insertion point—shows you where the next character will appear as you type. You can use the cursor-movement keys to move the cursor to different positions. As their arrows indicate, these keys let you move the cursor up, down, left, and right.

F. I am what I am. |

Cursor (or insertion point)

Cursor-movement keys

G. The Delete key erases characters to the right of the cursor. The Backspace key erases characters to the left of the cursor. In many applications, the Home and End keys let you move the cursor to the beginning or end of a line, or farther when used with a modifier key. Page Up and Page Down let you scroll quickly through a document, moving back or ahead one screen at a time.

Backspace key

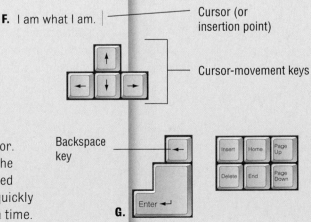

G.

For more information on the mouse and other pointing devices, see Lesson 2, "Interacting With the Computer."

USING THE MOUSE

The mouse makes your computer easy to use. In fact, Windows and Windows-based programs are mouse-oriented, meaning their features and commands are designed for use with a mouse.

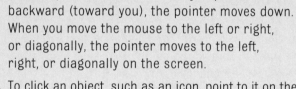

A.

A. This book assumes that you are using a standard two-button mouse. Usually, the mouse's left button is the primary button. You press ("click") it to select commands and perform other tasks. The right button opens special "shortcut menus," whose contents vary according to the program you are using.

B.

B. You use the mouse to move a graphical pointer around on the screen. This process is called pointing.

C. The pointer is controlled by the mouse's motions across your desktop's surface. When you push the mouse forward (away from you), the pointer moves up on the screen. When you pull the mouse backward (toward you), the pointer moves down. When you move the mouse to the left or right, or diagonally, the pointer moves to the left, right, or diagonally on the screen.

C.

❶ When the mouse moves...

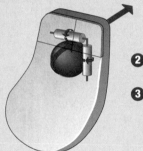

❷ ...the rolling mouse ball spins the rollers.

❸ The information from the spinning rollers is sent to the system software, which controls the pointer.

D. To click an object, such as an icon, point to it on the screen, then quickly press and release the left mouse button one time. Generally, clicking an object selects it, or tells Windows that you want to do something with the object.

E. To double-click an object, point to it on the screen, then quickly press and release the left mouse button twice. Generally, double-clicking an object selects and activates the object. For example, when you double-click a program's icon on the desktop, the program launches so you can use it.

F. To right-click an object, point to it on the screen, then quickly press and release the right mouse button one time. Generally, right-clicking an object opens a shortcut menu that provides options for working with the object.

G. You can use the mouse to move objects around on the screen. For example, you can move an icon to a different location on the Windows desktop. This procedure is often called drag-and-drop editing. To drag an object, point to it, press and hold down the left mouse button, drag the object to the desired location, then release the mouse button.

"click"

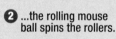

D.

"click click"

E.

"click"

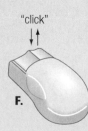

F.

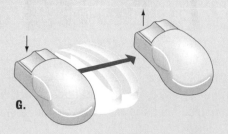

G.

Prerequisites

USING YOUR BROWSER AND THE WORLD WIDE WEB

This book features many Internet-related discussions, as well as exercises and review questions that require you to use the World Wide Web ("the Web"). This section is designed to help you learn the basic steps required for using a browser and navigating the Web.

A. To launch your browser, click the Start button on the Windows taskbar. When the Start menu opens, point to Programs. When the Programs menu opens, find the name of your browser and click it. Your browser will open on your screen.

B. A Web browser is software that enables you to view specially formatted Web pages. This illustration shows Netscape Navigator and names some of the the browser's most important tools.

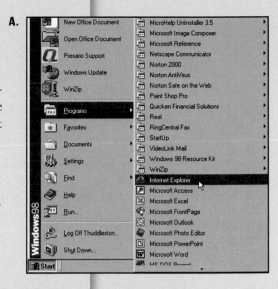

A.

Menu bar

Toolbar

Bookmarks list

Location/Address bar

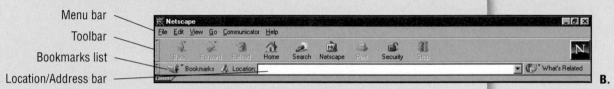

B.

C. You navigate the Web by moving from one Web page to another. A Web page is a document formatted with Hypertext Markup Language (HTML) tags. (A Web site is a collection of related Web pages.) Every Web page has a unique address called a uniform resource locator, or URL (pronounced as spelled: U-R-L). When you provide a URL for the browser, the browser loads that URL's page onto your PC.

C.

http://www.glencoe.com/

D. To navigate to a Web page, type a URL in the Location bar; then press Enter. For example, to go to the White House Web site, click in the Location (or Address) bar and type **http://www.whitehouse.gov/**. Then press Enter.

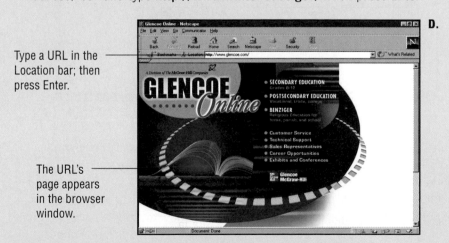

D.

Type a URL in the Location bar; then press Enter.

The URL's page appears in the browser window.

E. A hyperlink is simply a part of the Web page that is linked to a URL. When text has a hyperlink assigned to it, you can click it and "jump" from your present location to the URL specified by the hyperlink. Hyperlinked text looks different from normal text in a Web page; it is usually underlined, but can be formatted in any number of ways. When your mouse pointer touches hyperlinked text, the hyperlink's URL appears in the browser's status bar, and the pointer changes shape to resemble a hand with a pointing index finger (see page xviii).

Unit 5, "The Internet and Online Resources," provides a detailed look at many aspects of the Internet.

The mouse pointer is resting on hyper-linked text.

If you click the hyperlink, the browser will open the page with the URL shown on the status bar.

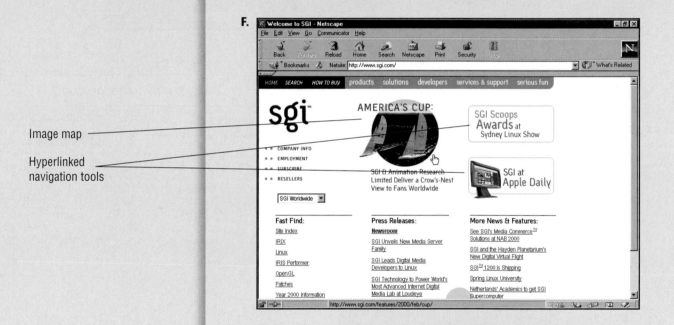

Image map

Hyperlinked navigation tools

F. Many Web pages provide pictures or graphical buttons—called navigation tools—that direct you to different pages, making it easier to find the information you need. Another popular tool is the image map, a single image that provides multiple hyperlinks. You can click on different parts of the image map to jump to different pages. When your mouse pointer touches a navigation tool or image map, it turns into a hand pointer, and the hyperlink's URL appears in the status bar of your browser.

G. The Back and Forward buttons return you to recently viewed pages, similar to flipping through a magazine. The Back button returns you to the previously opened Web page. After you use the Back button, you can click Forward to move forward again, returning to the last page you opened before you went back.

G.

Back   Forward

H. If you have saved any book-marks to pages you have visited earlier, you can open the Bookmarks (or Favorites) list, select a bookmark, and quickly return to that page.

I. When you type URLs into the Location bar, your browser saves them, creating a history list for the current session. You can choose a URL from this list and return to a pre-viously opened page without having to use the Back button or any other tools.

J. To close your browser, open the File menu and choose Close. You also can close the browser by clicking the Close button on the title bar. It may be necessary to close your Internet connection, too.

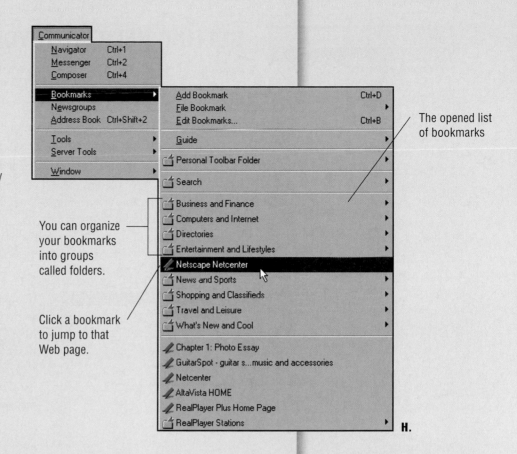

The opened list of bookmarks

You can organize your bookmarks into groups called folders.

Click a bookmark to jump to that Web page.

H.

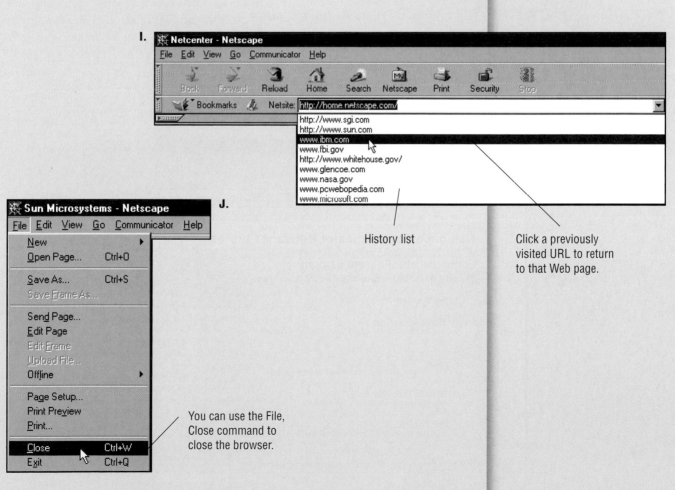

History list

Click a previously visited URL to return to that Web page.

You can use the File, Close command to close the browser.

1.

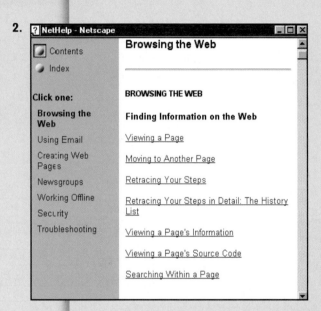

GETTING HELP WITH YOUR BROWSER

Although most browsers are easy to use, you may need help at some point. Newer browsers provide comprehensive Help systems, which can answer many of your questions about browsing and the World Wide Web.

1. Open the browser's Help menu, then choose Contents. (Depending on your browser, this option may be called Help Contents, Contents and Index, or something similar.)

2. A Help dialog box appears, listing all the topics for which help or information are available. Look through the list of topics and choose the one that matches your interest. When you are done, click the Close button on the window's title bar.

2.

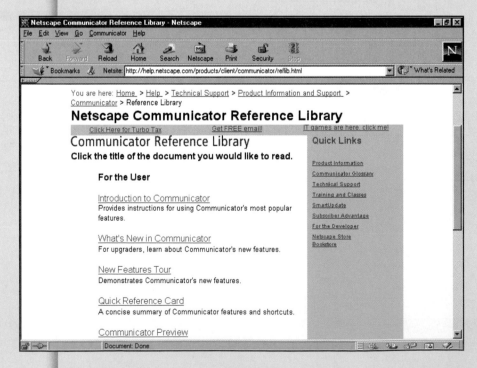

To get help from your browser maker's Web site, open your browser's Help menu and look for an option that leads you to the product's Web site. (In Netscape Navigator, you can get Web-based help information by clicking the Reference Library, Release Notes, or Product Information and Support options. In Microsoft Internet Explorer, click the Online Support option.) The resulting Web page will provide access to a knowledgebase of questions and answers, lists of frequently asked questions, links to help topics, and methods for getting in-depth technical support.

PETER NORTON'S®
Essential
Concepts

FOURTH EDITION

 **Glencoe**
McGraw-Hill

New York, New York   Columbus, Ohio   Woodland Hills, California   Peoria, Illinois

UNIT 1

The Computer and You

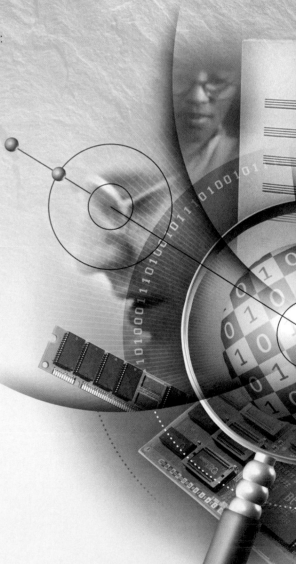

An Overview of Computer Systems

OVERVIEW:
Dissecting the Ultimate Machine

Have you ever watched an incredible scene in a movie or seen a drawing that looked so realistic you thought it was a photograph? Afterward, were you amazed to learn that it was done on a computer? If so, you are certainly not alone. We are endlessly surprised by the feats accomplished with the help of computers, and we marvel at their complexity. For this reason, many people assume that computers must be difficult to understand and use. Most of us do not realize, however, that computers are basically simple devices, and all computers have a great deal in common. Most computers—from the biggest to the smallest—operate on the same fundamental principles. They are all fabricated from the same basic types of components, and they all need instructions to run.

As a first step toward understanding and learning to use computers, this lesson gives you a peek at these fascinating machines. You will learn about the types of hardware that all computers use, and the types of software that make them run.

OBJECTIVES

- Name the four parts of a computer system.
- Identify four types of computer hardware.
- List five units of measure for computer memory and storage.
- Differentiate the two main categories of computer software.
- Differentiate the five most common types of computer systems.

THE COMPUTER SYSTEM DEFINED

What is a computer? In general terms, a **computer** is an electronic device used to process data, converting it into information that is useful to people. Any computer—regardless of its type—is controlled by programmed instructions, which give the machine a purpose and tell it what to do.

Computers come in many varieties, including the common **personal computer** or **PC** (designed to be used by just one person at a time). Other examples are tiny computers built into appliances and automobiles, and mainframe machines used to run businesses. Despite their differences in size and use, all these computers are part of a system. A complete **computer system** consists of four parts: hardware, software, data, and people (see Figure 1.1).

Figure 1.1
The computer system.

The mechanical devices that make up the computer are called **hardware.** In other words, hardware is any part of the computer you can touch. Hardware consists of interconnected electronic devices that you can use to control the computer's operation, input, and output. (The generic term **device** refers to any piece of hardware.)

Software (also known as **programs**) is a set of electronic instructions consisting of complex codes that make the computer perform tasks. Software tells the computer what to do. Some programs exist primarily for the computer's use and help the computer perform and manage its own tasks. Other types of programs exist primarily for the user and enable the computer to perform tasks, such as creating documents or drawing pictures.

Data consists of raw facts, which the computer stores and reads in the form of numbers. The computer manipulates data according to the instructions contained in the software and then forwards it for use by people or another computer. Data can consist of letters, numbers, sounds, or images. No matter what kind of data is entered into a computer, however, the computer converts it to numbers. Computerized data is **digital;** that is, it has been reduced to digits, or numbers.

Within the computer, data is organized into files. A computer **file** is simply a set of data or program instructions that has been given a name. A file that the user can open and use is often called a **document.** Although you may think of documents simply as text, a computer document can include many kinds of data. For example, a computer document can be a text file (such as a letter), a group of numbers (such as a budget), a video clip (which includes images and sounds), or any combination of these items. Programs are organized into files as well, but because programs are not considered data, they are not document files.

People are the computer operators, also known as **users.** It can be argued that some computer systems are complete without a person's involvement; however, no

computer is totally autonomous. Even if a computer can do its job without a person sitting in front of it, people still design, build, program, and repair computer systems. This lack of autonomy is especially true of personal computers, which are the focus of this book and which are designed for use by people.

HARDWARE: THE NUTS AND BOLTS OF THE MACHINE

The computer itself—the hardware—has many parts, but the critical components fall into one of four categories (see Figure 1.2):

1. Processor **3.** Input and output devices

2. Memory **4.** Storage

While any type of computer system contains these four types of hardware, this book focuses on hardware typically found in a personal computer.

The Processor

The procedure that transforms raw data into useful information is called **processing.** To perform this transformation, the computer uses two components: the processor and memory. (In Unit 2, you will learn how the computer uses instructions and how the computer's special language—the binary number system—enables a computer to represent data.)

The **processor** is like the brain of the computer in the way that it organizes and carries out instructions that come from either the user or the software. In a personal computer, the processor usually consists of one or more **microprocessors** (sometimes called "chips"), which are slivers of silicon or other material etched with many tiny electronic circuits. To process data, the computer passes electricity through the circuits to complete an instruction.

As shown in Figure 1.3, the microprocessor is plugged into the computer's motherboard. The **motherboard** is a rigid rectangular card containing the circuitry that connects the processor to the other hardware.

Figure 1.2
Types of hardware devices.

Figure 1.3
Processing devices.

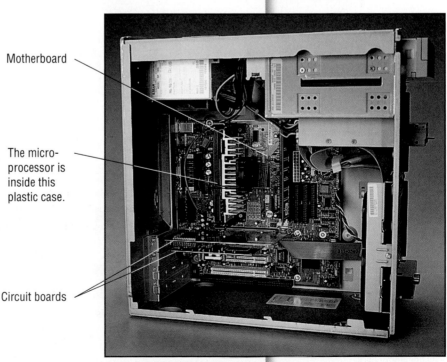

Motherboard

The microprocessor is inside this plastic case.

Circuit boards

Figure 1.4

The processors of modern personal computers are small, considering the amount of processing power they provide. Early PC microprocessors were not much larger than a thumbnail. Processors like Intel's Pentium III are somewhat larger.

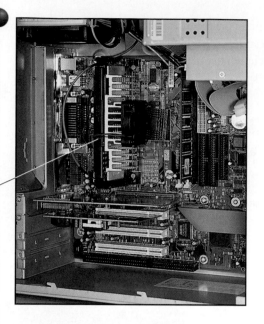

Central processing unit

The motherboard is an example of a **circuit board.** In most personal computers, many internal devices—such as video cards, sound cards, disk controllers, and other devices—are housed on their own smaller circuit boards, which are attached to the motherboard. Newer microprocessors, such as Intel's Pentium III, are large and complex enough to require their own dedicated circuit boards, which plug into a special slot in the motherboard. (Older PC microprocessors were single chips.) You can think of the motherboard as the master circuit board in a computer. Note that in newer personal computers, some devices are built directly onto the motherboard instead of being attached to it as a separate circuit board. This development promises to make computers smaller, faster, and less expensive.

As mentioned earlier, a personal computer's processor is usually a single chip or a set of chips contained on a circuit board. In some powerful computers, the processor consists of many chips and the circuit boards on which they are mounted. In either case, the term **central processing unit (CPU)** refers to a computer's processor (see Figures 1.4 and 1.5).

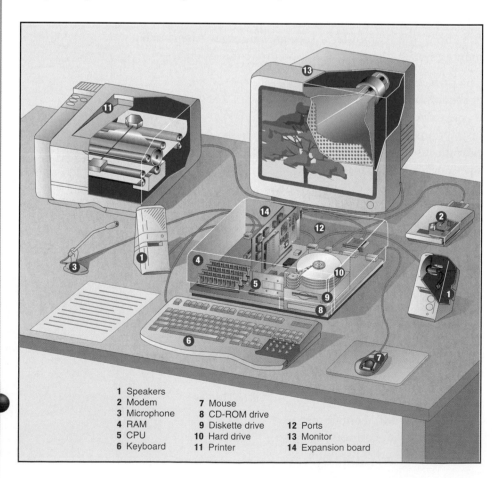

1 Speakers		
2 Modem	7 Mouse	
3 Microphone	8 CD-ROM drive	
4 RAM	9 Diskette drive	12 Ports
5 CPU	10 Hard drive	13 Monitor
6 Keyboard	11 Printer	14 Expansion board

Figure 1.5

Most personal computer systems include the types of hardware components shown here.

Memory

Memory is like an electronic scratch pad inside the computer. When you launch a program, it is loaded into and run from memory. Data used by the program is also loaded into memory for fast access. As you enter new data into the computer, it is also stored in memory—but only temporarily. The most common type of memory is called **random access memory,** or **RAM** (see Figures 1.5 and 1.6). As a result, the term *memory* is commonly used to mean RAM. (It is also sometimes called read/write memory because data is both written to and read from this memory.)

Perhaps the most important thing to remember about RAM is that it is volatile, which means that when you turn off your PC, everything in RAM disappears. For this reason, RAM needs a constant supply of power. The fact that RAM is volatile is why you should frequently save your data files to a storage device.

One of the most important factors affecting the speed and power of a computer is the amount of RAM it has. Generally, the more RAM a computer has, the more it can do and the faster it can perform certain tasks. The most common measurement unit for describing a computer's memory is the **byte**—the amount of memory it takes to store a single character, such as a letter of the alphabet or a numeral. When people talk about memory, the numbers are often so large that it is useful to use terms such as **kilobyte, megabyte, gigabyte,** and **terabyte,** which are defined in Table 1.1.

Figure 1.6
Random access memory (RAM).

RAM

Table 1.1	Units of Measure for Computer Memory and Storage			
Unit	Abbreviation	Pronounced	Approximate Value (bytes)	Actual Value (bytes)
Kilobyte	KB	KILl-uh-bite	1,000	1,024
Megabyte	MB	MEHG-uh-bite	1,000,000 (1 million)	1,048,576
Gigabyte	GB	GIG-uh-bite	1,000,000,000 (1 billion)	1,073,741,824
Terabyte	TB	TERR-uh-bite	1,000,000,000,000 (1 trillion)	1,099,511,627,776

Today's personal computers commonly have from 64 to 128 million (or 64 to 128 MB) bytes of memory. Newer generations of PCs feature more RAM than previous generations did because newer versions of operating systems and application software require ever-increasing amounts of RAM to operate efficiently. Adding RAM is a relatively inexpensive way to boost a system's overall performance. As a rule of thumb, therefore, the more RAM a computer has, the better. Note, too, that it is usually possible to add more RAM to a standard computer; some newer systems can be upgraded to nearly 1 GB of RAM.

Input and Output Devices

Computers would be useless if they did not provide interaction with users. They could not receive instructions or deliver the results of their work. **Input devices**

NORTON
ONLINE

Visit **www.glencoe.com/norton/online/** for more information on **RAM.**

accept data and instructions from the user or from another computer system (such as a computer on the Internet). **Output devices** return processed data back to the user or to another computer system. (You will learn more about specific types of input and output devices in Lesson 2.)

The most common input device is the **keyboard,** which accepts letters, numbers, and commands from the user. Another popular input device is the **mouse,** which lets you select options from on-screen menus. You use a mouse by moving it across a flat surface and pressing its buttons. Other popular input devices are trackballs, touchpads, joysticks, scanners, digital cameras, and microphones. The keyboard, mouse, and microphone are labeled in Figure 1.7.

Figure 1.7
The keyboard, mouse, and micro-phone are common input devices. Practically any new computer will come equipped with these three devices.

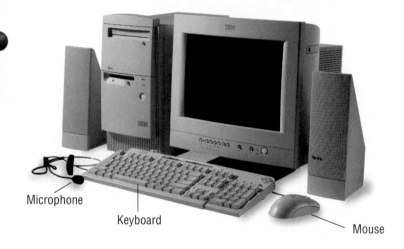

Microphone

Keyboard

Mouse

NORTON
ONLINE

Visit **www.glencoe.com/norton/online/** for more information on **input and output devices** of all types.

The most common output devices are the display screen, known as the **monitor,** and the **printer.** The computer sends output to the monitor when the user needs only to see the output. It sends output to the printer when the user needs a paper copy—also called a hard copy. Computers can accept sound as input, and they can use stereo speakers or headphones as output devices to produce sound. A monitor, a printer, and speakers are labeled in Figure 1.8.

Some types of hardware, such as **communications devices,** can act as both input and output devices. Communications devices connect one computer to another—a process known as networking. Among the many kinds of communications devices, the most common are modems, which enable computers to send information through telephone lines or cable television systems, and network interface cards (NICs), which let users connect a group of computers to share data and devices. (You will learn more about communications devices and networking in Lesson 4, "Networking Basics.")

Storage

A computer can function with only processing, memory, input, and output devices. To be really useful, however, it also needs a place to keep program files and data when it is not using them. The purpose of **storage** is to hold data and programs permanently.

Think of storage as an electronic file cabinet and RAM as an electronic worktable. When you need to work with a program or a set of data, the computer locates it in the file cabinet and puts a copy on the table. After you have finished working with the program or data, you put it back into the file cabinet. If you make changes

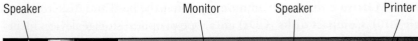

Speaker   Monitor   Speaker   Printer

Figure 1.8
The monitor, printer, and speakers are common output devices. Most new computers come equipped with a monitor and speakers. A printer is usually added to the computer system at extra cost.

to data while working on it, the changed data replaces the original data in the file cabinet (unless you put it in a different place in storage). There are three major distinctions between storage and memory:

A. There is more room in storage than in memory.

B. Contents are retained in storage when the computer is turned off. The programs and data you put into memory disappear when you shut down the computer.

C. Storage is very slow compared to memory, but it is much cheaper than memory.

Remember the distinction between storage and memory. Their functions are similar, but they work in different ways. Novice computer users often use the term *memory* when they actually mean *storage* or *disk*. This mistake can cause confusion.

The most common storage medium is the **magnetic disk.** A disk is a round, flat object that spins around its center. **Read/write heads,** which are similar to the heads of a tape recorder or VCR, are used to read data from the disk or write data onto the disk. Depending on the type of disk, the read/write heads may float just above the disk's surface or may actually touch the disk.

The device that holds a disk is called a **disk drive.** Some disks are built into the drive and are not meant to be removed; other kinds of drives enable you to remove and replace disks. Most personal computers have at least one nonremovable **hard disk** (or **hard drive**). In addition, there is also a **diskette drive,** which allows you to use removable **diskettes.** A hard disk can store far more data than a diskette can, so the hard disk serves as the computer's primary filing cabinet. Diskettes are used to load new programs or data onto the hard disk, trade data with other users, and make backup copies of the data on the hard disk.

Because you can remove diskettes from a computer, they are encased in a plastic or vinyl cover to protect them from fingerprints and dust. In older diskettes, this cover was thin, making the diskette seem flimsy, or "floppy." As a result, they came to be called **floppy disks** (see Figure 1.9).

Figure 1.9
Over the years, diskettes have shrunk while their capacity has increased greatly. The newest 3.5-inch diskette can hold more data than the older, larger diskettes.

The **CD-ROM drive** is the most common type after the hard and diskette drives (see Figure 1.10). **Compact disks (CDs)** are a type of optical storage device, identical to audio CDs, that can store about 74 minutes of audio or 650 MB of data, or about 450 times as much information as a diskette. The commercial type used in

Figure 1.10
Standard storage devices on most new computers include a hard disk, a floppy disk drive, and either a CD-ROM or DVD-ROM drive.

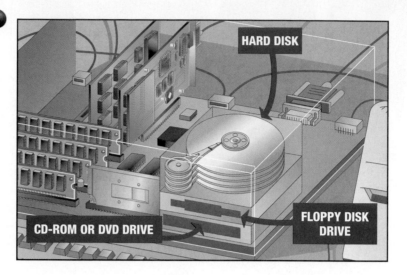

computers is called **Compact Disk Read-Only Memory (CD-ROM).** The name implies that you cannot change the information on the disk, just as you cannot record over an audio CD.

If you purchase a **CD-Recordable (CD-R)** drive, you have the option of creating your own CDs. A CD-R drive can write data to and read data from a compact disk. To write data, you must use a special CD-R disk, which can be written on only once, or a **CD-ReWritable (CD-RW)** disk, which can be written to multiple times.

An increasingly popular data storage technology is the **digital versatile disk** or **digital video disk (DVD),** which is revolutionizing home entertainment. Using sophisticated compression technologies, a single DVD (which is the same size as a standard compact disk) can store an entire full-length movie. DVDs can hold a minimum of 4.7 GB of data and as much as 17 GB. Future DVD technologies promise much higher storage capacities on a single disk. DVD drives can also locate data on the disk much faster than standard CD-ROM drives.

Figure 1.11
DVD players are now standard on many PCs.

NORTON ONLINE

Visit **www.glencoe.com/norton/online/** for more information on **storage** and **disks.**

DVDs require a special player (see Figure 1.11). The new players, however, can play audio, CD-ROM, and DVD disks, freeing the user from purchasing different players for each type of disk.

DVD drives are now standard equipment on many new personal computers. Users not only install programs and data from their standard CDs, but they can also watch movies on their PCs by using a DVD.

Answer the following questions by filling in the blank(s).

1. A(n) _____ is an electronic device used to process data.

2. There is more room in storage than in _____ in a computer.

3. A device that holds a disk is called a(n) _____ .

SOFTWARE: BRINGING THE MACHINE TO LIFE

NORTON ONLINE

Visit **www.glencoe.com/norton/online/** for more information on **operating systems**.

Computers are general-purpose machines; they can be applied to many different kinds of tasks. The ingredient that enables a computer to perform tasks is software, which consists of electronic instructions. These instructions tell the machine's physical components what to do; without them, a computer could not do anything at all. A specific set of instructions that drives a computer to perform a specific task is called a program. When a computer is using a particular program, it is said to be **running** or **executing** that program.

Although the array of programs available is vast and varied, most software falls into two major categories: **system software** and **application software** (see Figure 1.12). One major type of system software, the **operating system,** tells the computer how to use its own components. Examples of operating systems include Windows 2000, Windows NT, the Macintosh Operating System, UNIX, and DOS.

Application software tells the computer how to accomplish specific tasks, such as word processing or drawing, for the user. Examples of popular application programs are Microsoft Word, CorelDRAW, and Netscape Navigator.

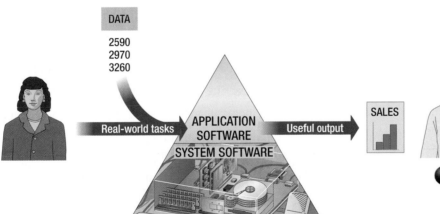

DATA

2590
2970
3260

Real-world tasks

APPLICATION SOFTWARE
SYSTEM SOFTWARE

Useful output

SALES

Figure 1.12
Application software and system software.

Operating Systems

When you turn on a computer, it goes through several steps to prepare itself for use. The first step is called the power-on self test (POST). The computer identifies the devices attached to it, calculates the amount of memory available, and determines whether the memory is functioning properly. This routine is initiated by a part of the system software located in **read-only memory (ROM),** a chip that contains brief, permanent instructions for starting the computer.

Next, the computer looks for an operating system, which is usually stored on the hard disk. The operating system tells the computer how to interact with the user and how to use devices such as the disk drives, keyboard, and monitor. When it finds the operating system, the computer loads a portion of it into memory. Because the operating system is necessary for controlling the computer's most basic functions, it continues to run until the computer is turned off.

After the computer finds and runs the operating system, it is ready to accept commands from an input device—usually the keyboard or a mouse—or from a program. At this point, the user can issue commands to the computer. A command might, for example, list the programs stored on the computer's disk or make the computer run one of those programs. Table 1.2 shows the process the computer follows at startup.

Table 1.2	The Startup Process	
Step	**Source of Instruction**	**Type of Instruction**
1	ROM	System self-check
2	Hard disk	System software loaded into memory
3	User	Controls hardware by issuing operating system commands or loads an application from a disk

Application Software

The operating system exists mostly for the benefit of the computer. Application software is required to make the computer useful for people, and it has been written to do almost every task imaginable. Here are some of the major categories of these applications:

◆ Word processing software for creating text-based documents such as letters

◆ Spreadsheets for creating numeric-based documents such as budgets

◆ Database management software for manipulating large sets of data

◆ Presentation programs for creating and presenting electronic slide shows

◆ Graphics programs for designing illustrations, manipulating photographs, etc.

◆ Multimedia authoring applications for building digital movies that incorporate sound, video, animation, and interactive features

◆ Entertainment and education software, many of which are interactive

◆ Web design tools and Web browsers, and other Internet applications such as newsreaders and e-mail programs

◆ Utilities that perform special tasks such as checking for viruses or sending a fax

◆ Games for a single player or multiple players

◆ Programming languages, such as C++, Visual Basic, and Java, which allow the user to create new applications

◆ Networking and communication software that let computers connect to one another and exchange data

NORTON
ONLINE

Visit **www.glencoe.com/norton/online/** for more information on all kinds of **application software**.

THE SHAPES OF COMPUTERS TODAY

Computers come in many sizes and ranges of power, and different types of computer systems have varying capabilities. Basically, today's computer systems fall into five categories (examples of these categories are illustrated on pages 14 and 15):

◆ **Supercomputers** are the most powerful computers made, and physically they are some of the largest. With the capability of performing billions of operations each second, these systems are devoted to some of the most complex computing tasks imaginable.

◆ **Mainframe computers** are used in large organizations where many people need access to the same information. In a traditional mainframe environment, each user works at a computer **terminal**—a monitor and a keyboard (and sometimes a pointing device, such as a mouse) wired to the mainframe.

There are basically two types of terminals. A dumb terminal does not have its own CPU or storage devices; these components are housed in the mainframe's system unit and are shared by all users. Each dumb terminal is simply an **input/output (I/O) device** that functions as a window into a computer located somewhere else. An intelligent terminal has its own processor and can perform some processing operations but does not usually provide any storage. Full-featured personal computers, instead of dumb or intelligent terminals, are more and more often being attached to mainframe systems.

◆ **Minicomputers** got their name at the time of their introduction in the 1960s because of their small size compared to other computers of the day. A minicomputer's capabilities are somewhere between mainframes and personal computers. For this reason, minicomputers are increasingly being called midrange computers.

Like mainframes, minicomputers can handle much more input and output than personal computers can. Although some minicomputers are designed for a single user, most are designed to handle multiple terminals. The most powerful minicomputers can serve the input and output needs of hundreds of users at a time. Like mainframes, minicomputers support attached terminals or personal computers.

◆ **Workstations** are specialized, single-user computers with many of the features of a personal computer but with the processing power of a minicomputer. Workstations typically use advanced processors and feature more RAM and storage capacity than personal computers. Workstations often have large, high-resolution monitors and accelerated graphics-handling capabilities, making them perfect for advanced design, animation, and video editing. Workstations are also used as servers on personal computer networks and as Web servers.

◆ **Microcomputers**—also called personal computers (PCs)—are the most widely used kind of computer today. The microcomputer category has grown tremendously and there are now several categories of microcomputers, each with its own capabilities, features, and purposes. Types of microcomputers include full-size desktop and tower models, **notebook computers** (also called **laptop computers**), **network computers (NCs),** and **handheld personal computers (H/PCs)** of various configurations.

NORTON
ONLINE

Visit **www.glencoe.com/norton/online/** for more information on **mainframe computers, supercomputers, minicomputers, workstations,** and **personal computers.**

VISUAL ESSAY: A COMPUTER FOR EVERY JOB

A

Supercomputers process huge amounts of data, and the fastest can perform more than 1 trillion calculations per second. This speed and power make supercomputers ideal for handling complex problems that require extreme calculating power, such as forecasting global weather patterns, analyzing nuclear fission, and mapping the human genome. This supercomputer is a Cray T90.

B

A mainframe system can house an enormous volume of data, literally millions of records. Large mainframe systems can handle the input and output requirements of several thousand terminals. The largest IBM S/390 mainframe, for example, can support 50,000 users simultaneously while executing more than 1,600,000,000 instructions per second.

C

Minicomputers are commonly used in network environments, handling the data-sharing needs of other computers on the network. Dozens or hundreds of personal computers can be connected to a network with a minicomputer acting as a server. Like mainframes, midrange computers are used as Web servers, handling thousands of transactions per day. Single-user minicomputers are commonly applied to sophisticated design tasks, such as animation and video editing. The HP 3000 shown here is a popular midrange computer used by medium- and large-sized businesses.

D

The traditional desktop model PC features a horizontally oriented system unit, on top of which many users place the monitor. Vertically oriented tower system units are also available for PCs.

E

The iMac is one of the more recent lines of personal computers from Apple.

F

F

Although this system looks like a personal computer, it is actually a powerful Ultra 60 workstation from Sun Microsystems.

G

As their name implies, notebook computers are about the shape of an 8.5- by 11-inch notebook. Also called laptop computers, they can operate on alternating (plug-in) current or special batteries. As shown here, some notebook systems can be plugged into a docking station (also called an expansion base). Docking stations provide ports that enable the notebook computer to connect to different devices in the same manner as a desktop system.

H

A network computer (NC) is a less powerful version of a personal computer, with minimal processing power, memory, and storage. Some types of network computers provide no storage at all. Network computers are designed to be connected to a network, a corporate intranet, or the Internet. The NC relies on the network for software and data storage and may even use the network's server to perform some processing tasks. The Sun JavaStation, shown here, is one type of network computer.

I

Many handheld personal computers (H/PCs) look like miniature notebook computers, with small displays and keyboards, but they are much smaller than even the tiniest full-featured notebook PC. Most H/PC systems do not provide disks, but memory can be added through PC Cards or other means. Software is abundant for these devices, most of which are Internet-capable and can connect to a full-size computer to exchange data. Many popular H/PC systems, like the HP Jornada shown here, provide various software packages and communications capabilities.

Molecule-Sized Computers?

Personal computing devices are getting smaller all the time. In fact, new types of limited-function handheld devices are not much larger than a credit card. These devices offer personal information management features by storing date book and contact information for their users. At some point, however, devices of that size (or even smaller) may offer the same computational power and features as today's most powerful desktop PCs.

But how small can computers be? Researchers are already answering that question by developing complete computer systems not much larger than a match head and chemical-based transistors so tiny that they function at the molecular level.

A Web Server on a Chip

In the summer of 1999, a graduate student at the University of Massachusetts announced that he had created a complete computer system not much larger than a match head—and for less than a dollar. H. Shrikumar's invention uses 512 bytes of program ROM and 16 bytes of RAM in a standard microprocessor chip. It can store enough data and instructions to host a complete Web server, which connects directly to the Internet. You can visit the Web site at **http://enablery.org/iPic**. The pages on this Web site are all served directly from this tiny computer.

Shrikumar's creation—named iPic—was not the first tiny microcomputer, but it proved that small computing devices can be made affordably and with enough power to perform various applications. For example, a mass-produced version of iPic (or a similar system) can be placed inside many kinds of appliances, enabling them to be connected by a network and accessed through the Internet.

Shrikumar envisions a home or workplace where all electronic appliances are networked together and all are controlled through a customized Web page. In his vision, a homeowner can open the Web page in a browser and make selections that turn lights on or off, set timers, adjust the home's temperature, activate security systems, set the VCR to record a program, and perform many other tasks. Because the iPic is so small and cheap, it is easy to imagine a house filled with such networked

appliances that are remotely controlled via a handheld device, such as a handheld computing device with an Internet connection.

Dress Yourself in Processors

Meantime, researchers at Hewlett-Packard Research Laboratories and the University of California at Los Angeles announced breakthroughs that may give the term *microcomputer* an entirely new meaning. In these systems, still in the theoretical stages, basic computer components are created from special chemical compounds rather than silicon and metal. The potential result

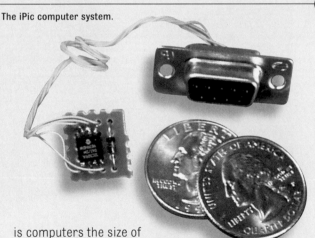

The iPic computer system.

is computers the size of molecules. Scientists foresee "stitching" these molecules together to create supercomputers that can sit in the palm of your hand. Computerized "fabrics" may someday be incorporated into clothing. In theory, computers can become part of anything. Such computers could take innumerable forms, and they could perform countless functions. Huge warehouses of data could be stored digitally in a device the size of a shoebox, with any byte instantly available.

Molecular-scale computer systems will not materialize soon, probably not for decades. Nonetheless, their promise is exciting, especially when you consider that a molecular computer—containing billions of molecules—could be more powerful than all the computers now running put together.

LESSON QUIZ

True/False

Answer the following questions by circling True or False.

True   False   **1.** To be considered complete, a computer system needs only hardware and software.

True   False   **2.** In a personal computer, the processor consists of one or more microprocessors.

True   False   **3.** When a computer is using a program, it is said to be processing the program.

True   False   **4.** Mainframe computers support only one user at a time.

True   False   **5.** Another name for a minicomputer is midrange computer.

Multiple Choice

Circle the word or phrase that best completes each sentence.

1. _____ is a set of electronic instructions that tells the computer what to do.
   A. Software   **B.** A program   **C.** Both A and B

2. The most common type of computer memory is called _____ .
   A. storage   **B.** RAM   **C.** neither A nor B

3. One major type of system software is called _____ .
   A. operating system software   **B.** application software   **C.** a program

4. In a traditional mainframe environment, each user works at a(n) _____ .
   A. network computer   **B.** terminal   **C.** H/PC

5. A _____ is a less powerful version of a PC, designed especially for use on a network.
   A. handheld computer   **B.** cellular phone   **C.** network computer

LESSON LABS

Complete the following exercises as directed by your instructor.

1. Using a computer, label each external device you can identify. Name each device and categorize it by type (storage, input, output). Of the types of devices described in this lesson, how many does your computer have? Are any significant devices missing?

2. With your instructor's help, remove the cover from a computer. Make a diagram of the computer's internal components and label as many of them as you can.

3. With your intructor's help, turn on a computer and watch the screen carefully as the system starts up. What do you see? Does the PC provide information about itself during the startup process? If so, what types of information can you gather about the system? Can you tell how much memory it has? What operating system does it use, and what is the version of that operating system?

LESSON 2

Interacting With the Computer

OBJECTIVES

- Identify the five key groups on a standard computer keyboard.
- Identify the five essential techniques for using a mouse.
- List three categories of alternative input devices.
- Name two categories of computer monitor.
- List the four criteria you should consider when evaluating monitors.
- List the three most commonly used types of printers.

OVERVIEW:
Input and Output

As you learned in Lesson 1, a computer system really needs a user to be complete. In the world of personal computers, the user interacts with the computer in two ways: by using input devices to enter data and commands for the computer to process, and by using output devices to see or hear the results of that processing.

From the user's point of view, input and output devices may be even more important than the CPU because you interact directly with these devices and only indirectly with the CPU. In fact, your ability to use input and output devices is critical to your overall success with the whole system. The skills you develop with these devices will make you a more well-rounded computer user.

This lesson introduces you to many of the input and output devices commonly used with PCs. You will learn the importance of these devices, the ways they enable you to interact with the computer, and the many tasks they enable you to perform on your PC.

THE KEYBOARD

The keyboard was one of the first peripherals to be used with computers, and it is still the primary input device for entering text and numbers. A relatively simple device, a standard keyboard includes about 100 keys. Keyboards for personal computers come in many styles, and the various models differ in size, shape, and feel. Except for a few special-purpose keys, most keyboards are laid out almost identically. Among IBM-compatible computers, the most common keyboard layout is the IBM Enhanced Keyboard. It has 101 keys arranged in five groups, as shown in Figure 2.1. In Macintosh computers, the keyboard layout is close to the IBM Enhanced Keyboard, but there are a few differences.

Figure 2.1
The standard keyboard layout found in IBM-compatible PCs.

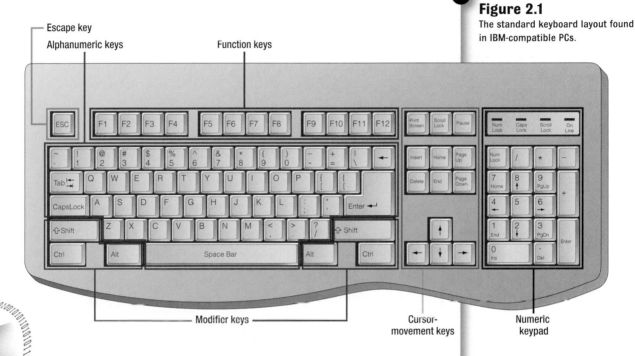

Standard computer keyboards include five groups of keys:

◆ **Alphanumeric keys** include the letters, numbers, and symbols found on a typewriter. The most common key arrangement is called the QWERTY layout because the first six keys on the top row of letters are Q, W, E, R, T, and Y. The alphanumeric key group includes a few additional keys with specific functions: the Tab, Caps Lock, Backspace, and Enter keys.

◆ **Modifier keys** are so named because they are used to modify the input of other keys. You press another key while holding down one of the modifier keys. On a PC, the modifier keys are Shift, Ctrl (for *control*), and Alt (for *alternate*). Macintosh computers also use Shift and Ctrl keys, and they function in much the same manner as their IBM-compatible counterparts. But Macintosh systems also offer a Command key and an Option (or Alt/Option) key (see Figure 2.2 on page 20).

◆ The **numeric keypad,** usually located on the right side of the keyboard, looks like an adding machine, with its ten digits and mathematical operators (+, −, *, and /). The numeric keypad

Figure 2.2
A Macintosh keyboard.

Option key   Command keys

features a Num Lock key, which is used to force the numeric keys to input numbers. When Num Lock is deactivated, the keys in the numeric keypad perform cursor-movement control and other functions.

◆ **Function keys** (F1, F2, and so on) are usually arranged in a row along the top of the keyboard. They allow you to input commands without typing long strings of characters or navigating menus or dialog boxes. The purpose of each function key depends on the program you are using. Most IBM-compatible keyboards have twelve function keys; most Macintosh systems have fifteen.

◆ The **cursor-movement keys** let you move around the screen. In many programs and operating systems, a mark on the screen appears where the next character you type will be entered. This mark, called the **cursor** or **insertion point,** can appear as a small box, a vertical line, or some other symbol that indicates your place on the screen (see Figure 2.3). Cursor-movement keys include the arrow keys, the Home and End keys, and the Page Up and Page Down keys.

Figure 2.3
The cursor.

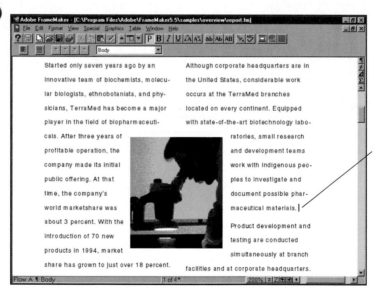

The cursor shows where the next letter typed on the keyboard will appear.

THE MOUSE AND ITS VARIANTS

If you bought a personal computer in the early 1980s, a keyboard would probably have been the only input device that came with it. Today, all new PCs come with a **pointing device** as standard equipment, as shown in Figure 2.4. If the computer is a desktop model, the pointing device is usually a mouse. A mouse is an input device that rolls around on a flat surface (usually on a desk or keyboard tray) and controls the pointer. The **pointer** is an on-screen object, usually an arrow, that is used to select text; access menus; and interact with programs, files, or data that appear on the screen. Figure 2.5 shows an example of a pointer in a program window.

A mouse lets you position the cursor anywhere on the screen quickly and easily without having to use the cursor-movement keys. You simply move the pointer

NORTON
ONLINE

Visit **www.glencoe.com/norton/online/** for more information on **mice.**

to the on-screen position you want, press the mouse button, and the cursor appears at that position. Instead of forcing you to type or issue commands from the keyboard, the mouse and mouse-based operating systems let you choose commands from easy-to-use menus and dialog boxes. The result is a much more intuitive way to use computers.

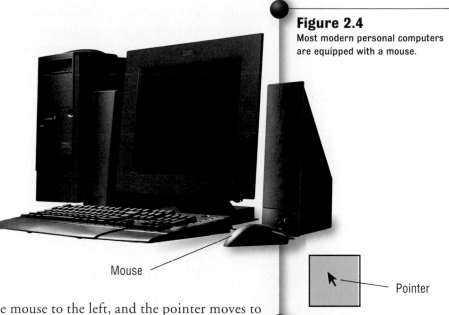

Figure 2.4
Most modern personal computers are equipped with a mouse.

Using the Mouse

You use a mouse to point to a location on the screen. Push the mouse forward across your desk, and the pointer moves up; push the mouse to the left, and the pointer moves to the left. To point to an object or location on the screen, you simply use the mouse to place the pointer on top of the object or location.

Mouse

Pointer

Figure 2.5
The mouse controls the pointer, which is used to interact with items on the screen.

You accomplish everything with a mouse by combining pointing with four other techniques: clicking, double-clicking, dragging, and right-clicking. Clicking, double-clicking, and dragging are illustrated in Figure 2.6.

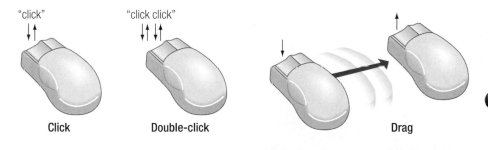

"click"

Click

"click click"

Double-click

Drag

Figure 2.6
Three mouse techniques.

Clicking something with the mouse means to move the pointer to the item on the screen and to press and release the mouse button once. **Double-clicking** an item means to point to it with the mouse pointer and then press and release the mouse button twice in rapid succession. **Dragging** an item means to position the mouse pointer over the item, press the mouse button, and hold it down as you move the mouse. As you move the pointer, the item is "dragged" along with it. You can then drop the item in a new position on the screen. This technique is called **drag-and-drop editing.**

Figure 2.7
The Microsoft mouse features two buttons. The Macintosh mouse features one button.

With Macintosh computers, most mice have only one button (see Figure 2.7). With IBM-compatible computers, most mice have two buttons. Clicking, double-clicking, and dragging are usually carried out with the left mouse button. (In multibutton mice, one button must be designated as the "primary" button. This button is referred to as the mouse button.) However, the operation known as **right-clicking** involves clicking the secondary button (usually the right one) on a two-button mouse. The right mouse button has special

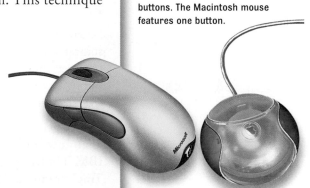

Figure 2.8

Trackballs come in many different shapes and sizes.

significance in Windows and Windows programs. Some mice have three or more buttons. The buttons' uses are determined by the computer's operating system, application software, and mouse-control software.

The Trackball

A **trackball** is a pointing device that works like an upside-down mouse (see Figure 2.8). You rest your thumb on the exposed ball and your fingers on the buttons. To move the pointer around the screen, you roll the ball with your thumb. Because you do not move the whole device, a trackball requires less space than a mouse. Trackballs gained popularity with the advent of laptop computers, which typically are used on laps or on small work surfaces without room for a mouse.

The Trackpad

The **trackpad** (also called a **touchpad**) is a stationary pointing device that many people find less tiring to use than a mouse or trackball. The movement of a finger across a small touch surface is translated into pointer movement on the computer screen. The touch-sensitive surface may be only 1.5 or 2 inches square, so the finger never has to move far. The trackpad's size also makes it suitable for a notebook computer. Some notebook models feature a built-in trackpad rather than a mouse or trackball (see Figure 2.9).

Trackpad

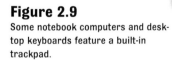

Figure 2.9

Some notebook computers and desktop keyboards feature a built-in trackpad.

Pointers in the Keyboard

Several computer manufacturers offer another space-saving pointing device, consisting of a small joystick positioned near the middle of the keyboard, typically between the *G* and *H* keys. The joystick is controlled with either forefinger. Two buttons that perform the same function as mouse buttons are just beneath the spacebar and are pressed with the thumb.

Several generic terms have emerged for this device; many manufacturers refer to it as an **integrated pointing device,** while others call it a 3-D point stick. On the IBM ThinkPad line of notebook computers, the pointing device is called the **TrackPoint** (see Figure 2.10).

Figure 2.10
IBM's ThinkPad comes with the TrackPoint pointing device. Several models of desktop keyboards are equipped with similar devices.

TrackPoint

ALTERNATIVE METHODS OF INPUT

Although the keyboard and mouse are the input devices people use most often, several other ways of getting data and commands into a computer are available. Because computer systems are so varied and because users' needs are becoming increasingly specialized, computer manufacturers are always developing new types of input devices and refining existing ones. There are three basic categories of alternative input devices (examples of these devices are illustrated on pages 24 and 25):

◆ **Devices for the Hand.** Other types of input devices designed for use by the hand include **touch screens** and **game controllers.** (Two common types of game controllers are **game pads** and **joysticks.**) Unlike keyboards and mice, many of these input devices are highly intuitive and easy to use without special skills or training.

◆ **Optical Devices.** Examples of optical devices are flatbed and handheld **bar code readers** and **image scanners** (sometimes simply called **scanners**). An optical device reads and analyzes different frequencies and intensities of light beams (such as those reflected off a bar code), then converts that data into numbers—digits—that the computer can use. This process is called **digitizing.** Bar code readers are used primarily to track information about products and packages. Scanners are generally used to create electronic versions of printed documents or photographs so they can be edited by a computer.

◆ **Multimedia Devices.** The most popular kinds of multimedia input devices are **microphones, PC video cameras,** and **digital cameras.** Nearly all modern PCs feature a built-in microphone, which accepts audio input (such as voice commands and dictated text) by converting sound waves into numeric data the computer can understand. PC video cameras work with a special video capture card in the PC to capture full-motion video, which can be saved to disk or transmitted over a network or Internet connection. Digital cameras are used to take snapshot-style pictures that can be stored and edited on the computer.

Visit **www.glencoe.com/norton/online/** for more information on **touch screens, game controllers, scanners, microphones, PC video cameras,** and **digital cameras.**

Pen-based systems—including many personal digital assistants and other types of handheld computers—use a "pen" for data input. (This pen-like device is sometimes called a stylus.) You hold the pen in your hand and write on a special pad or directly on the screen. You can also use the pen as a pointing device, like a mouse, to select commands.

Most touch-screen computers use sensors in or near the computer's screen to detect the touch of a finger. Touch screens are appropriate in environments where dirt or weather would render keyboards and pointing devices useless, and where a simple, intuitive interface is important.

Game controllers are an increasingly popular type of input device used with PCs. Two general types of game controllers are common: game pads and joysticks. Some controllers provide tactile feedback, such as vibrations or pulses, to help players "feel" the action in the game.

The bar code reader is a commonly used optical input device. Here, a flatbed bar code reader is used to enter a product's price at a computerized cash register. A light-sensitive detector identifies the bar code and converts the pattern into numeric digits. Then the bar code reader feeds that number to the computer as though the number had been typed on a keyboard.

Image scanners (also called scanners) convert any printed image into electronic form by shining light onto the image and sensing the intensity of the reflection at every point. Large-format, flatbed scanners produce high-resolution, digitized versions of documents. Graphic artists prefer this type of scanner because it yields the highest quality scans of photographs and other images.

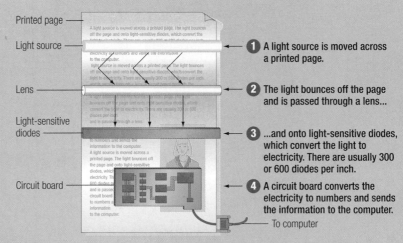

Printed page

Light source

Lens

Light-sensitive diodes

Circuit board

1. A light source is moved across a printed page.

2. The light bounces off the page and is passed through a lens...

3. ...and onto light-sensitive diodes, which convert the light to electricity. There are usually 300 or 600 diodes per inch.

4. A circuit board converts the electricity to numbers and sends the information to the computer.

To computer

This illustration shows how an image is scanned. Color scanners use filters to separate the components of color into the primary additive colors (red, green, and blue) at each point. Red, green, and blue are known as primary additive colors because they can be combined to create any other color. Processes that describe color in this manner are said to use RGB color.

Applications such as videoconferencing enable people to use full-motion video images, captured by a PC video camera, and transmit them to a limited number of recipients on a network or to the world on the Internet. Using video capture cards, the user can also connect other video devices, such as VCRs and camcorders, to the PC.

Digital cameras are portable, handheld devices that capture still images electronically. The digital camera digitizes the image, compresses it, and stores it on a disk or memory card. The user can then copy the information to a PC, where the image can be edited, copied, printed, embedded in a document, or transmitted to another user.

MONITORS

The keyboard is the most commonly used input device, and the monitor is the most commonly used output device on most personal computer systems. As you use your computer—whether you are typing, issuing commands, surfing the Internet, or even listening to music on the system's CD-ROM drive—hardly a moment goes by when you are not looking at your monitor.

Two basic types of monitors are used with PCs (see Figure 2.11). The first is the typical monitor that you see on a desktop computer. It looks a lot like a television screen and works the same way. This type of monitor uses a large vacuum tube, called a **cathode ray tube (CRT).** The second type, known as a **flat-panel display,** is used primarily with portable computers but is becoming an increasingly popular feature with desktop computers.

Figure 2.11
The most common types of monitors used with PCs.

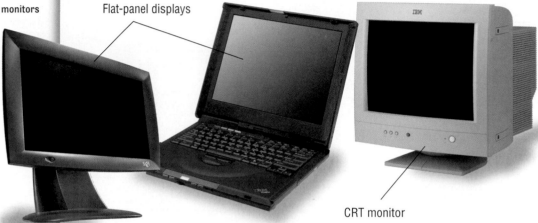

Flat-panel displays

CRT monitor

CRT Monitors

Figure 2.12 shows how a typical CRT monitor works. Near the back of the monitor's housing is an electron gun. The gun shoots a beam of electrons through a magnetic coil, which aims the beam at the front of the monitor. The back of the monitor's screen is coated with phosphors, chemicals that glow when they are struck by the electron beam. The screen's phosphor coating is organized into a grid of dots. The smallest number of phosphor dots that the gun can focus on is called a **pixel,** a contraction of the term *pic*ture *el*ement.

The electron gun does not just focus on a spot and shoot electrons at it. It systematically aims at every pixel on the screen, starting at the top left corner and scanning to the right edge. Then it drops down a tiny distance and scans another line, as shown in Figure 2.13.

Figure 2.12
How a CRT monitor creates an image.

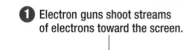

1 Electron guns shoot streams of electrons toward the screen.

2 Magnetic yoke guides the streams of electrons across and down the screen.

3 Phosphor dots on the back of the screen glow when the electron beams hit them.

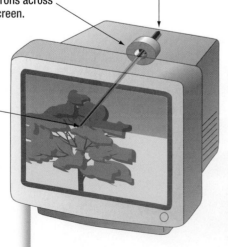

Flat-Panel Monitors

There are several types of flat-panel monitors, but the most common is the **liquid crystal display (LCD)** monitor. The LCD monitor creates images with a special kind of liquid crystal that is normally transparent but becomes opaque when charged with electricity. If you have a hand-held calculator or a digital watch, it most likely uses a liquid crystal display.

One disadvantage of LCD monitors is that, unlike phosphor, the liquid crystal does not emit light, so there is not enough contrast between the images and the background to make them legible under all conditions. The problem is solved by backlighting the screen. Although this makes the screen easier to read, it requires additional power. Another disadvantage of LCD monitors is their limited viewing angle—that is, the angle from which the display's image can be viewed clearly (see Figure 2.14).

① The electron gun scans from left to right,

② and from top to bottom,

③ refreshing every phosphor dot in a zig-zag pattern.

Figure 2.13
The scanning pattern of the CRT's electron gun.

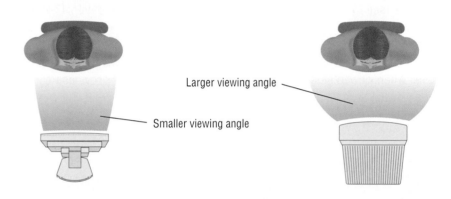

Larger viewing angle

Smaller viewing angle

Figure 2.14
Flat-panel displays typically have a smaller viewing angle than do CRT monitors.

There are two main categories of liquid crystal displays: passive matrix and active matrix. **Passive matrix LCD** relies on transistors for each row and each column of pixels, thus creating a grid that defines the location of each pixel. The color displayed by a pixel is determined by the electricity coming from the transistors at the end of the row and the top of the column.

Most notebooks that use passive matrix technology refer to their screens as dual-scan LCD. A **dual-scan LCD** scans through the pixels twice as often, creating a sharper image than a standard passive matrix LCD can.

Active matrix LCD technology assigns a transistor to each pixel, and each pixel is turned on and off individually. This enhancement allows the pixels to be refreshed much more rapidly than is possible in a dual-scan LCD. In addition, active matrix screens have a wider viewing angle than dual-scan screens. Active matrix displays are often called thin-film transistor (TFT) displays because many active matrix monitors are based on TFT technology, which employs as many as four transistors per pixel.

Although flat-panel monitors have so far been used primarily on portable computers, a new generation of large, high-resolution, flat-panel displays is gaining popularity among users of desktop systems (see Figure 2.15 on page 28).

NORTON
ONLINE

Visit **www.glencoe.com/norton/online/** for more information on **computer monitors**.

Comparing Monitors

When shopping for a monitor, first look closely at the display. Look at a screen full of text and examine how crisp the letters are, especially near the corners of the screen. Also, if you plan to work with graphics, display a picture with which you are familiar and see whether the colors look accurate. If possible, spend some time "surfing" the World Wide Web to display different pages and see how they look. Check the following specifications for any monitor you consider purchasing:

Figure 2.15

Flat-panel monitors for desktops are becoming increasingly popular.

◆ **Size.** Monitors are measured diagonally, in inches, across the front of the screen. For example, a 15-inch monitor measures 15 inches from the lower left to the upper right corner. But the picture on a 15-inch monitor usually measures about 13 inches diagonally. On a 17-inch monitor, the viewing area is a little over 15 inches (see Figure 2.16). Most new desktop systems are sold with 17-inch CRT monitors, and the norm may soon creep up to 19 inches or even 21 inches. Flat-panel monitors are rapidly gaining in size, too. Today, flat-panel displays rival CRT monitors in terms of viewing area, but they do not consume as much desktop space. When viewed side by side, a 17-inch flat-panel monitor provides nearly the same viewing area as a 17-inch CRT monitor.

Figure 2.16

Comparison of a 17-inch monitor to a 15-inch monitor.

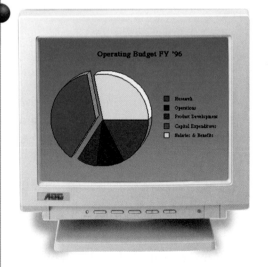
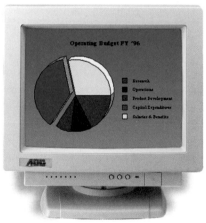

Visit **www.glencoe.com/norton/online/** for more information on **monitor manufacturers** and **monitor resolution.**

◆ **Resolution.** The **resolution** of a computer monitor is classified by the number of pixels on the screen, expressed as a matrix. For example, monitors that conform to the **Video Graphics Array (VGA)** standard operate at a resolution of 640 × 480—there are 640 pixels in each horizontal row and 480 pixels in each vertical column. The **Super VGA (SVGA)** standard expands resolutions to 800 × 600 and 1024 × 768. Because the actual resolution is determined by the video controller, not by the monitor itself, most monitor specifications list a range of resolutions. For example, most 17-inch monitors have pixel grids that allow for five settings: 640 × 480, 800 × 600, 1024 × 768, 1152 × 864, and 1280 × 1024 (see Figure 2.17).

◆ **Refresh Rate.** The **refresh rate** is the number of times per second that the monitor's electron guns scan every pixel on the screen. Refresh rate is measured in Hertz (Hz), or cycles per second. The monitor refreshes itself at least several dozen times each second. The refresh rate is an important concern because phosphor dots fade quickly after the electron gun passes over them. Therefore, if the screen is not refreshed often enough, it appears to flicker.

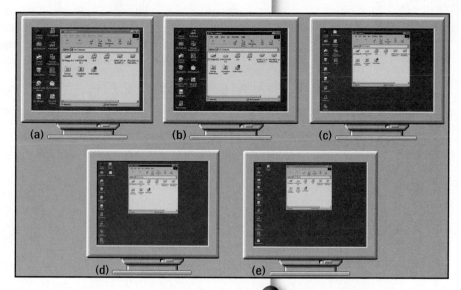

The problem is compounded because you may not even detect the flicker; in the long run it can still cause eyestrain. In general, a refresh rate of 72 Hz or higher should not cause eyestrain. Some monitors have different refresh rates for different resolutions. Make sure the refresh rate is adequate (at least 72 Hz) for the resolution you use.

◆ **Dot Pitch.** The last critical specification of a color monitor is the **dot pitch,** the distance between the phosphor dots that make up a single pixel. If these dots are not close enough together, the images on the screen will not be crisp (see Figure 2.18). Once again, it is difficult to detect slight differences in dot pitch, but blurry pixels will cause eyestrain anyway. In general, when you are looking for a color monitor, look for a dot pitch no greater than 0.28 millimeter.

Figure 2.17
Microsoft Windows 95 and 98 use this kind of illustration to show how screen items appear at different resolutions: (a) the monitor at a resolution of 640 × 480, (b) at 800 × 600, (c) at 1024 × 768, (d) at 1152 × 864, (e) at 1280 ×1024. Notice that more items can fit on the screen at higher resolutions, but the items appear smaller. These resolutions are typical for a 17-inch monitor.

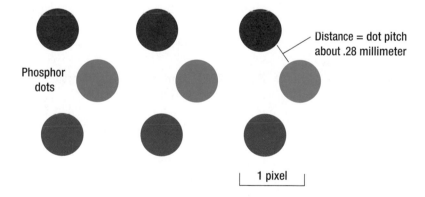

Figure 2.18
Dot pitch is the distance between the phosphor dots that make up a single pixel. The smaller the dot pitch, the crisper the display image.

Self Check

Answer the following questions by filling in the blank(s).

1. You use the mouse to control an on-screen item called the

   _____ .

2. In a CRT monitor, a(n) _____ aims a beam of electrons at the front of the monitor.

3. A disadvantage of LCD monitors is their limited _____ .

Norton Notebook

Whether you are shopping to equip a future office or to buy a home computer, you have quite a few monitor options to choose from. Basically, you can pick from two categories of desktop monitors: CRTs and flat-panel displays. Of course, you will get an LCD monitor if you buy a laptop system, but do not forget that most laptops have a port for connecting a desktop monitor. Both types of desktop monitor offer advantages and disadvantages.

In Some Ways, They Are All the Same

Flat-panel technology has made some big leaps in the last few years. Whereas flat-panel monitors used to be small, low-resolution devices found mostly on portable systems, they now rival CRT monitors feature for feature. When it comes to resolution, colors, dot pitch, refresh rate, and viewable area, flat-panel and CRT monitors compete head to head. Whatever monitor you buy, make sure it meets your requirements in each of these areas.

But in Other Ways, They Are Not

While all monitors may be created equal (or fairly equal) in terms of the resolutions and colors they can display, there are significant differences you need to consider:

◆ **Desktop Space Requirements.** Obviously, this is the criterion where CRT monitors cannot match flat-panels. A typical CRT monitor with a 15.8-inch viewable area stands about 19 inches high (including the base) and is about 16 inches wide and about 19 inches deep. A typical flat-panel monitor with a 15-inch viewable area stands about 18 inches high (including the base) and is about 16 inches wide, but it is only about 10 inches deep—4 inches without the base. Many flat-panel monitors can be hung on a wall or mounted on a swing-arm stand, further reducing their desktop space requirements.

◆ **Viewable Area.** CRT monitors offer viewable areas ranging from just over 13 inches to more than 22 inches. Flat-panels for the desktop range from about 14 inches to more than 18 inches, but larger viewing areas are being developed all the time.

◆ **Viewing Angle.** CRT monitors are usually hands-down winners in this category, but flat-panel systems are catching up. If you do not usually need to look at the monitor from an angle and if you do not typically have several people looking at the monitor

Flat-panel

Flat-panel monitors are becoming increasingly popular, but their cost is too high for many users.

CRT

at one time, the flat-panel's restricted viewing angle should not be a problem.

◆ **Screen Curvature.** CRT screens are flatter than they once were, and some higher-end models are almost completely flat. With most moderately priced CRTs, however, some curvature of the screen is normal and can easily be seen. If you use a computer for long periods, this curvature can cause minor distortions in the picture that lead to eyestrain. Because LCD monitors are flat, they do not pose this problem.

◆ **Power Consumption.** Flat-panel systems win in this category. CRT monitors consume a great deal of electricity to keep the screen refreshed. Conversely, LCD systems are energy efficient because of their tiny transistors. As an added benefit, flat-panel displays run cooler than CRTs.

◆ **Radiation Emissions.** CRT monitors emit low-level radiation. This radiation is not thought to be harmful, but it is there just the same. LCD monitors do not emit radiation.

◆ **Cost.** This category is usually the tie-breaker for shoppers who cannot decide between a flat-panel and CRT monitor. Despite their many advantages, flat-panel displays are much more expensive than CRT monitors. In fact, if you compare a flat-panel and CRT monitor with similar viewing areas, resolutions, and other features, the flat-panel system can cost three or four times as much as the CRT display.

The Video Controller

The quality of the images that a monitor can display is defined as much by the **video controller** as by the monitor itself. As shown in Figure 2.19, the video controller is an intermediary device between the CPU and the monitor. It contains the video-dedicated memory and other circuitry necessary to send information to the monitor for display on the screen. It consists of a circuit board that is attached to the computer's motherboard. Within the monitor's constraints, the controller's processing power determines the refresh rate, resolution, and number of colors that can be displayed.

Video controllers have increased dramatically in power and importance. There is a microprocessor on the video controller, which frees the CPU from the burden of making the millions of calculations required for displaying graphics. The speed of this chip limits the speed at which the monitor can be refreshed. Most video controllers today also include at least 4 MB of **video RAM,** or **VRAM** (in addition to the RAM that is connected to the CPU). VRAM is dual-ported: it can send a screen full of data to the monitor while receiving the next screen full of data from the CPU.

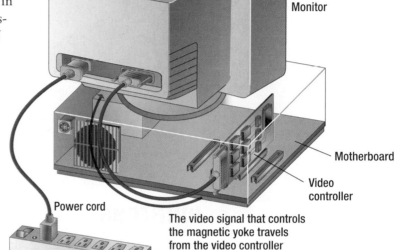

Figure 2.19
The video controller connects the CPU to the monitor.

Monitor

Motherboard

Video controller

Power cord

The video signal that controls the magnetic yoke travels from the video controller to the monitor.

SOUND SYSTEMS

Microphones are now important input devices, and speakers and their associated technology are key output systems. Today, when you buy a **multimedia PC,** you receive a machine that includes a CD-ROM (or DVD) drive, a high-quality video controller with plenty of video RAM, speakers, and a sound card (see Figure 2.20).

Visit **www.glencoe.com/norton/online/** for more information on **video controllers** and **PC audio technology.**

Figure 2.20
Speakers are common features on today's multimedia PCs.

The speakers attached to these systems perform like any other speaker does: they transfer a constantly changing electric current to a magnet, which pushes the speaker cone back and forth. The moving speaker cone creates pressure vibrations in the air—in other words, sound (see Figure 2.21).

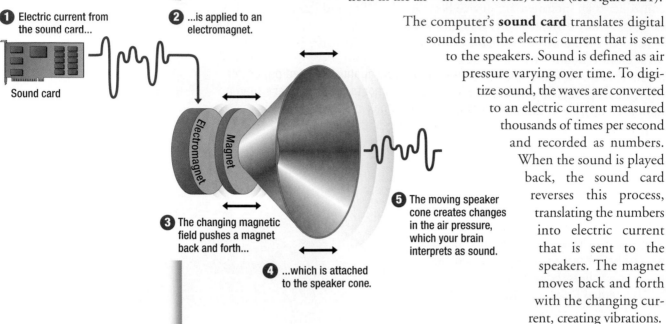

1 Electric current from the sound card...

Sound card

2 ...is applied to an electromagnet.

Electromagnet

Magnet

3 The changing magnetic field pushes a magnet back and forth...

4 ...which is attached to the speaker cone.

5 The moving speaker cone creates changes in the air pressure, which your brain interprets as sound.

The computer's **sound card** translates digital sounds into the electric current that is sent to the speakers. Sound is defined as air pressure varying over time. To digitize sound, the waves are converted to an electric current measured thousands of times per second and recorded as numbers. When the sound is played back, the sound card reverses this process, translating the numbers into electric current that is sent to the speakers. The magnet moves back and forth with the changing current, creating vibrations.

PRINTERS

Besides the monitor, the other important output device is the printer. An **impact printer** creates an image by pressing an inked ribbon against the paper, using pins or hammers to shape the image. The most common type of impact printer is the dot matrix printer.

Nonimpact printers use other means to create an image. Ink jet printers, for example, use tiny nozzles to spray droplets of ink onto the page. Laser printers work like photocopiers, using heat to bond microscopic particles of dry toner to specific parts of the page.

When buying a printer, one consideration is most important: that is, how do you plan to use the printer? Do you need to print only text, or are graphics capabilities also important? Do you need to print in color? Will you need to print a wide variety of fonts in many sizes? How quickly do you want your documents to be printed? When evaluating printers, four additional criteria are also important:

◆ **Image Quality.** Image quality, also known as print resolution, is usually measured in **dots per inch (dpi)**. The more dots per inch a printer can produce, the higher its image quality. Most medium-quality ink jet and laser printers can print 300 or 600 dots per inch, which is fine for most daily business applications. Professional-quality printers, used for creating colorful presentations, posters, or renderings, offer resolutions of 1800 dpi or more.

◆ **Speed.** Printer speed is measured in the number of **pages per minute (ppm)** the device can print. Most printers have different ppm ratings for text and graphics because graphics generally take longer to print. As print speed goes up, so does cost. Most consumer-level laser printers, for example, offer print speeds of 6 or 8 ppm, but high-volume professional laser printers can exceed 20 ppm.

- ◆ **Initial Cost.** It is possible to buy a quality ink jet printer for personal use for $100 or even less; low-end laser printers can be found for $250 or less. Professional-quality, high-output systems can range in price from $1000 to tens of thousands of dollars. Color printers (and the supplies to make them work) always cost more than black-and-white printers.

- ◆ **Cost of Operation.** The cost of ink or toner and maintenance varies with the type of printer. Many different types of printer paper are available, too, and the choice can affect the cost of operation. Low-quality recycled paper, for example, is fine for printing draft-quality documents and costs less than a penny per sheet. Glossy, thick photo-quality stock, used for printing photographs, can cost several dollars per sheet, depending on size.

Dot Matrix Printers

Dot matrix printers are commonly used in workplaces where physical impact with the paper is important, such as when the user is printing on carbon-copy or pressure-sensitive forms. A dot matrix printer creates an image by using a mechanism called a **print head,** which contains a cluster (or matrix) of short pins arranged in rows and columns. On receiving instructions from the PC, the printer can push any of the pins out, in any combination. By pushing out pins in various combinations, the print head can create alphanumeric characters (see Figures 2.22 and 2.23).

When pushed out from the cluster, the ends of the protruding pins strike a ribbon, which is held in place between the print head and the paper. When the pins strike the ribbon, they press ink from the ribbon onto a piece of paper. Where a single pin strikes the ribbon, a single dot of ink is printed on the page, hence the name, dot matrix. The more pins that a print head contains, the higher the printer's resolution. The lowest resolution dot matrix printers have only nine pins; the highest resolution printers have twenty-four pins.

Whereas other types of printers have their speed measured in pages per minute, dot matrix printers are measured in **characters per second (cps).** The slowest dot matrix printers create 50 to 70 characters per second; the fastest print more than 500 cps.

Ink Jet Printers

Ink jet printers create an image directly on the paper by spraying ink through tiny nozzles. Low-cost ink jet printers typically attain print resolutions of at least 360 dots per inch, and they can print from two to four pages per minute.

NORTON
ONLINE

Visit **www.glencoe.com/norton/online/** for more information on **dot matrix printers, ink jet printers,** and **laser printers.**

Figure 2.22
A dot matrix printer forms a character by creating a series of dots.

Figure 2.23
How a dot matrix printer creates an image.

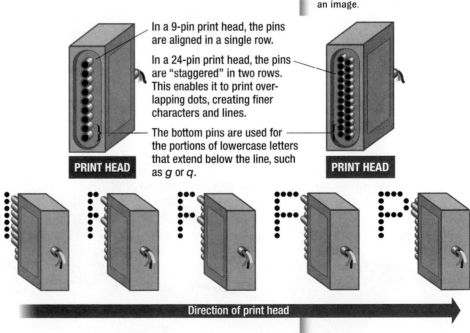

In a 9-pin print head, the pins are aligned in a single row.

In a 24-pin print head, the pins are "staggered" in two rows. This enables it to print overlapping dots, creating finer characters and lines.

The bottom pins are used for the portions of lowercase letters that extend below the line, such as *g* or *q*.

PRINT HEAD

PRINT HEAD

Direction of print head

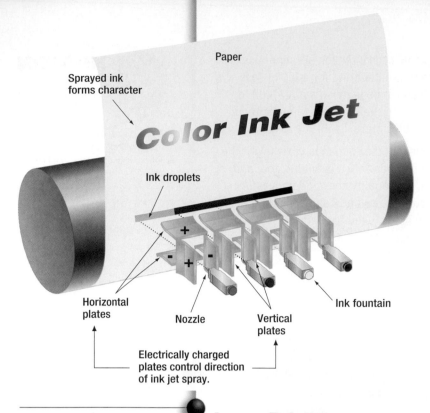

Paper

Sprayed ink
forms character

Color Ink Jet

Ink droplets

+   +
-   -   +

Horizontal
plates

Nozzle

Vertical
plates

Ink fountain

Electrically charged
plates control direction
of ink jet spray.

Ink jet printers offer a cost-effective way to print in color as well as black and white. Color ink jet printers have four ink nozzles: cyan (blue), magenta (red), yellow, and black (see Figure 2.24). These four colors are used in almost all color printing because it is possible to combine them to create any color in the visible spectrum. Notice that the colors are different from the primary additive colors (red, green, and blue) used in monitors. Printed color is the result of light bouncing off the paper, not color transmitted directly from a light source. Consequently, cyan, magenta, yellow, and black are sometimes called subtractive colors and color printing is sometimes called four-color printing.

Figure 2.24
How an ink jet printer creates an image.

Laser Printers

Laser printers are more expensive than ink jet printers, their print quality is higher, and most are faster. As their name implies, a laser is at the heart of these printers. A separate CPU and memory are built into the printer to interpret the data that it receives from the computer and to control the laser. The result is a complicated piece of equipment that uses technology similar to that in photocopiers. The quality and speed of laser printers make them ideal for offices where several users may need to share the same printer.

The laser in a laser printer can aim at any point on a drum, creating an electrical charge (see Figure 2.25). Toner, which is composed of tiny particles of oppositely charged ink, sticks to the drum in the places the laser has charged. Then, with pressure and heat, the toner is transferred off the drum onto the paper.

Figure 2.25
How a laser printer creates a printed page.

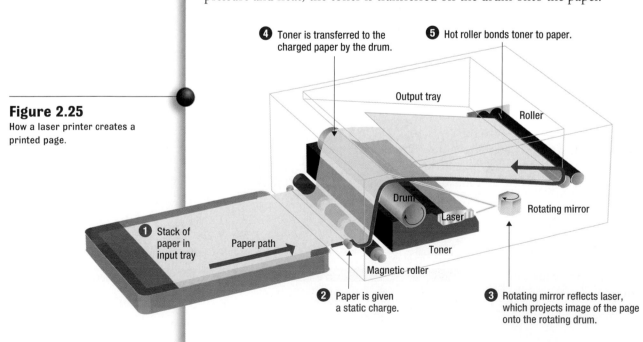

❹ Toner is transferred to the charged paper by the drum.

❺ Hot roller bonds toner to paper.

Output tray

Roller

Drum

Laser

Rotating mirror

❶ Stack of paper in input tray

Paper path

Toner

Magnetic roller

❷ Paper is given a static charge.

❸ Rotating mirror reflects laser, which projects image of the page onto the rotating drum.

LESSON QUIZ

True/False

Answer the following questions by circling True or False.

True   False   **1.** The keyboard keys labeled F1, F2, and so on, are called function keys.

True   False   **2.** On a two-button mouse, one button must be designated as the primary button.

True   False   **3.** A bar code reader is an example of a multimedia input device.

True   False   **4.** A cathode ray tube monitor looks and works much like a television screen.

Truc   False   **5.** The two categories of printers are impact and nonimpact.

Multiple Choice

Circle the word or phrase that best completes each sentence.

1. On standard keyboards, keys are usually arranged in _____ groups.
   A. three   **B.** five   **C.** eight

2. A _____ works like an upside-down mouse.
   A. trackball   **B.** trackpad   **C.** joystick

3. _____ monitors are most commonly used with desktop computers.
   A. Flat-panel display   **B.** Cathode ray tube (CRT)   **C.** Neither A nor B

4. In a monitor, _____ is the distance between the phosphor dots in a pixel.
   A. resolution   **B.** viewing angle   **C.** dot pitch

5. A laser printer creates an image by placing _____ at specific points on the page.
   A. toner   **B.** electric charges   **C.** neither A nor B

LESSON LABS

Complete the following exercises as directed by your instructor.

1. To check the mouse settings of your system, click the Start button to open the Start menu; then click Settings, Control Panel. The Control Panel dialog box opens. Double-click the Mouse icon to open the Mouse Properties dialog box. Click the tabs in the dialog box and inspect your settings. Experiment with the Pointer Speed and Show Pointer Trails tools and see how they affect the performance of your mouse. When you are finished, click Cancel.

2. Find out what type of printer is connected to your computer by clicking the Start button to open the Start menu; then click Settings, and Printers. The Printers window opens; if a printer is connected to your system (directly or through a network), it will appear in this window. If you see a printer, right-click its icon to open a shortcut menu. On this menu, choose Properties to open the Properties dialog box for the printer. Review the information about your printer; then close all dialog boxes.

VISUAL SUMMARY

LESSON 1: An Overview of Computer Systems

The Computer System Defined

- A computer is an electronic device used to process data, converting it into information that is useful to people.

- A complete computer system includes hardware, software, data, and people.

Hardware: The Nuts and Bolts of the Machine

- The hardware, or physical components, of a computer consists of a processor, memory, input and output (I/O) devices, and storage.

- The processing function is divided between the processor and memory.

- Memory holds data and program instructions as the CPU works with them.

- The role of input is to provide data from the user or another source. The function of output is to present processed data to the user or to another computer.

- Storage devices hold data and program instructions not currently being used by the CPU.

Software: Bringing the Machine to Life

- Programs are electronic instructions that tell the computer how to accomplish certain tasks. When a computer is using a particular program, it is running or executing the program.

- The operating system tells the computer how to interact with the user and how to use the attached hardware devices.

- Application software tells the computer how to accomplish tasks that the user requires.

The Shapes of Computers Today

- Supercomputers are the most powerful computers in terms of processing. They are useful for problems requiring complex calculations.

- Mainframe computers, which generally have many terminals or PCs connected to them, handle massive amounts of input, output, and storage.

- Minicomputers are smaller than mainframes but larger than micro-computers. They usually have multiple terminals.

- Workstations are powerful single-user computers that are used by engineers, scientists, and graphic artists. Like minicomputers, workstations are often used as network and Internet servers.

- Microcomputers are also known as personal computers. Many types of micro-computers, including desktop systems, notebook (or laptop) computers, and various types of handheld personal computers, are in general use.

LESSON 2: Interacting With the Computer

The Keyboard

- A standard computer keyboard has about 100 keys. Most keyboards follow a similar lay-out, with their keys arranged in five groups. Those groups include the alphanumeric keys, numeric keypad, function keys, modifier keys, and cursor-movement keys.

The Mouse and Its Variants

- The mouse is a pointing device that lets you control the position of a graphical pointer on the screen without using the keyboard.

- Using the mouse involves five techniques: pointing, clicking, double-clicking, dragging, and right-clicking.

- Variations of the mouse include trackballs, trackpads, and integrated pointing devices built into some keyboards.

Alternative Methods of Input

- There are many alternative input devices, each of which has special uses. Three categories of alternative input devices include those devices designed for use with the hand, optical input devices, and multimedia input devices.

- Hand-operated input devices include electronic pens, touch screens, and game controllers.

- Optical input devices include bar code readers and image scanners.

- Multimedia input devices include microphones, PC video cameras, and digital cameras.

Monitors

- Computer monitors are roughly divided into two categories: CRT and flat-panel displays.

- A CRT monitor works with one or more electron guns that aim a beam of electrons systematically at every pixel on the screen.

- Most LCD displays are either active matrix or passive matrix.

- When purchasing a monitor, you must consider its size, resolution, refresh rate, and dot pitch.

- The video controller is an interface between the monitor and the CPU that contains an on-board processor and memory, called video RAM.

Sound Systems

- Multimedia PCs generally come with sound systems that include a sound card, speakers, a CD-ROM or DVD drive, and a video controller. The sound card translates digital signals into analog signals that drive the speakers.

Printers

- Printers fall into two general categories: impact and nonimpact.

- When evaluating printers for purchase, you should consider four criteria: image quality, speed, initial cost, and cost of operation.

- A dot matrix printer (a common impact printer) uses a print head that contains a cluster of pins. The pins are used to press an inked ribbon against paper, thus creating an image.

- An ink jet printer is an example of a nonimpact printer. It creates an image by spraying tiny droplets of ink onto the paper.

- Laser printers are nonimpact printers. They use heat and pressure to bond tiny particles of toner (a dry ink) to paper.

UNIT REVIEW

KEY TERMS

After completing this unit, you should be able to define the following terms.

active matrix LCD, *27*
alphanumeric key, *19*
application software, *11*
bar code reader, *23*
byte, *7*
cathode ray tube (CRT), *26*
CD-Recordable (CD-R), *10*
CD-ReWritable (CD-RW), *10*
CD-ROM drive, *10*
central processing unit
   (CPU), *6*
characters per second
   (cps), *33*
circuit board, *6*
clicking, *21*
communications device, *8*
compact disk (CD), *10*
compact disk read-only
   memory (CD-ROM), *10*
computer, *4*
computer system, *4*
cursor, *20*
cursor-movement key, *20*
data, *4*
device, *4*
digital, *4*
digital camera, *23*
digital versatile disk
   (DVD), *10*
digital video disk (DVD), *10*
digitizing, *23*
disk drive, *9*

diskette, *9*
diskette drive, *9*
document, *4*
dot matrix printer, *33*
dots per inch (dpi), *32*
dot pitch, *29*
double-clicking, *21*
dragging, *21*
drag-and-drop editing, *21*
dual-scan LCD, *27*
executing, *11*
file, *4*
flat-panel display, *26*
floppy disk, *9*
function key, *20*
game controller, *23*
game pad, *23*
gigabyte (GB), *7*
handheld personal computer
   (H/PC), *13*
hard disk, *9*
hard drive, *9*
hardware, *4*
image scanner, *23*
impact printer, *32*
ink jet printer, *33*
input device, *7*
input/output (I/O) device, *13*
insertion point, *20*
integrated pointing device, *22*
joystick, *23*
keyboard, *8*

kilobyte (KB), *7*
laptop computer, *13*
laser printer, *34*
liquid crystal display
   (LCD), *27*
magnetic disk, *9*
mainframe computer, *13*
megabyte (MB), *7*
memory, *7*
microcomputer, *13*
microphone, *23*
microprocessor, *5*
minicomputer, *13*
modifier key, *19*
monitor, *8*
motherboard, *5*
mouse, *8*
multimedia PC, *31*
network computer (NC), *13*
nonimpact printer, *32*
notebook computer, *13*
numeric keypad, *19*
operating system, *11*
output device, *8*
pages per minute (ppm), *32*
passive matrix LCD, *27*
PC video camera, *23*
personal computer (PC), *4*
pixel, *26*
pointer, *20*
pointing device, *20*
printer, *8*

print head, *33*
processing, *5*
processor, *5*
program, *4*
random access memory
   (RAM), *7*
read-only memory (ROM), *11*
read/write head, *9*
refresh rate, *29*
resolution, *28*
right-clicking, *21*
running, *11*
scanner, *23*
software, *4*
sound card, *32*
storage, *8*
supercomputer, *13*
Super VGA (SVGA), *28*
system software, *11*
terabyte (TB), *7*
terminal, *13*
touchpad, *22*
touch screen, *23*
trackball, *22*
trackpad, *22*
TrackPoint, *22*
user, *4*
video controller, *31*
Video Graphics Array
   (VGA), *28*
video RAM (VRAM), *31*
workstation, *13*

KEY TERMS QUIZ

Fill in each blank with one of the terms listed under Key Terms.

1. Electronic instructions that tell the hardware what to do are known as _____ .

2. A(n) _____ is a powerful single-user computer often used for tasks such as advanced design, animation, and video editing.

3. A(n) _____ is a device that holds a disk.

4. A(n) _____ is a set of data or program instructions that has been given a name.

5. In addition to pointing, the four primary mouse techniques are _____ , _____ , _____ and _____ .

6. You use the mouse (or one of its variants) to position a(n) _____ on the screen.

7. A(n) _____ matrix LCD monitor assigns one transistor to each row and each column of pixels.

8. A monitor's _____ is classified by the numbers of pixels on the screen, expressed as a matrix.

9. A(n) _____ translates digital sounds into the electric current that is sent to the speakers.

10. A(n) _____ creates an image on paper by spraying ink through tiny nozzles.

REVIEW QUESTIONS

In your own words, briefly answer the following questions.

1. List the four key components of a computer system.
2. List the three major distinctions between storage and memory.
3. Computers fall into five categories. List them.
4. What is the difference between a "file" and a "document" in a computer?
5. How do you double-click an item with a mouse?
6. Name the two basic types of monitor used with PCs.
7. How does a dual-scan LCD monitor produce a clearer image than an ordinary passive matrix monitor?
8. List the four specifications you should consider when comparing monitors.
9. What unit of measure is used to express the speed of a dot matrix printer?
10. Color ink jet printers use four colors of ink. List them.

DISCUSSION QUESTIONS

As directed by your instructor, discuss the following questions in class or in groups.

1. Home computers are used more extensively than ever for tasks such as banking, investing, shopping, and communicating. Do you see this growth as having a positive or a negative impact on our society and economy? Do you plan to use a computer in these ways? Why?
2. Many computer users now think that a computer system is not complete unless it is equipped with a printer, a microphone, and speakers. Do you think this is true? Would you be happy (or able) to do your work at a PC that lacked these pieces of hardware? Why?

 **ETHICAL ISSUES** Computer skills can make a difference in a person's employability. With this thought in mind, discuss the following questions in class.

1. A factory is buying computerized systems and robots to handle many tasks, which means that fewer laborers will be needed. The company needs people to run the new equipment but wants to hire new workers who already have computer skills. Is the company obligated to keep the workers with no computer skills and train them to use the equipment? Are workers obligated to learn these new skills if they want to keep their jobs?

2. Commercially available PCs are currently configured for use by persons who do not suffer from physical impairments or disabilities. If a person with a physical impairment wants to use a computer, he or she may need to purchase special equipment or software. Do you think this necessity is fair? Should every PC be accessible to everyone, whether they have physical impairments or not?

UNIT LABS

You and the Computer

Complete the following exercises using a computer in your classroom, lab, or home. No other materials are needed.

1. **Explore Your Disk.** Once you are familiar with your computer's hardware, learn what resides on its hard disk. Take these steps:

   A. Click the Start button on the Windows taskbar to open the Start menu.

   B. On the Start menu, point to Programs. The Programs submenu will appear.

   C. Click Windows Explorer. The Exploring window will open.

   D. The left pane of the Exploring window lists the drives and folders on your system. Click any icon and its contents will appear in the right pane of the Exploring window.

   E. Close the Exploring window by clicking the Close button (with an **X** on it) in the top right-hand corner.

2. **Get Some Help.** If you do not know how to perform a task on your computer, turn to its online help system for answers and assistance. Browse your operating system's help system to learn more about your computer:

   A. Click the Start button on the Windows taskbar to open the Start menu.

   B. On the Start menu, click Help. The Windows Help window will appear.

   C. Click the Contents tab to see the categories of help topics. Click any category (with a closed book icon) to see which topics it contains.

   D. Click a topic (identified by a question mark). Its contents appear in the window's right pane.

   E. Click the Index tab to see an alphabetical list of all the terms covered by the help system. To see the help information associated with a term, click the term and then click Display.

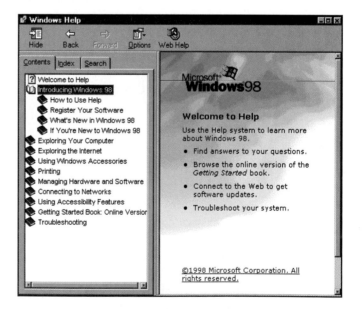

   F. Click the Search tab to search for help on a specific topic. In the text box, type a term (such as **print**); then click List Topics. When the topics appear in the list box, double-click on a topic to view its information. Search for help on these terms:

   - Finding documents
   - Copying files
   - Shutting down

   G. Close the help window by clicking the Close button (with an **X** on it) in the top right corner.

Internet Labs

To complete the following exercises, you will need a computer with an Internet connection and a Web browser. (For more information on using these tools, see "Prerequisites" at the front of this textbook.)

1. **Pick Your Favorite Pointing Device.** The Web is a great place to shop for computer equipment and to find information about new and different kinds of hardware. Visit these commercial Web sites for information on various types of pointing devices:

   - Gyration—**http://www.gyration.com/**
   - AVB Products—**http://www.avbtech.com/**
   - Cirque—**http://www.cirque.com/**
   - Logitech—**http://www.logitech.com/**
   - Razerzone—**http://www.razerzone.com/**
   - Hunter Digital—**http://www.footmouse.com/**

   When you are finished, decide which device will work best for you. Be prepared to tell your classmates about the device and explain why you selected it.

2. **Pick Your Dream Printer.** Visit these Web sites for information on printers:

   - Canon—**http://www.ccsi.canon.com/**
   - Epson—**http://www.epson.com/**
   - Hewlett-Packard—**http://www.hp.com/**
   - NEC Technologies—**http://www.nectech.com/**
   - Tektronix—**http://www.tek.com/**

   When you are finished, decide which device will work best for you. Be prepared to tell your classmates about the device and to explain why you selected it.

IBE Labs

If you have the Interactive Browser Edition (IBE) CD-ROM for this textbook, you may complete the following interactive exercises using the instructions provided in the IBE.

1. **Matching.** Play this game of word association.

2. **Labeling.** Drag-and-drop labels to "build" a computer system.

3. **What's Your Recommendation?** Based on the scenarios provided, make recommendations for users.

4. **Typing Test.** Use this exercise to test your typing skills.

UNIT 2

How Computers Work—Alone and in Groups

Manipulating and Storing Data

OVERVIEW:
The Difference Between Data and Information

It often seems as though computers must understand us because we understand the information they produce. However, all computers can do is recognize two distinct physical states produced by electricity, magnetic polarity, or reflected light. Essentially, all they can understand is whether a switch is on or off. In fact, the "brain" of the computer, the CPU, consists of several million tiny electronic switches, called **transistors.** A computer appears to understand information only because it contains so many transistors and operates at such phenomenal speeds, arranging and rearranging its individual on/off switches into patterns that are meaningful to us.

Data is the term used to describe the information represented by groups of on/off switches. Although the words *data* and *information* are often used interchangeably, there is an important distinction between them. In the strictest sense, data consists of the raw numbers that computers organize to produce information.

You can think of data as facts out of context, like the individual letters on this page. Taken individually, they do not tell you anything. Grouped together, however, they convey specific meanings. Just as a theater's marquee can combine thousands of lights to spell the name of the current show, a computer turns meaningless data into useful information, such as spreadsheets, graphs, and reports.

In this lesson, you will learn how computers process data and enable us to use it in informative ways. The following sections introduce the specific computing components that process and "remember" data, and those that store data so that it is always available for the user.

OBJECTIVES

- Explain why computers use the binary number system.
- List the two main parts of the CPU and explain how they work together.
- List three hardware factors that affect processing speed.
- List four common types of magnetic and optical storage devices.
- Explain how data is stored on the surface of magnetic and optical disks.

HOW COMPUTERS REPRESENT DATA

To a computer, everything is a number. Numbers are numbers; letters and punctuation marks are numbers; sounds and pictures are numbers. Even the computer's own instructions are numbers. When you see letters of the alphabet on a computer screen, you are seeing just one of the computer's ways of representing numbers. For example, consider this sentence: *Here are some words.* It may look like a string of alphabetic characters to you, but to a computer it looks like the string of ones and zeros shown in Figure 3.1.

Figure 3.1

The 1s and 0s that represent a sentence. The decimal system uses ten symbols, and it uses multiple digits for numbers above 9.

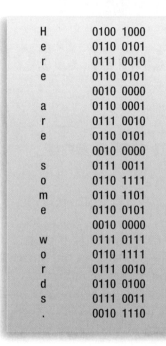

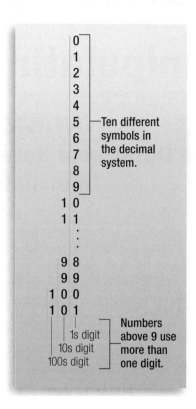

Computer data looks especially strange because people normally use base 10 to represent numbers. The system is called base 10, or the **decimal number system** (*deci* means "10" in Latin) because ten symbols are available: 0, 1, 2, 3, 4, 5, 6, 7, 8, and 9. When you need to represent a number greater than 9, you use two symbols together, as in 9 + 1 = 10. Each symbol in a number is called a digit, so 10 is a two-digit number.

In a computer, however, all data is represented by the state of the computer's electrical switches. A switch has only two possible states—on and off—so it can represent only two numeric values. To a computer, when a switch is off, it represents a 0; when a switch is on, it represents a 1 (see Figure 3.2). Because there are only two values, computers are said to function in base 2, which is also known as the **binary number system** (*bi* means "2" in Latin).

When a computer needs to represent a quantity greater than 1, it does the same thing you do when you need to represent a quantity greater than 9: it uses two (or more) digits.

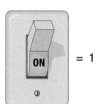

Figure 3.2

In a computer, data is represented by the state of electrical switches. An on switch represents a 1; an off switch represents a 0.

Bits and Bytes

When referring to computerized data, the value represented by each switch's state—whether the switch is turned on or off—is called a **bit.** The term *bit* is a combination of *b*inary dig*it.* A bit is the smallest possible unit of data a computer can recognize or use.

A group of 8 bits is called a byte (see Figure 3.3). There are enough different 8-bit combinations to represent up to 256 different values, including all the characters on the keyboard: all the letters (uppercase and lowercase), numbers, punctuation marks, and other symbols. If you refer to Figure 3.1, you will notice that each of the characters in the sentence *Here are some words.* is represented by 1 byte (8 bits) of data.

1 bit

Figure 3.3
One byte is composed of 8 bits.

8 bits = 1 byte

Text Codes

Early in the history of computing, programmers realized they needed a standard **text code**—a system they could all agree on—in which a series of numbers would be used to represent the letters of the alphabet, punctuation marks, and other symbols. The most popular systems that were invented are as follows:

◆ **EBCDIC.** The BCD (Binary Coded Decimal) system, defined by IBM for one of its early computers, was one of the first complete systems to represent symbols as groups of bits. BCD codes consisted of six-bit codes, which allowed a maximum of sixty-four symbols. The need to represent more characters led to IBM's development of **EBCDIC** (pronounced EB-si-dic), which stands for Extended Binary Coded Decimal Interchange Code. EBCDIC is an 8-bit code that defines 256 symbols. EBCDIC is still used in IBM mainframe and midrange systems but is rarely encountered in personal computers.

◆ **ASCII.** The American National Standards Institute's solution to representing symbols with bits of data was the ASCII character set. **ASCII** (pronounced AS-key) stands for the American Standard Code for Information Interchange. Today, the ASCII 8-bit character set is by far the most common in computers of all types. Table 3.1 on page 46 shows the first 128 ASCII codes.

◆ **Unicode.** An evolving standard for data representation, called the **Unicode** Worldwide Character Standard, provides 2 bytes—16 bits—to represent each letter, number, or symbol. With 2 bytes, enough Unicode codes can be created to represent more than 65,536 different characters or symbols, which is enough for every unique character and symbol in the world. A major advantage of Unicode is its compatibility with ASCII codes; the first 256 codes in Unicode are identical to the 256 codes used by ASCII systems.

Visit **www.glencoe.com/norton/online/** for more information on the **ASCII text code system** and the **Unicode text code system.**

Table 3.1 — The ASCII Table

ASCII Code	Decimal Equivalent	Character	ASCII Code	Decimal Equivalent	Character	ASCII Code	Decimal Equivalent	Character
0000 0000	0	Null prompt	0010 1011	43	+	0101 0110	86	V
0000 0001	1	Start of heading	0010 1100	44	,	0101 0111	87	W
0000 0010	2	Start of text	0010 1101	45	-	0101 1000	88	X
0000 0011	3	End of text	0010 1110	46	.	0101 1001	89	Y
0000 0100	4	End of transmit	0010 1111	47	/	0101 1010	90	Z
0000 0101	5	Enquiry	0011 0000	48	0	0101 1011	91	[
0000 0110	6	Acknowledge	0011 0001	49	1	0101 1100	92	\
0000 0111	7	Audible bell	0011 0010	50	2	0101 1101	93	]
0000 1000	8	Backspace	0011 0011	51	3	0101 1110	94	^
0000 1001	9	Horizontal tab	0011 0100	52	4	0101 1111	95	_
0000 1010	10	Line feed	0011 0101	53	5	0110 0000	96	`
0000 1011	11	Vertical tab	0011 0110	54	6	0110 0001	97	a
0000 1100	12	Form feed	0011 0111	55	7	0110 0010	98	b
0000 1101	13	Carriage return	0011 1000	56	8	0110 0011	99	c
0000 1110	14	Shift out	0011 1001	57	9	0110 0100	100	d
0000 1111	15	Shift in	0011 1010	58	:	0110 0101	101	e
0001 0000	16	Data link escape	0011 1011	59	;	0110 0110	102	f
0001 0001	17	Device control 1	0011 1100	60	<	0110 0111	103	g
0001 0010	18	Device control 2	0011 1101	61	=	0110 1000	104	h
0001 0011	19	Device control 3	0011 1110	62	>	0110 1001	105	i
0001 0100	20	Device control 4	0011 1111	63	?	0110 1010	106	j
0001 0101	21	Neg. acknowledge	0100 0000	64	@	0110 1011	107	k
0001 0110	22	Synchronous idle	0100 0001	65	A	0110 1100	108	l
0001 0111	23	End trans. block	0100 0010	66	B	0110 1101	109	m
0001 1000	24	Cancel	0100 0011	67	C	0110 1110	110	n
0001 1001	25	End of medium	0100 0100	68	D	0110 1111	111	o
0001 1010	26	Substitution	0100 0101	69	E	0111 0000	112	p
0001 1011	27	Escape	0100 0110	70	F	0111 0001	113	q
0001 1100	28	File separator	0100 0111	71	G	0111 0010	114	r
0001 1101	29	Group separator	0100 1000	72	H	0111 0011	115	s
0001 1110	30	Record separator	0100 1001	73	I	0111 0100	116	t
0001 1111	31	Unit separator	0100 1010	74	J	0111 0101	117	u
0010 0000	32	Blank space	0100 1011	75	K	0111 0110	118	v
0010 0001	33	!	0100 1100	76	L	0111 0111	119	w
0010 0010	34	"	0100 1101	77	M	0111 1000	120	x
0010 0011	35	#	0100 1110	78	N	0111 1001	121	y
0010 0100	36	$	0100 1111	79	O	0111 1010	122	z
0010 0101	37	%	0101 0000	80	P	0111 1011	123	{
0010 0110	38	&	0101 0001	81	Q	0111 1100	124		
0010 0111	39	'	0101 0010	82	R	0111 1101	125	}
0010 1000	40	(	0101 0011	83	S	0111 1110	126	~
0010 1001	41	)	0101 0100	84	T	0111 1111	127	Delete or rubout
0010 1010	42	*	0101 0101	85	U			

HOW COMPUTERS PROCESS DATA

Two components handle processing in a computer: the central processing unit, or CPU, and the memory. Both are located on the computer's motherboard (shown in Figure 3.4), the circuit board that connects the CPU to all the other hardware devices.

The CPU

The CPU is the "brain" of the computer, the place where data is manipulated. In large computer systems, such as supercomputers and mainframes, processing tasks may be handled by multiple processing chips. In the average microcomputer, the entire CPU is a single unit, called a microprocessor. Regardless of its construction, however, every CPU has at least two basic parts: the control unit and the arithmetic logic unit.

All the computer's resources are managed from the **control unit.** You can think of the control unit as a traffic cop directing the flow of data through the CPU, and to and from other devices. The control unit is the logical hub of the computer (see Figure 3.5). The CPU's instructions for carrying out commands are built into the control unit. The instructions, or **instruction set,** list all the operations that the CPU can perform.

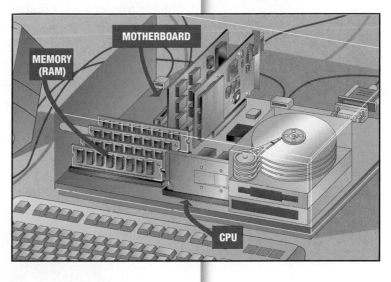

Figure 3.4
Processing devices.

Because all computer data is stored as numbers, much of the processing that takes place involves comparing numbers or carrying out mathematical operations. In addition to establishing ordered sequences and changing those sequences, the computer can perform two types of operations: arithmetic operations and logical operations. Arithmetic operations include addition, subtraction, multiplication, and division. Logical operations include comparisons, such as determining whether one number is equal to, not equal to, greater than, or less than another number.

Many instructions carried out by the control unit involve simply moving data from one place to another—from memory to storage, from memory to the printer, and so forth. When the control unit encounters an instruction that involves arithmetic or logic, however, it passes that instruction to the second component of the CPU, the **arithmetic logic unit,** or **ALU.** The ALU includes a group of **registers**—high-speed memory locations built directly into the CPU that are used to hold the data currently being processed. For example, the control unit might load two numbers from memory into the registers in the ALU. Then it might tell the ALU to divide the two numbers (an arithmetic operation), or to see whether the numbers are equal (a logical operation).

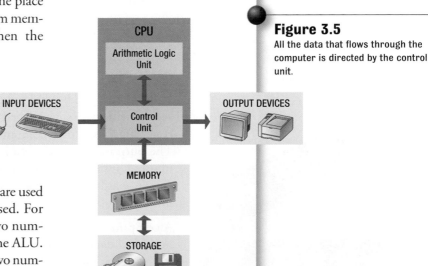

Figure 3.5
All the data that flows through the computer is directed by the control unit.

Memory

The CPU contains the basic instructions needed to operate the computer, but it cannot store entire programs or large sets of data permanently. The CPU contains registers, but they can hold only a few bytes at a time. In addition to registers, the CPU needs to have millions of bytes of randomly accessed space where it can quickly read or write programs and data while they are being used. This area is called memory. Physically, memory consists of chips either on the motherboard or on a small circuit board attached to the motherboard. This electronic memory allows the CPU to store and retrieve data quickly.

There are two types of built-in memory: permanent and nonpermanent (see Figure 3.6). Some memory chips always retain the data they hold, even when the computer is turned off. This type of memory is called **nonvolatile.** Other chips—in fact, most of the memory in a microcomputer—lose their contents when the computer's power is shut off. These chips have **volatile** memory.

Figure 3.6
The CPU is attached to two kinds of memory: RAM, which is volatile, and ROM, which is nonvolatile.

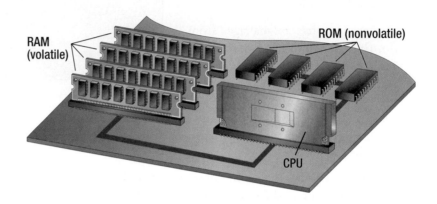

ROM

Nonvolatile chips always hold the same data; the data in them never changes during normal operations. In fact, putting data permanently into this kind of memory is called "burning in the data," and it is usually done at the factory. Because the data in these chips can only be read and used—and is not normally changed—the memory is called read-only memory (ROM). Among other things, ROM contains a set of start-up instructions so that the computer knows what to do when the power is first turned on.

Figure 3.7
On the top is a SIMM; on the bottom is an example of a DIMM.

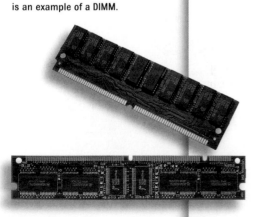

RAM

Memory that can be changed is called read-write memory or random-access memory (RAM). When people talk about computer memory in connection with microcomputers, they usually mean the volatile RAM. The purpose of RAM is to hold programs and data while they are in use. Physically, RAM consists of chips grouped together on small circuit boards called single in-line memory modules (SIMMs) or dual in-line memory modules (DIMMs). Both are shown in Figure 3.7.

A computer does not have to search its entire memory each time it must find data because the CPU uses a **memory address** to store and retrieve each piece of data. A memory address is a number that indicates a location on the memory chips, much as a post office box number indicates a slot into which mail is placed.

FACTORS AFFECTING PROCESSING SPEED

The circuitry design of a CPU determines its basic speed, but other components can make chips already designed for speed work even faster. Figure 3.8 shows how these components can be arranged on the motherboard.

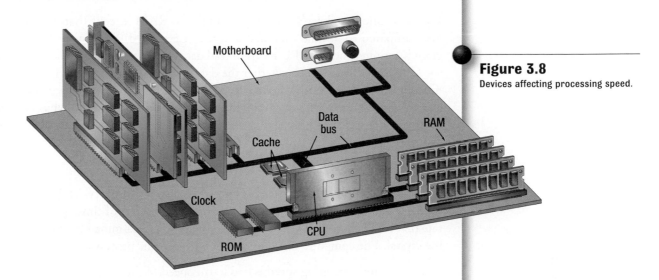

Figure 3.8
Devices affecting processing speed.

How Registers Affect Speed

The size of the registers, which is sometimes called the **word size,** indicates the amount of data with which the computer can work at any given time. The bigger the word size, the more quickly the computer can process a set of data. The registers in the first PCs could hold 2 bytes—16 bits—each. Most CPUs sold today, for both PCs and Macintosh computers, have 32-bit registers. Many newer PCs, as well as minicomputers and high-end workstations, have 64-bit registers.

Memory and Computing Power

The amount of RAM in a computer can have a profound effect on the computer's power. For one thing, more RAM means the computer can use bigger, more powerful programs, and those programs can access bigger data files.

More RAM can also make the computer run faster. The computer does not necessarily have to load an entire program into memory to run it. However, the greater the amount of the program that fits into memory, the faster the program runs. For example, a PC with 16 MB of RAM can run Microsoft Windows 98, even though the operating system actually occupies about 195 MB of disk storage space. When you run Windows, the program does not need to load all its files into memory to run properly. It loads only the most essential parts into memory. When the computer needs access to other parts of the program on the disk, it can unload, or **swap out,** nonessential parts from RAM back to the hard disk. Then the computer can load, or **swap in,** the program code or data it needs.

While this method is effective for managing a limited amount of memory, it can result in slow system performance because the CPU, memory, and disk are continuously occupied with the swapping process. However, if your PC has 64 MB of RAM (or more), you will notice a dramatic difference in how fast Microsoft Windows 98 runs because the CPU will need to swap instructions between RAM and the hard disk less often.

Visit **www.glencoe.com/norton/online/** for more information on **processor speeds.**

Cache Memory

Moving data between RAM and the CPU's registers is one of the most time-consuming operations a CPU must perform, simply because RAM is much slower than the CPU. A partial solution to this problem is to include a cache memory in the CPU. Since the late 1980s, cache memory has been built into most CPUs.

Cache (pronounced *cash*) **memory** is similar to RAM, except that it is extremely fast compared to normal memory, and it is used in a different way. When a program is running and the CPU needs to read data or program instructions from RAM, the CPU first checks to see whether the data is in cache memory. If the data that it needs is not there, it reads the data from RAM into its registers, but it also loads a copy of the data into cache memory. The next time the CPU needs that same data, it finds it in the cache memory and saves the time needed to load the data from RAM.

The Computer's Internal Clock

Every microcomputer has a **system clock,** driven by a quartz crystal. When electricity is applied, the molecules in the crystal vibrate millions of times per second, at a rate that never changes. The speed of the vibration is determined by the thickness of the crystal. The computer uses the vibrations to time its processing operations.

The computer's operating speed is tied to the speed of the system clock. **Hertz (Hz)** is a measure of cycles per second. **Megahertz (MHz)** means millions of cycles per second. For example, if a computer's clock speed is 300 MHz, it "ticks" 300 million times per second. As the system's clock speed increases, so does the number of instructions it can complete each second.

The Bus

In microcomputers, the term **bus** refers to the paths between the components of a computer. There are two main buses in a computer: the internal (or system) bus and the external (or expansion) bus. The system bus resides on the motherboard and connects the CPU to other devices that reside on the motherboard. An expansion bus connects other devices to the CPU.

The system bus has two parts: the data bus and the address bus (see Figure 3.9). The **data bus** is an electrical path that connects the CPU, memory, and the other hardware devices on the motherboard. Actually, the bus is a group of parallel wires. The number of wires in the bus affects the speed at which data can travel between hardware components. Because each wire can transfer 1 bit of data at a time, an 8-wire bus can move 8 bits at a time, which is a full byte. A 16-bit bus can transfer 2 bytes, and a 32-bit bus can transfer 4 bytes at a time. Newer computers have a 64-bit data bus, which transfers 8 bytes at a time.

The **address bus** is a set of wires similar to the data bus. The address bus, however, connects only the CPU and RAM and carries only memory addresses.

Figure 3.9

The motherboard includes an address bus and a data bus. The address bus leads from the CPU to RAM. The data bus connects the CPU to memory, as well as all the storage, input/output, and communication devices.

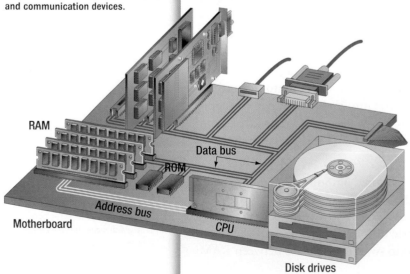

RAM

Data bus

ROM

Address bus

Motherboard

CPU

Disk drives

EXTENDING THE PROCESSOR'S POWER TO OTHER DEVICES

When you need to add a new piece of hardware to your computer, you need to know how to connect it to the bus. In some cases, you can plug the device into an existing socket, or port, on the back of the computer, as shown in Figure 3.10. When a port is not available, you must install a circuit board that includes the port you need.

Serial and Parallel Ports

Internally, a PC's components communicate through the data bus, which consists of parallel wires. Similarly, a **parallel interface** is a connection including eight or more wires through which data bits can flow simultaneously. Most computer buses transfer 32 bits simultaneously. However, the standard parallel interface for external devices like printers usually transfers 8 bits at a time over eight separate wires.

With a **serial interface,** data bits are transmitted one at a time through a single wire; however, the interface includes additional wires for the bits that control the flow of data. Inside the computer, a chip called a universal asynchronous receiver-transmitter (UART) converts parallel data from the bus into serial data that flows through a serial cable.

As you would expect, a parallel interface can handle a higher volume of data than a serial interface because more than 1 bit can be transmitted through a parallel interface simultaneously. Parallel ports are mostly used to connect printers.

Specialized Expansion Ports

In addition to the standard collection of expansion ports, many PCs include specialized ports. These ports allow the connection of special devices or extend the computer's bus in unique ways.

◆ **SCSI.** The **Small Computer System Interface** (**SCSI**, pronounced *scuzzy*) takes a different approach from those discussed so far and overcomes many of the constraints of a limited number of expansion slots on the motherboard. Instead of forcing the user to plug multiple cards into the computer's expansion slots, a single SCSI adapter extends the bus outside the computer by way of a cable. In other words, SCSI is like an extension cord for the data bus. Just as you can plug one extension cord into another to lengthen a circuit, you can also plug one SCSI device into another to form a daisy chain (see Figure 3.11).

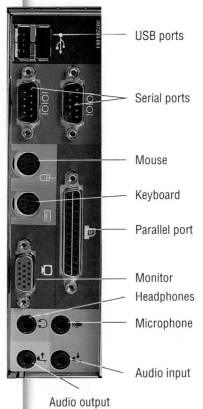

Figure 3.10
These ports are standard equipment on many newer PCs.

- USB ports
- Serial ports
- Mouse
- Keyboard
- Parallel port
- Monitor
- Headphones
- Microphone
- Audio input
- Audio output

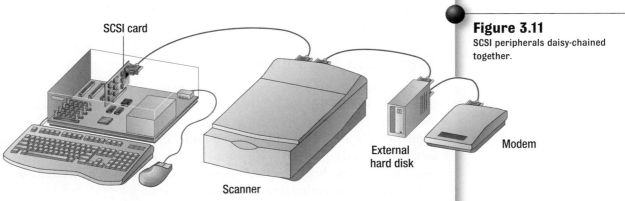

SCSI card

Scanner

External hard disk

Modem

Figure 3.11
SCSI peripherals daisy-chained together.

◆ **USB.** The **Universal Serial Bus (USB)** standard is rapidly gaining popularity on personal computers—both IBM-compatible systems and Macintosh systems. Because the USB standard allows 127 devices to be connected to the bus via a single port, many experts believe that USB will emerge as the single bus standard of the future. Today, most new computers feature at least one or two USB ports (see Figure 3.12).

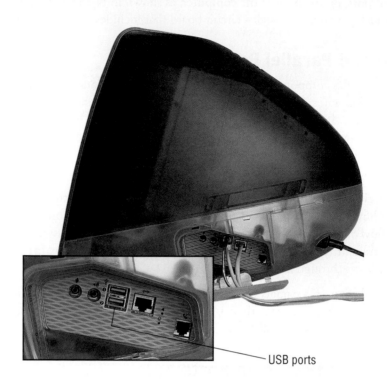

Figure 3.12
All new Macintosh computers and a growing number of IBM-compatible PCs feature one or more Universal Serial Bus (USB) ports. As many as 127 USB-compliant devices, including printers, keyboards, mice, video devices, and other peripherals, can be connected to a single USB port.

USB ports

◆ **IEEE 1394 (FireWire).** Like the USB standard, the **IEEE 1394** (or **FireWire**) standard extends the computer's bus to many peripheral devices through a single port. Because IEEE 1394-compliant technology is so expensive, however, it is not expected to become the dominant bus technology. It may gain wide acceptance as a standard for plugging video and other devices to the system bus.

◆ **MIDI.** The **Musical Instrument Digital Interface (MIDI)** has been in use since the early 1980s, when a group of musical instrument manufacturers developed the technology to enable electronic instruments to communicate. Since then, MIDI has been adapted to the personal computer. Many sound cards are MIDI-compliant and feature a special MIDI port. Using a MIDI port, you can plug a wide variety of musical instruments and other MIDI-controlled devices into the computer.

Expansion Slots and Boards

PCs are designed so that users can adapt, or configure, the machines to their particular needs. PC motherboards have two or more **expansion slots,** which are extensions of the computer's bus that provide a way to add new components to the computer. The slots accept **expansion boards,** also called cards, adapters, or sometimes just boards. Figure 3.13 shows a PC expansion board being installed. The board is being attached to the motherboard—the main system board to which the CPU, memory, and other components are attached.

Figure 3.13
An expansion card being inserted into an expansion slot.

PC Cards

Another type of expansion card—the **PC Card** (also initially called a Personal Computer Memory Card International Association or PCMCIA card)—is a small device about the size of a credit card (see Figure 3.14). This special device was initially designed for use in notebook computers and other computers that are too small to accept a standard expansion card. PC Cards are used for a wide variety of purposes and can house modems, network cards, memory, and even fully functioning hard disk drives.

CPUs USED IN PERSONAL COMPUTERS

For two decades after the birth of the personal computer, the biggest player in the PC CPU market was Intel Corporation. This situation began to change in 1998, however, when a number of leading computer makers (most notably Compaq and Gateway, as well as others) began offering lower-priced systems using chips made by AMD and Cyrix. These microprocessors were comparable in many respects to chips made by Intel but typically offered less performance at a lower price. That equation is quickly changing, however, because Intel's competitors are making rapid advances in their products' performance, while chip prices are becoming increasingly competitive.

Meantime, computer users watched the rebirth of Apple Computer, which nearly folded after losing most of its market share to competitors. Apple's savior, as it turned out, was an odd-looking PC named the iMac—a low-priced system that performed as well as higher-priced IBM-compatible PCs. Like other Macintosh systems, the iMac uses processors made by Motorola.

Intel Processors

The Intel Corporation is the world's largest manufacturer of microchips and is historically the leading provider of chips for PCs. In fact, Intel invented the microprocessor, the so-called computer on a chip, in 1971 with the 4004 model, which was used in handheld calculators. This invention led to the first micro-computers, which began appearing in 1975. Even so, Intel's success in this market was not guaranteed until 1981 when IBM released the first IBM PC, which was based on the Intel 8088 processor.

Figure 3.14
Small PC Card devices perform many different functions, providing memory, storage, communications, and other capabilities.

Since then, most IBM personal computers and compatibles based on IBM's design have been created around Intel's chips. Although the 8088 was the first chip to be used in an IBM PC, IBM actually used an earlier chip, the 8086, in a subsequent model, called the IBM PC XT. The chips that came later—the 80286, 80386, 80486, the Pentium, Pentium Pro, Pentium II, Pentium III, Celeron, and Xeon lines (see Figure 3.15)—correspond to certain design standards established by the 8086. This line of chips is called the 80x86 line. A list of Intel chips, along with their basic specifications, is shown in Table 3.2.

The basic structural design of each chip, known as the architecture, has grown steadily in sophistication and complexity. The architecture of the 8086 contained only a few thousand transistors, but today's powerful Pentium III Xeon processors contain 9.5 million. This complex design is primarily responsible for the continually increasing power and speed of the Intel processor line.

Figure 3.15
The Intel Pentium family of processors.

Advanced Micro Devices (AMD) Processors

In 1998, Advanced Micro Devices (AMD) emerged as a primary competitor to Intel's dominance in the IBM-compatible PC market. Until that time, AMD processors were typically found in low-end, low-priced home and small business computers. However, AMD proved that it could compete feature for feature with many of Intel's best-selling products and focused its efforts on two processor lines (see Figure 3.16):

Figure 3.16
The AMD K6-III and the AMD Athlon.

◆ **K6.** Known for years as a maker of budget processors, AMD burst into prominence with its K6 line of chips, which quickly became popular among major computer makers for both desktop and notebook PCs. While the K6 was not entirely compatible with Intel processors and initially performed at slower speeds, AMD continued to improve the line and eventually began to overtake Intel in some markets. In early 1999, AMD released the K6-III as a head-to-head competitor with the Pentium III.

Table 3.2 ▶ Intel Chips and Their Specifications

Model	Intro. Year	Data Bus Capacity	Register Size	Addressable Memory	Clock Speeds	Number of Transistors
8086	1978	16 bit	16 bit	1 MB	5 MHz, 8 MHz, 10 MHz	29,000
8088	1979	8 bit	16 bit	1 MB	5 MHz, 8 MHz	29,000
80286	1982	16 bit	16 bit	16 MB	6 MHz, 8 MHz, 10 MHz, 12 MHz, 25 MHz	134,000
80386	1985	32 bit	32 bit	4 GB	16 MHz, 20 MHz, 25 MHz, 33 MHz	275,000
80486	1989	32 bit	32 bit	4 GB	25 MHz, 33 MHz, 50 MHz, 66 MHz, 75 MHz, 100 MHz	1.2 million
Pentium	1993	64 bit	32 bit	4 GB	60 MHz, 66 MHz, 100 MHz, 120 MHz, 133 MHz, 150 MHz, 166 MHz	3.1 million
Pentium Pro	1995	64 bit	32 bit	64 GB	150 MHz, 166 MHz, 200 MHz	5.5 million
Pentium II	1997	64 bit	32 bit	64 GB	233 MHz, 266 MHz, 300 MHz, 333 MHz, 350 MHz, 400 MHz, 450 MHz	7.5 million
Pentium II Xeon	1998	64 bit	64 bit	64 GB	400 MHz, 450 MHz, and higher	7.5 million
Pentium II Celeron	1998	64 bit	64 bit	64 GB	266 MHz, 300 MHz, 333 MHz, 366 MHz, 400 MHz, 433 MHz, 466 MHz, 500 MHz	7.5 million*
Pentium III	1999	64 bit	64/128 bit	64 GB	450 MHz, 500 MHz, 550 MHz, 600 MHz, 750MHz, 1 GHz, and higher	9.5 million
Pentium III Xeon	1999	64 bit	64/128 bit	64 GB	500 MHz, 550 MHz, and higher	9.5 million

*Later versions of the Celeron processor have a total of 19 million transistors.

◆ **Athlon.** Upon its release in August 1999, AMD's Athlon processor was the fastest microprocessor available, operating at speeds up to 650 MHz. The Athlon outperformed the Pentium III in tests because it could perform more instructions at one time. Utilizing a bus speed of 100 MHz at the time of its release, the Athlon processor was actually designed to work with bus speeds of 200 MHz.

Self Check ✔

Answer the following questions by filling in the blank(s).

1. A PC uses the _____ number system.

2. _____ are high-speed memory locations built directly into the ALU.

3. The basic structural design of a processor is called its _____ .

Cyrix Processors

Cyrix began as a maker of specialized microchips, but in the mid-1990s the company began making processors that competed with Intel's products. Cyrix focuses its attention on the less-than-$1000 PC market, with its two processor lines:

◆ **MediaGX.** In 1997, Cyrix introduced the MediaGX processor, a Pentium-compatible microprocessor that integrated audio and graphics functions and operated at speeds of 233 MHz and higher. In 1999, however, Cyrix was sold by National Semiconductor, Inc., who maintained ownership of the MediaGX product line. At the time of the sale, National's announced intention was to market the MediaGX technology for use in smart appliances, network computers, and other small computing devices.

◆ **MII.** Under the auspices of its new owner, VIA Technologies, Inc., Cyrix continued to develop its MII line of microprocessors (see Figure 3.17). This Pentium II-class processor is used by various PC manufacturers.

Figure 3.17
The Cyrix MII processor.

Motorola Processors

Motorola Corporation is another major manufacturer of microprocessors for small computers. Apple's Macintosh computers use Motorola processors. Other computer manufacturers, including workstation manufacturers such as Sun Microsystems, have also relied heavily on Motorola chips. They were an early favorite among companies that built larger, UNIX-based computers, such as the NCR Tower series and the AT&T 3B series. Motorola offers two families of processor chips:

◆ **680x0.** Although the 68000 chip is best known as the foundation of the original Macintosh, it actually predates the Mac by several years. In fact, IBM considered using the 68000 in the first IBM PC. Although Motorola's 68000 chip (introduced in 1979) was more powerful than Intel's 8088, subsequent improvements to the Motorola chip were made in smaller increments than Intel's giant performance leaps. By the time Motorola introduced the 68060 chip in 1993, Intel was promoting the Pentium. In an attempt to regain market share, Motorola initiated the development of the new PowerPC chip.

◆ **PowerPC.** The PowerPC chip had an unusual beginning. Two industry rivals, IBM and Apple, joined forces with Motorola in 1991, ostensibly to dethrone Intel from its preeminence in the PC chip market. The hardware portion of their efforts focused on the PowerPC chip, the first of which was the 601. Following closely on its heels was the 603, a low-power processor suitable for notebook computers. Its successors, the 604 and 604e, are high-power chips designed for high-end desktop systems.

With the introduction of the 620 late in 1995, PowerPC chips established a new performance record for microprocessors. A handful of small 620-based machines working together offers about the same computing power as an IBM 370 mainframe. The PowerPC 750 chip (266 MHz) was released for desktop and mobile computers that need significant computing power in a low-voltage processor. The PowerPC 750 was designed for multimedia, small business, and mobile applications.

The G3 chip, released in 1998, provides even more power for such applications. Apple's iMac and Power Mac personal computer lines are built around the G3 chip and offer better performance and speed than Pentium II-based systems at a lower cost.

NORTON ONLINE

Visit **www.glencoe.com/norton/online/** for more information on **Cyrix** products and **Motorola's line of products.**

In 1999, Apple released the newest member of the PowerPC family—the G4—and described the processor as having "the heart of a supercomputer miniaturized onto a sliver of silicon." Apple's PowerMac G4 system (see Figure 3.18) is based on the G4 processor. Operating at speeds of 500 MHz and higher, the G4's 128-bit processor can perform 1 billion floating-point operations (one gigaflop) per second. The G4 processor features 1 MB of external cache and a bus speed of 100 MHz.

Figure 3.18
Apple's Power Mac G4 system is based on the powerful PowerPC G4 processor.

Visit **www.glencoe.com/norton/online/** for more information on **RISC** processors.

RISC Processors

Both the Motorola 680*x*0 and Intel 80*x*86 families are **complex instruction set computing (CISC)** processors. The instruction sets for these CPUs are large, typically containing 200 to 300 instructions.

A newer theory in microprocessor design holds that if the instruction set for the CPU is kept small and simple, each instruction will execute in much less time, allowing the processor to complete more instructions during a given period. CPUs designed according to this theory are called **reduced instruction set computing (RISC)** processors. RISC instruction sets are considerably smaller than those used by CISC processors. The RISC design, which is used in the PowerPC but was first implemented in the mid-1980s, results in a faster and less expensive processor (see Figure 3.19). Because of the way the Pentium and its spin-offs process instructions, they are called RISC-like, but their architecture is still based on complex instruction set computing.

Figure 3.19
This AlphaServer 1200 system is a RISC-based enterprise server. Some of the most powerful network servers and workstations are based on RISC technology.

Parallel Processing

An emerging school of thought on producing faster computers is to build them with more than one processor. This type of system uses **parallel processing** techniques; that is, the system harnesses multiple processors that share the processing workload. The result is a system that can handle a greater flow of data, complete more tasks in a shorter period of time, and deal with the demands of many input and output devices.

MAGNETIC STORAGE DEVICES

The purpose of storage devices is to hold data and program instructions—even when the computer is turned off—so they can be used whenever they are needed. This requirement involves the processes of writing data to the storage medium and reading data back from the storage medium. Writing data means recording data on the surface of the disk, where it is stored for later use. Reading data means retrieving the data from the disk's surface and transferring it into the computer's memory for use by the operating system or an application program.

Because they use the same medium (the material on which the data is stored), diskette drives, hard disk drives, and tape drives use similar techniques for writing and reading data. The surfaces of diskettes, hard disks, and magnetic tape are coated with a magnetically sensitive material, such as iron oxide, that reacts to a magnetic field.

Just as a transistor can represent binary data as on or off, the orientation of a magnetic field can be used to represent data. A magnet has one key advantage over a transistor: it can represent on and off without a continual source of electricity.

The surfaces of disks and magnetic tapes are coated with millions of tiny iron particles so that data can be stored on them. Each of these particles can act as a magnet, taking on a magnetic field when subjected to an electromagnet. The read/write heads of a hard disk drive, diskette drive, or tape drive contain electromagnets that generate magnetic fields on the storage medium as the head passes over the disk or tape.

As shown in Figure 3.20, the read/write heads record strings of 1s and 0s by alternating the direction of the current in the electromagnets. To read data from a magnetic surface, the process is reversed. The read/write head passes over the disk or tape while no current is flowing through the electromagnet. Because the storage medium has a magnetic field but the head does not, the storage medium charges the magnet in the head, which causes a small current to flow through the head in one direction or the other depending on the polarity of the field. The disk or tape drive senses the direction of the flow as the storage medium passes by the head, and the data is sent from the read/write head into memory.

Figure 3.20
Data being recorded by a read/write head.

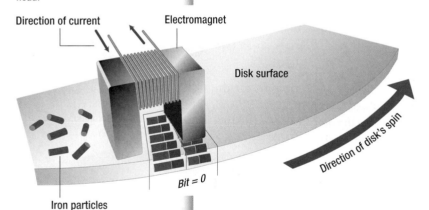

Direction of current

Electromagnet

Disk surface

Direction of disk's spin

Bit = 0

Iron particles

How Data Is Organized on a Magnetic Disk

Before the computer can use a diskette to store data, the disk's surface must be magnetically mapped so that the computer can go directly to a specific point on it without searching through data. This mapping process is called **formatting** or **initializing.** Even though new diskettes come preformatted, you may want to reformat a diskette whenever you want to delete all data from it. During formatting, you can also determine whether the disk's surface has bad spots, and you can copy important system files to the disk. You can format a floppy disk by using operating system commands (see Figure 3.21).

Hard disks must also be formatted so the computer can locate data on them. When you buy a computer, its hard disk has already been correctly formatted and probably already contains some programs and data. You can format your hard disk, if necessary, but the process is a little different from formatting a floppy disk.

Modern diskettes store data on both sides of the disk (numbered as side 0 and side 1), and each side has its own read/write head. What a disk drive does first when formatting a disk is create a set of magnetic concentric circles, called **tracks,** on each side of the disk. The number of tracks required depends on the type of disk. Most high-density diskettes, for example, have eighty tracks on each side of the disk. A hard disk may have several hundred tracks on each side of each platter. Each track is a separate circle, like the circles on a bull's-eye target. The tracks are numbered from the outermost circle to the innermost, starting from zero, as shown in Figure 3.22.

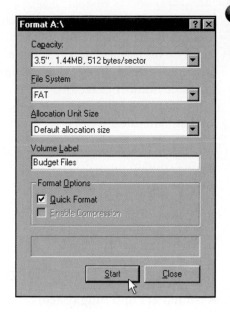

Figure 3.21
Formatting a floppy disk in Windows NT.

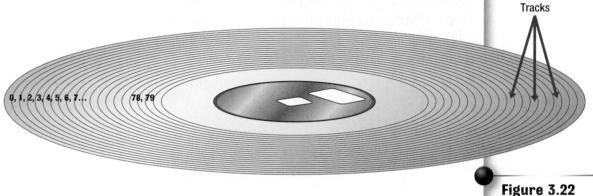

Figure 3.22
Tracks are concentric circles, numbered from the outside in.

Each track on a disk is also split into smaller parts. Imagine slicing up a disk like cutting a pie. As shown in Figure 3.23, each slice would cut across all the disk's tracks, resulting in short segments, or **sectors.** A sector is the smallest unit with which any disk drive (diskette drive or hard drive) can work. Each bit and byte within a sector can have different values, but the drive can read or write only whole sectors at a time. If the computer needs to change just 1 byte out of 512, it must rewrite the entire sector.

In both diskettes and hard disks, a sector can store up to 512 bytes (0.5 KB). All the sectors on the disk are numbered in one long sequence so that the computer can access each small area on the disk with a unique number. This scheme simplifies what would normally be a set of two-dimensional coordinates into a single numeric address.

Figure 3.23
Sectors on a disk, each with a unique number.

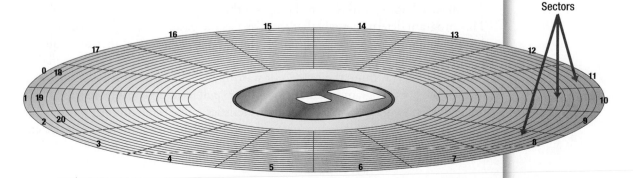

If a diskette has eighty tracks on each side, and each track contains eighteen sectors, then the disk has 1440 sectors (80 × 18) per side, for a total of 2880 sectors. This calculation is true regardless of the length of the track. The diskette's outermost track is longer than the innermost track, but each is still divided into the same number of sectors. All of a diskette's sectors hold the same number of bytes; that is, the shortest, innermost sectors hold the same amount of data as the longest, outermost sectors.

Because files are not usually a size that is an even multiple of 512 bytes, some sectors contain unused space after the end of the file. In addition, the Windows operating system allocates a group of sectors, called a **cluster,** to each file stored on a disk. Cluster sizes vary depending on the size and type of the disk, but they can range from four sectors for diskettes, to sixty-four sectors for some hard disks.

How the Operating System Finds Data on a Disk

A computer's operating system can locate data on a disk (diskette or hard drive) because each track and sector is labeled, and the location of all data is kept in a special log on the disk. The labeling of tracks and sectors is called performing a **logical format.** A commonly used logical format performed by Windows creates these four disk areas (see Figure 3.24):

◆ Master boot record (MBR)
◆ File-allocation table (FAT)
◆ Root folder or directory
◆ Data area

Figure 3.24
When a disk is formatted, these four areas are defined.

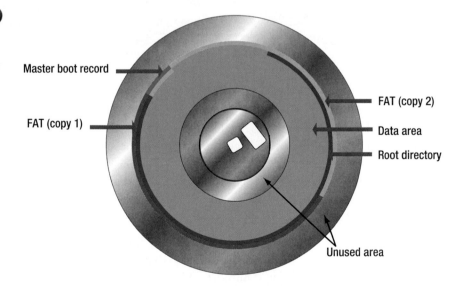

Master boot record

FAT (copy 1)

FAT (copy 2)

Data area

Root directory

Unused area

The **master boot record** is a small program that runs when you start the computer. This program determines whether the disk has the basic components necessary to run the operating system successfully. If the program determines that the required files are present and the disk has a valid format, it transfers control to the operating system, which continues the process of starting up. This process is called **booting** because the boot program makes the computer "pull itself up by its bootstraps." The boot record also describes other disk characteristics, such as the number of bytes per sector and the number of sectors per track—information that the operating system needs to access the data area of the disk.

The **file-allocation table (FAT)** is a log that records the location of each file and the status of each sector. When you write a file to a disk, the operating system checks the FAT for an open area, stores the file, and then identifies the file and its location in the FAT (see Figure 3.25).

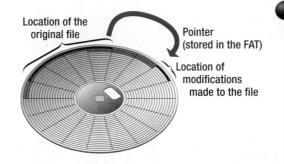

Location of the original file

Pointer (stored in the FAT)

Location of modifications made to the file

Figure 3.25
When new data must be added to a file and there is no more room next to the cluster where the original data is stored, the operating system records the new information in an unused cluster on the disk. The FAT lists both clusters, and a pointer at the end of the first cluster connects it to the second.

Users do not see the information listed in the FAT, but they often use the information. A **folder,** also called a **directory,** is a tool for organizing files on a disk. Folders can contain files or other folders, so it is possible to set up a hierarchical system of folders on your computer, just as you have folders within other folders in a file cabinet. The top folder on any disk is known as the root. (Experienced computer users may refer to this folder as the **root folder** or **root directory.**) When you use the operating system to view the contents of a folder, the operating system lists specific information about each file in the folder. Figure 3.26 shows a typical folder listing on a Windows NT system. The part of the disk that remains free after the boot sector, FAT, and root folder have been created is called the **data area** because that is where files are actually stored.

Figure 3.26
A Windows NT folder listing.

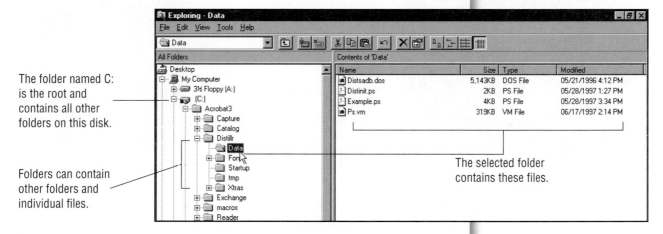

The folder named C: is the root and contains all other folders on this disk.

Folders can contain other folders and individual files.

The selected folder contains these files.

Diskettes (Floppy Disks)

Figure 3.27 shows a diskette and a diskette drive. The drive includes a motor that rotates the disk on a spindle and read/write heads that can move to any spot on the disk's surface as the disk spins.

Diskettes spin at approximately 300 revolutions per minute. Therefore, the longest it can take to position a point on the diskette under the read/write heads is the amount of time required for one revolution—about 0.2 second.

Figure 3.27
Parts of a diskette and diskette drive.

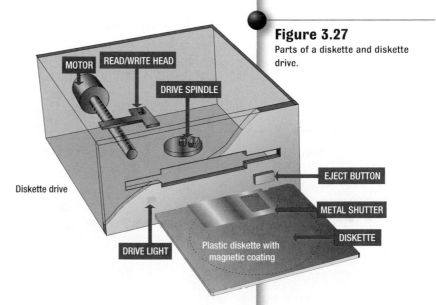

MOTOR · READ/WRITE HEAD · DRIVE SPINDLE · Diskette drive · EJECT BUTTON · METAL SHUTTER · DISKETTE · DRIVE LIGHT · Plastic diskette with magnetic coating

The most common uses of diskettes are as follows:

◆ Moving files between computers that are not connected through network or communications hardware

◆ Loading new programs onto a system

◆ **Backing up** (the process of creating a duplicate set of files) data or programs, the primary copy of which is stored on a hard disk drive

During the 1980s, most PCs used 5.25-inch diskettes. Today, the 3.5-inch diskette has almost completely replaced its 5.25-inch cousin (see Figure 3.28). The size refers to the diameter of the disk and is not an indication of the disk's capacity. The 5.25-inch type is encased in a flexible vinyl envelope with an oval cutout that allows the read/write head to access the disk. The 3.5-inch diskette is encased in a hard plastic shell with a sliding metal shutter. When the disk is inserted into the drive, the shutter slides back to expose the disk's surface to the read/write head.

Figure 3.28
A 5.25-inch diskette (left) and a 3.5-inch diskette (right).

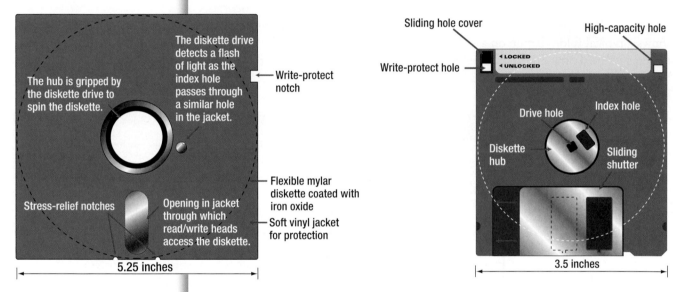

Both types of diskette have evolved from lower to higher densities. The **density** of the disk is a measure of the capacity of the disk surface (see Table 3.3). The higher the density, the more closely the iron-oxide particles are packed, and the more data the disk can store. Early versions of diskettes were double density (DD). However, double-density diskettes have been almost completely replaced by high-density (HD) diskettes, which provide more storage.

Table 3.3	Formatting Specifications for Floppy Disks							
Diameter (Inches)	Type	Tracks	Sectors/ Track	Sectors	Bytes/ Sector	Total Bytes	Bytes Expressed in KB	MB
5.25	Double density (DD)	40	9	720	512	368,640	360	.36
5.25	High density (HD)	80	15	2400	512	1,228,800	1200	1.2
3.5	Double density (DD)	80	9	1440	512	737,280	720	.7
3.5	High density (HD)	80	18	2880	512	1,474,560	1440	1.44
3.5	Extra-high density (ED)	80	36	5760	512	2,949,150	2880	2.88

Hard Disks

Although a shift toward optical technology is occurring, the hard disk is still the most common storage device for all computers. Much of what you have learned about diskettes and diskette drives applies to hard disks as well. Like diskettes, hard disks store data in tracks and sectors. Physically, however, hard disks look different from diskettes.

A hard disk includes one or more metal platters mounted on a central spindle, like a stack of rigid diskettes. Each platter is covered with a magnetic coating, and the entire unit is encased in a sealed chamber. Unlike diskettes, where the disk and drive are separate, the hard disk and drive are a single unit. It includes the hard disk, the motor that spins the platters, and a set of read/write heads (see Figure 3.29).

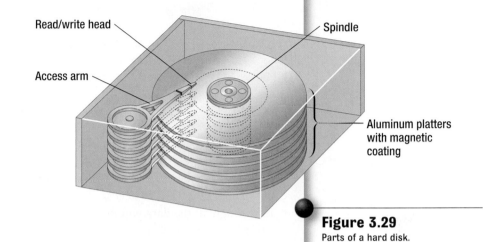

Visit **www.glencoe.com/norton/online/** for more information on **floppy disk drives** and **hard disks**.

Figure 3.29
Parts of a hard disk.

Hard disks have become the primary storage device for PCs because they are convenient and cost-efficient. In both speed and capacity, they far outperform diskettes. A high-density 3.5-inch diskette can store 1.44 MB of data. In contrast, hard disks offer capacities from about several hundred megabytes or more. Most PCs now come with hard disks of at least 6.8 GB, but minimum capacities are continually increasing.

Two important physical differences between hard disks and diskettes account for the differences in performance. First, hard disks are sealed in a chamber, and second, the hard disk consists of a rigid metal platter (usually aluminum), rather than flexible mylar.

The rigidity of the hard disk allows it to spin much faster than diskettes. The hard disks found in most PCs spin between 3600 rpm and 7200 rpm. (Compare this rate to a diskette's spin rate of 300 rpm.) Some new high-performance hard disks can spin as fast as 10,000 rpm. The speed at which the disk spins is a big factor in the drive's overall performance.

Figure 3.30
Read/write heads on each side of each platter, except the bottom of the last platter.

Not only do hard disks pack data more closely together, they also hold more data because they usually include multiple platters, stacked one on top of another. To the computer system, this configuration means that the disk has more than two sides. Larger-capacity hard disk drives may use twelve platters, but both sides of every platter are not always used.

With hard disks, the number of sides that the disk uses is specified by the number of read/write heads. For example, a particular hard disk drive might have six disk platters (that is, twelve sides), but only eleven heads, indicating that one side is not used to store data. Often this is the bottom side of the bottom disk, as shown in Figure 3.30.

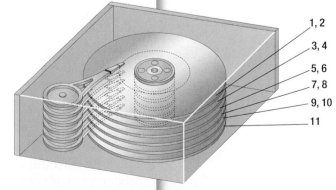

Figure 3.31
A cylinder on a hard disk.

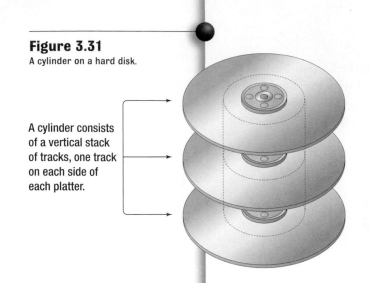

A cylinder consists of a vertical stack of tracks, one track on each side of each platter.

Because hard disks are actually a stack of platters, the term **cylinder** is used to refer to the same track across all the disk sides, as shown in Figure 3.31. For example, track 0 (the outermost track) on every disk is cylinder 0.

Like diskettes, hard disks generally store 512 bytes of data in a sector, but because of their higher tolerances, hard disks can have more sectors per track—fifty-four, sixty-three, or even more sectors per track are not uncommon.

Tape Drives

The best use of tape storage is for data that you do not use often, such as backup copies of your hard disk. Because a tape is a long strip of magnetic material, the tape drive has to write data to it serially—one byte after another. Serial access is inherently slower than the direct access provided by media such as disks. When you want to access a specific set of data on a tape, the drive has to scan through all the data you do not need to get to the data you want. The result is a slow access time. With capacities as high as 50 GB, 100 GB, and higher, however, tape offers an inexpensive way to store a lot of data on a single cassette.

OPTICAL STORAGE DEVICES

Popular alternatives to magnetic storage systems are optical systems. The most widely used type of optical storage medium is the compact disk (CD), which is used in CD-ROM, DVD-ROM, CD-Recordable, CD-ReWritable, and PhotoCD systems.

CD-ROM

The familiar audio compact disk is a popular medium for storing music. In the computer world, however, the medium is called compact disk, read-only memory (CD-ROM). CD-ROM uses the same technology used to produce music CDs. If your computer has a CD-ROM drive, a sound card, and speakers, you can play audio CDs with your PC.

Data is laid out on a CD-ROM disk in a long, continuous spiral that starts at the outer edge and winds inward to the center. On a full CD-ROM, the spiral of data stretches almost three miles long! Data is stored in the form of lands, which are flat areas on the metal surface, and pits, which are depressions or hollows. As Figure 3.32 shows, a land reflects the laser light into the sensor (indicating a data bit of 1), and a pit scatters the light (indicating a data bit of 0). A standard compact disk can store 650 MB of data, or about 70 minutes of audio.

DVD-ROM

Standard compact disks and CD-ROM drives are beginning to be replaced on computer systems by digital video disk read-only memory (DVD-ROM), also called digital video disk or digital versatile disk. DVD-ROM is a high-density medium capable of storing a full-length movie on a single disk the size of a CD. DVD-ROM achieves such high storage capacities by using both sides of the disk,

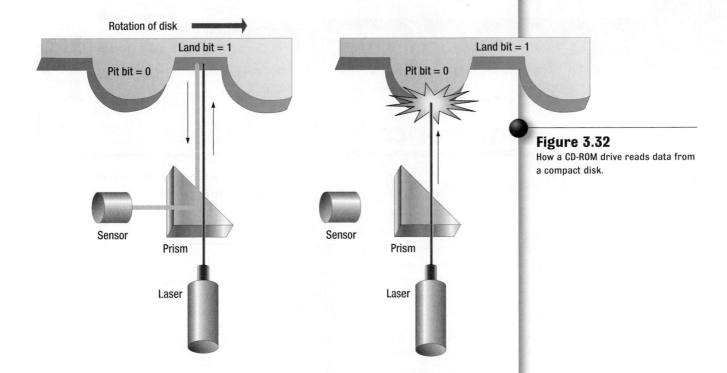

Figure 3.32
How a CD-ROM drive reads data from
a compact disk.

special data-compression technologies, and extremely small tracks for storing data. The latest-generation DVD-ROM disks actually use layers of data tracks, effectively doubling their capacity.

Each side of a standard DVD-ROM disk can hold up to 4.7 GB. Therefore, these two-sided disks can contain as much as 9.4 GB of data. Dual-layer DVD-ROM disks can hold 17 GB of data.

CD-Recordable, CD-ReWritable, and PhotoCD Drives

For large quantities, CD-ROM disks can be produced by manufacturers with expensive duplication equipment. For fewer copies or even single copies, a CD-Recordable (CD-R) drive can be attached to a computer as a regular peripheral device. CD-R drives allow you to create your own CD-ROM disks that can be read by any CD-ROM drive. After information has been written to part of the CD, that information cannot be changed. With most CD-R drives, however, you can continue to record information to other parts of the disk until it is full.

Using newer-generation CD-ReWritable (CD-RW) drives, users can write and overwrite data onto compact disks again and again. Users thus can leverage the high storage capacity of compact disks but revise the data on them in the same manner as a floppy disk.

One popular form of recordable CD is PhotoCD, a standard developed by Kodak for storing digitized photographic images on a CD. Many film developing stores now have PhotoCD drives that can store your photos and put them on a CD. You can then put the PhotoCD in your computer's CD-ROM drive (assuming that it supports PhotoCD, and most do) and view the images on your computer. You can also paste them into other documents. With a PhotoCD, you can continue to add images until the disk is full. After an image has been written to the disk using a field of lasers, however, it cannot be erased or changed.

NORTON
ONLINE

PRODUCTIVITY Tip

Insurance for Your Data

Backing up your data simply means making a copy of it, separate from the original version on your computer's hard disk. You can back up the entire disk, programs and all, or you can back up your data files. If your original data is lost, you can restore the backup copy and resume your work with no more than a minor inconvenience. Here are some tips to help you start a regular backup routine.

Choose Your Medium

The most popular backup medium is the floppy disk, but you may need dozens of them to back up all your data files. A tape drive or CD-RW drive may be a perfect choice if the medium provides enough storage space to back up your entire disk. When choosing your own backup medium, make sure it can store everything you need. It should also enable you to restore backed-up data and programs with little effort.

If your PC is connected to a corporate network, the network administrator may set aside room on the server for your data files. Some companies even provide automatic backup services for their employees. If you aren't sure about your company's backup options, check with your network manager.

Remote backup services are a growing trend. For a fee, such a service can connect to your computer remotely (via an Internet or dial-up connection) and back up your data to their servers. You can restore data remotely from such a system.

Make Sure You Have the Right Software

For backing up your entire hard disk to a high-capacity device, use the file-transfer software that came with the device. Your operating system may also have a built-in backup utility that works with various devices. The critical issue when choosing backup software is that the software should enable you to organize your backups, perform partial backups, and restore selected files at will. If you are backing up data files to a floppy disk or some other low-capacity medium, you can use the operating system's file copying commands.

Set a Schedule and Stick to It

Your first backup should be a full backup—everything on your hard disk—and it should be repeated once a

Online backup services like @Backup can back up your system's hard drive over an Internet connection, on any schedule.

week. Beyond that, you can do a series of partial backups—either incremental (files that have changed since the last partial backup) or differential (files that have changed since the last full backup).

Keep Your Backups Safe

Be sure to keep your disks or tapes in a safe place. Experts suggest keeping them somewhere away from the computer. If your computer is damaged or stolen, your backups won't suffer the same fate. Some organizations routinely ship their media to a distant location, such as a home office or a commercial warehouse, or store them in weatherproof, fireproof vaults. Home users may want to keep their backups in a fireproof box. Companies often keep three or more full sets of backups, all at different sites. Such prudence may seem extreme, but where crucial records are at stake, backups can mean the life or death of a business.

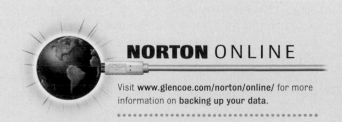

NORTON ONLINE

Visit **www.glencoe.com/norton/online/** for more information on **backing up your data.**

LESSON QUIZ

True/False

Answer the following questions by circling True or False.

True   False   **1.** Unicode is by far the most commonly used character set.

True   False   **2.** The control unit contains a list of all the operations that the CPU can perform.

True   False   **3.** The basic structural design of a microchip is called its architecture.

True   False   **4.** Parallel processing uses multiple processors to share the workload.

True   False   **5.** The physical materials on which data is stored are called storage media.

Multiple Choice

Circle the word or phrase that best completes each sentence.

1. The _____ handles processing in a computer.
  A. CPU   **B.** memory   **C.** both A and B

2. The CPU uses a _____ to store and retrieve each piece of data in memory.
  A. control unit   **B.** cache   **C.** memory address

3. The instruction set for a _____ processor usually contains 200 to 300 instructions.
  A. CISC   **B.** SMP   **C.** RISC

4. In a _____ interface, data bits are transmitted one at a time through a single wire.
  A. parallel   **B.** serial   **C.** neither A nor B

5. A _____ is an example of a magnetic storage device.
  A. hard disk drive   **B.** CD-ROM drive   **C.** neither A nor B

LESSON LABS

Complete the following exercises as directed by your instructor.

1. Using the list of ASCII characters in Table 3.1, compose a sentence with at least six words using ASCII text codes. Swap your ASCII sentence with someone else in class; then translate his or her sentence into English. Time yourself. How long did it take? What does this length of time tell you about the speed of a computer's processor?

2. Take a blank floppy disk, or one that contains unimportant data, and format it:

  A. Make sure the disk's write-protect tab is closed. Place the disk in your diskette drive.

  B. Click the Start button; then click Programs, Windows Explorer. When the Exploring window opens, search in the left pane for the floppy disk drive's icon.

  C. Right-click the floppy disk icon. When the shortcut menu appears, select Format.

  D. In the Format dialog box, choose a disk capacity. (Your selection depends on whether the disk is double-density or high-density.) Select the Quick (erase) option; then click in the Label box and type a label. Finally, make sure the "Display summary when finished" option is checked, and click Start.

  E. Choose Close twice. Remove the disk from the drive.

Networking Basics

OBJECTIVES

- List the four benefits of using a network.
- Differentiate between LANs and WANs.
- Identify three common network topologies.
- Name four common network media.
- List four examples of network operating system software.

OVERVIEW:
Sharing Data Anywhere, Anytime

When PCs first appeared in businesses—and software programs were designed for a single user—there were few obvious advantages to connecting PCs. As computers spread throughout business, however, and as developers began offering complex, multi-user software (software designed for multiple users), many companies quickly learned the importance of connecting PCs together. **Data communications,** the electronic transfer of information between computers, became a major focus of the computer industry. The Internet also spurred the spread of data communications. For these reasons, networking technology has become the most explosive area of growth in the entire computer industry. The demand for larger, faster, higher-capacity networks has increased as businesses have realized the value of networking their computer systems.

When most people think of a network, they imagine several computers in a single location sharing documents and devices such as printers. Networks, however, can include all the computers and devices in a department, a building, or multiple buildings spread over a wide geographic area.

By interconnecting many individual networks into a massive single network (like the Internet), people around the world can share information as though they were across the hall from one another. The information they share can be much more than text documents. Many networks carry voice, audio, and video traffic, allowing videoconferencing and collaboration that were not possible just a few years ago.

THE USES OF A NETWORK

A **network** is a way to connect computers together so that they can communicate, exchange information, and share resources in real time (see Figure 4.1). Four of the most compelling benefits provided by networks are discussed in the following sections.

Simultaneous Access

It is a fact of business computing that multiple employees often need access to the same data at the same time. Without a network that enables file sharing, workers typically keep separate copies of data on different disks, and universally updating the data becomes difficult.

Figure 4.1
In most offices, personal computers are connected to form a network.

Businesses can solve this problem by determining which data is used by more than one person, then storing that data on a **network server** (or just **server**)—a central computer that provides a storage device and other system resources that all users can share. If the server stores data files for users to access, it is commonly called a **file server.** The business can store a single "master" copy of a data file on the server, and employees can access it whenever they need to.

In addition to using the same data files, most office workers also use the same programs. In an environment where PCs are not networked, a separate copy of each program must be installed on every computer. This practice can be expensive. Here are two solutions to this problem:

◆ **Site Licenses.** One solution is to purchase a **site license** for an application. Under a site license, a business purchases a single copy (or a few copies) of an application and then pays the developer for a license to copy the application onto a specified number of computers. Under a site license, each user has a complete, individual copy of the program running on his or her PC, but the business generally pays less money than it would by purchasing a complete copy of the software for each user.

◆ **Network Versions.** Another solution is to connect users' computers to a central network server and thus allow users to share a **network version** of a program. In a network version, only one copy of the application is stored on the server, with a minimum number of supporting files copied to each employee's computer. When employees need to use a program, they simply load it from the server into the RAM of their own desktop computers, as shown in Figure 4.2.

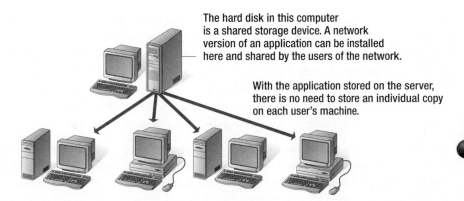

The hard disk in this computer is a shared storage device. A network version of an application can be installed here and shared by the users of the network.

With the application stored on the server, there is no need to store an individual copy on each user's machine.

Figure 4.2
Using a network version of an application.

Shared Peripheral Devices

Perhaps the best incentive for small businesses to link computers in a network is to share peripheral devices, especially expensive devices such as high-volume laser printers.

Although printer costs have fallen considerably over the years, it still is not cost-effective for each user in an organization to have his or her own printer. Aside from the duplicated cost of purchasing multiple printers, maintenance contracts and other factors (such as the cost of supplies) increase the overall cost of ownership. Sharing a laser printer on a network makes the cost much less prohibitive and also centralizes management of the printer.

Personal Communications

One of the most far-reaching applications of data communications is **electronic mail (e-mail),** a system for exchanging written messages (and voice and video messages) through a network. E-mail is a cross between the postal system and a telephone answering system.

In an e-mail system, each user has a unique identifier, typically referred to as an e-mail address. To send someone an e-mail message, you must use a special e-mail program that works with the network to send and receive messages. You enter the person's e-mail address and then type the message. When you are finished, you can click an icon and the message is sent to the e-mail address. After reading the message, the recipient can save it, delete it, forward it to someone else, or respond by sending back a reply message. Figure 4.3 shows the process for sending and receiving e-mail.

Visit **www.glencoe.com/norton/online/** for more information on **networks** and **e-mail**.

1 Sender composes e-mail message and sends it.

2 Message is stored on the server.

3 Server alerts recipient that there is a message.

4 When the recipient is ready to read the message, the recipient's computer retrieves it from the server.

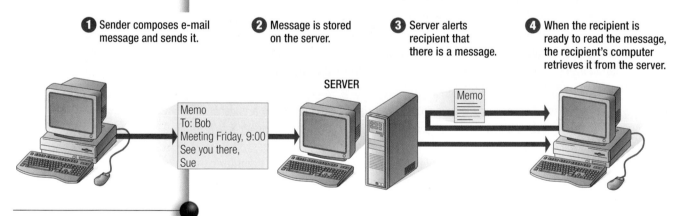

Figure 4.3
Sending and receiving e-mail over a typical network.

In addition to sending a text message, many systems allow you to attach data files—such as spreadsheet files or word-processed documents—to your message (see Figure 4.4). An e-mail system allows people to share files even when they do not have access to the same storage devices. For example, a local area network may also have a connection to a large information network, such as America Online or the Internet. In this case, the person on the local network can share files with anyone on the large information network simply by attaching data files to e-mail messages.

In addition to e-mail, the spread of networking technology is adding to the popularity of teleconferencing and videoconferencing. A **teleconference** is a virtual meeting in which people in different locations conduct discussions by typing messages to each other. Each message can be seen by all the other people in the teleconference.

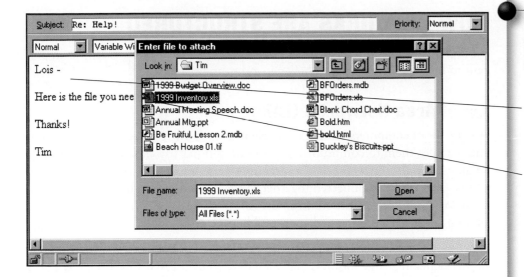

Teleconferencing software has become more sophisticated, adding features such as a shared scratch pad where diagrams or pictures can be drawn or electronically pasted.

If users have the necessary hardware (a PC video camera, microphone, and speakers) and software, they can actually see and speak to each other as they meet online instead of merely typing messages. This process is known as **videoconferencing** (see Figure 4.5).

Easier Backup

In business, data is extremely valuable, so making sure that employees back up their data is critical. One way to address this problem is to keep all valuable data on a shared storage device that employees access through a network. Often the person managing the network has the responsibility of making regular backups of the data on the shared storage device from a single, central location. Network backup software is also available and allows backups to be made of files stored on employees' hard drives. With this method, files do not have to be copied to the central server before they can be backed up.

HOW NETWORKS ARE STRUCTURED

To understand the different types of networks and how they operate, it is important to know something about how networks can be structured.

Local Area Networks (LANs)

A network of computers located relatively near each other and connected in a way that enables them to communicate with one another (by cable, infrared link, or small radio transmitter) is called a **local area network (LAN).** A LAN can consist of two or three PCs connected together to share resources, or it can include hundreds of computers of different kinds. Any network that exists within a single building, or even a group of adjacent buildings, is considered a LAN.

It is often helpful to connect different LANs together. For example, two different departments in a large business may each have its own LAN, but if there is a need for data communications between the departments, then it may be necessary to create a link between the two LANs. To understand how this connection is possible, you need to understand how networks transmit data and how different types of networks can share data. On a network, data is sent in small groups called packets. A **packet** is a group of bits that includes a header, payload, and control elements that are transmitted together (see Figure 4.6). Think of a packet as one sentence or a group of numbers being sent at one time.

Figure 4.6
An e-mail message, divided into packets.

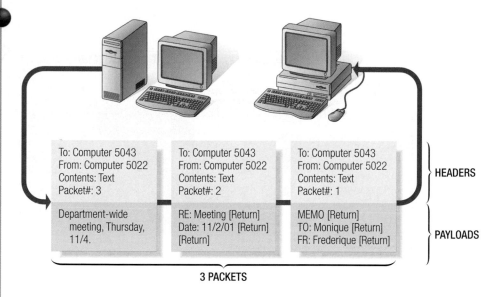

The payload is the part of the packet that contains the actual data being sent. The header contains information about the type of data in the payload, the source and destination of the data, and a sequence number so that data from multiple packets can be reassembled at the receiving computer in the proper order. Each LAN is governed by a **protocol,** which is a set of rules and formats for sending and receiving data. An individual LAN may utilize more than one protocol. Some of the most common protocols in use today include TCP/IP, IPX/SPX, NetBEUI, and DLC.

If two LANs are built around the same communication rules, then they can be connected with one of two devices:

◆ **Bridge.** A **bridge** is a relatively simple device that looks at the information in each packet header and forwards data that is traveling from one LAN to

another. Bridges forward data from one network to another but are not suitable in many large organizations because they can connect only two LANs.

◆ **Router.** A **router** is a more complicated device that stores the routing information for networks. Like a bridge, a router looks at each packet's header to determine where the packet should go and then determines a route for the packet to take to its destination.

If you need to create a more sophisticated connection between networks, you need a **gateway,** a computer system that connects two networks and translates information from one to the other. Packets from different networks have different kinds of information in their headers, and the information can be in various formats. The gateway can take a packet from one type of network, read the header, and then encapsulate the entire packet into a new one, adding a header that is understood by the second network, as shown in Figure 4.7.

Figure 4.7
How a gateway forwards a packet from one type of network to a different type of network.

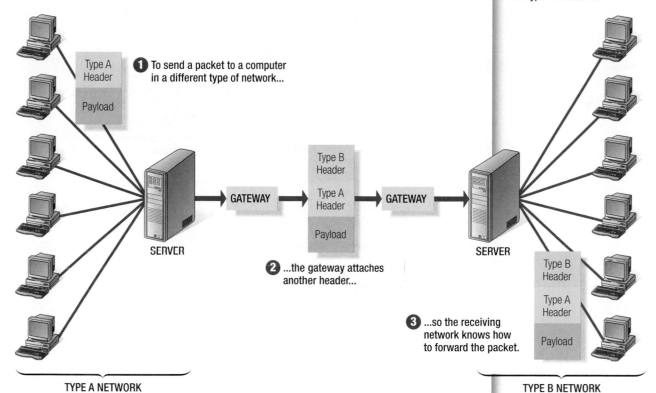

① To send a packet to a computer in a different type of network...

② ...the gateway attaches another header...

③ ...so the receiving network knows how to forward the packet.

TYPE A NETWORK

TYPE B NETWORK

Wide Area Networks (WANs)

Typically, a **wide area network (WAN)** is two or more LANs connected together, generally across a wide geographical area. For example, a company may have its corporate headquarters and manufacturing facility in one city and its marketing office in another. Each site needs resources, data, and programs locally, but it also needs to share data with the other site. To accomplish this feat of data communication, the company can attach routers connected over public utilities (such as telephone lines) to create a WAN.

Note, however, that a WAN does not have to include any LAN systems. For example, two distant mainframe computers can communicate through a WAN, even though neither one is part of a local area network.

Server-Based Networks

Describing a network as a LAN or a WAN gives a sense of the physical area the network covers. However, this classification does not tell you anything about how individual computers on a network, called **nodes,** interact with one another.

Many networks include not only nodes but also a central computer with a large hard disk used for shared storage. As you saw earlier, this central computer is known as the file server, network server, or just the server. Files and programs used by more than one user (at different nodes) are generally stored on the server.

One relatively simple implementation of a network with nodes and a file server is a **file server network** (see Figure 4.8). This network is a hierarchical arrangement in which each node can have access to the files on the server but not necessarily to files on other nodes. When a node needs information from the server, it requests the entire file containing the information. In other words, the file server is used simply to store files and forward (or send) them to nodes that request them.

Figure 4.8

A simple LAN with a file server.

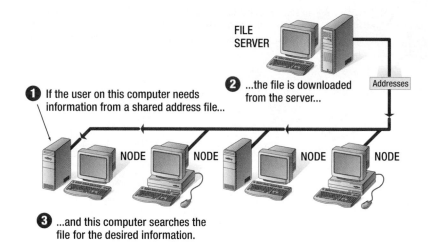

1 If the user on this computer needs information from a shared address file...

2 ...the file is downloaded from the server...

FILE SERVER

Addresses

NODE NODE NODE NODE

3 ...and this computer searches the file for the desired information.

Client/Server Networks

One popular type of server-based network is **client/server** computing, a hierarchical strategy in which individual computers share the processing and storage workload with a central server (see Figure 4.9). This type of arrangement requires specialized software for both the individual node and the network server. It does not, however, require any specific type of network. Client/server software can be used on LANs or WANs, and a single client/server program can be used on a LAN where all the other software is based on a simple file server relationship.

Client/server software is valuable to large, modern organizations because it distributes processing and storage workloads among resources efficiently. Thus, users receive the information they need faster.

Client/server computing is also a commonly used model on the Internet. Users typically have client software that provides an easily used interface for interacting with this giant WAN. Other types of processing, such as receiving, storing, and sending e-mail messages, are conducted by remote computers running the server part of the software.

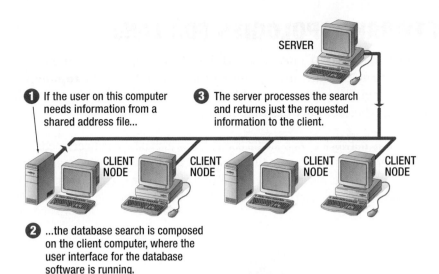

Figure 4.9
Distribution of processing in a client/server computing model.

SERVER

1 If the user on this computer needs information from a shared address file...

3 The server processes the search and returns just the requested information to the client.

CLIENT NODE   CLIENT NODE   CLIENT NODE   CLIENT NODE

2 ...the database search is composed on the client computer, where the user interface for the database software is running.

Peer-to-Peer Networks

In a **peer-to-peer network** (sometimes called a workgroup), all nodes on the network have equal relationships to all others, and all have similar types of software that support the sharing of resources (see Figure 4.10).

Peer-to-peer networks do not necessarily use a server. Instead, each node has access to at least some of the resources on all other nodes, so the relationship is nonhierarchical. If they are set up correctly, many multi-user operating systems give users access to files on hard disks and printers attached to other computers in the network.

Figure 4.10
A peer-to-peer network.

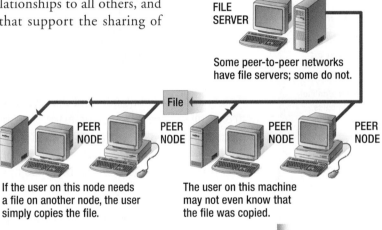

FILE SERVER

Some peer-to-peer networks have file servers; some do not.

File

PEER NODE   PEER NODE   PEER NODE   PEER NODE

If the user on this node needs a file on another node, the user simply copies the file.

The user on this machine may not even know that the file was copied.

Self Check

Answer the following questions by filling in the blank(s).

1. A(n) _____ is a central computer that provides storage and other resources that users can share.

2. _____ is a system for exchanging written messages over a network.

3. A(n) _____ is a network that does not necessarily use a server.

NORTON ONLINE

Visit **www.glencoe.com/norton/online/** for more information on **client/server technology** and **peer-to-peer networks**.

NETWORK TOPOLOGIES FOR LANs

In addition to the size of a network and the relationship between the nodes and the server (if any), another distinguishing feature of LANs is the **topology**—the physical or logical layout of the cables and devices that connect the nodes of the network. There are three basic topologies:

◆ **Bus.** A **bus network** uses a single conduit, to which all the network nodes and peripheral devices are attached (see Figure 4.11). Each node is connected in series to one cable. A special device called a terminator is attached at the cable's start and end points. A terminator stops the signals so they do not "bounce" back down the cable.

Figure 4.11
A LAN with bus topology.

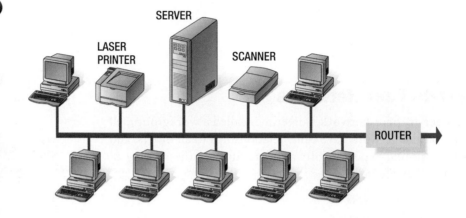

The bus topology has inherent disadvantages. Keeping data transmissions from colliding requires some extra circuitry and software, and a broken connection can bring down (or "crash") all or part of the network, rendering it inoperable so that users cannot communicate until the connection is repaired. The primary advantage of the bus topology is that it uses the least amount of cabling of any topology.

◆ **Star.** The **star network** is the most common topology in use today. In a star network, a device called a hub is placed in the center of the network; that is, all nodes are connected to the central hub and communicate through it. Groups of data are routed through the hub and sent to all the attached nodes, thus eventually reaching their destinations. Figure 4.12 shows the star topology.

Some hubs—known as intelligent hubs—can monitor traffic and help pre-vent collisions. In a star topology, a broken connection (between a node and the hub) does not affect the rest of the network. If you lose the hub, however, all nodes connected to that hub are unable to communicate.

◆ **Ring.** The **ring topology** connects the nodes of the network in a circular chain, with each node connected to the next. The final node in the chain connects to the first to complete the ring, as shown in Figure 4.13 on page 78. With this methodology, each node examines

Figure 4.12
A LAN with star topology.

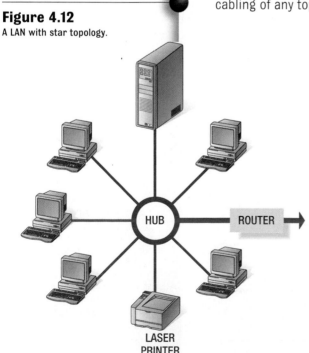

COMPUTERS
in your career

Careers in Networking

Two of the most popular (and best paying) computer-related fields are networking and data communications. Most large organizations have existing networks that must be maintained, repaired, and updated as the company grows or shrinks. When companies merge, networks must be combined to create a seamless interface for the organization. Many times two or more networks that use different topologies, network operating systems, and protocols must be merged into one large network. As these networks are merged, there must be a limited amount of downtime so employees can continue processing data for the company. Careers relating to networking and data communications require training in a wide range of computing and networking topics.

Some of the careers relating to networking and data communications are listed below:

◆ **Network Administrators.** These individuals are responsible for managing a company's network infrastructure. Some of the jobs in this career field include designing and implementing networks, setting up and managing users' accounts, installing and updating network software and applications, and backing up the network. To succeed as a network administrator, you should gain experience in the major network operating systems, including Novell NetWare, Windows NT 4.0 Server, and Windows 2000 Server. You should also have experience with major operating systems, such as Windows 98, MS-DOS, Apple Macintosh, and UNIX. You might also consider earning certification from Novell or Microsoft.

◆ **Information Systems (IS) Managers.** IS managers are responsible for managing a team of information professionals, including network administrators, software developers, project managers, and other staff. Jobs in the IS management field differ according to the needs of the company, but many IS managers maintain project lists, oversee project management, perform database administration, and possibly do some programming. IS managers should possess experience and skills in a wide range of networking and computing areas, including network operating system experience, operating system experience, database knowledge, and management abilities.

◆ **Data Communications Managers.** These managers are responsible for setting up and maintaining Internet, intranet, and extranet sites. Often data communications managers are also responsible for designing and establishing an organization's telecommuting initiative. This responsibility often requires experience with several technologies, including networking, data communications, remote access software, and Internet technologies. If you are interested in a career in data communications, learn as much as you can about these technologies.

Networking is one of the most rapidly growing fields in the computing industry.

77

Figure 4.13
A LAN with ring topology.

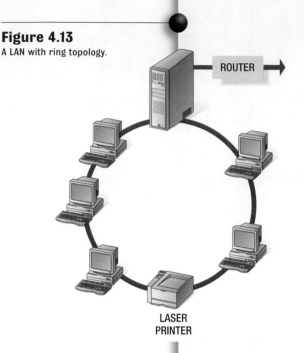

LASER
PRINTER

data that is sent through the ring. If the data—known as a token—is not addressed to the node examining it, that node passes it along to the next node in the ring.

The ring topology has a substantial advantage over the bus topology. There is no danger of collisions because only one packet of data may traverse the ring at a time. Like the bus topology, however, if the ring is broken, the entire network cannot communicate until the ring is restored.

Network designers consider several factors in determining which topology, or combination of topologies, to use. Among the factors considered are the type of computers currently installed, the type of cabling currently in place (if any), the cost of the components and services required to implement the network, the distance between each computer, and the speed with which data must travel around the network.

NETWORK MEDIA AND HARDWARE

No matter what their structure, all networks rely on media to link their nodes and/or servers together. You may recall that, when referring to data storage, the term *media* refers to materials for storing data, such as magnetic disks and tape. In network communications, however, the term refers to the wires, cables, and other means by which data travels from its source to its destination. The most common media for data communications are twisted-pair cable, coaxial cable, fiber-optic cable, and wireless links.

Figure 4.14
Shielded (top) and unshielded (bottom) twisted-pair wire is the most common medium for computer networks.

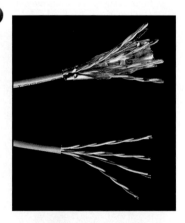

Twisted-Pair Cable

Twisted-pair cable normally consists of two wires individually insulated in plastic, then twisted around each other and bound together in another layer of plastic insulation. Except for the plastic coating, nothing shields this type of wire from outside interference, so it is also called unshielded twisted-pair (UTP) wire. Some twisted-pair wire is also encased in a metal sheath and therefore is called shielded twisted-pair (STP) wire. Figure 4.14 shows what UTP and STP look like.

Indoor wiring for telephones uses twisted-pair wire, so this type of wire is often called telephone wire. Because it was readily available and inexpensive, telephone wire gained early favor as a conduit for data communications. Today, however, most twisted-pair wire used for network communications is made to more demanding specifications than voice-grade telephone wire.

Sometimes network media are compared by the amount of data they can transmit each second. The difference between the highest and lowest frequencies of a transmission channel is known as **bandwidth.** Simply stated, the higher a medium's bandwidth, the more data it can transmit at any given time. As more users transmit data over a network, however, the bandwidth decreases, thereby slowing down all transmissions. Bandwidth is expressed in cycles per second (hertz) or in bits per second.

NORTON
ONLINE

Visit **www.glencoe.com/norton/online/** for more information on **network media.**

Coaxial Cable

Coaxial cable, sometimes called coax (pronounced CO-axe), is similar to the cabling used in cable TV systems. There are two conductors in coaxial cable. One is a single wire in the center of the cable, and the other is a wire mesh shield that surrounds the first wire, with an insulator between (see Figure 4.15).

Coaxial cable can carry more data than older types of twisted-pair wiring. However, it is also more expensive and has become less popular as twisted-pair technology has improved.

Figure 4.15
Coaxial cable.

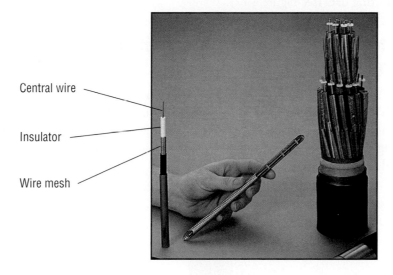

Central wire

Insulator

Wire mesh

Fiber-Optic Cable

A **fiber-optic cable** is a thin strand of glass that transmits pulsating beams of light rather than electric frequencies (see Figure 4.16). When one end of the strand is exposed to light, the strand carries the light all the way to the other end—bending around corners along the way. Because light travels at a much higher speed than electrical signals, fiber-optic cable can easily carry data at more than 1 billion bits per second. Because of improvements in transmission hardware, however, fiber-optic cable transmission speeds have drastically improved and now approach 100 Gbps. Fiber-optic cable is also immune to the electromagnetic interference that is a problem for copper wire. Fiber-optic cable offers extraordinary bandwidth. It is extremely fast and can carry an enormous number of messages simultaneously. Fiber-optic cable is also a secure transmission medium.

Figure 4.16
Fiber-optic cable.

The disadvantage of fiber-optic cable is that it is more expensive than twisted-pair and coax, and it is more difficult to install. Special equipment is required to cut the cable and install connectors; as a result, fiber-optic line can be difficult to splice. Also, great care must be taken when bending fiber-optic cable. As costs have come down, however, fiber-optic cable has become increasingly popular, and it is now revolutionizing

Strands of glass

several communications industries. Telephone and cable television companies, especially, have been moving from twisted-pair wire and coaxial cables to fiber-optic cables.

Wireless Links

Today, wireless technologies are competing with twisted-pair, coaxial, and fiber-optic cable. Its advantage is the flexibility that it offers in terms of the network layout. **Wireless communication** relies on radio signals or infrared signals for transmitting data (see Figure 4.17).

The Network Interface Card, Network Protocols, and Cabling Specifications

Cables are used to link a network together in a topology, as described earlier. When cables cannot be used, a wireless implementation may be an alternative, but data transmission speeds can suffer greatly as a result. Regardless of the wiring and topology, each computer on the network still needs a hardware component to control the flow of data.

Figure 4.17
Connecting LANs using microwave requires a direct line of sight between the two antennas.

The device that performs this function is the **network interface card (NIC),** commonly called a network card. This printed circuit board fits into one of the computer's expansion slots and provides a port on the back of the PC, where the network cable can be attached. Network software works with the operating system and tells the computer how to use the NIC. Both the network software and the NIC must adhere to a network protocol, as discussed earlier.

Another critical specification of a network is the cabling equipment (also called the network technology) used to create a LAN. The most common types of network technology include Ethernet, Fast Ethernet, and Token Ring.

Ethernet

Currently, **Ethernet** is the most common network technology used. Ethernet was originally designed for a bus topology and thick coaxial cable, but most new network installations use an Ethernet star topology with either twisted-pair or fiber-optic cables as the medium. With Ethernet, if two nodes transmit simultaneously, the collision is detected and they retransmit one at a time. As you might guess, collisions are few in a small network. On a large network, access time can become noticeably delayed as collisions become more prevalent.

The original implementations of Ethernet, which used coaxial cable, were called 10Base-5 and 10Base-2. The most popular implementation of Ethernet—called 10Base-T—uses a star topology and twisted-pair wires and can achieve transmission speeds up to 10 Mbps.

Fast Ethernet

100Base-T, also known as **Fast Ethernet,** is available using the same media and topology as Ethernet, but different network interface cards are used to achieve speeds of up to 100 Mbps. Still other implementations of Ethernet are pushing transmission speeds even higher.

Token Ring

IBM's network technology is the **Token Ring.** The controlling hardware in a Token Ring network transmits an electronic token—a small set of data—to each node on the network many times each second, that is, if the token is not already in use by a specific node. A computer can copy data into the token and set the address where the data should be sent. The token then continues around the ring, and each computer along the way looks at the address until the token reaches the computer with the address that was recorded in the token. The receiving computer then copies the contents of the token and sends an acknowledgment to the sending computer. When the sending computer receives the acknowledgment from the receiving computer, it resets the token's status to empty and transmits it to the next computer in the ring.

NETWORK SOFTWARE

The group of programs that manages the resources on the network is often called the **network operating system (NOS).** Here are some of the popular network operating systems:

Visit **www.glencoe.com/norton/online/** for more information on **network operating systems.**

- ◆ **Microsoft Windows NT Server 4.0.** This network operating system provides a graphical, Windows 9*x*–style user interface and is ideal for administering small and medium-size networks. Many companies that have invested in Microsoft Windows 3.11, Windows 95, and Windows 98 use Windows NT Server as their NOS, and an example of the interface is shown in Figure 4.18. Windows NT Server also operates with many other network operating systems.

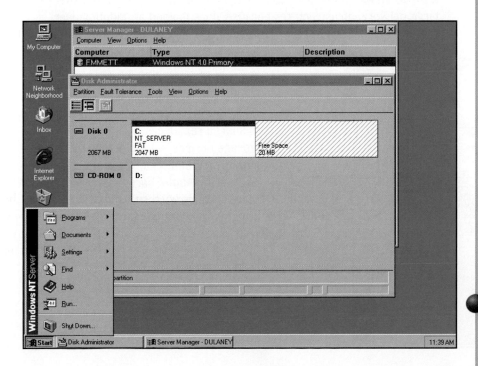

Figure 4.18
The graphical interface in Windows NT Server 4.0.

◆ **Novell NetWare.** One of the most popular network operating systems in terms of the number of installations, NetWare (developed by Novell, Inc.) can be used to run networks with different topologies, including Ethernet and Token Ring. NetWare also includes support for various hardware platforms, such as Mac, PC, and UNIX hosts and servers.

Figure 4.19

The graphical interface from Windows NT 4.0 carries over, with modifications, to Windows 2000.

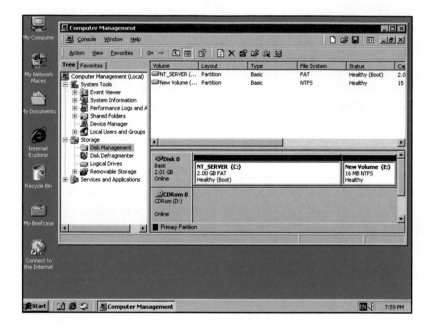

◆ **Microsoft Windows 2000.** Microsoft Windows 2000 is the next release of—and a radical departure from—Windows NT. Windows 2000 (shown in Figure 4.19) adds Plug and Play capabilities and an enterprise directory model (known as Active Directory) while maintaining the graphical user interface. With these features and scalability/expandability, it is ideal for administering networks ranging from small to enterprise-wide.

Figure 4.20

The AppleShare NOS allows for networking between Macintosh machines.

◆ **Banyan Vines.** The Vines NOS is commonly found in installations that have large network infrastructures because Vines is good at updating user information on multiple servers connected to each other on the same network.

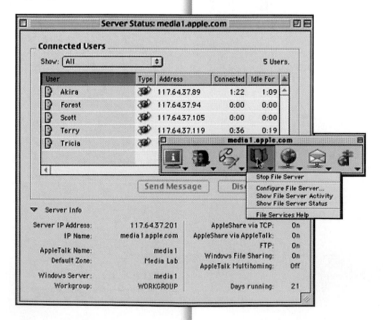

◆ **AppleShare.** AppleShare is used by Apple Macintosh users to network with one another (see Figure 4.20). AppleShare provides access to shared resources, such as printers and storage devices, and to centralized servers. In many installations, you will find networks comprising AppleShare networks along with servers running other network operating systems, such as Windows NT Server.

◆ **Linux.** Linux has garnered a large share of the small business and home market for providing Internet and networking services. An "open" operating system, it is a cost-effective alternative to other operating systems for sharing files, applications, printers, modems, and Internet services.

LESSON QUIZ

True/False

Answer the following questions by circling True or False.

True   False   **1.** A network is a way to connect computers together so they can communicate, exchange information, and share resources.

True   False   **2.** Electronic mail is a system for exchanging written messages through a network.

True   False   **3.** On a network, data is sent in small groups called payloads.

True   False   **4.** Typically, a wide area network is two or more LANs connected together.

True   False   **5.** Twisted-pair cable may be either shielded or unshielded.

Multiple Choice

Circle the word or phrase that best completes each sentence.

1. _____ is one of the benefits of using a network.
   A. Simultaneous access   **B.** Shared peripheral devices   **C.** Both A and B

2. If a server stores data files for users to access, it is commonly called a(n) _____ .
   A. file server   **B.** application server   **C.** both A and B

3. A _____ is a virtual meeting in which people in different locations conduct a discussion by typing messages to each other.
   A. teleconference   **B.** videoconference   **C.** network operating system

4. A _____ is a networking device that stores the routing information of each computer on each of the LANs it connects.
   A. bridge   **B.** router   **C.** server

5. A _____ network places a hub in the center of the network nodes.
   A. bus   **B.** ring   **C.** star

LESSON LABS

Complete the following exercises as directed by your instructor.

1. To view your network adapter card settings, right-click the Network Neighborhood icon on the desktop; then choose Properties from the shortcut menu. When the Properties dialog box opens, click the Configuration tab and double-click the network adapter that appears. The card's properties will appear. _Do not make any changes to these settings._ Write down the settings and close all dialog boxes.

2. To view your network protocol settings, right-click the Network Neighborhood icon on the desktop; then choose Properties from the shortcut menu. When the Properties dialog box appears, click the Configuration tab, select a protocol from the list, and click the Properties command button. _Do not make any changes to these settings._ Write down the settings and close all dialog boxes.

LESSON 3: Manipulating and Storing Data

How Computers Represent Data

- Computer data is reduced to binary numbers because computer processing is performed by transistors that have only two possible states: on and off.

- A single unit of data is called a bit; 8 bits make up 1 byte. In the most common character-code set, ASCII, each character consists of 1 byte of data.

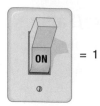 = 1

How Computers Process Data

- A microcomputer's processing takes place in the central processing unit, the two main parts of which are the control unit and the arithmetic logic unit (ALU).

- Random-access memory (RAM) is volatile (or temporary). Programs and data can be written to and erased from RAM as needed. Read-only memory (ROM) is nonvolatile (or permanent). It holds instructions that run the computer when the power is first turned on.

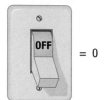 = 0

Factors Affecting Processing Speed

- The size of the registers determines the amount of data the computer can use at one time.

- The amount of RAM can affect speed because the CPU can keep more of the active program and data in memory.

- Cache memory is a type of high-speed memory that contains the most recent data and instructions that have been loaded by the CPU.

- The faster the CPU's clock, the more instructions the CPU can process each second.

- The width of the data bus determines how many bits can be transmitted at a time between the CPU and other devices.

Extending the Processor's Power to Other Devices

- External devices—such as those used for input and output—are connected to the system by ports on the back of the computer.

- Most computers come with a serial port and a parallel port.

- If the computer does not have the right type of port for an external device, you can install an expansion board that provides the appropriate type of port.

CPUs Used in Personal Computers

- Intel, AMD, Cyrix, and Motorola make CPUs for personal computers. All PCs use CISC processors.

- Instruction sets for RISC processors are smaller than those used in CISC chips, enabling the processor to process more instructions per second.

- Multiple processors can be used in a single system, enabling them to share processing tasks. This type of system is called a parallel processing system.

Magnetic Storage Devices

- Magnetic storage devices work by polarizing tiny pieces of iron on the magnetic medium. Read/write heads create magnetic charges on the medium.

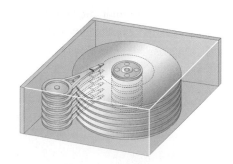

■ Before a magnetic disk can be used, it must be formatted—a process that maps the disk's surface and creates tracks and sectors where data can be stored.

Optical Storage Devices

■ CD-ROM uses the same technology as a music CD does; a laser reads lands and pits from the surface of the disk.

■ DVD-ROM technology is a variation on standard CD-ROM. DVD disks offer capacities up to 17 GB. Other popular variations on CD-ROM are CD-Recordable and CD-ReWritable.

LESSON 4: Networking Basics

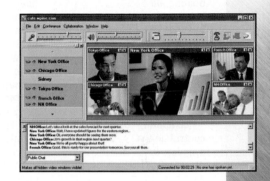

The Uses of a Network

■ A network is a way to connect computers for data communication.

■ The biggest benefits of networking are simultaneous access, peripheral sharing, streamlined communications, and easier backups.

■ Many networks are built around a central computer called a network server that provides a storage device and other resources that users can share.

How Networks Are Structured

■ A local area network (LAN) consists of computers that are relatively near one another.

■ Typically, a wide area network (WAN) is the result of connecting two or more LANs together through public utilities.

■ In a file server network, the server provides storage and file sharing services for the nodes. In a client/server network, nodes and the server share the storage and processing chores.

■ A peer-to-peer network is a small network that usually does not include a central server.

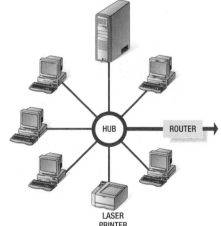

Network Topologies for LANs

■ A topology is the physical layout of the cables and devices that connect the nodes of a network. The three basic topologies are bus, star, and ring.

Network Media and Hardware

■ When used in the context of networks, the term *media* refers to the wires, cables, and other means by which data travels from its source to its destination.

■ The most common media for data communications are twisted-pair wire, coaxial cable, fiber-optic cable, and wireless links.

■ The most common types of network technology include Ethernet, Fast Ethernet, and Token Ring.

Network Software

■ A network operating system manages the resources on a network. Common network operating systems include Windows 95, Windows 98, Windows 2000, Windows NT, NetWare, Banyan Vines, and others.

UNIT REVIEW

KEY TERMS

After completing this unit, you should be able to define the following terms.

address bus, 50
arithmetic logic unit (ALU), 47
ASCII, 45
backing up, 62
bandwidth, 78
binary number system, 44
bit, 45
booting, 60
bridge, 72
bus, 50
bus network, 76
cache memory, 50
client/server, 74
cluster, 60
coaxial cable, 79
complex instruction set
    computing (CISC), 57
control unit, 47
cylinder, 64
data area, 61
data bus, 50
data communications, 68
decimal number system, 44
density, 62

directory, 61
EBCDIC, 45
electronic mail (e-mail), 70
Ethernet, 80
expansion board, 52
expansion slot, 52
Fast Ethernet, 81
fiber-optic cable, 79
file-allocation table (FAT), 60
file server, 69
file server network, 74
FireWire, 52
folder, 61
formatting, 58
gateway, 73
hertz (Hz), 50
IEEE 1394, 52
initializing, 58
instruction set, 47
local area network (LAN), 72
logical format, 60
master boot record, 60
megahertz (MHz), 50
memory address, 48

Musical Instrument Digital
    Interface (MIDI), 52
network, 69
network interface card
    (NIC), 80
network operating system
    (NOS), 81
network server, 69
network version, 69
node, 74
nonvolatile, 48
packet, 72
parallel interface, 51
parallel processing, 57
PC Card, 53
peer-to-peer network, 75
protocol, 72
reduced instruction set
    computing (RISC), 57
register, 47
ring topology, 76
root directory, 61
root folder, 61
router, 73

sector, 59
serial interface, 51
server, 69
site license, 69
Small Computer System
    Interface (SCSI), 51
star network, 76
swap in, 49
swap out, 49
system clock, 50
teleconference, 70
text code, 45
Token Ring, 81
topology, 76
track, 59
transistor, 43
twisted-pair cable, 78
Unicode, 45
Universal Serial Bus (USB), 52
videoconference, 71
volatile, 48
wide area network (WAN), 73
wireless communication, 80
word size, 49

KEY TERMS QUIZ

Fill in each blank with one of the terms listed under Key Terms.

1. People use the _____ number system to represent numbers, but computers use the _____ number system.

2. The CPU's _____ lists all the operations that the CPU can perform.

3. The electronic transfer of information between computers is called _____ .

4. The size of a computer's registers is called its _____ .

5. A disk's _____ records the location of each file and the status of each sector.

6. You can organize the files on a disk by setting up _____ .

7. The individual computers on a network are referred to as _____ .

8. A(n) _____ is a network of computers located relatively near each other.

9. You can connect computers together to communicate and exchange information by using a(n) _____ .

10. The physical layout of wires and devices that connect the network's nodes is called the _____ .

REVIEW QUESTIONS

In your own words, briefly answer the following questions.

1. What is the difference between data and information?

2. How many characters or symbols can be represented by one 8-bit byte?

3. In computers made today, what are the most common register sizes?

4. What is a data bus?

5. What is the primary difference between a CISC processor and a RISC processor?

6. List the primary types of magnetic and optical storage.

7. Describe how a computer's operating system can locate data on a disk's surface.

8. List and describe the benefits that networks provide.

9. How do networks help businesses save money?

10. How can a network enhance the personal communications of its users?

DISCUSSION QUESTIONS

As directed by your instructor, discuss the following questions in class or in groups.

1. Because the Unicode text code system is so large and can include so many characters, what benefits would developers and users enjoy if the system were universally adopted for operating systems and application software?

2. Fiber-optic cable is much faster than other kinds of network media. Why, then, do you think it is not more widely used?

 **ETHICAL ISSUES**   Computers are becoming more powerful all the time. Many people see this increasing power as a source of limitless benefits, but others view it as a threat. With this thought in mind, discuss the following questions in class.

1. As technology improves, the pace of life increases. It can be argued that computer technology, to a large extent, has made Americans a less patient culture than it was a decade ago. People become frustrated, for example, when a printer does not work fast enough, or when Web pages do not download instantly. Do you think this statement is true? Should we restrain our urge to make life faster?

2. CD-ReWritable (CD-RW) devices are getting cheaper and more popular. They let you create backups and store data in a safe format. But people also use them to make illegal duplicates of software and audio CDs. If you had a CD-RW system, would you consider illegal duplication? Do you think such copying should or should not be illegal?

You and the Computer

Complete the following exercises using a computer in your classroom or lab. No other materials are needed.

1. **Plug It In.** With your instructor observing, turn your computer and monitor off and unplug them from their power source. Then take these steps:

   A. Move to the back of the computer and inspect all the cables plugged into it. Which devices are connected to the PC and by which cables? Which port is connected to each device? Make a chart of these connections.

   B. Unplug each connection. After all students have unplugged their devices, switch places with someone and reconnect all the devices. Does the other student's system have the same connections as yours? If not, can you reconnect all its devices correctly?

   C. Return to your PC. Use your chart to see whether your system has been reconnected correctly. If not, correct the other student's mistakes. When you are sure all devices are plugged into the right ports, reconnect the PC and monitor to their power source. Turn the PC on and make sure everything is working correctly.

2. **Check Out Your Network.** If your computer is connected to a network, you can use Windows tools to view the other nodes and servers connected to the network. Take the following steps:

   A. On the Windows desktop, double-click the Network Neighborhood icon. The Network Neighborhood window opens.

   B. Double-click the Entire Neighborhood icon. If your PC is part of a network, it should expand to display a list of all the PCs, servers, and other devices connected to the network.

   C. Right-click any item in the list; then choose Properties from the shortcut menu. Review the properties of several parts of the network. Do not make any changes to any of the settings or information.

   D. When you are done, close any dialog boxes that may be open; then close the Network Neighborhood window.

Internet Labs

To complete the following exercises, you need a computer with an Internet connection and a Web browser. For more information on using these tools, see "Prerequisites" at the front of this textbook.

1. **Backup Online.** Suppose you want to back up the hard disk on your home computer, but you do not want to research, purchase, and set up a backup system.

Instead, you decide to check out some online backup services that can back up your data over the Internet. Here are a few online backup services. Visit their Web sites and decide which service would be best for your needs.

- @Backup—**http://www.backup.com/**
- BackJack Online Backup Service—**http://www.backjack.com/**
- Data Protection Services, LLC—**http://www.dataprotection.net/**
- NetMass, Inc.—**http://www.systemrecovery.com/**

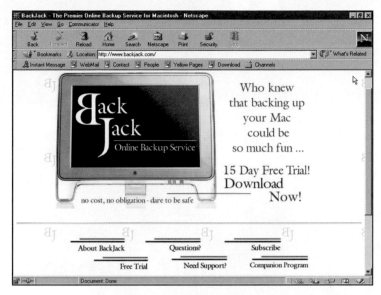

2. **Network Operating Systems.** Visit the following Web sites and gather as much information as you can about each company's network operating system:

- Apple Computer, Inc., makers of AppleShare—**www.apple.com/**
- Artisoft, Inc., makers of LANtastic—**www.artisoft.com/**
- Microsoft Corp., makers of Windows—**www.microsoft.com/**
- Novell, Inc., makers of NetWare—**www.novell.com/**

IBE Labs

If you have the Interactive Browser Edition (IBE) CD-ROM for this textbook, you may complete the following interactive exercises using the instructions provided in the IBE.

1. **Trivia.** Choose a category; then test your knowledge of networks.

2. **Drag-and-Drop.** Build a flowchart to show how a computer processes data.

3. **Association Game.** Challenge your understanding of storage technology by arranging information correctly in a table.

4. **Click the Switch.** Turn switches on and off to view how characters are represented in ASCII.

UNIT 3

Introduction to Software

UNIT OBJECTIVES

Define the terms *operating system* **and** *user interface.*

Name four major functions of the operating system.

Identify six commonly used PC operating systems.

Identify the four primary types of productivity applications.

Identify five interface components found in windowed productivity applications.

UNIT CONTENTS

This unit contains the following lessons:

Operating Systems

OVERVIEW: The Role of the Operating System

An operating system (OS) is a software program, but it is different from the other software programs on your computer. The OS is the computer's master control program. It provides you with the tools (commands) for interacting with the PC.

When you issue a command, the OS translates it into code that the machine can use. The OS also ensures that the results of your actions are displayed on screen, printed, and so on.

The operating system performs the following functions:

▶ Provides the instructions to display the on-screen elements with which you interact. Collectively, these elements are known as the user interface.

▶ Loads other programs into the computer's memory so that you can use them.

▶ Coordinates how programs work with the hardware as well as with other software.

▶ Manages the way information is stored on and retrieved from disks.

OBJECTIVES

● Identify four components found in most graphical user interfaces.

● Describe the operating system's role in running software programs.

● Explain how the operating system enables users to manage files.

● List three ways the operating system manages the computer's hardware.

● Identify one key feature of each common PC operating system.

OPEN

SAVE

PRINT

COPY

PASTE

THE USER INTERFACE

With an operating system, you see and interact with a set of items on the screen: the **user interface.** In the case of most current operating systems, the user interface looks like a collection of objects on a colored background (see Figure 5.1).

Graphical User Interfaces

Most current operating systems, including all versions of Windows, the Macintosh operating system, OS/2, and some versions of UNIX, provide a **graphical user interface** (**GUI,** pronounced GOO-ee). Apple Computer introduced the first successful GUI with its Macintosh computer in 1984. Graphical user interfaces are so called because you use a mouse (or some other type of pointing device) to point at graphical objects on the screen. Figure 5.2 shows the Windows 98 interface with the Start menu open, a program running, and a dialog box open.

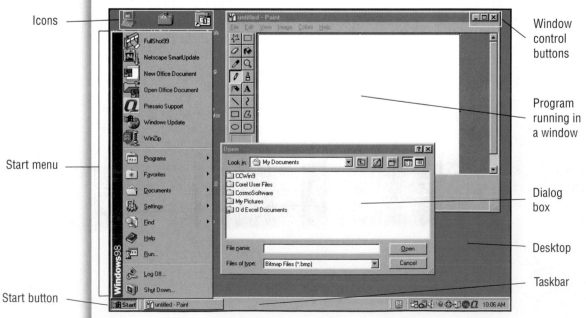

The Desktop

Software makers call the colored area you see on screen the **desktop** because they want you to think of it as just like the surface of a desk. The pictures, too, stand for items you might have in your office. In the case of Windows, these items include My Computer, a Recycle Bin, an Inbox, and a Briefcase.

Icons

Icons are pictures that represent the parts of the computer you work with—printers, fonts, document files, folders (a way to organize files into logical groups), disk drives, programs, and so on. Software designers try to design the icons so that they look like what they represent, thus making it easier to identify the icon you need. In Figure 5.3, for example, the Paintshop Pro icon represents the Paintshop Pro program, which resides on the computer's disk.

You interact with your computer's resources by activating the icons that represent them, and this activation is done most easily by using a pointing device, such as a mouse. With most GUI-based operating systems, rules for using the mouse to interact with icons are fairly consistent:

◆ You click an icon to **select** it. This action indicates that you plan to work with it.

◆ You double-click on an icon to **choose,** or **activate** it. For instance, you double-click the icon of a word processing program to load that program into memory and start using it. This action is also called launching the program.

◆ If you click an icon and hold down the mouse button, you can drag the mouse to move the icon to another location on the desktop. Sometimes you drag an icon to another icon to perform an action. For example, to move a file you can drag its icon from one folder icon to another.

◆ With Windows 9*x*, Windows NT, and Windows 2000 operating systems, you can right-click many parts of the desktop, and you will see a small menu (called a **shortcut menu** or a **context menu**) containing the most common commands associated with that part.

Although icons generally look like the object they represent, another class of symbols, called buttons, generally look the same from program to program. **Buttons** are areas of the screen you can click to cause something to happen. Most buttons feature a name and/or a picture surrounded by a black border. You may find many kinds of buttons in your program windows and dialog boxes; each button enables you to perform a specific task. For example, the Open button and the Cancel button are found in many dialog boxes (see Figure 5.2).

The Taskbar and the Start Button (Windows Only)

Whenever you start a program in certain versions of Windows (including Windows 95, Windows 98, Windows 2000, or Windows NT version 4.0 or later), a button for it appears on the **taskbar**—an area at the bottom of the screen whose purpose is to display buttons for the programs you are running. The **Start button** (see Figure 5.4) is a permanent feature of the taskbar. You click it to open the **Start menu** (see Figure 5.2). From the Start menu, you can click a program icon to start a program, choose Help to find information to assist you, or choose Shut Down when you are ready to turn off your computer.

Figure 5.3
If icons like these appear on your operating system's desktop, you can use them to launch programs or to access different devices on your computer.

Visit **www.glencoe.com/norton/online/** for more information on **graphical user interfaces.**

Figure 5.4
The Start button is a standard feature of the Windows 95, 98, 2000, and NT operating systems. You use it to open the Start menu, which provides access to the programs and devices on your disk.

Introduction to Software 93

Programs Running in Windows

In a graphical operating system, you can launch a program by choosing its program icon on the desktop. (In Windows 95, Windows 98, and Windows 2000, you can also launch a program by choosing its name from the Start menu.) The program is then loaded into memory and begins to run. A running program may take up the whole screen, or it may appear in a rectangular frame, called a **window.** Windows give you access to all the resources on your computer. For example, you can view the contents of a disk in a window, run a program and edit a document inside a window, view a Web page in a window, or change system settings in a window. A different window appears for each resource you want to use.

Most windows share many of the characteristics shown in Figure 5.5. For example, all windows include a **title bar** across the top that identifies the window's contents. Below the title bar, most programs contain a menu bar and toolbars that give you quick access to options and commands. Many windows also provide **scroll bars** with scroll arrows and scroll boxes, which enable you to view the different parts of the program or file that do not fit in the window.

Figure 5.5

Typical components of a program window in a graphical user interface.

Click the Minimize button to reduce the program to a button on the taskbar.

Click the Maximize button to make the window fill the entire screen.

Click the Close button to close the window altogether.

Title bar

Menu bar

Toolbar

Scroll arrow

Scroll box

Scroll bar

Scroll arrow

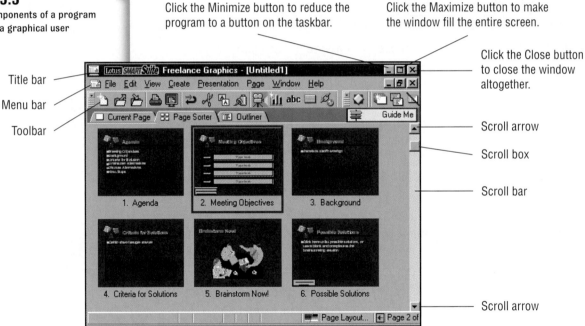

Graphical operating systems enable you to have multiple programs and resources running at the same time, but you can work in only one window at a time. The window that is currently in use is called the **active window;** it is the window where your next action will take effect. If you have multiple windows open (see Figures 5.6 and 5.7), you can identify the active window in several ways:

◆ Unless all open windows are arranged side by side, the active window will appear on top of the other windows. Inactive windows appear to be in the background.

◆ The active window's title bar is highlighted—that is, it is displayed in color. The title bar of an inactive window is "grayed out," meaning that it appears in gray rather than in color.

◆ If you are using a Windows system with a taskbar, the active window's taskbar button is highlighted—that is, it appears to be "pushed in." An inactive program's taskbar button appears to be "popped out."

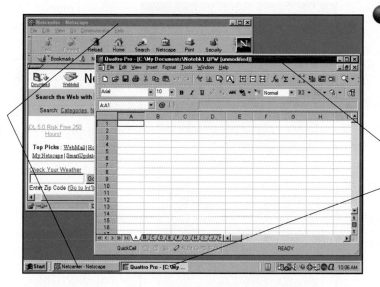

Netscape Navigator is in the background. Its title bar is grayed out and its taskbar button is not highlighted.

Figure 5.6
Two programs running under Windows 98. Quattro Pro is the active program.

Quattro Pro is on top, ready to be used. Its title bar and taskbar button are highlighted.

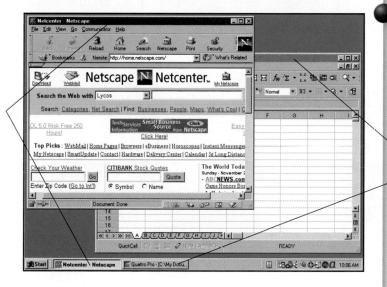

Netscape Navigator is now the active program. Its title bar and taskbar button are highlighted.

Figure 5.7
The same two programs running under Windows 98. Now, Netscape Navigator is active.

Quattro Pro is now in the background. Its title bar is grayed out and its taskbar button is no longer highlighted.

If you have more than one window open, you must select the window you want to use before you can access its contents. The process of moving from one open window to another is called **task switching,** and different operating systems let you task switch in different ways. In any graphical operating system, you can simply click in any open window to make it active. Your OS may also provide a special dialog box or a keyboard shortcut for performing task switching. In Windows 95, Windows 98, and Windows 2000, you can also click an open program's taskbar button to activate its window.

Menus

Although you initiate many tasks by clicking icons and buttons, you can also start tasks by choosing commands from lists called **menus.** You have already seen the Start menu, which appears when you click the Start button in some versions of Windows.

Figure 5.8

The File menu in WordPerfect. Notice that if any keyboard shortcuts are available, you can see them on the menu.

The most standard type of menu appears at the top of many windows in a horizontal list of menus called the **menu bar.** When you click a menu's name, a menu "drops down" and displays a list of commands. For this reason, these menus are sometimes called pull-down menus or drop-down menus. Many programs feature a File menu, for example, which typically contains commands for opening, closing, saving, and printing files. Figure 5.8 shows the File menu in WordPerfect. To execute or run one of the commands listed in the menu, you click it.

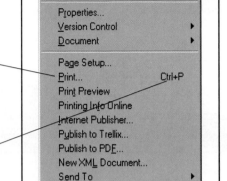

The underlined F indicates that you can press Alt+F to open the File menu.

With the File menu open, you can press P to execute the Print command.

As a one-step shortcut, you can press Ctrl+P to execute the Print command without opening the File menu.

Dialog Boxes

Dialog boxes are special-purpose windows that appear when you need to tell a program (or the operating system) what to do next. A dialog box is so named because it conducts a "dialog" with you as it seeks the information it needs to perform a task. Figure 5.9 shows a typical dialog box.

Figure 5.9

A dialog box can provide a wide variety of tools, thus allowing you to perform specialized tasks in an application or operating system.

Click a tab to display different "pages" of the dialog box. The Index section is currently visible.

Option buttons let you select one option from a set of choices.

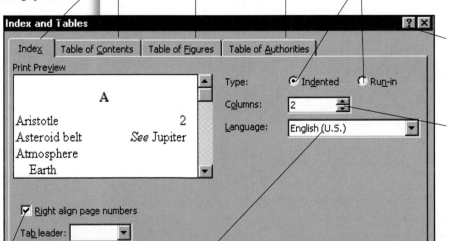

The Help button provides information about the tools of the dialog box.

Spinner (or counter) buttons usually contain numbers. Use the controls to increase or decrease the value.

These three buttons are called command buttons. Click one to initiate an action right away. If a button's name is followed by an ellipsis (…), then a second dialog box appears.

Click a check box to turn a feature on or off.

A drop-down list works like a pull-down menu. Click the arrow to open the list, then make a selection.

The OK button applies the options you select in the dialog box.

The Cancel button closes the dialog box without making any changes.

Command-Line Interfaces

The graphical user interface has become the standard because the Macintosh and Windows operating systems use it. For years, however, computer operating systems used **command-line interfaces,** which are environments that use typewritten commands rather than graphical objects to execute tasks and process data.

During the 1980s, the most popular of these command-line interfaces were Microsoft's MS-DOS, its near twin PC-DOS from IBM, and UNIX. Users interact with a command-line interface by typing strings of characters at a **prompt** on screen. In DOS, the prompt usually includes the identification for the active disk drive (a letter followed by a colon), a backslash (\), and a greater-than symbol, as in C:\>. DOS is still available in Windows for those who want to run DOS programs or to work with DOS keyboard commands.

RUNNING PROGRAMS

The operating system provides a consistent interface between programs and the user; and it is also the interface between those programs and other computer resources (such as computer memory, a printer, or another program). Programmers write computer programs with built-in instructions—called **system calls**—that request services from the operating system. (They are "calls" because the program has to call on the operating system to provide some information or service.) For example, when you want your word processing program to retrieve a file, you use the Open dialog box to list the files in the folder that you specify (see Figure 5.10). To provide the list, the program calls on the operating system.

NORTON
ONLINE

Visit **www.glencoe.com/norton/online/** for more information on **command-line interfaces.**

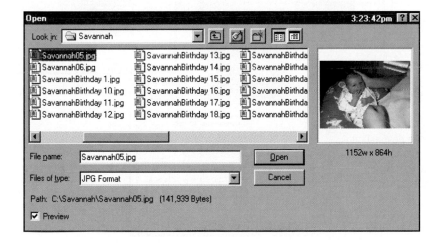

Figure 5.10
The Open dialog box in FullShot 99, an image-management program.

Some other services that an operating system provides to programs, in addition to listing files, are as follows:

◆ Saving the contents of files to a disk for permanent storage

◆ Reading the contents of a file from disk into memory

◆ Sending a document to the printer and activating the printer

◆ Providing resources that let you copy or move data from one document to another, or from one program to another

◆ Allocating RAM among various programs that you may have open

◆ Recognizing keystrokes or mouse clicks and displaying characters or graphics on the screen

Sharing Information

In many types of applications, you may want to move chunks of data from one place in a document to another. For example, you may want to copy a chart from a spreadsheet program and place the copy in a document in a word processor (see Figure 5.11.) Most newer operating systems accomplish this feat with a feature known as the **Clipboard.** The Clipboard is a temporary storage space (in the computer's memory) for data being copied or moved.

To move a paragraph in a word-processed document, select the paragraph; then choose the **Cut** command, which removes the data and places it on the Clipboard. (If you want to leave the original data in place, you can use the **Copy** command, which makes a copy of the data and stores it on the Clipboard but does not remove the original.) After placing the insertion point where you want to place the paragraph, choose the **Paste** command, which copies the Clipboard's contents back into the document.

Figure 5.11
Using the Clipboard to copy a chart from an Excel document to a WordPro document.

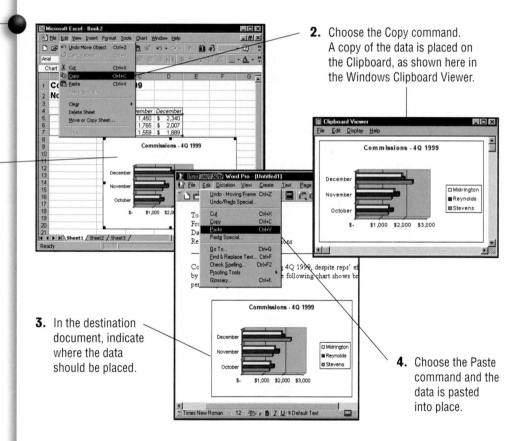

1. Select the desired data—in this case, a chart in Excel.

2. Choose the Copy command. A copy of the data is placed on the Clipboard, as shown here in the Windows Clipboard Viewer.

3. In the destination document, indicate where the data should be placed.

4. Choose the Paste command and the data is pasted into place.

The Clipboard can also be used to move data from one document to another. For example, you can copy an address from one letter to another and thereby avoid rekeying it. The real versatility of the Clipboard, however, stems from the fact that it is part of the operating system, not a particular application. As a result, you can use the Clipboard to move data from one program to another.

The versatility of the Clipboard has been extended with a feature known in Windows as **OLE,** which stands for **Object Linking and Embedding.** A simple cut and paste between applications results in object embedding. The data, which is known as an object in programming terms, is embedded in a new type of document. It retains the formatting that was applied to it in the original application, but its relationship with the original file is destroyed; that is, it is simply part of the new file.

NORTON
ONLINE

Visit **www.glencoe.com/norton/online/** for more information on **data sharing, multitasking,** and **file management.**

Object linking adds another layer to the relationship: the data that is copied to and from the Clipboard retains a link to the original document, so that a change in the original document also appears in the linked data.

Multitasking

Since the mid-1990s, all PC operating systems have been able to multitask, which is a computer's version of being able to "walk and chew gum at the same time." **Multitasking** means much more than the capability to load multiple programs into memory. Multitasking means being able to perform two or more procedures—such as printing a multiple-paged document, sending e-mail over the Internet, and typing a letter—all simultaneously.

MANAGING FILES

The files that the operating system works with may be programs or data files. Most programs you purchase come with any number—possibly thousands—of files. When you use the programs, you often create your own data files, such as word processing documents, and store them on a disk under names that you assign to them. The operating system is responsible for keeping track of all these files so that it can copy any one of them into RAM at a moment's notice.

The operating system keeps track of different disks or disk drives by assigning names to them. For example, on IBM and compatible computers, diskette drives are assigned the letters A and B, and hard disk drives are designated as the C drive and up. CD-ROM drives have the first available letter following the hard drives—often the letter D.

When there are hundreds of files on a disk, finding the one you want can be time-consuming. To find files quickly, you can organize them using folders. Figure 5.12 shows a list of the main folder of a hard disk, as shown in the Windows Explorer utility. Notice how file names are accompanied by the file sizes in bytes, and the date and time when the files were last modified. Also notice that there are several folders in the list. Folders can contain other folders, so you can create a structured system known as a hierarchical file system.

Figure 5.12
The Exploring window, showing the contents of the hard disk.

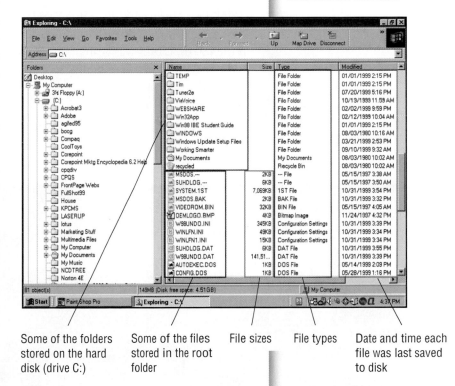

Some of the folders stored on the hard disk (drive C:)

Some of the files stored in the root folder

File sizes

File types

Date and time each file was last saved to disk

MANAGING HARDWARE

The operating system is the intermediary between programs and hardware. Following are three ways in which the operating system serves as the go-between to keep hardware running smoothly:

◆ **Processing Interrupts.** The operating system responds to requests to use memory and other devices, keeps track of which programs have access to which devices, and coordinates everything the hardware does so that various activities do not overlap and cause the computer to become confused and stop working. For example, if you tell the operating system to list the files in a folder, it sends an interrupt request (IRQ) to the computer's CPU.

◆ **Drivers.** The operating system often provides complete programs for working with special devices, such as printers. These programs are called **drivers** because they allow the operating system and other programs to activate and use—that is, "drive"—the hardware device.

◆ **Networking.** The operating system can also allow you to work with multiple computers on a network. A network server's operating system manages the flow of data on the file server and around the network.

Visit **www.glencoe.com/norton/online/** for more information on **UNIX** and its variants.

OPERATING SYSTEMS IN REVIEW

The following sections introduce you to the primary operating systems used on personal computers, chronologically, in order of their appearance on the desktop.

UNIX

UNIX (pronounced YOO-niks) is older than all the other PC operating systems, and in many ways it served as a model for them. Initially developed by Bell Labs in the 1970s, UNIX was geared toward uses in telecommunications systems. Today, many specific versions of UNIX exist, including A/UX for the Mac, AIX for IBM high-end workstations, Solaris for Sun Microsystems workstations, OpenVMS for Alpha workstations, SCO UNIX, XENIX, and others.

UNIX is an incredibly powerful and flexible operating system that can run on a single computer or a network. It provides multitasking and allows multiple users to work from more than one keyboard and monitor attached to a single CPU. UNIX also supports multiprocessor systems and runs on many different types of computers.

Figure 5.13
Window-based GUIs, like this one, make UNIX systems more user-friendly.

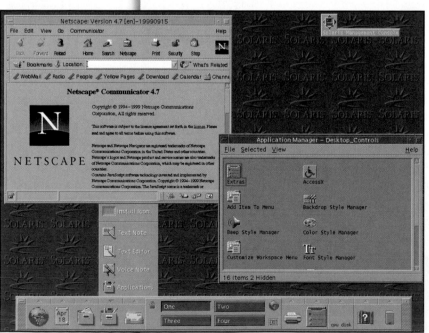

UNIX is not for the faint of heart because of its command-line interface and cryptic instructions, and the fact that it requires many commands to do even simple tasks. In an attempt to make UNIX more user-friendly, developers have created windows-based GUIs for UNIX, such as MOTIF and OpenLook, based on a windowing standard called X-Windows (see Figure 5.13).

DOS

Microsoft's **MS-DOS** (which stands for Microsoft Disk Operating System), along with IBM's PC-DOS (Personal Computer Disk Operating System), was once the most common of all the PC operating systems. DOS was developed in the 1970s and was distributed on some of the earliest commercial PCs. DOS won the early operating system marketing wars because IBM chose to license it as the standard operating system for the IBM PC. Therefore, it became the operating system for the huge market of IBM-compatibles and was the dominant PC operating system throughout the 1980s.

Among DOS's strengths were its reliability and stability. On a properly configured system, DOS and DOS programs ran well; crashes and lock-ups were rare. Most users needed to learn only a small set of commands. Although the DOS prompt is not an elegant interface, it was not terribly hard to use once you mastered the commands you used most frequently.

NORTON ONLINE

Visit **www.glencoe.com/norton/online/** for more information on **DOS** and the **Macintosh operating system**.

The Macintosh Operating System

The Macintosh is a purely graphical machine and brought the first truly graphical user interface to consumers. In its early days (in the mid-1980s), the Macintosh's integration of hardware and operating system, along with its GUI, made it popular among users who did not want to deal with DOS's command-line interface. Another big advantage of the Macintosh was that all its applications looked alike and functioned similarly, making them easier to learn than DOS applications, most of which had their own unique look and feel. Now that GUIs have become the standard, it is difficult to appreciate how big a breakthrough the Macintosh interface was.

The **Macintosh operating system** (or the **Mac OS**) was also ahead of Windows with many other features, such as built-in network support and **Plug and Play** hardware support. Plug and Play means that you can attach a new piece of hardware to the system and the OS detects it automatically. The Mac OS also provides multitasking and allows data sharing across different applications (see Figure 5.14). Such features quickly made even die-hard DOS enthusiasts envious and led Microsoft to develop the Windows operating environment for the IBM-compatible market.

Figure 5.14

Before the advent of Windows, the Mac OS enabled users to run multiple applications in a graphical user interface.

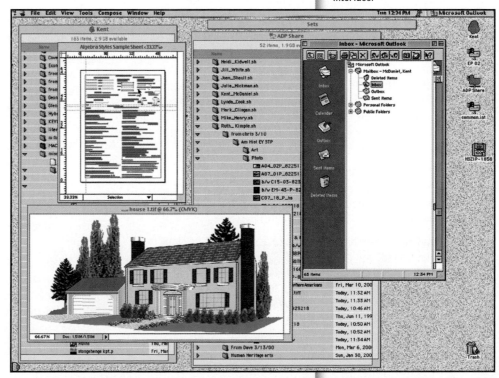

PRODUCTIVITY Tip

Do-It-Yourself Tech Support

If you want to learn a new feature in a program or need help solving a problem, the answers may be on your hard disk or the Internet.

Using Local Online Help

Most commercial operating systems and applications include an online help system that is installed on your computer with the software. New-generation help systems include descriptions, tips, audio/video demonstrations, hyperlinks, and links to Internet-based resources.

To find help on your hard drive, open the help system and look for answers. To get help with the Windows OS, for example, click the Start button and choose Help from the Start menu. In any Windows application, click the Help menu and choose Contents or Help Topics. A Help window appears, providing tools that let you search for help in different ways. Remember the following tips:

◆ **Be Patient.** You may not find your answer immediately. Be prepared to try again.

◆ **Learn Different Search Options.** Most Windows-based help systems are divided into three sections, each providing different options for finding help. The Contents section displays help topics in a hierarchical list. The Search section lets you search all topics to find those topics whose title contains a specific term. The Index tab displays all the key terms in the help system; select one or more terms. Then get a list of help topics that contain those terms.

◆ **Think of the Problem in Different Ways.** For example, if you want help with making characters bold in your document, the terms *bold*, *format*, *font*, and *style* may bring up the right answers.

◆ **Use Bookmarks and Annotations.** Most help systems let you bookmark specific help topics so you can find them again quickly. You can also add your own notes to specific topics.

Using Remote Online Help

Many software makers provide several remote online help resources that you can access over the Internet.

◆ **Web-Based Technical Support.** Many software companies have a "Support" or "Help" link on their Web home page.

The online help system is often the last place users turn for help; in fact, it should be the first place you look.

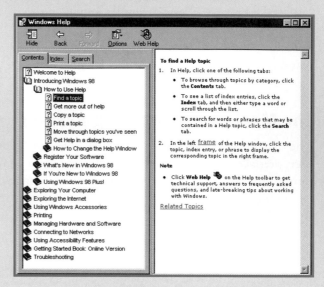

◆ **FAQs.** Most software companies have Web sites with lists of frequently asked questions (FAQs).

◆ **E-Mail Help.** At the company's Web site, you may find an option that lets you describe a problem and submit a request for help. A support technician will investigate the problem, or an automated system will send you a list of possible solutions.

◆ **Knowledgebases.** A knowledgebase is a sophisticated database containing detailed information about a specific topic. To use a knowledgebase, type a term or phrase, or describe a problem. After your text is matched against a database, you are presented with a list of possible solutions.

◆ **Newsgroups.** Large software companies sponsor newsgroups on the Internet. Using your newsreader, you can access these newsgroups, post questions for other users to answer, or participate in discussions about specific products and technical issues.

Before you use any remote online help resource, read all the information the company provides about it. Look for notices about fees, registration, and proof of product ownership.

Windows 3.x

In the mid-1980s, Microsoft accepted the popularity of the Macintosh computer and users' desire for a GUI. Microsoft's solution was **Windows,** a GUI that ran on top of DOS, replacing the command-line interface with a point-and-click system. Windows, therefore, was not originally an operating system but an **operating environment,** an interface that disguises the underlying operating system.

The first version of Windows did not work or sell well, and the second version also was not a success. Not until Microsoft released Windows 3.0 in 1990 did the product really take off. Windows 3.0 was reasonably stable and succeeded in providing a GUI (as shown in Figure 5.15) and the capability to load more than one program into memory at a time. Users could also run DOS programs under Windows, either in full-screen mode (so the screen looked like a DOS system) or within a window.

During the early 1990s, Windows 3.0, Windows 3.1, and Windows 3.11 (called Windows for Workgroups) became the market leaders and eventually were installed on most new PCs, running on top of DOS. (The term **Windows 3.x** is used when referring to more than one member of the Windows 3 family.)

OS/2 Warp

After the introduction of the Intel 80286 processor in 1982, IBM and Microsoft teamed up to develop **OS/2 Warp,** a multitasking, GUI-based operating system for Intel microprocessors. Unlike Windows 3.x, OS/2 was a true operating system (see Figure 5.16).

OS/2 provides networking support, true multitasking, and multiuser support. OS/2 also enables users to run OS/2-specific applications as well as programs written for DOS and Windows 3.x. OS/2 became the first OS to provide built-in speech recognition technology. Like UNIX, it can run on a wide range of hardware platforms.

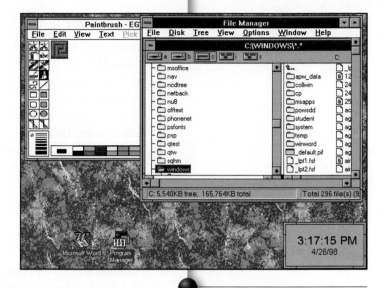

Figure 5.15
The interface for Windows 3.x has a lot in common with the Macintosh OS. Users can work with files and programs by clicking desktop icons to open windows.

Visit **www.glencoe.com/norton/online/** for more information on **Windows 3.x** and **OS/2 Warp.**

Figure 5.16
The OS/2 Warp interface.

Windows NT

Microsoft released **Windows NT,** a 32-bit operating system for PCs, in 1993. Windows NT (New Technology) was originally designed as the successor to DOS, but by the time it was ready for release, it had become too large to run on most of the PCs in use at the time. As a result, Microsoft repositioned Windows NT to be a high-end operating system designed primarily for powerful workstations and network servers. (With Windows NT released, Microsoft went back to the drawing board to create a more consumer-oriented version of Windows to replace DOS on home and office PCs. The result was Windows 95, which is discussed later.)

At the time of its release, Windows NT addressed the market for the powerful 32-bit, networked workstations that used some of the most powerful CPUs on the market. Because these types of computers fell into two primary categories, Microsoft separated Windows NT into two distinct products:

◆ **Windows NT Workstation.** Although **Windows NT Workstation** looks almost identical to consumer versions of Windows, its underlying operating system is almost completely different. Windows NT Workstation is designed to take better advantage of today's computers and also runs on a broader range of CPUs than do other versions of Windows. As its name implies, Windows NT Workstation is typically used on individual, stand-alone PCs that may or may not be part of a network.

◆ **Windows NT Server.** **Windows NT Server** incorporates all the same features as Windows NT Workstation but has additional capabilities. Microsoft fine-tuned Windows NT Server to function as an operating system for file and print servers and on other systems that provide services for other computers on a LAN or the Internet. Windows NT Server offers expanded security features for grouping and authenticating users and controlling their access to network resources.

Visit **www.glencoe.com/norton/online/** for more information on **Windows NT, Windows 95,** and **Windows 98.**

Self Check

Answer the following questions by filling in the blank(s).

1. MOTIF and OpenLook are examples of _____ for UNIX.

2. The _____ brought the first truly graphical user interface to consumers.

3. Windows 3.x is called a(n) _____ because it is not a true operating system.

Windows 95 and Windows 98

In 1995, Microsoft released **Windows 95,** a complete operating system and a successor to DOS for desktop computers. Windows 95 is a 32-bit multitasking operating system with a revised GUI. All the strengths of Windows 95, which followed the Windows 3.x series, had already existed in other operating systems—most notably the Macintosh and Windows NT.

Windows 95 can run almost any DOS or Windows 3.x program (see Figure 5.17). Thus, if a company had already invested in many such programs, it could continue to use its familiar programs while migrating to the new operating system.

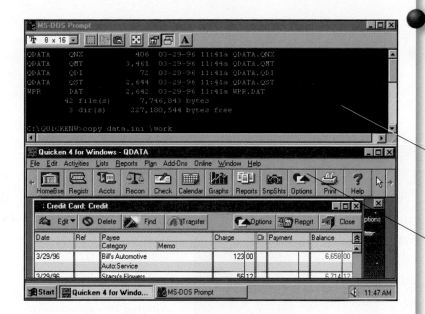

Figure 5.17
Windows 95 is designed primarily to run 32-bit applications but can run older 16-bit applications designed for Windows 3.*x* and DOS.

DOS, running in a window

A 16-bit application written for Windows 3.*x*

For users of Windows 3.*x,* Windows 95 has several attractions. It offers 32-bit processing; for programs designed with 32-bit processing in mind, the operating system can exchange information with printers, networks, and files in 32-bit pieces instead of 16-bit pieces, as in Windows 3.*x* and DOS. For information moving in the computer, the effect is like doubling the number of lanes on an expressway.

Windows 95 has a graphical interface that is a welcome improvement over Windows 3.*x.* The Windows Explorer, for example, improves on earlier Microsoft operating systems for working with files. Windows 95 also allows users to type file names of up to 256 characters and to have spaces in those names—features that had not been available on DOS-based PCs.

In addition, Windows 95 offers a Plug and Play standard for connecting new hardware. Another Windows 95 asset is compatibility with networking software such as NetWare and Microsoft Windows NT Server. With networks, too, you can simply identify the network operating system when you install Windows 95, and Windows 95 will be compatible with it.

Many experts considered **Windows 98** to be an update to Windows 95, rather than a major Windows operating system upgrade. In other words, the differences from Windows 95 to Windows 98 are not as significant as the differences from Windows 3.*x* to Windows 95. However, one key change in Windows 98 is the inclusion of the Internet Explorer Web browser. A new feature, called the Active Desktop, lets you browse the Internet and local computer in a similar manner (see Figure 5.18). Active Desktop enables you to integrate Internet resources such as stock tickers and news information services directly on your Windows desktop. If you have an active Internet connection, the information will update automatically.

Windows 98 also adds support for new and emerging technologies and expands other hardware

Figure 5.18
The Windows 98 Active Desktop lets the operating system function like a Web browser.

support, including Universal Serial Bus devices, DVD, and OnNow (which enables computers to be booted and ready to use almost instantly). One interesting feature of Windows 98 is its capability to support up to eight monitors at one time. This new feature is ideal for certain applications such as computer-aided design to provide large desktops and the capability to separate application and document windows. It's also a great feature for many online and interactive games.

Figure 5.19
Although Linux is typically considered to be a server platform, an increasing number of software companies are porting their applications to Linux.

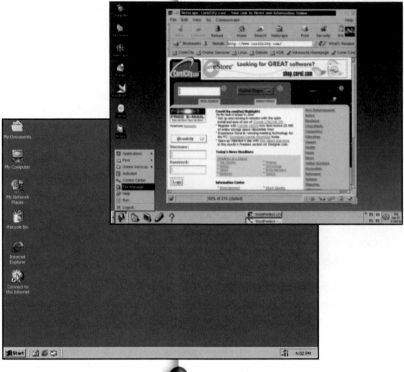

Linux

Between the release of Windows 95 and Windows 98, the computer world's attention focused on another new operating system, called **Linux** (pronounced LIH-nuhks). In fact, Linux is a new version of UNIX, developed by a worldwide cooperative of programmers, and is freely distributed by various sources. Even though Linux is considered a "freeware" operating system, industry experts have been impressed by its power, capabilities, and rich feature set. Like UNIX, Linux is a full 32-bit, multitasking operating system that supports multiple users and multiple processors. Also like UNIX, Linux can run on nearly any computer and can support almost any type of application. Native Linux is driven by a command-line interface, but a windows-based GUI is also available (see Figure 5.19).

Figure 5.20
The Windows 2000 desktop.

Windows 2000

Windows 2000 combines the user-friendly interface and features of Windows 98 with the file system, networking, power, and stability of Windows NT (see Figure 5.20). New and improved features include the following:

◆ **Improved Setup and Installation.** Although Plug and Play has existed for a few years, the protocol has improved. Windows 2000 also includes the new Windows Installer to make software installation easier.

◆ **Improved Internet Features.** Although casual users may not see much of a difference, network administrators can look forward to new features that make it easier to blend workstations, servers, intranets, and the Internet into one seamless unit.

◆ **Improved Networking.** Its networking features make Windows 2000 easier for administrators to set up and run a network and allow less experienced users to run office networks.

◆ **Improved Disk Management.** Windows 2000 includes a more flexible method of dividing and accessing hard drive space as well as adding drive-maintenance programs like Disk Defragmenter, which were missing in Windows NT.

NORTON ONLINE

Visit www.glencoe.com/norton/online/ for more information on **Linux** and **Windows 2000**.

LESSON QUIZ

True/False

Answer the following questions by circling True or False.

True   False   **1.** Graphical user interfaces are so called because you point at graphical objects.

True   False   **2.** You interact with icons by using the keyboard.

True   False   **3.** All windows are unique because none share any of the same characteristics.

True   False   **4.** MS-DOS stands for Microsoft Disk Operating System.

True   False   **5.** Windows 3.*x* replaced DOS as the operating system of computers on which it was installed.

Multiple Choice

Circle the word or phrase that best completes each sentence.

1. In a GUI, you work in the _____ window.
   A. active   **B.** biggest   **C.** program

2. Graphical operating systems often let you choose commands from lists, called _____ .
   A. command lines   **B.** menus   **C.** neither A nor B

3. In a command-line interface (such as DOS), you enter commands at a _____ .
   A. dialog box   **B.** window   **C.** prompt

4. In Windows 98, the _____ feature lets you browse the Internet and local resources in a similar manner.
   A. GUI   **B.** Active Desktop   **C.** Universal Serial Bus

5. One of the primary attractions of Linux is the fact that it _____ .
   A. can be acquired at no cost   **B.** can run on almost any computer   **C.** both A and B

LESSON LABS

Complete the following exercise as directed by your instructor.

Use your operating system's tools to find files:

A. Click the Start button, point to Programs, and click Windows Explorer.

B. Click Tools, click Find, and then click Files or Folders.

C. In the Named text box, type ***.txt**. This tells Windows to search for all files with the file-name extension *txt*.

D. From the Look in drop-down list, choose your computer's hard disk (typically C:).

E. If the Include subfolders check box is not selected (with a check mark), click it once.

F. Click Find Now. Windows conducts the search and displays the results at the bottom of the Find: All Files dialog box.

G. Repeat the search, specifying ***.wri**, ***.doc**, and ***.gif** as your search criteria. When you are finished, close the Find: All Files dialog box and the Exploring window.

Productivity Software

OBJECTIVES

- List three types of formatting you can perform in a word processor.
- Identify four types of data that can be entered in a worksheet.
- Describe the process of creating a presentation.
- Differentiate between the terms *database* and *database management system (DBMS)*.
- List three basic tasks that a DBMS enables users to perform.

OVERVIEW:
The Way We Work Has Changed Forever

There are very few professions that have not been affected by computer technologies. Over the past two decades, computers have found their way into the workplace in many different forms with many different uses. Nowhere has this change been more evident than in the office and school, where millions of people use personal computers to perform information-related tasks. To manage different types of information, these workers use specialized software packages that fall into the category of productivity applications.

As their name implies, productivity applications are designed to help users be more productive in their daily work. They have replaced once-common workplace tools like typewriters, erasers, and ledger books and have helped many people reduce or even eliminate the need for filing paper-based documents.

This lesson introduces the four most commonly used types of productivity applications: word processing software, spreadsheet programs, presentation programs, and database management systems. You will learn about the primary uses for each type of software and some of the general features common to each type.

WORD PROCESSING SOFTWARE

Word processing software (also called a **word processor**) is an application that provides extensive tools for creating all kinds of text-based documents. This definition does not mean that word processors work only with text. Word processors enable you to incorporate images in your documents and can help you design and lay out a document so it looks like the product of a professional print shop.

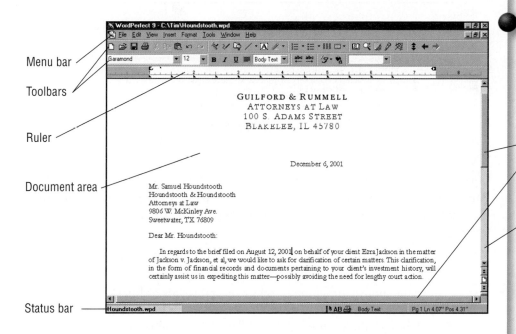

Menu bar
Toolbars
Ruler
Document area
Status bar
Scroll boxes
Scroll bar

Figure 6.1
WordPerfect's interface features tools that are commonly found in word processing programs.

The Word Processor's Interface

The word processor's main editing window, called the **document area** (or **document window**), is where you view the document. A word processor also provides several sets of tools (see Figure 6.1). These tools include a menu bar displaying titles of command categories, from which you can select hundreds of commands and options. One or more **toolbars** provide tools that resemble buttons; these buttons represent frequently used commands, such as those for printing and for selecting text styles.

A **ruler** shows you the positioning of text, tabs, margins, indents, and other elements across the page. Horizontal and vertical scroll bars with scroll boxes let you scroll through a document that is too large to fit inside the document area. Most word processors also offer a **status bar** across the bottom of the window, with information about your position in the document, the page count, and the status of keyboard keys.

Entering and Editing Text

You create a document by typing text using the keyboard—a process known as entering text. In a new document, the program places a blinking insertion point in the upper left corner of the document window. As you type text, the insertion point advances across the screen, showing you where the next character will be placed.

NORTON
ONLINE

Visit **www.glencoe.com/norton/online/** for general information on **word processing software**.

When your text reaches the right edge of the screen, the word processor automatically moves the insertion point to the next line (see Figure 6.2.) This feature is called **word wrap.** The only time you need to press Enter is to start a new paragraph.

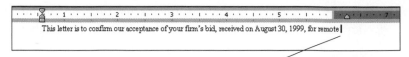

When the insertion point reaches the end of a line...

...it automatically moves down to the next line.

Figure 6.2
Word wrap.

One advantage of word processing software over the typewriter is that it enables you to change text without retyping the entire page. Instead, you retype only the text that needs to be changed. Changing an existing document is called **editing.**

A **block** is a contiguous group of characters, words, lines, sentences, or paragraphs in your document that you mark for editing. To mark text for editing, you select text by using the mouse (dragging to select several words or lines), the keyboard (using Shift and the arrow keys to select characters, words, or lines), or both (using Ctrl while clicking to select entire sentences). When you select text, it changes color—becoming **highlighted,** as shown in Figure 6.3.

Figure 6.3
The paragraph that appears as white text against a black background has been highlighted; it is a selected block of text.

flow, or a burst of waves, the reservoir cushions the banks from changing forces. A UPS is like a reservoir for electricity. As your electricity fluctuates, the UPS absorbs and supplements the flow.

To fully appreciate how helpful a UPS is, take the water analogy one step further and think of the plumbing in your home. If someone is drawing water when you start a shower, the other person notices a drop in the water pressure and you notice that the water pressure isn't as high as it should be. Then, if someone else flushes a toilet, you can expect the flow of cold water to momentarily drop even more. When the toilet finishes filling up, you can expect a sudden return of the cold water. And, when the original person drawing water stops, you notice a sudden increase in water pressure. Once you're through fiddling with the faucets, you appreciate how nice a personal reservoir could be. The electricity in your home works much the same way, so a UPS goes a long way to even out the flow as various appliances are turned on an off.

What Are the Most Common Electrical Problems?
Electrical problems come in all types, from the nearly harmless minor fluctuation in the voltage level, to

After you select text, you can change it in many ways. You can erase the entire selected block by pressing the Delete key or by typing any other text over the selected block. You can change the formatting of the selection, by making it bold or underlined, for example, or by changing the font. You can also copy or move the block from one part of the document to another or even from one document to another. In a word processor, moving text is as easy as dragging the block to a new location, a technique called drag-and-drop editing. The same effect can be accomplished by cutting or copying the block to the Clipboard and then pasting it to a new location.

To **deselect** a selected block of text, click the mouse anywhere on the screen or press any arrow key. The text is displayed again normally.

Formatting Text

Most word processing features are used to format the document. Most formatting features fall into one of three categories: character formats, paragraph formats, and document formats.

Character Formats

Character formatting is used to control the attributes of individual characters:

◆ **Fonts.** The term **font** refers to the characteristics of the letters, symbols, and punctuation marks in your document. There are two general categories of fonts: monospace and proportional (see Figure 6.4). Fonts also fall into two additional broad categories: serif and sans serif (see Figure 6.5).

◆ **Type Size.** The size of a font is measured in points (see Figure 6.6).

◆ **Type Styles.** In addition to the font and type size, the appearance of characters can be controlled with type styles (which are often referred to as attributes or effects). The most common styles used in documents are **bold**, *italics*, and underlining. Less commonly used style attributes include ~~strikethrough~~, superscript, subscript, SMALL CAPS, and many others.

> This is the Courier font, which is monospaced.
>
> This is the Times font, which is proportional.

> Berkeley is a serif font.
>
> Helvetica is a sans serif font.

This is 10 point Times type.

This is 12 point Times type.

This is 14 point Times type.

This is 16 point Times type.

This is 18 point Times type.

Paragraph Formats

Word processing software creates a **paragraph** each time you press the Enter key. A group of sentences is a paragraph, but a two-word heading (like the one above this paragraph) is also defined as a paragraph. **Paragraph formatting** includes settings applied to one or more entire paragraphs:

◆ **Line and Paragraph Spacing.** A setting known as line spacing controls the amount of space between each line of text in a paragraph. Lines can be single-spaced or double-spaced or set to any spacing you want. Paragraph spacing refers to the amount of space between each paragraph.

◆ **Indents.** Indents determine how close each line of a paragraph comes to the margins (the white borders around a page's edge).

◆ **Alignment.** Alignment refers to the orientation of the lines of a paragraph with respect to the margins. There are four alignment options—left, right, center, and justified (or full justification)—as shown in Figure 6.7.

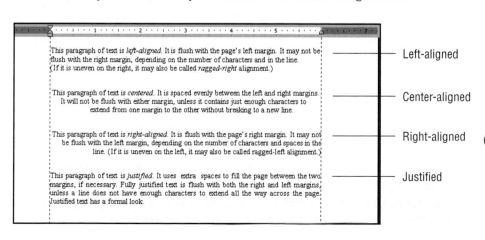

This paragraph of text is *left-aligned*. It is flush with the page's left margin. It may not be flush with the right margin, depending on the number of characters and in the line. (If it is uneven on the right, it may also be called *ragged-right* alignment.) — Left-aligned

This paragraph of text is *centered*. It is spaced evenly between the left and right margins. It will not be flush with either margin, unless it contains just enough characters to extend from one margin to the other without breaking to a new line. — Center-aligned

This paragraph of text is *right-aligned*. It is flush with the page's right margin. It may not be flush with the left margin, depending on the number of characters and spaces in the line. (If it is uneven on the left, it may also be called ragged-left alignment.) — Right-aligned

This paragraph of text is *justified*. It uses extra spaces to fill the page between the two margins, if necessary. Fully justified text is flush with both the right and left margins, unless a line does not have enough characters to extend all the way across the page. Justified text has a formal look. — Justified

Figure 6.4

In a monospaced font, each character occupies the same amount of horizontal space. In a proportional font, characters take up only as much space as they need.

Figure 6.5

Serif fonts have decorative lines and curls at the ends of strokes. Sans serif fonts do not.

Figure 6.6

Type sizes.

NORTON ONLINE

Visit **www.glencoe.com/norton/online/** for more information on **formatting** documents and **fonts**.

Figure 6.7

The vertical dotted lines represent the left and right margins on the page. Notice how the different paragraph alignments adjust the text in relation to the margins.

Figure 6.8
Four kinds of tab stops.

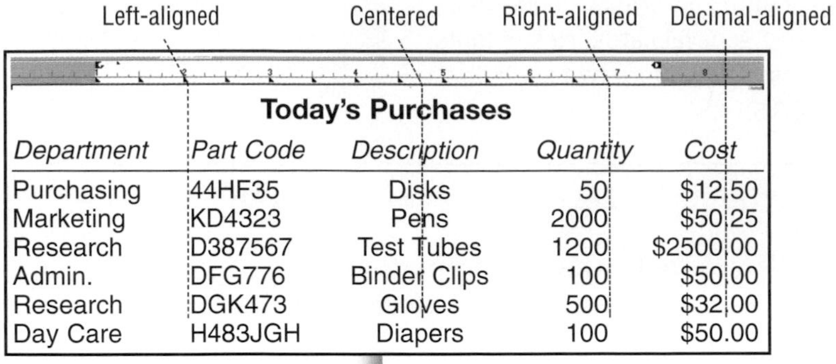

| Left-aligned | Centered | Right-aligned | Decimal-aligned |

Today's Purchases

Department	Part Code	Description	Quantity	Cost
Purchasing	44HF35	Disks	50	$12.50
Marketing	KD4323	Pens	2000	$50.25
Research	D387567	Test Tubes	1200	$2500.00
Admin.	DFG776	Binder Clips	100	$50.00
Research	DGK473	Gloves	500	$32.00
Day Care	H483JGH	Diapers	100	$50.00

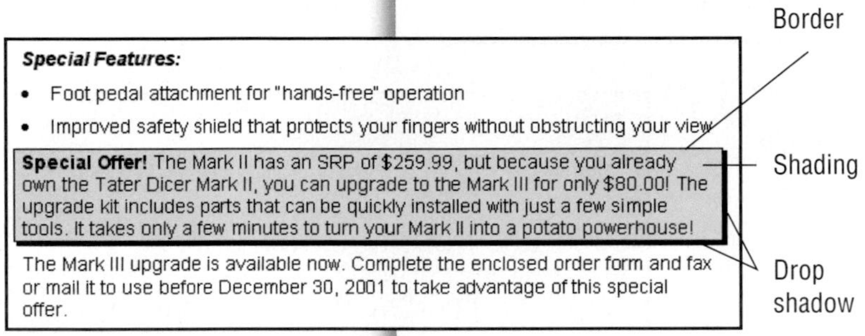

Special Features:

- Foot pedal attachment for "hands-free" operation
- Improved safety shield that protects your fingers without obstructing your view

Special Offer! The Mark II has an SRP of $259.99, but because you already own the Tater Dicer Mark II, you can upgrade to the Mark III for only $80.00! The upgrade kit includes parts that can be quickly installed with just a few simple tools. It takes only a few minutes to turn your Mark II into a potato powerhouse!

The Mark III upgrade is available now. Complete the enclosed order form and fax or mail it to use before December 30, 2001 to take advantage of this special offer.

Border

Shading

Drop shadow

Figure 6.9
A paragraph formatted with a border, shading, and a drop shadow.

◆ **Tabs.** The keyboard's Tab key moves the insertion point forward (to the right) until it encounters a tab stop (or just tab), inserting a fixed amount of space in the line. A tab stop is a position, both on screen and in the document, usually measured from the left margin of the document. Tabs are used most often to align columns of text accurately or to create tables. Word processors provide at least four different types of tab stops so that you can align columns in different ways, as shown in Figure 6.8.

◆ **Borders and Shading.** Paragraphs can be formatted with borders or shading, as shown in Figure 6.9. A border is a line, often called a rule, that is drawn on one or more sides of a paragraph. Shading consists of a pattern or color that is displayed as a background to the text in a paragraph. A drop shadow is a partial shadow around a bordered paragraph, which creates the illusion that the paragraph is floating above the page.

Document Formats

Document formatting refers to the settings that apply to an entire document:

◆ **Margins.** Margins are the white borders around the edge of the page where the text is not allowed to go. Every document has top, bottom, left, and right margins, and in any document all four margins can be the same or different.

◆ **Page Size.** Normally, documents are set up to fit on 8.5- by 11-inch pieces of paper, a standard known as letter-size paper. You can, however, set up your document for other standard sizes such as legal size (8.5 by 14 inches).

◆ **Orientation.** The dimensions of the document are also determined by the orientation of the paper. By default, documents are set up with portrait orientation, as shown in the pages of this textbook. However, you can always switch to landscape orientation in which the text is printed parallel to the widest page edge.

◆ **Headers and Footers.** Long documents generally include headers, footers, or both. Headers and footers are lines of text that run along the top and bottom, respectively, of every page. They may include the document's name and the page number or other information.

◆ **Columns.** Columns are popular and effective formats for certain types of documents. Newsletters, for example, typically are laid out in a two- or three-column format. Columns make it easy to read a document quickly and open the door for other special formatting techniques.

- **Sections.** Sometimes, a column layout is appropriate for only one part of a document, while a normal page-wide layout suits the rest of the document better. For this reason, word processors allow you to divide a document into sections and apply a different format to each section. In Figure 6.10, the document's top section is a page-wide heading. The second section is a three-column format.

Special Features of Word Processing Programs

All modern word processing programs are rich in features, many of which have nothing to do with text editing or formatting. Most word processors include the following special features, among others:

- **Spell Checkers.** If your word processor features a spell checker, you can enable it to catch spelling mistakes as you type. You can also use the spell checker to review an entire document for potential spelling errors. A spell checker works by matching each word in your document against a built-in dictionary containing standard spellings. If the utility encounters a word that has no match in the dictionary, it lets you know. A good spell checker will provide options for replacing the word, ignoring the word, or adding the word to the spelling dictionary.

- **Tables.** Although tabs can be used to set up rows and columns of information in a document, word processors provide features that let you create **tables** in just a few steps. The size of a table is limited only by the amount of page space that can be devoted to it, and tables can be formatted in dozens of ways.

- **Mail Merge.** A **mail merge** is the process of combining a form letter with the contents of a database, usually a name and address list, so that each copy of the letter has one entry from the database printed on it.

- **Graphics.** Using a word processor, you can add graphical images—photos, drawings, or clip art—to your documents. In fact, the process is simple. You set the cursor where you want the graphic to appear, tell the word processing program that you want to insert a graphic, and then locate the graphic file.

- **Sounds.** In addition to graphics, you can embed sound files in your documents, as shown in Figure 6.11. You embed the sound file in much the same way that you embed a graphical file. The only difference is that an icon appears in the document. Clicking the icon plays the sound file, if the PC has a sound card and speakers. Although sound files are of no value in printed documents, they can be useful in documents that are distributed electronically— on disk, online, or across a network.

Figure 6.10
A two-section document, with different document formats in each section.

Figure 6.11
Documents can contain both graphics and sounds.

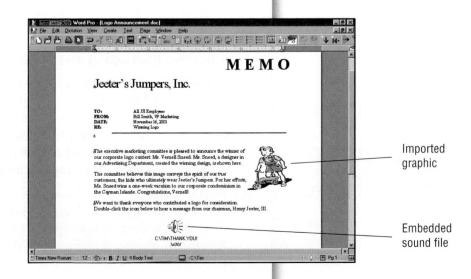

Imported graphic

Embedded sound file

113

◆ **Templates. Templates** are predesigned documents that are blank, except for preset margins, fonts, paragraph formats, headings, rules, graphics, headers, or footers. You can open a document template, type your text into it, and save it. Templates free users from manually formatting complex documents, such as memos, fax cover sheets, reports, résumés, and other types of business, legal, or academic documents and forms (see Figure 6.12). You can even create new templates.

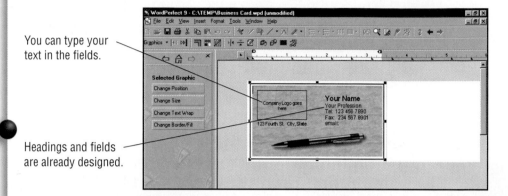

You can type your text in the fields.

Headings and fields are already designed.

Figure 6.12
Predesigned templates make it easy to create professional documents, from business cards to newsletters.

◆ **HTML Capabilities.** Word processors can convert documents into HTML format so they can be viewed in a Web browser. The resulting Web page contains not only the original text but is formatted with HTML tags so that headings, body text, bulleted lists, and other elements will appear in a standard Web format. (You will learn more about Web pages and HTML in Unit 5, "The Internet and Online Resources.")

SPREADSHEET PROGRAMS

A **spreadsheet** program is a software tool for entering, calculating, manipulating, and analyzing sets of numbers. Spreadsheets have a wide range of uses—from family budgets to corporate earnings statements, and all sorts of tasks in between.

You can set up a spreadsheet to show information in any number of ways, such as the traditional row-and-column format (which the spreadsheet takes from its predecessor, the ledger book), or a slick report format with headings and charts.

The Spreadsheet's Interface

Like a word processing program, a spreadsheet lets you work in a main document area (also called a document window), which displays your data and various tools. Figure 6.13 shows Microsoft Excel 2000. In a spreadsheet program, you actually work in a document called a **worksheet** (or sheet, as it is also called), and you can collect related worksheets in a **workbook.** Worksheets can be named, and a workbook can contain as many individual worksheets as your system's resources will allow.

A typical spreadsheet interface also provides a menu bar, toolbars, and a special **formula bar,** where you can create or edit data and formulas in the worksheet. Scroll bars help you navigate a large worksheet, and at the bottom of the window, a status bar tells you specific information about the worksheet, such as the sum of a selected group of numbers.

NORTON
ONLINE

Visit **www.glencoe.com/norton/online/** for a wide variety of information on **spreadsheets.**

An empty worksheet (one without any data) looks like a grid of rows and columns. The intersection of any column and row is called a **cell,** as shown in Figure 6.13. You interact with a spreadsheet primarily by entering data into individual cells. A typical worksheet contains thousands of individual cells, allowing you to enter and manipulate huge arrays of data.

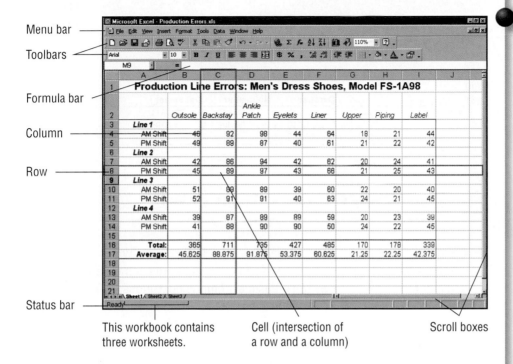

Menu bar

Toolbars

Formula bar

Column

Row

Status bar

This workbook contains three worksheets.

Cell (intersection of a row and a column)

Scroll boxes

Figure 6.13
Microsoft Excel's interface features tools common to nearly all Windows and Macintosh spreadsheets.

Entering Data in a Worksheet

The process of entering data in a worksheet is simple. Using the mouse or arrow keys, you select a cell to make it active. The active cell is indicated by a **cell pointer,** a rectangle that makes the active cell's borders look bold.

To navigate the worksheet, you need to understand its system of **cell addresses.** All spreadsheets use row and column identifiers as the basis for their cell addresses. If you are working in the cell where column B intersects with row 3, for example, then cell B3 is the active cell.

A worksheet's cells can hold different types of data, including the following:

◆ **Labels.** Worksheets can contain text, called **labels.** In spreadsheets, text is referred to as a label because it is usually used to identify a value or series of values (as in a row or column heading) or to describe the contents of a specific cell (such as a total). Labels help you make sense of a worksheet's contents (see Figure 6.14 on page 116).

◆ **Values.** In a spreadsheet, a **value** is any number you enter or that results from a computation. You might enter a series of values in a column so that you can total them. Or you might enter several different numbers that are part of an elaborate calculation.

◆ **Dates.** A date may be added to a worksheet simply to indicate when it was created, or a date function may be used to update when the worksheet is opened. Spreadsheets can also use dates in performing calculations. An example might be when calculating late payments on a loan. If the spreadsheet knows the payment's due date, it can calculate late fees based on that date.

Figure 6.14

The cell pointer highlights the active cell, where you can enter and edit data. Labels help organize the information in a worksheet.

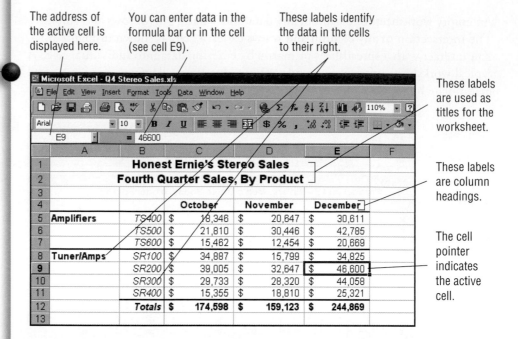

The address of the active cell is displayed here.

You can enter data in the formula bar or in the cell (see cell E9).

These labels identify the data in the cells to their right.

These labels are used as titles for the worksheet.

These labels are column headings.

The cell pointer indicates the active cell.

◆ **Formulas.** The power of the spreadsheet lies in **formulas,** which calculate numbers based on values or formulas in other cells. You can create many kinds of formulas manually to do basic arithmetic operations, calculus or trigonometric operations, and so on.

Cell References and Ranges

Formulas typically refer to the values in other cells throughout the worksheet. To reduce time and errors, you can use a cell reference in formulas. A **cell reference** tells the formula to look up the contents of the referenced cell; this feature saves you the trouble of typing the referenced cell's contents into the formula. If the referenced cell's contents change, the change is reflected automatically in the formula that refers to the cell.

The most common method is to refer to the cell by its address, such as A1, B10, or Y254. Therefore, if you want to add the values in cells B13 and C16, your formula might look like this: =B13+C16.

A cell reference can refer to one or more cells in the same worksheet, in a different worksheet from the same workbook, or in a different workbook. Sophisticated worksheets that draw data from many different sources may use dozens—or even hundreds—of formulas containing cell references.

If your formula uses cells that are contiguous, you can refer to all the cells at once as a **range** (also called a block). For example, in Excel, the formula =SUM(B4,C4,D4) can be written =SUM(B4:D4). The SUM formula calculates the total of the values in a specified range of cells. Ranges can consist of a group of cells in a column, a row, or even a group that includes several rows and columns. For example, a range of B5:D9 includes the whole block that has B5 as the upper left corner and D9 as the lower right corner.

Functions

Spreadsheets come with many built-in formulas, called **functions,** that perform specialized calculations automatically. You can include these functions in your own formulas. Some functions are simple, such as the COUNT function, which counts how many values are in a range of cells. Many functions, however, are complex. You may not know the mathematical equations for a loan payment or the depreciation of an asset using the double declining balance method, but by using spreadsheet functions, you can arrive at the answer.

You add **arguments** within the parentheses of the function. Arguments are the values (often cell references) that the function uses in its operation. The number and type of arguments used depend on the function.

The most commonly used function is the SUM function (see Figure 6.15), which adds a list of numbers to get a total. In the following formula, the SUM function's argument is a range: @SUM(D9..D5). This formula adds the values in the five cells that comprise the range D5 through D9.

Editing and Formatting a Worksheet

Like word processors, spreadsheet programs are extremely accommodating when you want to make changes. To change a label or a date, you simply select its cell and make the desired changes. You can edit any part of a formula or function manually simply by selecting its cell and making your changes in the formula bar. Spreadsheet programs make it easy to move, copy, or delete the contents of cells. You can also insert or delete rows and columns. You can add new sheets to a workbook or delete worksheets you no longer need.

When you move formulas and data to a new location, the spreadsheet adjusts the cell references automatically for formulas based on that data. In Figure 6.16, for example, the second-quarter totals in cells D8 and D9 can be copied to create third-quarter totals without having to reenter the cell references. In Figure 6.17, the second-quarter formulas were copied to create the third-quarter formulas. The spreadsheet program created the proper formulas automatically (based on the existing formulas), summing the third-quarter months.

Relative and Absolute Cell References

The spreadsheet program changes the formulas when you copy them because it remembers that the

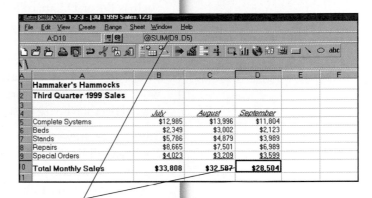

Figure 6.15
An example of the SUM function in a Lotus 1-2-3 worksheet.

This cell contains a SUM function, which adds the values in the cells above it.

Figure 6.16
Copying formulas.

The formulas in these two cells,

which compute totals for these two ranges...

...were copied to these two cells.

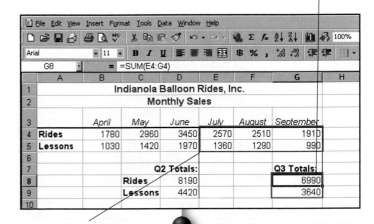

The resulting formulas automatically adjust to compute the totals for these two ranges.

Figure 6.17
The copied formulas.

formulas being copied will reference the same rows as the original, but it will automatically change the column reference when the formulas are moved to a new column. For this reason, when they are used in formulas, cell references such as B4 or D7 are called **relative cell references.** In Figure 6.16 on page 117, cell D8 contains the formula =SUM(B4:D4). When it was copied to cell G8, the program changed the formula automatically to =SUM(E4:G4) so that it would add the July, August, and September sales in row 4 (see Figure 6.17 on page 117). This feature saved the time of having to type the formula. When you work with long lists of formulas, the time saved can be tremendous, and you will make fewer keyboard mistakes.

Sometimes, however, you don't want the formulas to change as you copy them. You want all the formulas, no matter where they are, to refer to a specific cell. For example, if the current interest rate is in cell A1 and several formulas are based on that rate, you want to be able to copy the formulas without the reference to cell A1 changing. In this case, you use an **absolute cell reference,** which is usually written using the dollar sign ($). For example, A1 is a relative cell reference, and A1 is an absolute cell reference.

Formatting Values, Labels, and Cells

Spreadsheet programs offer numerous formats specifically for numbers. Numbers can appear as dollars and cents, percentages, dates, times, and fractions. They can be shown with or without commas, decimal points, and so forth.

In addition to number formats, spreadsheets also offer a choice of fonts and type styles, shadowed borders, and more. You can also create special effects by adding graphics, such as clip art, to your worksheets.

Honest Ernie's Stereo Sales
Fourth Quarter Sales By Product

		October	November	December
Amplifiers	TS400	$18,346	$20,647	$30,611
	TS500	$21,810	$30,446	$42,785
	TS600	$15,462	$12,454	$20,669
Tuner/Amps	SR100	$34,887	$15,799	$34,825
	SR200	$39,005	$32,647	$46,600
	SR300	$29,733	$28,320	$44,058
	SR400	$15,355	$18,810	$25,321
	Totals	$174,598	$159,123	$244,869

Figure 6.18
A spreadsheet containing data about stereo sales.

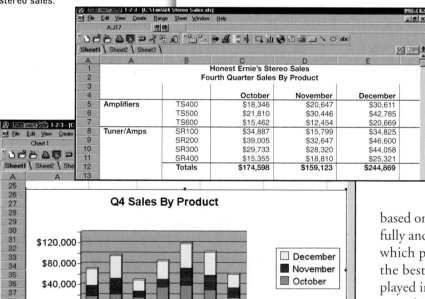

Figure 6.19
The data from Figure 6.18 is now summarized in a chart.

Adding Charts

A popular feature of spreadsheet software is the capability of generating charts based on numeric data. Charts make data easier to understand—especially when presenting data to an audience.

For example, the worksheet in Figure 6.18 lists total sales of various stereo components over a three-month period. Making quick conclusions based on this data is difficult. You must look carefully and do some mental arithmetic to determine which products sold best and which month had the best sales. But when the information is displayed in a chart, as in Figure 6.19, you can easily see which products have performed best and which month had the best sales results.

Analyzing Data in a Worksheet

When your worksheet's basic format is complete, you can use the worksheet to analyze the data.

Even adding totals is a simple form of analysis, but you may need more. Three useful techniques are as follows:

◆ **What-If Analysis. What-if analysis** is the process of using a spreadsheet to test how alternative scenarios affect numeric results. All spreadsheets allow you to do simple what-if analyses. You can easily change one part of a formula or a cell that it refers to and see how that affects the rest of the worksheet.

A more sophisticated type of what-if analysis is to create a table that automatically calculates the results based on any number of assumptions. Figure 6.20 shows such a table, which calculates the monthly mortgage payment for several possible interest rates.

Figure 6.20
Monthly mortgage payments based on different interest rates.

B7		= =PMT(B4/12,B5*12,-B3)				
	A	B	C	D	E	F
1	Mortgage Payment Examples					
2				Other Possible Interest Rates		
3	Total Mortgage:	125000				
4	Interest Rate:	8.25%		7.50%	$1,158.77	
5	Years Paid:	15		7.75%	$1,176.59	
6				8.00%	$1,194.57	
7	Monthly Payment:	$1,212.68		8.25%	$1,212.68	
8				8.50%	$1,230.92	
9						

◆ **Goal Seeking. Goal seeking** finds values for one or more cells that make the result of a formula equal to a value you specify. In Figure 6.21, cell B7 is the result of the Payment (PMT) formula. In this case, you know the maximum monthly payment you can afford is $1200, so you want cell B7 to be your starting point. The bank is offering an interest rate of 8.25% over 15 years. The total mortgage, cell B3, can be calculated from the monthly payment, years paid, and interest rate.

◆ **Sorting.** Another helpful data-analysis tool is sorting. When you **sort** data, you arrange it in a specific manner, based on certain criteria, such as by date, by dollar amount, or alphabetically. After data is sorted in a given manner, it may be easier to perform calculations on the results.

Spreadsheet programs offer the capability of creating, arranging, and selecting data in lists. They do not offer the same database capabilities as relational database management programs, but they can handle many simple database tasks.

B7		= =PMT(B4/12,B5*12,-B3)
	A	B	C
1	Mortgage Payment Examples		
2			
3	Total Mortgage:	$ 123,693	
4	Interest Paid:	8.25%	
5	Years Paid:	15	
6			
7	Monthly Payment:	$1,200.00	
8			

Figure 6.21
The result of a goal-seeking operation.

Self Check

Answer the following questions by filling in the blank(s).

1. In a word processor, a mark called the _____ shows you where your next character will be typed in the document.

2. When you enter text in a worksheet cell, the text is called a(n) _____ .

3. The values a function uses in its operation are called _____ .

PRESENTATION PROGRAMS

If you have ever attended a seminar or lecture that included slides or overhead transparencies projected on a wall screen—or displayed on a computer screen or

video monitor—then you probably have seen the product of a modern presentation program. **Presentation programs** enable the user to create and edit colorful, compelling presentations that can be displayed in various ways and used to support any type of discussion.

Presentation programs are used to produce a series of **slides**—single-screen images that contain a combination of text, numbers, and graphics (such as charts, clip art, or pictures), often on a colorful background. Slides can be simple or sophisticated. Depending what you want to do, you can turn a basic slide show into a multimedia event using the built-in features of presentation programs.

The Presentation Program's Interface

The typical presentation program displays a slide in a large document window and provides a wide array of tools for designing and editing slides. Presentation programs provide many of the features found in word processors (for working with text), spreadsheets (for creating charts), and paint programs (for creating and editing simple graphics). You can add elements to the slide by typing or making menu or toolbar choices, and dragging. As you work on the slide, you see exactly how it will look when it is shown to an audience.

Figure 6.22 shows a slide being designed in Microsoft PowerPoint 2000, a popular presentation program. Note that the status bar says that the presentation contains five slides. A presentation can contain a single slide or hundreds. Most presentation programs let you save a set of slides as a group in one file so that you can open the related slides and work with them together.

Figure 6.22

Interface features of Microsoft PowerPoint 2000, a popular presentation program.

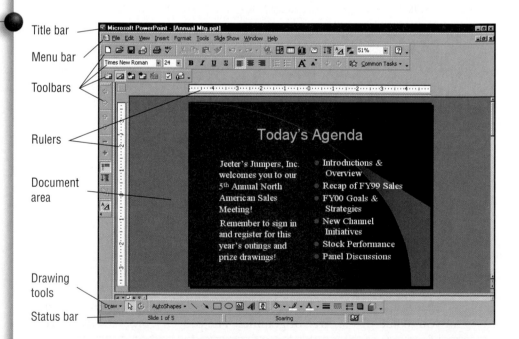

A windowed presentation program includes a menu bar, one or more toolbars (for managing files, formatting, drawing, and doing other tasks), rulers, slide-viewing or navigation buttons that let you move from one slide to another, a status bar, and other tools.

Creating a Presentation

Creating a presentation is simple; choose the type of slide you want to create and then start adding the content. A complete presentation usually includes multiple slides arranged in a logical series. You can insert new slides anywhere, copy slides from other presentations, and reorder the slides any way you want.

You can create slides from scratch (starting with a blank slide), but it is easier and faster to work with one of the presentation program's many templates. Like a template in a word processor, a presentation template is a predesigned document that already has finished fonts, a layout, and a background. Presentation programs provide dozens of built-in templates (see Figure 6.23).

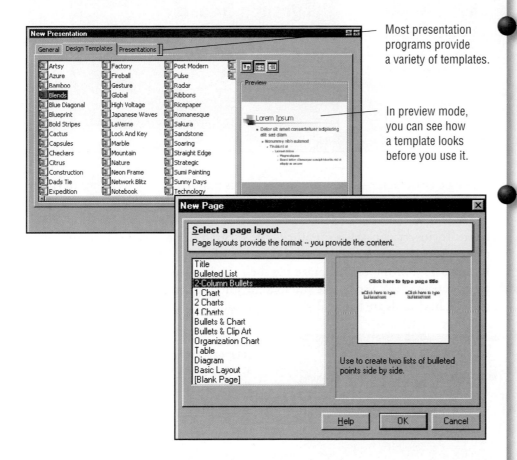

Most presentation programs provide a variety of templates.

In preview mode, you can see how a template looks before you use it.

Figure 6.23
Choosing a presentation template in PowerPoint.

Figure 6.24
Choosing a slide type in Lotus Freelance Graphics.

After you select a template, you can assemble a presentation quickly by creating individual slides. To create a slide, you can choose a slide type, as shown in Figure 6.24. Presentation programs provide several types of slides that can hold varying combinations of titles, text, charts, and graphics. You can choose a different type for each slide in your presentation, if you want.

After you select a slide type, the blank slide appears in the document window, ready for you to add text, charts, or graphics. The program provides special **text boxes** and **frames** (special resizable boxes for text and graphical elements) to contain specific types of content. These special boxes often contain instructions telling you exactly what to do. To add text to a text box, simply click in the box to place the insertion point there and then type your text, as shown in Figure 6.25 on page 122. The text is formatted automatically, but you can easily reformat the text later using many of the same formatting options available in word processors.

Visit **www.glencoe.com/norton/online/** for more information on **creating slides for a presentation.**

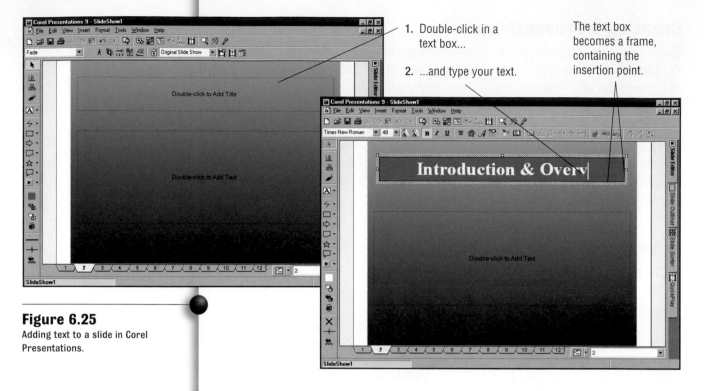

1. Double-click in a text box...

2. ...and type your text.

The text box becomes a frame, containing the insertion point.

Figure 6.25
Adding text to a slide in Corel Presentations.

Adding charts, tables, clip art, or other graphics is nearly as easy, as shown in Figure 6.26. When you choose a slide type that contains a chart or table, for example, you can create the chart or table in a separate window and then insert it in the slide. To insert clip art or another type of graphic in a slide, you can select the appropriate image from your software's collection of graphics (as shown in Figure 6.27), or import an image file such as a scanned photograph or clip art. Built-in paint tools also enable you to draw simple graphics and add them to your slides. These tools are handy if you want to add callouts to elements of a slide.

Figure 6.26
Creating a chart in PowerPoint.

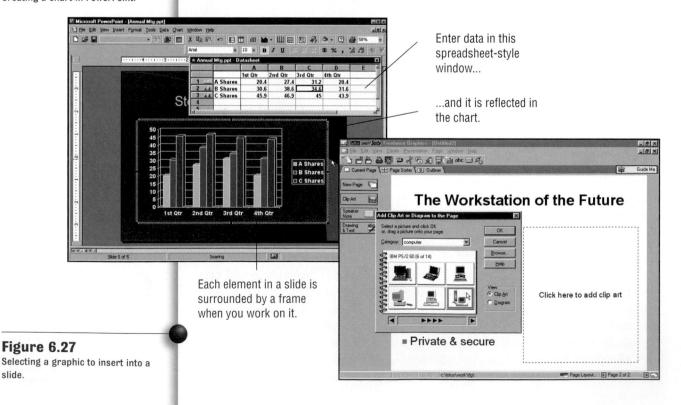

Enter data in this spreadsheet-style window...

...and it is reflected in the chart.

Each element in a slide is surrounded by a frame when you work on it.

Figure 6.27
Selecting a graphic to insert into a slide.

Formatting Slides

Because presentation programs are like a combination of a word processor, spread-sheet, and paint program, you can format slides easily in many ways:

◆ **Formatting Text.** Formatting text in a presentation program is like formatting text in a word processor. Text in slides is usually in the form of titles, headings, and lists. Although a text box can hold multiple paragraphs, the paragraphs themselves are usually quite short. Most often, these paragraphs are formatted with bullets. To format text, you select it and then apply formats by using the toolbars or options from the Format menu.

◆ **Resizing Frames.** When you add a chart or graphic to a slide, you may need to resize it to allow better spacing for other elements on the slide. Sometimes it is necessary to resize text boxes, too, if you type more or less text than the box can hold by default. Resizing is easy using frames that surround most of the elements in a slide. To resize a frame, click it; several **handles** will appear around it, as shown in Figure 6.28. Handles are small boxes (usually white or black in color) that you can drag to resize the frame. The frame expands or shrinks depending on which direction you drag the handle.

Figure 6.28
Resizing a frame.

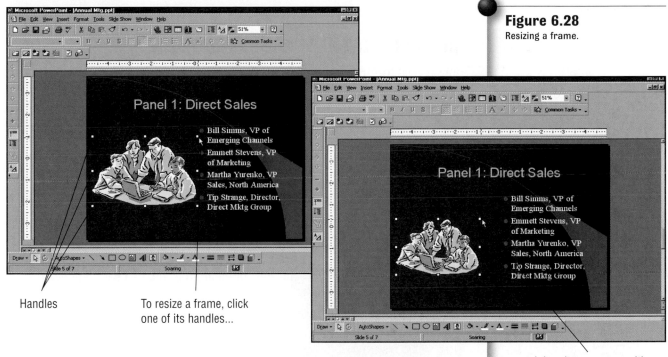

Handles

To resize a frame, click one of its handles...

...and drag it to a new position.

◆ **Adding Colors.** Colors enable you to create a wide range of moods for your presentations. Therefore, it is important to choose colors carefully. You should also make sure that the slides' colors complement one another and do not make any text difficult to read (see Figure 6.29 on page 124).

◆ **Adding a Background or Shading.** You can add depth to a plain presentation by giving it a shaded background and by placing borders around certain elements. Borders separate different elements and help hold the viewer's attention on individual parts of the slide. Shaded backgrounds provide depth and can make static information appear dynamic. A gradient fill, as shown in Figure 6.30 on page 124, changes color as it moves from one part of the slide to another. This effect can almost make the slide appear as if it is in motion.

Figure 6.29
Setting a color scheme for a presentation.

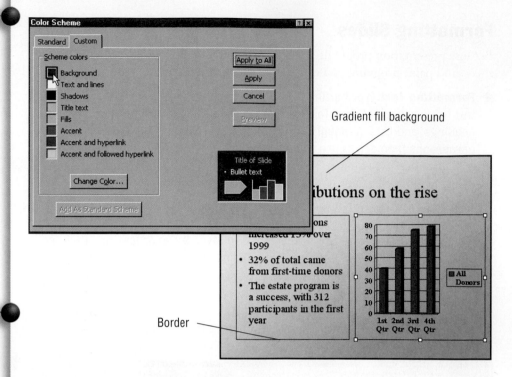

Gradient fill background

Border

Figure 6.30
Borders and backgrounds can make a dull presentation more appealing.

Special Features of Presentation Programs

Some special features found in presentation programs include the following:

◆ **Outlining.** Like any document with more than one part, a good presentation should be outlined; that is, it should be organized so information flows logically. An outlining tool enables you to organize your slides' contents as you create them, by moving them around and viewing them in order (see Figure 6.31).

◆ **Annotations.** Speakers often prepare a set of notes (called **annotations**) to accompany their slides. Using a presentation program, you can prepare notes for each slide as you create your presentation. You can set up notes so they are visible only to you, or you can print them with or without the actual slide.

◆ **Animation.** You can use animation tools to make text pop up or crawl onto the screen, or to make slides build themselves by adding individual pieces of text that appear as you introduce them to the audience. You can also create animated **transitions,** an effect that causes slides to blend together. Popular transitions are the "fade" (where the first slide fades and the next appears slowly) and the "blind" (where the first slide seems to disappear behind a closing Venetian blind, and the next slide appears as the blind reopens).

Figure 6.31
Editing a presentation in the Outline view of Microsoft PowerPoint.

- **Sound and Video.** Slide presentations can be full-fledged multimedia events. You can embed a sound or video object into a slide, then play the object by double-clicking its icon during a presentation. All the multimedia objects can be played directly from the computer, assuming that you have the appropriate sound and video display hardware.

- **Other Embedded Objects.** You can embed different types of objects, such as links to Web pages or other applications, in a presentation. When you click such a link in a slide, the Web page opens in a browser window, or the other application launches.

- **Web Page Conversion.** Like word processors and other types of applications, presentation programs let you save your slides in HTML format to use as Web pages.

- **Embedded Multimedia.** Today's presentation programs enable you to incorporate many different types of media into a slide show. If you present the slides directly from the PC instead of printing and placing them on a slide or overhead projector, you can actually embed different media objects, such as audio files, QuickTime movies, or animation, in your slides. They can play without interrupting the flow of the presentation to start another application, such as an audio or video player.

Figure 6.32
You can get the best results from your slide shows if you present them directly from the PC's disk using a display device that is appropriate for the audience and room size.

Presenting Slide Shows

At one time, presentations required the use of a projector (slide or overhead) and a hard-copy version of the content, either on 35-mm slides or overhead transparencies. The presenter had to display each slide manually in a preset order. Jumping to a slide out of sequence meant finding the right slide, pulling it, displaying it, and getting the presentation back on track. This change could be difficult when dealing with many slides or an impatient audience.

Thanks to presentation programs, you can present your slides directly from the computer's disk, along with any audio or video files that you associate with your slides (see Figure 6.32). Your audience can view slides in several ways:

- **On the PC's Screen.** If you are presenting slides to a few people, your PC's monitor might be adequate. Of course, the larger the monitor, the better your audience can see the slides. Also, note that flat-panel monitors are not well suited for this purpose because of their limited viewing angle. If you want to show slides to more than three or four people at a time, consider a different way to display them.

- **On a Large-Format Monitor.** Large-format monitors can display your slides at the proper resolution and size for a larger audience to view comfortably. These devices are expensive and more difficult to transport than a standard monitor, but they may be the best solution for some presentation settings.

- **On a Television Screen.** Using a **PC-to-TV converter,** you can connect your computer to a standard television set and view the PC's video output on the television monitor. While this option may sound like a convenient solution,

there are many compatibility issues to consider (not all converters work with all televisions, for example), and televisions do not display images at the same resolution as a PC monitor. As a result, image quality may suffer when a PC-to-TV converter is used.

◆ **From a PC Projector.** Portable, high-resolution PC projectors are expensive but can be the perfect way to display slides to a large audience. These projectors plug into one of the PC's ports and accept the system's video output. New-generation projectors can display crisp images in only semi-darkened rooms, and a projector displays at the same resolution as the PC's monitor.

DATABASE MANAGEMENT SYSTEMS

To make large collections of data useful, individuals and organizations use computers and an efficient database management system. Like a warehouse, a **database** is a repository for collections of related data or facts. A **database management system (DBMS)** is a software tool that allows multiple users to store, access, and process data or facts into useful information.

Database management is one of the primary reasons people use computers. A DBMS makes it possible to perform many routine tasks that would otherwise be tedious, cumbersome, and time-consuming. Many large companies and organizations rely heavily on a commercial or custom DBMS to handle immense data resources.

The Database

A database contains a collection of related items or facts, arranged in a specific structure. The most obvious example of a noncomputerized database is a telephone directory. (Telephone companies use an electronic database program to produce their printed phone books.)

Before learning more about the powers of electronic databases, you need to learn how data is organized within a database and some common database terms. To help you visualize how a database stores data, think about a typical address or telephone book, like those shown in Figure 6.33.

Figure 6.33
Data is stored in tables. A table is divided into records, and each record is divided into fields.

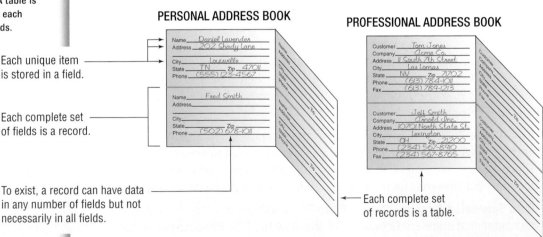

Each unique item is stored in a field.

Each complete set of fields is a record.

To exist, a record can have data in any number of fields but not necessarily in all fields.

Each complete set of records is a table.

Three of the most important terms to know about databases are listed below:

◆ **Fields.** Each piece of information in the address/telephone book is stored in its own location, called a **field.** For example, each entry in the address/phone book has a field for Name, as well as fields for Address, City, State, Zip Code, and Phone Number. Each unique type of information is stored in its own field.

◆ **Records.** One full set of fields—that is, all the related information about one person or object—is called a **record.** Therefore, all the information for the first person is record 1, all the information for the second person is record 2, and so on.

◆ **Tables.** A complete collection of records makes a table.

After you have a structure for storing data (whether it is a printed address/telephone book or an electronic table), you can enter and view data, create reports, and perform other tasks with the data. For example, you might create a report that lists customers by ZIP code. These extra tools, along with the tables, combine to form a database, as shown in Figure 6.34.

Figure 6.34
A database consists of tables and all the supporting documents.

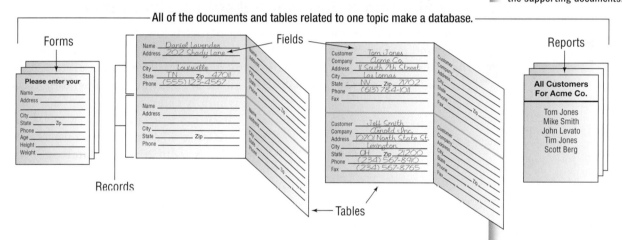

Look at the arrangement of the customer information table shown in Figure 6.35 on page 128. The table consists of a set number of named columns (fields) and an arbitrary number of unnamed rows (records). It organizes each record's data by the same set of fields, but it can store any number of records. For example, if you are storing employee data, you can have an unlimited number of employees, at least theoretically. But there are a finite number of facts, or fields, about each employee. The only limit is the storage capability of the disk. Any one record in the table does not necessarily have data in every field. For a record to exist, however, it must have data in at least one field. An employee, for example, must have a name. It is not an optional fact about an employee. Therefore, it will always be present in the record for each employee.

The order of fields in a table strictly defines the location of data in every record. A telephone number field, for example, must contain a record's telephone number—it cannot contain a person's name or ZIP code. Similarly, the set of fields in any one table provides a sensible definition of the database for those who must access its data. For instance, you would expect to find the part number for a radiator in an inventory of auto parts, but you should not expect to view an employee's payroll record in the same table.

Figure 6.35

A customer information table in
Lotus Approach.

Field name

Field

Record

Figure 6.36

Linked fields in relational database
tables.

Table names

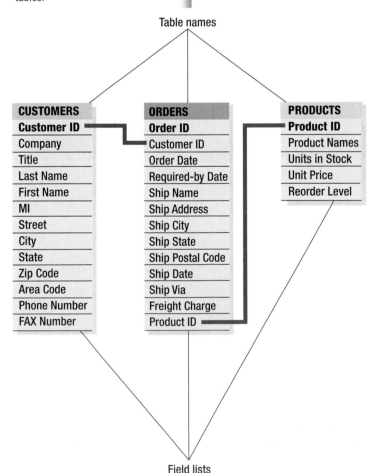

Field lists

Flat-File and Relational Database Structures

Many early database applications and some current low-end applications could access and manipulate only one table at a time. Each table was stored in its own file, as were any related documents. In these cases, there is no reason to use the term *table,* because the table and the database are one and the same. Often, the table is simply called a file or just "the database." To be more precise, however, a database file that consists of a single data table is called a **flat-file** (or sequential file) **database.** Flat-file databases are useful for certain single-user or small-group situations, especially for maintaining lists such as addresses or inventories. Data that is stored, managed, and manipulated in a spreadsheet is similar to a flat-file database.

Although easy to learn and use, flat-file database systems can be difficult to maintain and are limited in their power. When numerous files exist (one for each table or related document), there is often a lot of data redundancy, which increases the chance for errors, wastes time, and uses excess storage space. Adding, deleting, or editing any field requires that you make the same changes in every file that contains the same field.

In a **relational database**—a database made up of a set of tables—a common field existing in any two tables creates a relationship between the tables. As shown in Figure 6.36, a Customer ID Number field in both the Customers table and the Orders table links the two tables, while a Product ID field links the Orders and Products tables.

The relational database structure is easily the most prevalent in today's business organizations. In a business, a typical relational database would likely contain data tables such as the following:

- Customer information
- Order information
- Vendor information
- Employee information
- Inventory information

Visit **www.glencoe.com/norton/online/** for more information on **relational databases**.

Multiple tables in this kind of database make it possible to handle many data management tasks. Consider these examples:

- The customer, order, and inventory tables can be linked to process orders and billing.
- The vendor and inventory tables can be linked to maintain and track inventory levels.
- The order and employee tables can be linked to control scheduling.

The DBMS

Perhaps the biggest asset of a DBMS is its capability to provide quick access and retrieval from large databases. Because database files can grow extremely large (many gigabytes—millions of records—on large systems), recalling data quickly is not a trivial matter. A DBMS, especially when it is running on powerful hardware, can find any speck of data in an enormous database in minutes—sometimes even in seconds or fractions of a second. Instead of searching through every row in the database, DBMS systems build complex indexes internally (similar to an index in a book) that enable the system to retrieve records at incredible speeds.

Although you can perform many tasks with a DBMS, including creating and designing the database itself, data management tasks fall into one of three general categories:

- Entering data into the database
- Sorting the data—that is, arranging or reordering the database's records
- Obtaining subsets of the data

Equally important, a DBMS provides the means for multiple users to access and share data in the same database by way of networked computer systems.

Working With a Database

The DBMS interface presents the user with data and the tools required to work with the data. You work with the tools of the interface to perform data management functions:

- Creating tables
- Entering and editing data
- Viewing data
- Sorting records
- Querying the database
- Generating reports

Creating Tables

The first step in building any database is to create one or more tables. As you know, tables hold the raw data that the DBMS will work with. To create a new database, you must first determine what kind of data will be stored in each table. In other words, you must define the table's fields. Defining the fields is a three-step process:

1. Name the field.   **2.** Specify the field type.   **3.** Specify the field size.

When naming the field, indicate as briefly as possible what the field contains. Figure 6.37 shows a database table with clearly named fields.

Figure 6.37
Clearly named fields.

	Stock No	Vendor No	Equipment Class	Model	Part No	Description
1	900.00	3,820.00	Vehicle	DV-100	T-5100	Underwater Diver Vehicle
2	912.00	2,014.00	Vehicle	18-DV	7160-00	Underwater Diver Vehicle
3	1,313.00	3,511.00	Air Regulators	MK-200/G200	12-200-000	Regulator System
4	1,314.00	5,641.00	Air Regulators	TR-200	6832-14A	Second Stage Regulator
5	1,316.00	3,511.00	Air Regulators	MK-10/G200 B	12-502-000	Regulator System

Table : C:\...\stock.db

Field names

Specifying the field type requires knowledge of what kind of data the DBMS can understand. Most modern database systems can work with seven predefined field types (see Figure 6.38).

Figure 6.38
Field types.

Counter field
Text field
Date field
Numeric field

Logical field
Binary field
Memo field

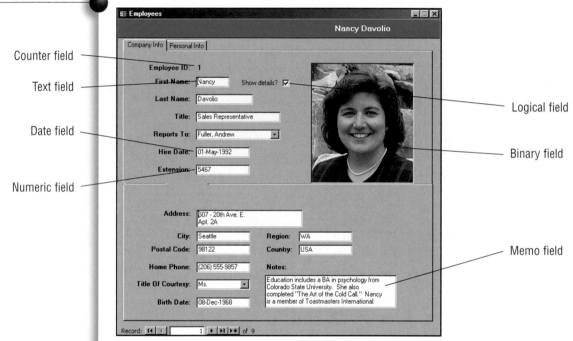

◆ **Text fields** (also called character fields or alphanumeric fields) accept any string of alphanumeric characters that are not used in calculations. Such an entry might be a person's name, a company's name, an address, a telephone number, or any other textual data.

◆ **Numeric fields** store purely numeric data such as currency, percentages, statistics, quantities, or any other value that can be used in calculations. The data itself is stored in the table strictly as a numeric value, even though the DBMS can display the value with formatting characters such as dollar or percent signs, decimal points, or comma separators.

◆ A **date field** or **time field** stores date or time entries. This field type converts a date or time entry into a numeric value, just as dates and times are stored internally as serial numbers in spreadsheet cells.

◆ **Logical fields** (also called Boolean fields) store one of only two possible values. You can apply almost any description for the data (yes or no, true or false, on or off, and so forth). For example, a Catalog field in a Customer table can tell a customer service representative whether a customer has ordered a new catalog (Yes) or not (No).

◆ **Binary fields** store binary objects, or BLOBs. A **BLOB (Binary Large OBject)** can be a graphic image file such as clip art, a photograph, a screen image, a graphic, or formatted text. A BLOB can also be an audio file, video clip, or other object, as shown in Figure 6.39.

◆ In some DBMSs, **counter fields** (sometimes called autonumber fields) store a unique numeric value that the DBMS assigns to each record. Because it is possible for two records to have identical data in some tables (such as two employees with the same name), a counter field ensures that every record will have a completely unique identification. Counter fields may also be used for creating records that number sequentially, such as invoices.

◆ Because most field types have fixed lengths that restrict the number of characters in an entry, **memo fields** (also called description fields) provide fields for entering notes or comments of any length.

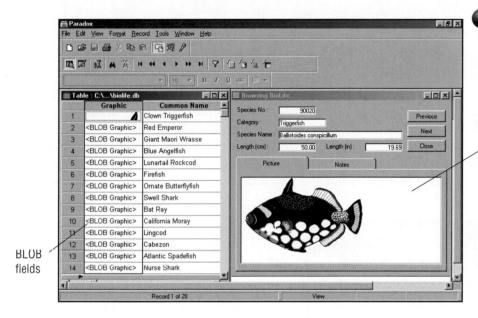

Figure 6.39
Binary fields allow graphic images and other nontext items to be stored in a database.

Binary field containing a graphic

BLOB fields

Entering and Editing Data

After the table has been set up, data can be entered. In most cases, entering data is a matter of typing characters at the keyboard. Entering data in a database table is much like entering data in a spreadsheet program. The process can have more pitfalls than you might expect, however, especially if it is being done by someone other than the user who set up the tables. For example, the DBMS might not handle a number correctly if the user enters it with a dollar sign—even though the number will be displayed as a dollar amount. If the data is entered with an inconsistent mix of upper- and lower-case letters, the DBMS may not be able to sort the data properly or locate records.

Most DBMSs allow you to create a data entry **form** to make data entry easier (see Figure 6.40 on page 132). The form is nothing more than a custom view of the table that typically shows one record at a time and includes special controls and labels that make data entry less confusing. For example, you can include controls that move the insertion point automatically to the next field when the typist presses the Enter or Tab key, or you can convert all the input into capital letters to maintain data consistency. You can even direct input into multiple tables, which really makes life easier for a typist who does not know about the underlying structure of the DBMS and database tables.

NORTON
ONLINE

Visit **www.glencoe.com/norton/online/** for more information on **database forms.**

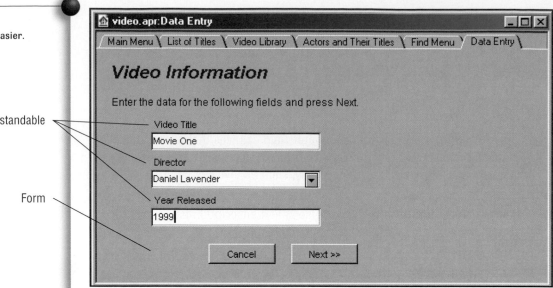

Understandable labels

Form

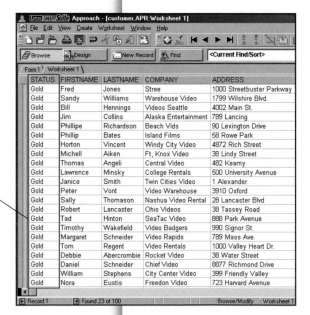

Filtered column

Viewing Data

The way data appears on screen contributes to how well users can work with it. You have already seen examples of data presented in two-dimensional, worksheet-style tables. With many DBMS products, the table view (sometimes called the datasheet view) is what you use to create a database table and to modify field specifications. This view is also suitable for viewing lists of records grouped together in some meaningful way, such as all customers who live in the same city.

Sometimes viewing the entire table is unwieldy because there are too many entries. **Filters** are DBMS features for displaying a selected list or subset of records from a table. The visible records satisfy a condition that the user sets. A filter tells the DBMS to display those records that satisfy the condition, while hiding—or filtering out—those that do not. For example, you can create a filter that displays only those records that have the data "Gold" in the Status field, as shown in Figure 6.41.

As shown in Figure 6.42, a DBMS also allows you to create forms for viewing records. These forms are similar in design to those used in data entry, but they are used to display existing data instead of receiving new data. By using forms, you can create simple, easily understood views of your data that show only one record at a time. You can also create complex forms that display related information from multiple tables.

Sorting Records

One of the most powerful features of a DBMS is its capability to sort a table of data, either for a printed report or for display on screen. As you learned in the discussion of spreadsheets, sorting arranges records according to the contents of one or more fields. For example, in a table of products, you can sort records into numerical order by product ID or into alphabetical order by product name.

Figure 6.42
This form lets the user work with information for a single record.

TERS

career

obs

rise software application. Many people
ses every day without even realizing it.

ost computer users do not work with
, such as a contact management,
ediary between the user and the

all centers or help desks interact with
dd and edit information about cus-
mation stored in a help desk's data-
d fix those problems in new versions.
BMS to store the data relevant to that
. Other software engineers design,
e of the fastest growing careers in the

ced database professionals is high,
relational databases. Database develop-
ds and order-entry tools, generate com-
velopers are skilled in programming
query languages such as SQL. They are
s.

design, and construct corporate data-
structed, database administrators are
olved with altering the database based

COMPU
in your c

Database-Related Jo

Database technologies touch the work lives of millions of people each day. You do not have to be a database expert, however, to work with a database management system or enterp work with databa

◆ **Secretaries, Clerks, Data-Entry Specialists, and Telemarketers.** M a true DBMS on a daily basis. Instead, most work with a front-end progran order-entry, or accounts payable/receivable system, that acts as an inter actual database.

◆ **Help Desk and Product Support Specialists.** Persons who work at c large databases of product and customer information and continuously a tomer complaints, problems, and suggestions. By drawing from the infor base, product designers can find unpopular features in their products an

◆ **Software Engineers.** Some commercially developed software uses a D software. Software engineers design, develop, and test these application develop, and test the DBMS application itself. Software engineering is on computer industry.

◆ **Database Programmers and Developers.** The demand for experien especially for high-end users who can develop forms and set up comple ers create custom tools for corporate databases, create special front e plicated queries, develop report-generation macros, and more. These d languages such as COBOL, Visual Basic, Java, and C, as well as database familiar with powerful databases such as Sybase, DB2, Oracle, and othe

◆ **Database Administrators.** Database administrators typically lay out bases using the DBMS software. After the corporate databases are con asked to develop backup, load, and unload strategies. They are often in on system enhancements and upgrades to the DBMS software.

◆ **System Analysts.** Many organizations hire system analysts to review and update the operation of their enterprise applications. The analyst must be well-versed in database concepts and terminology and must understand how the organization uses its DBMS and data tables to store, retrieve, and manage data. Analysts frequently assist managers in designing queries and reports that draw data from the database or in creating forms that make data input easier or more efficient.

134

LESSON QUIZ

True/False

Answer the following questions by circling True or False.

True   False   **1.** Word processing programs are designed to work with text only.

True   False   **2.** As you enter text in a word processor, you do not need to press Enter at the end of a line unless you want to start a new paragraph.

True   False   **3.** A spreadsheet and a worksheet are the same.

True   False   **4.** As you create a slide presentation, you can rearrange slides in any order you like.

True   False   **5.** A flat-file database uses only one data table.

Multiple Choice

Circle the word or phrase that best completes each sentence.

1. Most word processors feature one or more _____ , which provide tools that resemble buttons.
   A. menu bars   **B.** toolbars   **C.** status bars

2. On the screen, selected text is _____ .
   A. highlighted   **B.** deleted   **C.** neither A nor B

3. To navigate a worksheet, you should understand its system of _____ .
   A. cell addresses   **B.** spreadsheets   **C.** neither A nor B

4. A presentation _____ is a predesigned document, with fonts, a layout, and a background.
   A. format   **B.** template   **C.** program

5. A _____ tells the DBMS to display records that satisfy a condition while hiding those that do not.
   A. form   **B.** filter   **C.** report

LESSON LABS

If a spreadsheet is installed on your computer, complete the following exercise as directed by your instructor.

Practice using a worksheet:

A. In your worksheet's document area, type numbers in cells A1 through A5.

B. Using the mouse, select all the values in this range. (Click in cell A1. Then drag the mouse pointer down through cell A5.)

C. Click in cell A6 and type =**SUM(A1:A5)**. Press Enter. The total of the values in cells A1 to A5 should appear in cell A6. If it does not, ask your instructor for help.

D. Click in cell A3 and press Delete. The value in the cell disappears; cell A6's total changes.

E. Issue the Undo command. (There should be an Undo tool on the toolbar. If not, ask your instructor for assistance.) The value is returned to cell A3 and the total in cell A6 updates once more.

F. Click in cell B6 and type =**A6*0.05**. Press Enter. The formula's result appears in cell B6.

G. Close the spreadsheet program by clicking the Close button. If the program prompts you to save the worksheet, choose No.

LESSON 5: Operating Systems

The User Interface

- Most modern operating systems employ a graphical user interface (GUI) in which users control the system by pointing and clicking graphical objects on the screen.

- A GUI is based on the desktop metaphor. Icons, windows, menus, dialog boxes, and other graphical objects appear on the desktop.

- Some older operating systems, such as DOS and UNIX, use command-line interfaces that the user controls by typing commands at a prompt.

Running Programs

- The operating system manages all the other programs that run on the PC. Some operating systems, such as Windows, allow programs to share information.

- Modern operating systems support multitasking, which is the capability of running multiple processes simultaneously.

Managing Files

- The operating system keeps track of all the files on each disk.

- Users can make their own file management easier by creating a hierarchical file system that includes folders and subfolders arranged in a logical order.

Managing Hardware

- The operating system uses interrupt requests (IRQs) to maintain organized communication with the CPU and other pieces of hardware.

- The operating system provides the software necessary to link computers and form a network.

Operating Systems in Review

- UNIX was the first multi-user, multitasking operating system available for use on PCs.

- DOS features a command-line interface.

- The Mac OS brought the first truly graphical user interface to consumers.

- Windows 3.0, 3.1, and 3.11 brought a graphical user interface and multitasking capabilities to PCs that ran DOS.

- IBM's OS/2 Warp was the first true GUI-based operating system for Intel-based PCs.

- Microsoft's Windows NT was originally meant as a replacement for DOS. Microsoft issued two versions: Windows NT Workstation and Windows NT Server.

- Windows 95 was Microsoft's first true GUI-based, 32-bit OS for Intel PCs.

- The features of Windows 98 include advanced Internet capabilities, an improved user interface, and enhanced file system performance, among others.

- Linux is a recently developed version of UNIX and is available free or at a low cost from various sources.

- Windows 2000 features the same interface and features of Windows 98, with the file system, networking, power, and stability of Windows NT.

LESSON 6: Productivity Software

Word Processing Software

- A word processor provides tools for creating, editing, and formatting text documents. Word processors provide three types of formatting: character, paragraph, and document.

- Word processors allow you to add graphics and sound files to your documents and provide special features such as tables, mail merge, spell checking, and more.

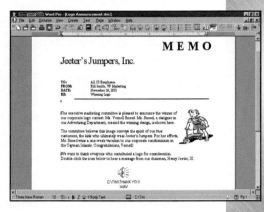

Spreadsheet Programs

- Spreadsheet programs provide tools for working with numerical data. In a spreadsheet program, you work in a worksheet. Worksheets can be collected into workbooks.

- A worksheet contains a series of columns and rows. Each row-and-column intersection is called a cell. Cells actually contain the data in the worksheet. Each cell is identified by a cell address, which is the combination of the cell's column letter and row number.

- Formulas are used to perform calculations in the worksheet. Formulas can use cell references to use data in other cells. A function is a predefined formula provided by the spreadsheet program.

- Goal seeking and sorting are common data analysis tools found in spreadsheets.

Presentation Programs

- Presentation programs allow you to create a series of slides that can be used to support a discussion.

- Slides can be formatted with different fonts, colors, backgrounds, and borders. Using frames, you can resize many of the elements in a slide.

- Presentation programs provide various special features that enable you to annotate your slide show, create transitions, convert slides to HTML documents, and more.

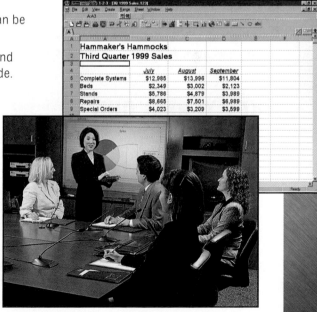

Database Management Systems

- A database is a repository for collections of related data or facts. A database management system (DBMS) is a software tool that enables many users to add, view, and work with the data in a database.

- Flat-file databases are two-dimensional tables of fields and records. They cannot form relationships with other tables. Relational databases are powerful because they can form relationships among different tables.

- Forms are custom screens for displaying and entering data that can be associated with database tables and queries.

- Filters let you browse through selected records that meet a set of criteria.

- Queries are user-constructed statements that set conditions for selecting and manipulating data.

- Reports are user-generated sets of data, usually printed as a document.

UNIT REVIEW

KEY TERMS

After completing this unit, you should be able to define the following terms.

absolute cell reference, *118*
activate, *93*
active window, *94*
annotation, *124*
argument, *117*
binary field, *131*
binary large object
   (BLOB), *131*
block, *110*
button, *93*
cell, *115*
cell address, *115*
cell pointer, *115*
cell reference, *116*
character formatting, *111*
choose, *93*
Clipboard, *98*
command-line interface, *97*
context menu, *93*
Copy, *98*
counter field, *131*
Cut, *98*
database, *126*
database management
   system (DBMS), *126*
date field, *130*
deselect, *110*
desktop, *93*
dialog box, *96*
document area, *109*

document formatting, *112*
document window, *109*
driver, *100*
editing, *110*
field, *127*
filter, *132*
flat-file database, *128*
font, *111*
form, *131*
formula, *116*
formula bar, *114*
frame, *121*
function, *116*
goal seeking, *119*
graphical user interface
   (GUI), *92*
handle, *123*
highlight, *110*
icon, *93*
label, *115*
Linux, *106*
logical field, *130*
Macintosh Operating
   System (Mac OS), *101*
mail merge, *113*
memo field, *131*
menu, *95*
menu bar, *96*
MS-DOS, *101*
multitasking, *99*

numeric field, *130*
Object Linking and
   Embedding (OLE), *98*
operating environment, *103*
OS/2 Warp, *103*
paragraph, *111*
paragraph formatting, *111*
Paste, *98*
PC-to-TV converter, *125*
Plug and Play, *101*
presentation program, *120*
prompt, *97*
query, *133*
range, *116*
record, *127*
relational database, *128*
relative cell reference, *118*
report, *133*
ruler, *109*
scroll bar, *94*
select, *93*
shortcut menu, *93*
slide, *120*
sort, *119*
spreadsheet, *114*
Start button, *93*
Start menu, *93*
status bar, *109*
system call, *97*
table, *113*

taskbar, *93*
task switching, *95*
template, *114*
text box, *121*
text field, *130*
time field, *130*
title bar, *94*
toolbar, *109*
transition, *124*
UNIX, *100*
user interface, *92*
value, *115*
what-if analysis, *119*
window, *94*
Windows, *103*
Windows 3.*x*, *103*
Windows 95, *104*
Windows 98, *105*
Windows 2000, *106*
Windows NT, *104*
Windows NT Server, *104*
Windows NT
   Workstation, *104*
word processing
   software, *109*
word processor, *109*
word wrap, *110*
workbook, *114*
worksheet, *114*

KEY TERMS QUIZ

Fill in each blank with one of the terms listed under Key Terms.

1. In a graphical user interface, _____ represent the parts of the computer you work with, such as files or printers.

2. All windows include a(n) _____ across the top, which identifies the window's contents.

3. The process of moving from one open window to another is called _____ .

4. You interact with a command-line interface by typing strings of characters at a(n) _____ .

5. Word processors enable you to perform three basic types of formatting: _____ , _____ , and _____ .

6. In a worksheet, a column letter and row number combine to form a(n) _____ .

7. _____ are built-in formulas that perform specialized calculations automatically.

8. A(n) _____ is designed to hold text content in a slide.

9. In a database table, each row represents a(n) _____ .

10. A(n) _____ is a DBMS feature for displaying a selected list of records from a table.

REVIEW QUESTIONS

In your own words, briefly answer the following questions.

1. What are the four primary functions that an operating system performs?

2. Where do graphical user interfaces get their name?

3. In later versions of Windows, what happens when you right-click many parts of the desktop?

4. What is the function of windows in a graphical user interface?

5. In a word processor, what makes a block of text?

6. What is the difference between a spreadsheet and a worksheet?

7. Name the four kinds of data you can enter in a worksheet.

8. What effect can you use to make a slide appear as if it is in motion?

9. What is a form?

10. What does it mean to query a database?

DISCUSSION QUESTIONS

As directed by your instructor, discuss the following questions in class or in groups.

1. Discuss the benefits of using the object linking and embedding (OLE) capabilities of newer operating systems. Can you envision a task where this capability would be helpful? What types of documents might you create that could benefit from OLE?

2. Do you think that using a spell checker for all your final documents is a sufficient substitute for proofreading? Explain your answer.

ETHICAL ISSUES

Many people believe that software is simply becoming too powerful. With this thought in mind, discuss the following questions in class.

1. Many observers believe that by including so many features (such as disk defragmenters, file management tools, and Internet applications) in its operating systems, Microsoft has taken market share away from other companies that might develop and sell such tools to Windows users. Do you agree, or do you feel that an operating system should include such extras?

2. Spreadsheets give us fast access to data and analysis. Some say that this fast access is partly to blame for our numbers-oriented society, where companies are run by numbers with little apparent regard for issues like product quality, customer satisfaction, or loyalty to employees. Do you agree?

UNIT LABS

You and the Computer

Complete the following exercises using a computer in your classroom, lab, or home. No other materials are needed.

1. **Take a Tour of Windows.** If you use Windows 98, you can take a multimedia tour of the operating system to learn about its features. Take the following steps:

   A. Click the Start button to open the Start menu. Point to Programs, Accessories, System Tools. Click Welcome To Windows. The Welcome to Windows 98 window opens.

   B. Click Discover Windows 98, and the tour begins. Follow the instructions on the screen to complete the tour. (You can close the tour at any time by clicking the Close button.)

   C. When you finish the tour, close the Welcome to Windows 98 window.

2. **Copy and Paste.** You can create documents in one application that contain data from a different application. Try this process now using your word processor and spreadsheet. Take the following steps:

   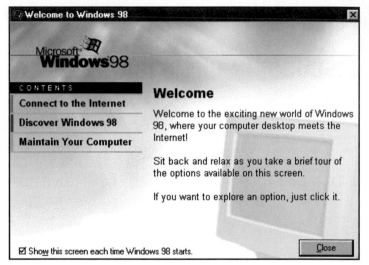

   A. Launch your word processor and your spreadsheet. Switch to the word processor.

   B. Type three short paragraphs of text, pressing Enter after each one. Move the insertion point to the beginning of the third paragraph, and press Enter to create a blank paragraph. Press the up arrow button to move the insertion point to the blank paragraph.

   C. Switch to the spreadsheet program. Fill cells A1 through D5 with data of any kind. Now select the entire range.

   D. Issue the Copy command in your spreadsheet program. The cells' data is copied.

   E. Switch to the word processor, and issue the Paste command.

   F. In the word processor, select the spreadsheet data and see what changes you can make to it.

   G. Close both applications without saving either document.

Internet Labs

To complete the following exercises, you will need a computer with an Internet connection and a Web browser. (For more information on using these tools, see "Prerequisites" at the front of this textbook.)

1. **Get the Latest on Windows 2000.** If you do not have Windows 2000 yet, chances are good that you will be using it eventually. Learn about the OS by finding the latest information at the following Web sites:

- Microsoft Corp. Visit Microsoft's main Windows 2000 page at **http://www.microsoft.com/windows2000/default.asp**

- Windows Magazine. For a series of articles and links on Windows 2000, visit **http://www.winmag.com/win2000/**

- Planet IT Windows 2000 Technology Center. For articles, reviews, and technical information relating to Windows 2000 in enterprise settings, visit **http://www.planetit.com/techcenters/windows_2000**

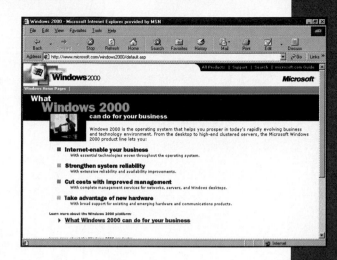

2. **Pick Your Suite.** The most popular word processors and spreadsheet applications are available as part of larger application suites. A suite is a collection of programs, such as a word processor, spreadsheet, database, presentation program, and more. Visit the Web sites of the three leading makers of application suites and research their products.

- Microsoft Corp.—
http://www.microsoft.com/
(Look for information on the Microsoft Office 2000 application suite.)

- Corel Corp.—
http://www.corel.com/
(Look for information on the WordPerfect Office 2000 application suite.)

- Lotus Development Corp.—
http://www.lotus.com/
(Look for information on the SmartSuite Millenium Edition application suite.)

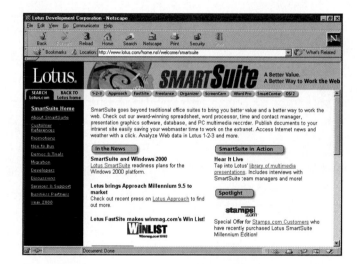

IBE Labs

If you have the Interactive Browser Edition (IBE) CD-ROM for this textbook, you may complete the following interactive exercises using the instructions provided in the IBE.

1. **Presentation Programs or Databases?** Match the terms with the correct type of software.

2. **Drag-and-Drop.** Create a flowchart showing the functions of an operating system.

3. **Association Game.** Challenge your understanding of productivity software by arranging information correctly in a table.

4. **Format a Document.** Choose formatting options and see the results.

UNIT 4

Computer Graphics and New Media

UNIT OBJECTIVES

List two key uses for graphics software.

Identify the primary graphics file formats.

List six important types of graphics software.

Explain the basic concepts of multimedia and new media.

Describe the process used in developing multimedia content.

UNIT CONTENTS

This unit contains the following lessons:

Graphics

OVERVIEW:
Graphics, Graphics Everywhere

You may not realize how much of the imagery you see during a typical day is created on a computer. From postage stamps to magazine illustrations, from billboards to television programs, all kinds of graphic images are created and edited using computers and graphics software. Computer graphics programs—and the designers who use them—have become so proficient that it can be impossible to tell a hand-drawn illustration or a photograph from a computer-generated graphic.

With the computer's ability to mimic traditional artists' media, graphics software allows artists to do with a computer what they once did with brushes, pencils, and darkroom equipment. Similarly, architects and engineers now do most of their design and rendering work on computers—even though many were trained in traditional paper-based drafting methods. By using the computer, they produce designs and renderings that are not only highly accurate but also aesthetically pleasing.

Graphics software has advanced a great deal in a short time. In the early 1980s, most graphics programs were limited to drawing simple geometric outlines, usually in one color. Today, graphics software offers advanced drawing and painting tools and almost unlimited color control. Everywhere you look, you see the products of these powerful tools. Their results can be subtle or stunning, obviously artificial, or amazingly lifelike.

This lesson introduces you to the basics of computer graphics. You will learn about the types of file formats that computer artists routinely use, various methods for getting images inside a computer, and the types of software currently used in graphic design.

OBJECTIVES

● Identify three computer platforms widely used in graphic design.

● Define the terms *bitmap* and *vector*, and differentiate these types of graphics.

● Identify four means for loading graphics files into a computer.

● List the key categories of graphics software and their uses.

COMPUTER PLATFORMS USED FOR GRAPHICS

Just as traditional artists must know the capabilities of their brushes and cameras, today's computer-based artist must have a wide-ranging knowledge of graphics software, the hardware platforms on which it runs, and the formats in which the data can be stored. The most popular hardware platforms in graphics are:

◆ **Macintosh Computers.** In 1984, the introduction of the Apple Macintosh computer and MacPaint software ushered in the era of "art" on the personal computer. With a pointing device and a black-and-white WYSIWYG monitor that displayed images just as they would print, the Macintosh computer allowed users to manipulate shapes, lines, and patterns with great flexibility. (**WYSIWYG,** pronounced *wizzy wig,* stands for "What You See Is What You Get" and is used to describe monitors and software that display documents as they will appear when printed.) Graphic artists also appreciated the Macintosh's easy-to-use graphical interface, with enhancements such as sophisticated typefaces and the capability to magnify images and undo mistakes.

Figure 7.1

Some of the most sophisticated design and illustration tools were created specifically for the Macintosh platform. Today, almost all important graphics software is available for both Windows-based PC and Macintosh users.

Within a few years, the graphics world had embraced the Macintosh as a serious production tool. With the release of more powerful graphics software and the advent of the Postscript page-description language (which enabled accurate printing of complex images), the Macintosh became the tool of choice for computer artists (see Figure 7.1).

◆ **Windows-Based PCs.** In the late 1980s, Microsoft's Windows brought many of the same Macintosh capabilities to IBM PCs and compatibles, greatly expanding that market for graphics software. At the same time, PC hardware was also becoming more graphics-capable, with the advent of high-resolution, high-color monitors and video cards. Today, PCs and Macintosh

Figure 7.2

Many current movies, television programs, and commercials rely heavily on computer-generated special effects. Before being transferred to film, these virtual landscapes and characters are created on workstations and personal computers in a wide variety of commercial and proprietary software.

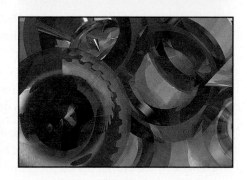

Figure 7.3
Today, the majority of advertisements, magazine covers, and posters are created using graphics software.

systems provide basically the same capabilities when it comes to running graphics software. A wide array of graphics programs is now available for both platforms.

◆ **UNIX-Based Workstations.** Workstations provide another important platform for computer graphics. These specialized, single-user computers possess extremely powerful and fast CPUs, large-capacity hard disks, high-resolution displays, sophisticated video cards, and lots of RAM. Many workstations use the UNIX operating system; some use graphics software written especially for the workstation. Professional graphic artists and designers typically use workstations made by Sun Microsystems and SGI. Because of their expense, workstations typically are reserved for the most demanding graphics projects, such as animation, high-resolution mapping, technical drafting, and cinematic special effects (see Figures 7.2 and 7.3).

NORTON ONLINE

Visit **www.glencoe.com/norton/online/** for more information on **bitmaps** and **vectors**.

TYPES OF GRAPHICS FILES

You can create and save graphics files in many different ways using one of several widely supported file formats. These formats are divided into two basic groups:

◆ **Bitmaps.** A grid whose cells are filled with a color. This grid is called a **bitmap** (see Figure 7.4). The individual cells in the grid can all be filled with the same color or each cell can contain a different color. The term *raster* is sometimes used to describe bitmap images. You may also see bitmap images referred to as bitmapped images.

Figure 7.4
If you magnify a bitmap, you can see its individual pixels.

◆ **Vectors.** A set of **vectors,** which are mathematical equations describing the size, shape, thickness, position, color, and fill of a closed graphical shape or of lines (see Figure 7.5).

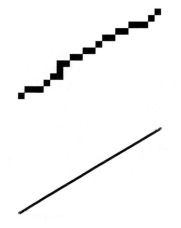

Figure 7.5
This vector is defined as a line stretching between two endpoints, not as a set of pixels.

The text in Figure 7.6 has been generated with a bitmap-based program. In other words, the text is composed of tiny blocks called pixels.

Figure 7.6
The text is a simple bitmap image.

Congratulations!

Visit **www.glencoe.com/norton/online/** for more information on **graphic file formats**.

Perhaps more than other types of computer-generated documents, graphics files require users to understand and work with different file formats. A **file format** is a standardized method of encoding data for storage, and there are many types of file formats. A graphics program uses a file's format to determine the type of data contained in the file and how the data is organized.

Nearly all bitmap-based graphics programs can use any of the file formats listed in Table 7.1. For this reason, these formats are said to be **compatible** with such programs. For example, most bitmap-based programs can open, read, and save files in GIF format and convert it to a different bitmap format, such as TIF.

Table 7.1	Standard Formats for Bitmap Graphics
Format	**Description**
BMP	(BitMaP) A graphics format native to Windows and OS/2. BMP is widely used on PCs for icons and wallpaper. Some Macintosh programs can also read BMP files. The BMP file format is not recommended for use with high-quality graphics images or photographs because it uses only 256 unique colors.
PICT	(PICTure) The native format defined by Apple for the Mac. It is widely used on Macs but less so on PCs.
TIFF	(Tagged Image File Format) Bitmap format defined in 1986 by Microsoft and Aldus and widely used on both Macs and PCs. This format is usually the best to use when exchanging bitmap files that will be printed or edited further.
JPEG	(Joint Photographic Experts Group) JPEG is often abbreviated as JPG (pronounced JAY-peg). This bitmap format is common on the World Wide Web and is often used for photos and other high-resolution (24-bit or millions of colors) images that will be viewed on screen.
GIF	(Graphic Interchange Format) Like JPEG images, GIF images are often found on World Wide Web pages. Unlike JPEG images, GIF images are reduced to 256 or fewer unique colors.
PNG	(Portable Network Graphics) This format was developed as an alternative to GIF and JPEG. PNG, like JPEG, can store color images in a small amount of space, but PNG files can also store transparency information the way GIF files do. The PNG format was designed mainly for use in Web pages.

Most vector-based programs create and save files in proprietary file formats. These formats are either **incompatible** with (that is, cannot be used by) other programs or not totally supported by other programs. In the latter case, other programs may use import filters to use these proprietary formats. Import filters never work perfectly because the program using the import filter will not have the same features as the program that created the file. This lack of commonality has forced developers to create "universal" file formats, which enable users of one program to work with files created in other programs.

Only a handful of common file formats exist for vector graphics, such as Data Exchange Format (DXF) and Initial Graphics Exchange Specification (IGES). These "universal" formats should enable you to create a vector file in one program, such as AutoCAD, and use it in another program, such as CorelDRAW or Visio.

GETTING IMAGES INTO YOUR COMPUTER

The majority of graphics programs allow the user to create images from scratch, building simple lines and shapes into complex graphics. If you begin with an existing image, you can edit or enhance it by using graphics software. If the image you start with is already a graphics file, then getting it into your computer is a matter of importing the file into the program that you want to use. Doing so simply requires the file to be in a format that is compatible with your program. There are, however, other building blocks with which you can start:

◆ **Scanners.** A scanner is a little bit like a photocopy machine except that, instead of copying the image to paper, it transfers the image directly into the computer (see Figure 7.7). If the image is on paper or a slide, a scanner can convert it into a digital file that a computer can manipulate. The scanner is an input device attached to the computer by a cable and controlled by software. This software may accompany the scanner or may be included with a graphics program. The result of scanning an image is a bitmap file. Tools are available for translating these images into vector formats.

◆ **Digital Cameras.** Digital cameras are another way to import images into a computer (see Figure 7.8). These devices store digitized images (in on-board flash memory, on removable media such as a PC Card or floppy disk) for transfer into a computer. Many are small and easy to use and include software and cables or infrared connections for the transfer process. Once again, the resulting file is generally a bitmap.

NORTON
ONLINE

Visit **www.glencoe.com/norton/online/** for more information on **scanners** and digital cameras.

Figure 7.7
A scanner is a valuable tool for graphic artists because it allows them to convert printed images into bitmap files that can be stored on a computer and manipulated with graphics software.

Figure 7.8
A digital camera stores an image as a bitmap file rather than an exposed piece of film.

◆ **Clip Art.** For the nonartist or for the artist looking for an easy way to start or enhance digital artwork, **clip art** is available from many vendors. The term *clip art* originated with the existence of large books filled with page after page of professionally created drawings and graphics that could be cut out, or "clipped," from the pages and glued to a paper layout.

Today, clip art is commonly available on CD-ROM, on diskettes, or via commercial online services. Many word processing and presentation programs also feature a selection of clip art. Clip art can be found in both bitmap and vector formats. The variety of clip art ranges from simple line drawings and cartoons to lush paintings and photographs (see Figure 7.9).

Figure 7.9

Many newer application programs provide built-in libraries of clip art. You can also purchase large collections of clip art or download clip art from various online sources.

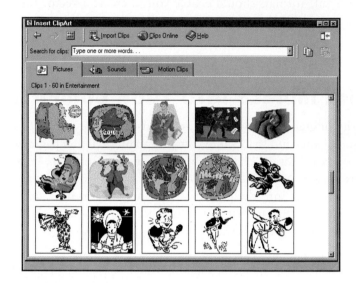

◆ **Electronic Photographs.** Graphic artists commonly use traditional photos that have been converted into digital format by scanning. Digitizing a photo always involves some type of scanner, but the process has become sophisticated in recent years, ensuring high-resolution, professional-quality digital images. Photos are often digitized at special processing labs that scan the images and save the resulting files in a format called PhotoCD (see Figure 7.10). Kodak created the PhotoCD (PCD) format as a standard means for recording photographic images and storing them on a compact disk.

Figure 7.10

The computer shown here is used to convert pictures into a digital format and store them on PhotoCDs.

Answer the following questions by filling in the blank(s).

1. *Raster* is another term for _____ .

2. A(n) _____ is a standardized method of encoding data for storage.

3. _____ are commonly stored in PhotoCD format.

GRAPHICS SOFTWARE

There are five major categories of graphics software, which designers frequently use in combination:

- Paint software
- Photo-manipulation software
- Draw software
- Computer-aided design (CAD) software
- 3-D modeling and animation software

Paint Programs

Paint programs are bitmap-based graphics programs. Paint programs range from the simple (with only a handful of tools) to the complex, with tools that have names like paintbrush, pen, chalk, watercolors, airbrush, crayon, and eraser. Because paint programs keep track of each and every pixel placed on a screen, they can also perform tasks that are impossible with traditional artists' tools.

Paint programs lay down pixels in a process comparable to covering a floor with tiny mosaic tiles. Changing an image created with a paint program is like scraping tiles off the floor and replacing them with different tiles. This dot-by-dot approach allows a high degree of flexibility, but it has a few drawbacks. For example, after you create a circle or make an electronic brush stroke, you can erase or tinker with the individual pixels, making minor adjustments until the image is exactly what you want. On the other hand, you cannot change the entire circle or stroke, especially if you have painted over it, because the software does not recognize bitmaps as a circle or brush stroke after they are created. They are simply a collection of pixels (see Figure 7.11).

Although there are exceptions, most paint programs are also not well suited to handling text. Even though many provide an easy way to add text to an image, after that text is placed it becomes just another collection of pixels. If you misspell a word, you cannot simply backspace over the faulty text and retype it, as you would in a word processor. Instead, you must select the word (or a portion of it), delete the selected portion, and replace it (see Figure 7.12).

Figure 7.11
This circle was created using a paint program. As you zoom into the circle, making it larger on the screen, you can see the pixels that comprise it.

The last *m* should be an *e*.

Party Timm!!!

The artist selects the letter for deletion.

Party Timm!!!

Party Tim   !!!

When the letter is deleted, so is the background.

Figure 7.12
This text was drawn in a paint program that does not allow layering. To correct the misspelling, the artist must select the letter *m* and delete it. Because the letters replaced the background color instead of being layered on top of it, the deletion also removes part of the background.

Visit **www.glencoe.com/norton/online/** for more information on **paint programs**.

This process can be difficult if you place the text over another part of the image. Many newer paint programs enable you to layer a new part of an image over existing parts, leaving the older parts intact if you move or erase the new part. In these cases, you can delete or edit text without affecting the rest of the image. If your paint program does not provide layering, however, existing portions of the image are replaced by—that is, their pixels are recolored with—any new part that you add to the image.

These limitations aside, paint programs provide the tools to create some spectacular effects. More sophisticated paint programs can make brush strokes that appear thick or thin, soft or hard, messy or neat, opaque or transparent. Some allow you to change media with a mouse click—turning your paintbrush into chalk or a crayon or giving your "canvas" a texture like rice paper or eggshell (see Figure 7.13).

Figure 7.13
Chalk, watercolors, and textures are a few of the effects available in sophisticated paint programs.

Photo-Manipulation Programs

When scanners made it easy to transfer photographs to the computer at high resolution, a new class of software was needed to manipulate these images on the screen. A cousin of paint programs, **photo-manipulation programs** now take the place of a photographer's darkroom for many tasks. Although most often used for simple jobs such as sharpening focus or adjusting contrast, photo-manipulation programs are also used to modify photographs in ways far beyond the scope of a traditional darkroom. The picture shown in Figure 7.14, for example, has obviously been subjected to electronic manipulation.

Because photo-manipulation programs edit images at the pixel level, just as paint programs do, they can control precisely how a picture will look. They are also used to edit nonphotographic images and to create images from scratch. The advent of these programs has caused an explosion in the use of computers to modify images.

Photo-manipulation programs can accomplish some amazing tasks. After a photograph has been brought into the computer, usually by scanning or from a digital camera or PhotoCD, the artist can change or enhance the photo at will, down to individual pixels.

Figure 7.14
This image demonstrates how a photo-manipulation program can be used to combine a traditional photograph with computer-generated graphics effects.

White lines come from scratches on the original film.

Using the airbrush tool, the artist can blend them into the background.

Figure 7.15
Repairing a scratched image with an airbrush tool.

For example, if a photo has dust spots, or someone's eyes look red from a flash, the artist can draw just the right number of appropriately colored pixels in the affected areas to correct the problem (see Figure 7.15). Photo-manipulation programs are frequently used to correct color and brightness levels in photographs, to apply special effects, and to combine different parts of images so they look like a complete image.

Photo-manipulation programs also contain tools that can alter the original image drastically, in effect causing photos to lie. For example, if a photograph of a group of people has been scanned into the computer, special tools can erase the pixels that form the image of one of these people and replace them with pixels from the background area—effectively removing the person from the photo. There are even tools that can move objects in a scene or create a collage of several different images (see Figure 7.16). Architects use these kinds of tools to show how a new building can change a city's skyline.

Figure 7.16
The keyhole in this photo has been partially erased and replaced with parts of a new background—the cow.

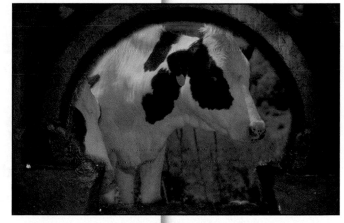

Draw Programs

Draw programs are vector-based graphics programs that are well suited for work when accuracy and flexibility are as important as coloring and special effects. Although they do not possess the pixel-pushing capability of paint programs, draw programs can be used to create images with an "arty" look and have been adopted as the primary tool of many designers. You see the output of draw programs in everything from cereal box designs to television show credits.

Draw programs work by defining every line as a mathematical equation, or vector. These programs are sometimes referred to as object-oriented programs because each item drawn—whether it is a line, square, rectangle, or circle—is treated as a separate and distinct object from all the others. (Some designers and draw programs use the term *entity* rather than *object*, but the concept is the same.) All objects

NORTON
ONLINE

Visit **www.glencoe.com/norton/online/** for more information on **photo-manipulation programs** and **draw programs**.

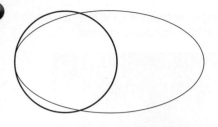

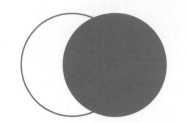

Figure 7.17
Simply by clicking and dragging in a draw program, you can change a circle into an oval. You can use similar techniques to change squares to rectangles and to modify other shapes.

Figure 7.18
Because this circle was created with a draw program, it can be filled with a color (green, in this case), moved, and copied.

created in modern draw programs consist of an outline and a fill. The fill can be nothing at all, a solid color, a vector pattern, a photo, or something else. For example, when you draw a square with a draw program, the computer remembers it as a square of a fixed size at a specific location, that may or may not be filled, and not as a bunch of pixels that are in the shape of a square.

Draw programs offer two advantages over paint programs. First, when objects are created, they remain objects to the computer. After you draw a circle, you can return to it later and move it intact by dragging it with the mouse, even if it has been covered with other shapes or lines. You can change the circle's shape into an oval; you can change the size of the circle, change its color, or fill its interior with a color, a blend of colors, or a pattern (see Figures 7.17 and 7.18). You can make these changes without affecting any other objects in the drawing.

For similar reasons, draw programs are also superior to paint programs in their handling of text. Because the computer treats text characters as objects rather than as collections of dots, the text can be colored, shaded, scaled, tilted, or even joined to a curvy line with little effort (see Figure 7.19).

Figure 7.19
Draw programs make it easy to color text. Lines of text can be bent or distorted. Text can also be forced to follow a curvy line.

Computer-Aided Design Programs

Computer-Aided Design (CAD), also known as Computer-Aided Drafting or Computer-Aided Drawing, is the computerized version of the hand-drafting process that used to be done with a pencil and ruler on a drafting table. CAD is used extensively in technical fields, such as architecture, and in mechanical, electrical, and industrial engineering.

Unlike drawings made using paint or drawing programs, CAD drawings are usually the basis for the actual building or manufacturing process—for a house, an engine, or an electrical system. CAD programs are so precise that they can produce designs accurate down to the micrometer—or one-millionth of a meter. This accuracy extends to the other end of the scale, as well. If you want to draw a full-scale, three-dimensional version of the Earth, you can do it. In fact, it has already been done! See Figure 7.20.

Three-dimensional (3-D) design got its start in CAD programs during the late 1980s as a way of allowing designers to view their designs from all possible angles

on screen. Today, most CAD programs provide different ways to design, display, animate, and print 3-D objects, called **models.** For example, **wireframe models** represent 3-D shapes by displaying their outlines and edges, as shown in Figure 7.21. Many CAD programs also work with **solid models.** This type of modeling works by giving the user a representation of a block of solid material. The user can apply different operations to shape the material by cutting, adding, and combining.

Once a model is finished, CAD programs can render the image, shading in the solid parts and creating output that looks almost real. Figure 7.22 shows a rendered image of the wireframe model from Figure 7.21. A solid model would look the same.

3-D Modeling Programs

Whether you are aware of it or not, you are constantly exposed to elaborate 3-D imaging in movies, television, and print. Many of these images are now created with a special type of graphics software, called **3-D modeling software,** that enables users to create electronic models of three-dimensional objects without using CAD software. Fast workstations or PCs coupled with 3-D modeling programs can lend realism to even the most fantastic subjects.

Figure 7.21
A 3-D wireframe model.

Figure 7.22
A rendering of the 3-D wireframe model. If the model had been solid rather than wireframe, the rendering would look almost the same.

There are four different types of 3-D modeling programs. (Three of these types are illustrated in Figures 7.23, 7.24, and 7.25 on page 154.) Each uses a different technique to create three-dimensional objects:

◆ Surface modelers build objects by stretching a surface—like a skin—over an underlying wireframe structure.

◆ Solid modelers do the same thing as surface modelers but also understand thickness and density. This feature can be important if you need to punch a hole through an electronic object.

◆ Polygonal modelers combine many tiny polygons to build objects—similar to the way one would build a geodesic dome out of many perfectly fitted triangles.

◆ Spline-based modelers build objects, either surface or solid, using mathematically defined curves that are rotated on an axis to form a 3-D shape.

NORTON
ONLINE

Visit **www.glencoe.com/norton/online/** for more information on **galleries of 3-D images.**

Figure 7.23
This gear is an example of a CAD model rendered with surface modeling techniques.

Figure 7.24
This CAD model of a spray nozzle was created using solid modeling techniques.

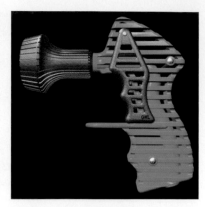

Figure 7.25
This model demonstrates how polygonal modeling techniques can be used.

Figure 7.26
Images from a traditional, manually drawn animation. Although computers speed up the animation process tremendously, they still work on the same idea: generate hundreds or thousands of individual images, and then display them in rapid succession to create the illusion of motion.

Animation

An outgrowth of the 3-D explosion is computer-based animation. Since the creation of filmmaking, animation was possible only through a painstaking process of hand-drawing a series of images (called cels), as shown in Figure 7.26, and then filming them one by one. Each filmed image is called a **frame.** When the film is played back at high speed (around 30 frames per second for high-quality animation), the images blur together to create the illusion of motion on the screen. The process of manually creating a short animation—even just a few seconds' worth—can take weeks of labor.

Computer-generated imagery (CGI) has changed the world of animation in many ways. Although computer animation works on the same principles as traditional animation (a sequence of still images displayed in rapid succession), computer animators now have highly sophisticated tools that take the drudgery out of the animation process and allow them to create animations more quickly than ever.

Computer animators also have the advantage of being able to display their animations on the computer screen or to output them to CD-ROM, videotape, or film.

An added bonus of computer animation is the capability of animating three-dimensional characters and create **photorealistic** scenes. The computer-generated image looks so realistic that it could be mistaken for a photograph of a real-life object (see Figure 7.27). These capabilities make computer-generated characters difficult to distinguish from real ones. Good examples are the dinosaurs in *Godzilla*, the space ships in *Galaxy Quest*, and the eerie landscapes of *The Matrix*.

Figure 7.27
Computer-generated animation is often so lifelike that it is hard to distinguish from the real thing.

GRAPHICS AND THE WORLD WIDE WEB

Perhaps even more than 3-D design and animation, the World Wide Web has aroused intense curiosity and interest in computer graphics because nearly anyone can create and post a Web page, and the World Wide Web can support many types of graphics. By using basic paint and draw software as described earlier in this lesson, it is easy to create or edit graphics for use on a Web page. Such graphics include simple items such as bullets and horizontal rules, more complicated images such as logos, and complex artwork and photographs. If you have spent any time surfing the Web, you may agree that graphics elements truly enhance the viewing experience and can make even a simple page look elegant (see Figure 7.28 on page 157).

Although a Web page might look like one big graphic, most pages are actually collections of graphics and text elements combined by the browser according to codes embedded in the content of the page. (You will learn more about Web pages in Unit 5, "The Internet and Online Resources.") If any navigation buttons, icons, bullets, bars, or other graphics appear on the page, they are separate graphics files that are being displayed at the same time.

When a Web page designer creates a Web page, he or she usually begins by adding the text elements to an HTML-format file. By surrounding the text elements with special codes—called HTML tags, the designer can cause different pieces of text to be displayed in different ways by the Web browser. Tags tell the Web browser what information to display and how to display it.

NORTON
ONLINE

Visit **www.glencoe.com/norton/online/** for more information on **using graphics in Web pages.**

COMPUTERS
in your career

Computer Graphics and Design

Few areas of computing are as wide open as the field of computer graphics. If you are an artist or aspire to be a designer, consider adding computer-based design tools to your list of skills. By transferring their drawing and design skills to the computer, many of today's professional graphic artists have greatly expanded their portfolios and client lists. Here are just a few areas where computer-based graphics are used routinely:

◆ **Web Page Designers.** No Web site is complete unless it is graphically rich and filled with navigation tools. Web designers use programs such as Adobe Photoshop, Adobe Illustrator, and many others to create graphics for their pages. Good designers bring a sense of color and balance to the Web page and use graphics to enhance the site's message as well as to make it more visually appealing and easier to navigate.

◆ **Architects and Engineers.** If you have studied drafting, you can apply that skill to computer-aided drafting tools and find a career in architecture or engineering as a designer or drafter. (In fact, nearly all drafting classes teach computer-based drafting as well as manual drafting skills.) Computer drafting tools are used in a huge array of design fields, from building and construction to aerospace and product packaging. In the world of computer design, you are limited only by your imagination and willingness to learn, as you can work in 2-D, 3-D, animation, programming, and many other segments of the field.

◆ **Product Designers.** From shampoo bottles to automobiles, from initial specifications to modeling and visualization, most product design is done on the computer.

◆ **Advertising Designers.** Computer graphics have exploded in popularity among advertising agencies, which use computers to create everything from magazine ads to program-length television infomercials. Advertisers are continually pushing the envelope in computer-based and character animation as they seek to give personality to the items they hope to sell.

◆ **Game Designers and Filmmakers.** These fields are perhaps at the pinnacle of computer graphics today because they use the most sophisticated tools available to create complex effects for use in video games and movies. These designers use every tool available to obtain the desired results, from simple paint packages to advanced particle-generating effects software, as well as high-end workstations.

◆ **Animators.** Until a few years ago, animation was done almost exclusively by hand. Today's animators use a wide variety of computerized systems to create animation— from the simple, two-dimensional cartoons you see on Saturday-morning television to complex 3-D animation of normally inanimate objects (such as dancing cereal boxes). Professional animators work on all different platforms and use out-of-the-box software as well as sophisticated custom programs that make computer-generated animation seem as realistic as possible.

Computer hardware and graphics software are used in almost every design field.

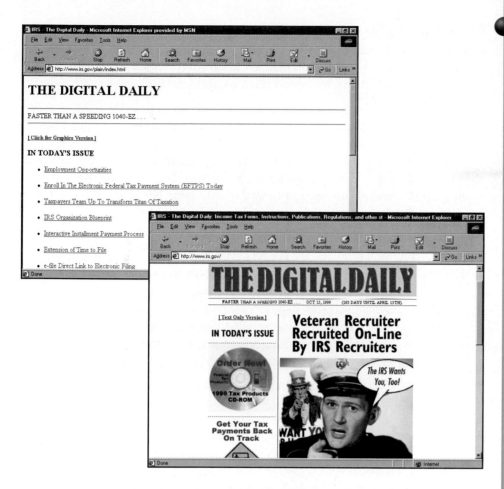

Figure 7.28
Graphics can make nearly any Web page easier to use or simply more appealing visually. On the left is a text-only version of the Internal Revenue Service's home page. On the right is the graphics-enabled version.

The designer can also add tags that tell the browser to display graphics, as shown in Figure 7.29, and a single Web page can hold many individual graphics. On the Web server, the designer must store all the graphics files required by the Web page. When the user's browser encounters the tags for a graphic, the server sends the graphics file to the browser. The HTML tags help the browser organize the graphics, text, and other design elements on the page.

These tags in the HTML file...

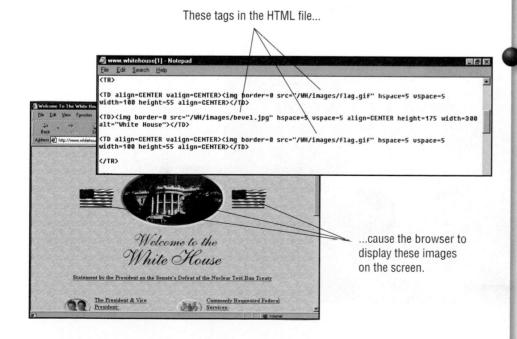

...cause the browser to display these images on the screen.

Figure 7.29
These two screens show a Web page's source code and the results in a browser. On the top, you can see the tags that format text and display graphics. On the bottom, you can see how the browser interprets the tags and displays the information.

The designer can use various methods to incorporate graphics in a Web page. The graphics can be placed almost anywhere on the page, aligned in different ways, sized, incorporated in tables, and used as backgrounds. Graphics files are used to create buttons and bullets, horizontal rules, navigational tools, and much more.

Whenever possible, designers use graphics of the highest possible resolution and color depth. On the World Wide Web, however, image quality often must be sacrificed to reduce file size and download times. Whenever your browser encounters a graphic in a Web page, it must download the graphic file from the Web server to your disk and then display it on screen. If the file is large or if the page contains many graphics, download time can be annoyingly slow. Therefore, Web designers have adopted a few standards to ensure that their pages download as quickly as possible:

◆ **Resolution.** Web graphics are always saved and displayed at a resolution of 72 pixels per inch (ppi), even though it is possible to save pictures at a much higher resolution, because monitors have a fixed display resolution of 72 ppi. As Figure 7.30 demonstrates, higher resolution settings do not necessarily improve the appearance of an image when it is displayed on a standard monitor. Higher-resolution images also require more storage space and take longer to download to the user's computer.

◆ **Color Depth.** Although most computer screens can display colors of up to 24 or even 32 bits (called true color), the files that take advantage of these color settings can be large. Generally, Web designers use only two file formats—GIF and JPG—that have specific color settings and specific uses. The maximum color depth for a GIF file is 8 bits, or 256 colors. JPG images are always 24-bit images. Savvy designers use JPG images for images with lots of colors in them, such as photos, photorealistic images, and images that contain complex gradients. Designers use the GIF format when they want to create animated GIFs or create background transparency (such as shapes that are not rectangles or squares).

◆ **Image Size.** Although it is possible to save images that are larger than the user's display space, Web designers try to avoid this practice. When a Web page requires a large graphic, designers try to ensure that the graphic is not so large that it will run off the edge of the user's screen at 800 × 600 screen resolution.

◆ **File Formats.** Although just about any graphics file format can be used on a Web page, browsers support only the GIF, JPG, and PNG file formats without requiring the use of special plug-in software. Generally, browsers can open and view images in GIF, JPG, and PNG formats directly in the browser window, although PNG-format images are not commonly used.

Figure 7.30
These three images were saved at different resolutions: 72 ppi, 144 ppi, and 244 ppi, from left to right. Note that the quality of the image does not improve much with the change in resolution.

LESSON QUIZ

True/False

Answer the following questions by circling True or False.

True   False   **1.** In 1984, the IBM-PC ushered in the era of "art" on the personal computer.

True   False   **2.** Vector images use groups of dots to define entities.

True   False   **3.** Paint programs are bitmap-based.

True   False   **4.** Draw programs are sometimes called object-oriented programs.

True   False   **5.** CAD drawings are usually the basis for a building or manufacturing process.

Multiple Choice

Circle the word or phrase that best completes each sentence.

1. A _____ is a group of dots.
  A. bitmap   **B.** vector   **C.** format

2. A file format is _____ .
  A. always proprietary   **B.** a method of encoding data for storage   **C.** neither A nor B

3. A(n) _____ can convert a printed image into digital format.
  A. photocopy machine   **B.** electronic photograph   **C.** scanner

4. The images that make up an animation are called _____ .
  A. objects   **B.** vectors   **C.** frames

5. A Web designer can use _____ to tell a browser to display an image.
  A. HTML tags   **B.** color depth   **C.** both A and B

LESSON LABS

Complete the following exercises as directed by your instructor.

1. Your hard disk may already contain a collection of graphic images. To find out if there are any useful images on your hard disk, launch Windows Explorer and select the icon for your hard disk. On the menu bar, click Tools, point to Find, and then click Files or Folders. The Find dialog box appears. Click in the Named box; then type *.**GIF**, *.**JPG**. (This will search the disk for all files in the GIF and JPG formats.) In the Look in box, select the icon for your hard disk; then check the Include subfolders check box. Click Find Now. If Windows finds any files, they appear in the bottom half of the dialog box. To view any of these files, double-click its name. When you are done, close the Find dialog box and any other applications.

2. Windows Paint is a basic bitmap-based paint program that is almost always installed with Windows. To launch the program, click the Start menu, point to Programs, point to Accessories, and then click Windows Paint. Experiment with the program's drawing tools to create a simple image. Print and save the image, if your instructor approves; then close Paint.

Understanding Multimedia

OBJECTIVES

- Define the terms *multimedia*, *interactivity*, and *new media*.
- Explain how different types of media are used to create multimedia events.
- Describe the six phases of the multimedia design process.
- Name three ways in which multimedia content is commonly distributed.

OVERVIEW:
Bringing Content to Life

As technology improves, consumers become more and more demanding. In an era of high-speed communications, we not only want to receive information immediately—we also want it in multiple ways at one time. This demand explains why television news channels commonly feature text that "crawls" across the bottom of the screen while an announcer talks and videotaped images roll. It explains why Web sites now feature graphics, animation, and sound as well as text and hyperlinks.

This demand extends to the way we work, learn, and entertain ourselves. Simple, one-dimensional content is no longer acceptable to most of us. Information, lessons, games, and shopping are more appealing and hold our attention longer if we can approach and arrange them in different ways, even on a whim. These demands and technological advances have worked hand in hand to propel the art and science of multimedia to new levels, resulting in products that weave together text, graphics, animation, audio, and video.

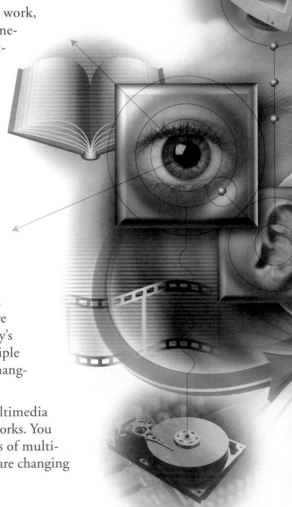

When we use these products—whether a Web-based encyclopedia or a CD-ROM video game, we are doing more than working with a computer program. We are experiencing a multimedia event. Today's multimedia products appeal to multiple senses at one time and respond to our changing needs with ever-increasing speed.

This lesson introduces you to basic multimedia concepts and explains how multimedia works. You will learn about some of the applications of multimedia technologies and how new media are changing the way we work and play.

MULTIMEDIA, INTERACTIVITY, AND NEW MEDIA DEFINED

For much of history, information was presented via a single, unique medium. In this context, a medium is simply a means of conveying information. Sound, such as the human voice, is one type of medium, and for centuries before written language came into widespread use, speech was the primary way of exchanging information. Eventually, people began telling stories (and leaving a record of their lives) through drawings and paintings, such as the famous cave paintings found in France. The creation of written language gave people another medium for expressing their thoughts.

Today, people commonly use speech, sounds, music, text, graphics, animation, and video to convey information. These are all different types of media (*media* is the plural of *medium*), and each has traditionally been used to present certain types of information.

Multiple Media = Multimedia

People long ago discovered that messages are more effective (that is, the audience understands and remembers them more easily) when they are presented through a combination of different media. This kind of message is what is meant by the term **multimedia**—using more than one type of medium at a time.

In practice, you can say that even the simplest speech-and-text presentation is a multimedia event because it uses more than one unique medium to deliver a message. As an example, consider a teacher who uses a chalkboard in the classroom so she can use written text to support a spoken lecture (see Figure 8.1). At a more advanced level, people use movies and television to combine multiple types of media (sound, video, animation, still graphics, and text) to create different kinds of messages, to inform or entertain in unique and meaningful ways.

Figure 8.1
It does not take much to create a basic multimedia event. Simply by using text to underscore the important points of a spoken message, you incorporate two unique media. The number of media types used is not important, as long as the author has complete control of each and the presenter delivers the message in a clear and engaging way.

Interactivity: Just Add Users

The computer, however, has taken multimedia to an even higher level by enabling us to use many different media simultaneously. A printed encyclopedia, for example, is basically pages of text and pictures. In a multimedia version, however, the encyclopedia's pictures can move, a narrator's recorded voice can provide the text, and the user can move around at will by clicking hypertext links and using navigational tools. By combining different types of media to present the message, the encyclopedia's developer improves the chances that users will understand the information.

Of course, the same point can be made about television programming, because it uses various media at the same time. Computer technologies, however, enable

NORTON
ONLINE

Visit www.glencoe.com/norton/online/ for more information on the **basics of multimedia** and **interactivity**.

PC-based multimedia products to go one step further. Because the computer can accept input from the user, it can host **interactive** multimedia events, involving the user unlike any book, movie, or television program.

Interactivity has been defined in many ways, but in the realm of multimedia the term means that the user and program respond to one another; the program continually provides the user with a range of choices from which the user selects to direct the flow of the program. This level of interactivity is the primary difference between computer-based multimedia programs and other kinds of multimedia events. Most television programs, for example, require the viewer only to sit and observe (see Figure 8.2). Computers, however, make it possible to create **interactive media** that enable people to respond to—and even control—what they see and hear. By using the PC to control the program, the user can make choices, move freely from one part of the content to another, and in some cases customize the content to suit a specific purpose.

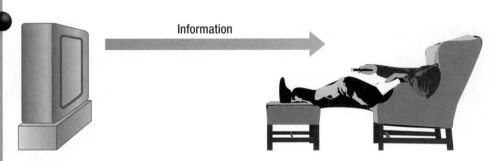

Information

Figure 8.2

Traditional medium with one-way communication. Although the viewer can select different programs to watch, television does not yet provide the level of interactivity currently available in computer-based interactive media products.

By accepting input from the user, interactive media create a **feedback loop,** which generally works like this:

1. To start the loop, the user launches the interactive media program and chooses the content.

2. The program responds by displaying the content, along with choices (navigation tools, links to other topics, controls for displaying different types of content, and so on) for the user.

3. The user responds by making a choice, such as moving to a different place in the program or selecting different content.

4. The program responds by fulfilling the user's selection, which usually comes with a new set of options for the user to choose.

5. The process continues—sometimes at a rapid and complex pace, as in the case of many computer games—until the user stops the program (see Figure 8.3).

Interactive media programs are effective (and successful) because they provide this give-and-take with the user. You will find this level of interactivity in practically any popular multimedia product, whether the program is a video game, a CD-based reference tool, an electronic test bank, or a shopping site on the Web (see Figure 8.4).

Figure 8.3

Interactive media with feedback loop. By choosing options continually and using the joystick to guide the action on-screen, the user can control the flow of the program's content.

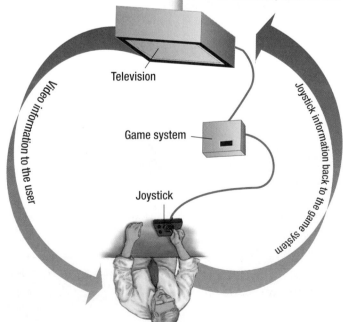

Video information to the user

Television

Game system

Joystick

Joystick information back to the game system

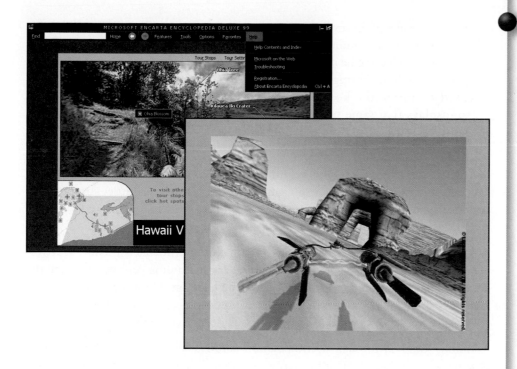

The New Media

Interactivity involves more than just a computer and a mouse. The **new media** (a term encompassing all types of interactive multimedia technologies) bring into play different communication technologies, such as cable TV, telephone lines, private networks, the Internet, and others. The new media are created by a convergence of many types of technology, enabling individuals and large groups to communicate and convey information using computers and communications systems.

At the core of new media is a concept known as **digital convergence.** Computers are used to create all kinds of digital content, from plain text to video. This digital information can travel to the consumer along the same path—perhaps via a CD-ROM disk, a cable TV wire, or a satellite transmission. Rather than delivering movies on film or videotape, music on tapes or compact disks, and books on the printed page, different kinds of content can now reach the computer or cable TV box in the same way. Thus, various content comes together, converging into one digital stream.

INFORMATION IN LAYERS AND DIMENSIONS

Multimedia developers continually struggle to find ways to make their products more appealing to users, whether the product is a fast-paced action game, a tutorial on disk, or an e-commerce Web site. A basic strategy in multimedia development is to provide information that is layered and multidimensional. This strategy may mean giving the user multiple pieces of information simultaneously—such as a rotating 3-D image of a motor, an audio description of its function, and pop up text boxes that provide more information when the user points at certain parts of the graphic. In a multidimensional presentation, the user has the option of experiencing the information from different perspectives; for example, one user may prefer to see only an animated demonstration of a landscaping project, while another may prefer to read a text description.

NORTON
ONLINE

Visit **www.glencoe.com/norton/online/** for more information on **new media** and **digital convergence.**

One way to make plain text and pictures inviting to an audience is to add time-based content, such as audio, cartoon animation, and video. It is important, however, that the added media do more than merely mimic the static text and graphics content. It would be boring indeed to watch a video of someone reading a passage of text that appears on the screen. But if the text is a scene from *Hamlet* and the video displays that same scene with Sir Laurence Olivier's film portrayal, then the video enlivens the printed text.

Multimedia and online encyclopedias, such as the Microsoft Encarta Web site (**www.encarta.com/**), use sound, animation, and video clips to enliven many of their text articles. For example, in an article about the space shuttle, you can view diagrams of the shuttle, photos and backgrounds of crew members, and videos of shuttle launches and missions.

A major challenge accompanies the large volume of multimedia content that arrives via a compact disk, DVD, Web site, or online service: finding your way through the text, pictures, and other media available in the presentation. This large volume of multimedia content is where the interactivity component comes into play. The user is responsible for deciding when to go to a particular place within the collection of data.

Wending your way through electronic information is commonly called **navigation.** The person who wrote the information is responsible for providing the user with on-screen aids to navigate. In software that mimics the old format of books, the navigation aid might be a simple palette of left- and right-facing arrow icons to navigate backward or forward one page. Because authors of digital content are not bound by the physical constraints of pages, they can also provide buttons that allow you to jump to locations outside the normal, linear sequence (see Figure 8.5).

Figure 8.5
This product displays a popular method of navigation in multimedia programs. By clicking the appropriate button, you can move forward or backward through the product's content.

REWIND BACK 1 STOP PAUSE ADV.1 PLAY F-FWRD

Visit **www.glencoe.com/norton/online/** for more information on **hypermedia.**

The term **hypermedia** has evolved to describe the environment that allows users to click on one type of media to navigate to the same or other type of media. If you have spent any time surfing the Web or using disk-based multimedia products, you probably have seen various types of hypermedia tools. In a Web page devoted to The Beatles, for example, clicking on a photo of the band might bring up a page containing biographies of the band members or a gallery of additional photos. A click on such a link may automatically connect you to a related item on a computer in another state or another country—and it appears on your screen as if it were coming from your own hard disk (see Figure 8.6).

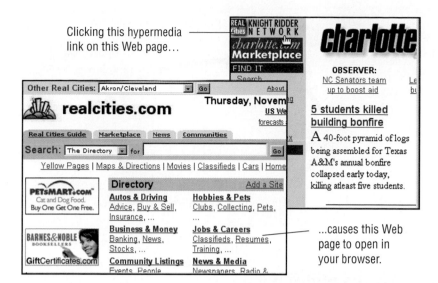

Clicking this hypermedia link on this Web page...

...causes this Web page to open in your browser.

Figure 8.6
In any Web page, clicking a hyperlinked word or image opens a new Web page in your browser window. The first and second page may be on the same Web server, or they may be on different servers many miles apart. The purpose of hypermedia links is to make information of all kinds, and in all locations, appear as a seamless whole so that accessing different types of information becomes as simple as flipping through the pages of a magazine.

Hypermedia can also exist on a smaller scale. You may have already used hypermedia in the Windows Help system. Clicking a hyperlinked word may display a pop-up window that provides a definition of a term or a list of additional links. Other links may open separate Help windows, providing helpful information on a different topic.

Self Check

Answer the following questions by filling in the blank(s).

1. The level of _____ differentiates computer-based multimedia programs and other kinds of multimedia events.

2. New media are created by a(n) _____ of many types of technology.

3. _____ is the concept behind the hyperlinks found in World Wide Web pages.

CREATING NEW MEDIA CONTENT

To capture and hold the user's attention and to remain competitive with other products, a multimedia program must provide three features:

◆ Information, action, or a story line that compels the user to interact with the program

◆ A wide assortment of media types that are cleverly and seamlessly interwoven

◆ Flexibility in navigation, enabling the user to move around or even redirect the flow of content

As a result, creating effective multimedia can be a challenging process. To cover all the bases, a multimedia development team usually involves people with various skills who adhere to a complex but well-defined development process. Figure 8.7 on page 166 shows an overview of the multimedia development process. The following sections discuss each step of this process in greater detail.

NORTON ONLINE

Visit **www.glencoe.com/norton/online/** for more information on **multimedia development**.

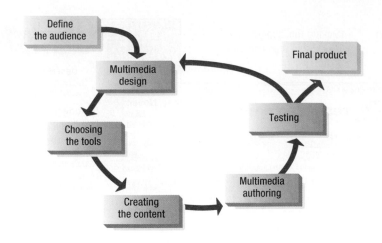

Defining the Audience

Understanding the audience is the most essential issue that developers must tackle, and it is discussed in detail long before actual development work begins. To define the audience for their product, developers ask questions such as these:

◆ What specific interest will the product fulfill, and who possesses this interest?

◆ What assumptions can be made about the audience?

◆ What do users expect to gain by using the program?

◆ How much time will users want to spend exploring this content?

◆ What media will deliver the message best or provide the right impact for this user?

◆ What method or methods will be used to distribute the product? Floppy disk? CD-ROM? DVD? Dial-up Internet? Broadband Internet? Intranet?

In reality, the preceding list is short. Development teams may spend weeks or months trying to define their product's users, getting to know the consumer's every want, need, and wish. Marketers may be recruited to interview prospective customers or meet with focus groups to seek consumer reactions to competing products (see Figure 8.8).

Design and Storyboarding

Planning the overall design is often the longest part of the development process. Much of this work is done without any computers. A common way to start is by composing an outline of the sequences and blocks of information that will appear on the screen. Such an outline can take many forms, depending on the type of product to be developed. For example, suppose you are developing a multimedia dictionary. Your outline may resemble an outline for a book, including a list of terms to be defined, but with the addition of lines and arrows to indicate important links that must be provided within the information. If you are developing a CBT product, on the other hand, the outline may be considerably more complex, with placeholders for text, narration or animation that plays on cue, quizzes, links to Web sites, and much more.

Figure 8.8
Developers seldom work in isolation when creating a new product. They frequently enlist the help of marketers, who may use focus groups to determine what consumers want from a specific type of product or to get reviews about competing products.

Techview

VIRTUAL REALITY

Virtual reality (VR)—the computer-generated simulation of a real or imagined physical space—is probably the ultimate multimedia experience because it immerses you in a completely artificial environment. VR environments typically produce one of three possible image types:

◆ **Simulations of Real Places.** You might find yourself in a virtual room, car, or cave.

◆ **Simulations of Imaginary Places.** In this kind of simulation, you could be riding alongside King Arthur or battling aliens.

◆ **Simulations of Real Things That Do Not Exist.** In this kind of simulation, you could walk through a building that has not been built yet.

Uses for Virtual Reality

People use these VR simulations in many situations:

◆ **Training.** VR simulations of air combat, space shuttle flights, or nuclear reactor meltdowns provide excellent low-cost training areas.

◆ **Document and Facilities Management.** Virtual reality allows you to file electronic documents visually. Using such a system, you can create a virtual model of a factory and then attach maintenance records to each item within the factory.

◆ **Design.** By building a prototype in VR, a designer can work out design and construction flaws before the product leaves the drawing board.

◆ **Entertainment.** VR games and adventures are the ultimate fantasy experience.

VR Hardware and Software

VR technology appears in the following formats:

◆ **On-Screen.** Images are displayed on a computer screen. The user is outside the environment, which limits the "reality" effect.

NORTON ONLINE

Visit **www.glencoe.com/norton/online/** for more information on **virtual reality**.

There are many different head-mounted VR displays. Using such a device, the wearer feels immersed in the virtual environment, without distractions from outside.

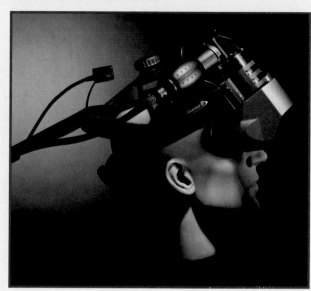

◆ **Head-Mounted Displays.** Developers have created helmets and goggles that display stereoscopic images close to the user's eyes. The images block the outside world and create the illusion of a world that wraps around the wearer. As the wearer turns his or her head, tracking devices tell the computer to change the image, allowing the wearer to look around the virtual environment rather than stare straight ahead.

◆ **Rooms.** These rooms, called Cave Automatic Virtual Environments (CAVEs), contain complex projection and stereo equipment that create a complete virtual world. The user can move around the room and move objects with the aid of a wand.

◆ **Clothing.** Developers are working on VR clothing, like chest pads and gloves, that provide tactile feedback when you touch a virtual object.

The most impressive VR equipment costs hundreds of thousands of dollars. Nevertheless, home users can experience convincing VR using low-end equipment and a home PC. Of course, even low-end VR hardware is not cheap. While you can spend as little as $99 on a pair of goggles, a top-of-the-line home-user helmet can easily cost more than $500.

Now is the time to determine how much information—text, graphics, clickable objects—will be presented on each screen. It is also the time to establish a navigation methodology for the user. Will there be a navigation bar with arrows leading from scene to scene, or will there be text or graphic objects that the user will click to jump around the entire program? Will the user always be able to return to a single starting point? Will the content change without input from the user?

When a program includes a great deal of animation or many different scenes, the best design aid is the storyboard. Used by film directors for productions ranging from thirty-second television commercials to feature-length motion pictures, the **storyboard** consists of sketches of the scenes and action. A storyboard helps the author recognize gaps in logic or flaws in the flow of the content. Some multimedia authoring programs provide facilities for drawing and organizing the frames of a storyboard, and stand-alone storyboarding programs are available (see Figure 8.9). Many experienced multimedia designers create storyboards simply by using a word processor or drawing program.

Figure 8.9
Creating a storyboard.

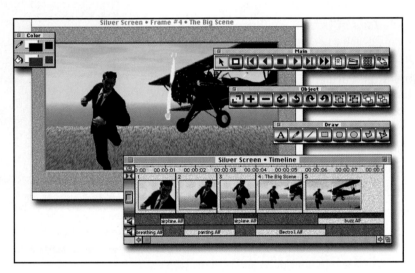

Tools, Creating Content, and Authoring

Because multimedia includes different kinds of content, creating it involves many types of software. Creating text often requires a word processor; working with digital images requires graphics software; using video requires a video-capture program and editing software; and sound often requires its own editing software. HTML is commonly used in interactive multimedia programs as well as Web pages, so HTML editors are an important tool in the developer's arsenal (see Figure 8.10). Similarly, products such as Macromedia's Shockwave, which enables developers to incorporate interactive animation into multimedia products and Web pages, are increasingly common tools in content development.

When the content is ready, it is assembled in a process called **multimedia authoring.** This process requires still another type of software that can understand all the different types of media, combine them, control the sequences in which they appear, and create navigational tools and an interface for the user.

Macromedia Director is one of the most popular programs for combining all the elements of a multimedia presentation (see Figure 8.11). In it, the multimedia author assembles each element—text, graphics, sound, and video—into separate tracks. The program helps the author to synchronize all the elements so that, for example, a crash sound effect is heard precisely when two animated objects collide.

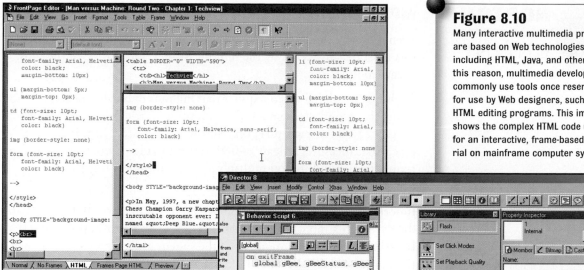

Figure 8.10
Many interactive multimedia products are based on Web technologies, including HTML, Java, and others. For this reason, multimedia developers commonly use tools once reserved for use by Web designers, such as HTML editing programs. This image shows the complex HTML code used for an interactive, frame-based tutorial on mainframe computer systems.

Figure 8.11
Developers use multiple tools to create the individual components of a multimedia program. Then they rely on a multimedia authoring application such as Macromedia Director to incorporate everything into a seamless product for the user.

Testing

It is vital that the program be tested by the kinds of people who will be using it. With this testing, the programmer can locate any flaws ahead of time and repair them before unleashing the finished product on the world.

As with the testing of any software product, it is helpful for the program's author(s) to watch users navigate through the product. The kinds of problems to watch for are any locations in the product where the user does not know what to do next. Is the user struggling to read a font size too small for descriptive text? Is the user following navigational paths that lead quickly to the desired information, or are there times when the user seems lost in the multimedia maze?

Before a program is ready for release, it may need to go through several testing-and-revision cycles so that everyone is comfortable with the finished product. As part of the planning process, sufficient time must be built into the schedule for the testing cycles. Most software developers and programmers employ firms to test the software, or they have their own testing departments.

TECHNOLOGIES THAT SUPPORT NEW MEDIA

Since the first PC-based multimedia products appeared, developers have worked to create new technologies that will allow graphics, audio, video, and user feedback to work more seamlessly. As a result, dozens of specialized file formats, audio/video platforms, and programming techniques have become available.

Today's most sophisticated multimedia products incorporate any number of these technologies, resulting in smoother animation, audio and video streams that flow without interruption, and a heightened level of interactivity. These technologies are being used in products of all kinds, from games to Web sites, and are found both in CD-ROM-based and Web-based multimedia events.

MPEG and JPEG

Even though a modern multimedia PC can display multimedia content, other factors must be considered by the multimedia developer. One of the most important is data compression.

High-quality digital video requires that millions of bits be transmitted to the monitor every second. Remember, the monitor is attached to a video controller, which assigns 24 bits to each pixel on a full-color monitor. Monitors display a grid of pixels that measures at least 640 × 480, and video requires at least fifteen image frames per second. If you multiply all these numbers together, you get the number of bits it takes to display digital video.

It does not matter whether the information comes from a CD-ROM and is being displayed on a monitor or comes through a cable box and is being displayed by the television—the components of the system usually are not capable of transmitting, processing, and displaying the digital information fast enough. The capacity for data transmission is known as bandwidth. Somewhere in a computer system, there is almost always a bottleneck in the bandwidth. When it comes to video, one potential solution is data compression.

Data compression typically uses mathematical analyses of digital source material to strip away unnecessary bits of data prior to sending it across the wire. This process is called **encoding** and results in image files of a much smaller size than would be possible if they were not encoded. At the receiving end (for example, inside a modern cable TV converter or direct-broadcast satellite receiver), the compressed file undergoes a **decoding** process, and the missing bits are quickly reinserted to produce a copy that is extremely close to the original in quality and detail. Special hardware or software may be required to decode compressed files of certain types.

Among the most common multimedia compression schemes currently being used are **JPEG** (pronounced JAY-peg, for Joint Photographic Experts Group), which is commonly used for high-resolution still images, and **MPEG** (pronounced EM-peg, for Motion Picture Experts Group), which is used for full-motion video files (see Figure 8.12). To play MPEG-format audio or video files, you need an MPEG-compliant player, such as Windows Media Player. There are other MPEG-compliant players available, many of which can be downloaded from various sources on the Internet.

Figure 8.12

Many of the most colorful, high-resolution images on Web pages are JPEG-format graphics (right). MPEG compression allows high-quality video and audio to be viewed on the computer screen, whether the source is a compact disk or the Internet (left).

QuickTime and QuickTime VR

The **QuickTime** multimedia file format was developed for use on Apple computers and allowed users to play high-quality audio and video files on the desktop. Today, QuickTime is available for use on Windows-based PCs and Macintosh computers.

To play QuickTime-format files on your desktop, you need either the Apple QuickTime Player or a QuickTime plug-in that will work with your browser. (The plug-in will enable the browser to play QuickTime content directly in the browser window.) The QuickTime Player supports a wide variety of multimedia file formats (see Figure 8.13).

An adaptation of the QuickTime format, called **QuickTime VR,** enables developers to create virtual reality-like environments from flat, two-dimensional images. By stitching together a series of images (such as a series of photographs creating a panoramic view of an entire room or the interior of a car), QuickTime VR can be used to create immersive environments that look and feel a great deal like artificial three-dimensional environments created by expensive VR workstations. You can view QuickTime VR movies in the QuickTime Player or in a Web browser that includes the QuickTime plug-in, as shown in Figure 8.14.

Figure 8.13
Apple's QuickTime Player is commonly used on the Internet for playing music videos, movie trailers, and other streaming video or audio files.

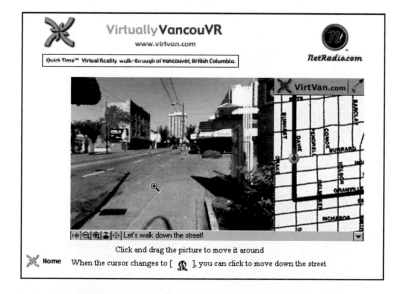

Figure 8.14
Using QuickTime VR movies, the Virtually VancouVR Web site enables you to navigate up and down any street of Vancouver, British Columbia.

Video for Windows (AVI Format)

The **Video for Windows** format was developed by Microsoft as a way to store compressed audio and video information. Video for Windows files use the file-name extension *AVI,* which stands for audio-video interleave. AVI-format files do not provide the resolution or speed available from MPEG, QuickTime, and other audio/video formats. Because AVI files require no special hardware or software, however, they can be played on any Windows computer.

NORTON
ONLINE

Visit **www.glencoe.com/norton/online/** for more information on **QuickTime** and **AVI**.

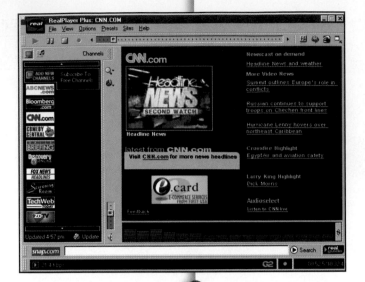

RealAudio and RealVideo

RealNetworks first released the RealAudio Player in 1995, and the program quickly became the standard for playing streaming audio over the Internet. Now called the **RealPlayer,** the product incorporates **RealAudio** and **RealVideo** technologies and can play streaming audio and video broadcast from a World Wide Web site.

The terms *streaming audio* and *streaming video* refer to technologies that enable high-quality audio and video data to be transmitted over an Internet connection. The quality of the streaming audio and video, of course, depends on the speed of your Internet connection and the processing power of your PC. Streaming capabilities are essential to many types of multimedia Web sites, such as the CNN and Weather Channel sites, that broadcast their programming live over the Internet (see Figure 8.15). By using RealNetworks' technologies, artists such as Jimmy Buffet, the Rolling Stones, and others provide music and videos over the Web and can actually broadcast live concerts online.

Figure 8.15
Using RealPlayer technology, Web sites such as CNN Headline News Online can broadcast its television programming over the World Wide Web.

Shockwave

Macromedia Corp. created a stir in 1997 with the release of its Shockwave plug-in. **Shockwave** is part of a suite of products that allows developers to add multimedia content (such as audio, video, and animation) to Web pages. Web designers can create multimedia content and compress it into a Shockwave-format file that can be displayed directly in a Web page. Even though the Shockwave plug-in is required to view "Shocked" Web sites, the Shockwave material appears in the browser window, not in a separate window.

One advantage that Shockwave offers to Web designers is its ability to accept user input. For instance, you may be able to click on or roll your mouse pointer over a Shockwave animation to redirect the animation, cause a different event to occur, or initiate a hypertext jump. Because Shockwave supports user interaction, it can be used to develop online games, puzzles, and other types of fun interactive content (see Figure 8.16).

Visit **www.glencoe.com/norton/online/** for more information on **RealAudio,** **RealVideo,** and **Shockwave.**

Figure 8.16
Using Shockwave content, developers can create interactive games, like this online football game, which can be played live on the Web.

DISTRIBUTING NEW MEDIA CONTENT

An important part of the multimedia development process is understanding how a product will be distributed to its users. Currently, multimedia content is typically delivered to users by one of three means: CD-ROM (or DVD-ROM), the Internet or some sort of network connection, or television. Of course, each delivery technology has its own set of unique strengths and weaknesses. Each delivery method affects the product's ability to use certain technologies, or the user's ability to interact with and direct the content.

CD-ROM

Perhaps the most obvious way to deliver multimedia content is on a compact disk. Because of their large storage capacities, low cost, and ease of use, compact disks were the obvious early choice of multimedia developers who needed a way to put their products in the hands of consumers. Early CD-ROM titles such as *Myst* and *Encarta* were very successful and proved that PCs and gaming consoles could support a wide range of audio and video technologies, hypermedia, and other important types of multimedia content.

Figure 8.17
Despite advances in other delivery technologies, compact disks remain the leading delivery mechanism for multimedia products. Because nearly all new PCs include a CD-ROM drive and other multimedia components, the user base for disk-based products is huge and growing.

By incorporating new technologies such as MPEG, Java, Shockwave, and other formats that allow tightly compressed streaming media, the performance of CD-based products continues to improve. By correlation, the number of products on CD-ROM continues to grow at a tremendous pace (see Figure 8.17).

The Internet

For several years, experts have envisioned the Internet (and, by extension, the individual networks that tie into the Internet) as the ultimate vehicle for multimedia delivery. Consumers have heard endless promises that, because it supports two-way interaction between users and servers, the Internet will someday become *the* place to go for online gaming, shopping, education, and other multimedia experiences—even interactive virtual reality. This dream, however, has been hampered by two problems: limited bandwidth and a lack of technologies that support streaming multimedia content. Fortunately, both problems are getting smaller with time.

As you read earlier, several technologies have recently been developed to support multimedia on the Web. Using plug-in technologies that are powerful but small in size, developers can customize the browser interface to display almost any type of content (see Figure 8.18 on page 174).

Bandwidth is becoming less of an issue for two reasons. First, Web designers are using compression technologies to ensure that Web pages (especially multimedia components) download and function faster than ever. Web sites are also shifting more processing functions away from the server and onto the user's computer, requiring less downloading and uploading time, and freeing the server from certain tasks. These advances make better use of existing bandwidth. Also, more Internet users are adopting high-speed connections.

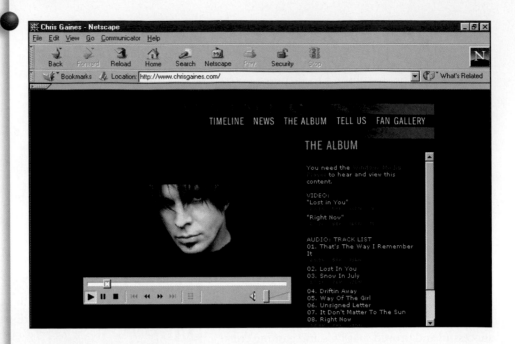

As a result, the availability of online multimedia has exploded. Internet users can easily find games (including multiplayer games involving thousands of participants), music videos, radio and television broadcasts, reference materials, and distance learning resources. These multimedia products perform online with nearly the same speed and responsiveness as CD-ROM-based products.

Television

Television has long been the king of multimedia delivery vehicles. Television, however, is not interactive. It is extremely limited in the types and amount of feedback it can accept from the audience because television has traditionally been a one-way medium. Content travels from the broadcaster to the user, but not vice versa (changing channels does not count). Until recently, it has been difficult or impossible for the viewer to respond in any meaningful way to a television program.

Figure 8.19
Television is slowly becoming more interactive, but only through the addition of technologies such as game devices and Internet connections.

Currently, interactive television is possible to a limited extent, and only because additional technologies have been incorporated with television. You can use your television for playing interactive video games, for example, but this activity is possible only with the addition of a game console and control devices. The games themselves are separate from the television programming you receive through an aerial, cable, or satellite transmission (see Figure 8.19).

Many regional cable television providers are starting to offer high-speed Internet services over existing cable connections. The user simply connects a cable modem to the PC and uses the cable's high bandwidth to carry Internet and broadcast content.

LESSON QUIZ

True/False

Answer the following questions by circling True or False.

True   False   **1.** A medium is simply a means of conveying information.

True   False   **2.** PC-based multimedia events are said to be interactive because they can accept input from the user, unlike a book, movie, or television program.

True   False   **3.** Digital convergence is the practice of using individual technologies in distinct ways, separate from one another.

True   False   **4.** Users of multimedia products are generally more interested in multimedia features than the information, action, or story line offered by the product.

True   False   **5.** The multimedia development process usually involves the efforts of a group of people.

Multiple Choice

Circle the word or phrase that best completes each sentence.

1. The practice of using more than one type of medium at the same time is called _____ .
   A. interactivity   **B.** multimedia   **C.** a computer game

2. In a _____ , the user and program respond to one another.
   A. feedback loop   **B.** head-mounted display   **C.** new media

3. Wending your way through electronic information is called _____ .
   A. interactivity   **B.** multimedia   **C.** navigation

4. Multimedia developers often use a(n) _____ to organize the product.
   A. storyboard   **B.** encoder   **C.** map

5. A problem with television as a distribution method for multimedia content is television's lack of _____ capabilities.
   A. interactive   **B.** streaming   **C.** decoding

LESSON LABS

Complete the following exercises as directed by your instructor.

1. Determine whether your PC is multimedia capable by taking stock of its hardware features. How fast is the processor and how much RAM is available? Does the computer have a color monitor, sound card and speakers, and a CD-ROM (or DVD-ROM) drive? What, if any, components does your system lack that would enable it to support multimedia programs better?

2. To find out if any multimedia software is installed on your system, click the Start button, point to Programs, and inspect the Programs menu. Look for programs like Windows Media Player, QuickTime Player, RealPlayer, and others. Are there any games or reference products installed? If so, look them up and launch them.

LESSON 7: Graphics

Computer Platforms Used for Graphics

- The era of art on personal computers started in 1984 with the release of the first Apple computers. With the advent of Windows, IBM-compatible PCs caught up with the Macintosh in terms of graphics performance. Today, PCs are also used extensively in the graphics and design fields.

- Workstations are reserved for the most demanding graphics applications.

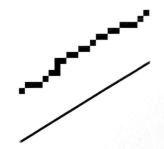

Types of Graphics Files

- Bitmap graphics define images as a series of dots. Vectors define objects in a drawing by using mathematical equations to pinpoint their location and other features.

- A file format is a means of encoding data for storage. There are many different file formats used with graphics.

- Not all file formats work in all programs. This problem is called incompatibility. To solve this problem, developers have created universal file formats that are compatible across various software applications.

Getting Images Into Your Computer

- Scanners enable the user to digitize hard-copy images, such as photographs, so they can be stored and edited in a computer.

- A digital camera stores images in its memory or on a disk until it can be loaded into a computer.

- Clip art and electronic photographs are images that are already available in digital form.

Graphics Software

- Paint programs work with bitmap images and function by managing the individual pixels that make up an image.

- Photo-manipulation programs work with bitmap images and are used to edit digitized photographs.

- Draw programs work with vectors and give the designer a great deal of flexibility in editing an image.

- Computer-Aided Design (CAD) software is used in technical design fields, such as architecture and engineering, to create three-dimensional (3-D) wireframe and solid models of objects that will be built or manufactured.

- Three-dimensional modeling programs are used to create spectacular visual effects.

- Computers can create animation for use in various fields, including games and movies.

Graphics and the World Wide Web

- Using HTML tags and simple graphics, you can add images to a Web page easily.

- The GIF and JPG image formats are the most widely used formats on the World Wide Web.

LESSON 8: Understanding Multimedia

Multimedia, Interactivity, and New Media Defined

■ A medium is a unique means of communicating information, such as speech or text. Multimedia is the use of more than one unique medium at a time.

■ Multimedia programs are described as being interactive if they accept input from the user and thus allow her or him to direct the flow of information or action in the program.

■ The term *new media* is used to describe the combination of multimedia programming and communications technologies that enable multimedia to be distributed in different ways (such as on disk, via the Internet, or over television).

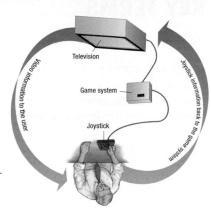

Information in Layers and Dimensions

■ In layered multimedia, multiple types of information may be presented simultaneously. In multidimensional programming, the user can approach information in different ways, such as a text-only description or an animation demonstration.

■ Navigation is the act of moving through electronic information, using navigation tools.

■ When the user chooses a hypermedia link, the program moves to a different piece of information, possibly represented by a different type of media.

Creating New Media Content

■ The development process involves defining the audience, designing the product, choosing development tools, creating content, multimedia authoring, and testing.

■ Using basic tools such as outlines and storyboards, designers lay out and organize the content and flow of the information for their products.

■ Because a multimedia product can use many types of media, designers use a variety of tools, ranging from text editors to video editors, to create individual components.

■ After the components of a multimedia product are created, the developer uses multimedia authoring tools to assemble them into a single working program.

Technologies That Support New Media

■ MPEG, AVI, and QuickTime formats are technologies that allow full-motion video files to be compressed and played back on a PC, whether from a CD or the Internet.

■ The RealAudio and RealVideo formats are the current standard for streaming audio and video played over an Internet connection.

■ Formats such as Macromedia's Shockwave enable developers to create animations that not only display within a browser but also accept input from the user.

Distributing New Media Content

■ The three primary means of distributing new media content are CD-ROM (or DVD-ROM), the Internet, and television.

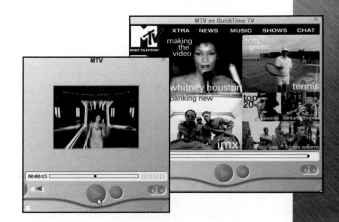

UNIT REVIEW

KEY TERMS

After completing this unit, you should be able to define the following terms.

bitmap, *145*
clip art, *148*
compatible, *147*
Computer-Aided Design (CAD), *152*
computer-generated imagery (CGI), *154*
decode, *170*
digital convergence, *163*
draw program, *151*
encode, *170*
feedback loop, *162*
file format, *146*
frame, *154*
hypermedia, *164*
incompatible, *147*
interactive, *162*
interactive media, *162*
interactivity, *162*
JPEG, *170*
model, *153*
MPEG, *170*

multimedia, *161*
multimedia authoring, *168*
navigation, *164*
new media, *163*
paint program, *149*
photo-manipulation program, *150*
photorealistic, *155*
QuickTime, *171*
QuickTime VR, *171*
RealAudio, *172*
RealPlayer, *172*
RealVideo, *172*
Shockwave, *172*
solid model, *153*
storyboard, *168*
3-D modeling software, *153*
vector, *145*
Video for Windows, *171*
wireframe model, *153*
WYSIWYG, *144*

KEY TERMS QUIZ

Fill in each blank with one of the terms listed under Key Terms.

1. Paint and photo-manipulation programs work with _____ images.

2. With CAD programs, you can create various types of _____ to represent 3-D objects.

3. Someone who is not an artist can use _____ as an easy way to start or enhance digital artwork.

4. If a file format and program do not work together, they are said to be _____ .

5. Graphics files are composed of either bitmaps or a set of _____ .

6. The term _____ refers to the use of more than one type of medium at the same time.

7. By accepting input from the user, interactive media create a(n) _____ .

8. According to the concept of _____ , when various technologies are used, different types of content can converge into a single digital stream.

9. Wending your way through electronic information is commonly called _____ .

10. The _____ format is commonly used for high-resolution, moving images on multimedia products.

REVIEW QUESTIONS

In your own words, briefly answer the following questions.

1. What two products ushered in the era of "art" on personal computers?
2. What kind of images do draw programs enable the user to work with?
3. What device can be used to convert images on paper into a digital graphics file?
4. Where does the term *clip art* come from?
5. What limitations are there with bitmap-based paint programs?
6. Why are CAD programs so accurate?
7. What does the term *interactive media* mean?
8. List the basic steps involved in developing a multimedia product.
9. Why is data compression such an important issue for multimedia developers?
10. Explain how hypermedia allows a user to navigate through digital content without necessarily following a linear sequence.

DISCUSSION QUESTIONS

As directed by your instructor, discuss the following questions in class or in groups.

1. As cheaper and more powerful computers are developed, in what areas of our lives do you think we will see more sophisticated graphics?
2. Think about the issues that must be addressed by television, cable, and satellite companies as interactivity becomes a more integral part of television programming. What interactive programming can you envision? Will television shows and movies as we know them still be produced in thirty years?

ETHICAL ISSUES

Computers and graphics software provide ever-more powerful creative tools to artists and designers. But is there a downside to the explosion of computer graphics? With this thought in mind, discuss the following questions in class.

1. Magazines commonly retouch photographs before printing them, especially on covers. In some cases, editors make the subjects look different from what they look like in reality, and not always for the better. Should this type of retouching be regulated, or do you see it as harmless? Support your position.

2. It is increasingly common to find copyrighted images being used on Web sites, distributed in newsgroups and chat rooms, and in other places. These images are often used without the knowledge or permission of the owner. Do you believe that once an image is digitized, it enters the public domain and no longer belongs to its creator? Why or why not?

UNIT LABS

You and the Computer

Complete the following exercises using a computer in your classroom, lab, or home. No other materials are needed.

1. **Check Your Settings.** The way your PC displays graphics depends a great deal on your monitor's settings. You can easily check your settings and change them if you need better graphics performance. In this exercise, you will learn how to check monitor settings, but do not change them without your instructor's permission. Take the following steps:

   A. Click the Start button, point to Settings, and then click Control Panel. The Control Panel window opens.

   B. Double-click the Display icon. The Display Properties dialog box opens.

   C. Click the Settings tab. Check the settings in the Colors and Screen Area boxes and write them down.

   D. To see the other available color settings for your system, click the Colors drop-down arrow. Review the settings and write them down. (Is yours set to the highest possible color setting?) Then click outside the list to close it without changing anything.

   E. To see the other available resolution settings for your monitor, drag the Screen Area slider control to the right and left. It should display the available settings. Return the slider to its original position.

   F. Click Cancel to close the Display Properties dialog box; then close the Control Panel window.

2. **Set Your Volume.** If your computer has a set of speakers, you can use the Windows volume control to set the volume, mute the speakers, and possibly to configure special effects, such as a 3-D spatializer (if any such effects are installed). Take the following steps:

   A. On the Windows taskbar, double-click the speaker icon. The Volume Control dialog box opens.

   B. Use the slider controls to set the volume and balance for your PC's speakers. If you are not sure which setting to use, simply set them in the middle.

   C. Click the Advanced button to view any other options that may be available for your system. Check these settings, but do not change them.

   D. Close all open dialog boxes; then test your speaker volume by opening the Control Panel window and double-clicking the Sounds icon. When the Sounds Properties dialog box opens, select a sound from the Events list; then click the play button under Preview. Close the dialog box and the Control Panel window.

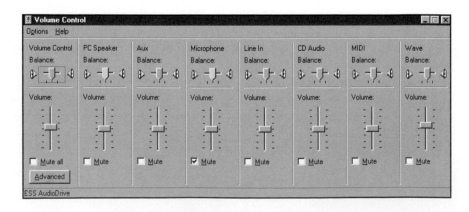

Internet Labs

To complete the following exercises, you will need a computer with an Internet connection and a Web browser. (For more information on using these tools, see "Prerequisites" at the front of this textbook.)

1. **Find Some Interesting Software.** Visit these Web sites for information on a few graphics programs:

- Adobe Systems, Inc.—Adobe makes graphics and desktop publishing programs. Visit **http://www.adobe.com/** and click the Products link.

- JASC, Inc.—JASC makes the PaintShop Pro paint program as well as other graphics tools. Visit **http://www.jasc.com/** and click the Products link.

- Microsoft Corp.—Visio 2000 produces various drawing tools that make the creation of technical drawings easy for people with no design experience. Visit **http://www.microsoft.com/office/visio/** and click the Visio 2000 Overview Tour link.

- Autodesk, Inc.—Autodesk makes CAD, 3-D, animation, and other products used in architecture, engineering, and movie and game design. Visit **http://www.autodesk.com/** and click the Products and Solutions link.

- Macromedia, Inc.—Macromedia makes the Shockwave and Flash plug-ins tools for creating content that use them. The company produces various design tools for graphics, multimedia, and the Web. Visit **http://www.macromedia.com/** and click the Products link.

2. **Check Out Some Audio/Video Players.** Several audio and video players are available for use on a PC. Visit these Web sites for information on a few players:

- RealNetworks, Inc.—For information about RealPlayer, visit **http://www.real.com/**

- Microsoft Corp.—For information about Windows Media Player, visit **http://www.microsoft.com/windows/mediaplayer/default.asp**

- Apple Computer, Inc.—For information on QuickTime and QuickTime VR, visit **http://wwww.apple.com/quicktime/**

IBE Labs

If you have the Interactive Browser Edition (IBE) CD-ROM for this textbook, you may complete the following interactive exercises using the instructions provided in the IBE.

1. **Multimedia or New Media?** Classify the examples provided.

2. **Labeling.** This exercise focuses on types of graphics software.

3. **Scavenger Hunt.** Answer questions about graphics files to reveal pieces of a puzzle.

4. **Build a Multimedia Presentation.** Combine media elements on a screen.

UNIT 5

The Internet and Online Resources

UNIT OBJECTIVES

List two reasons for the Internet's creation.

Describe the two parts of an Internet address.

Name five major features of the Internet.

List two ways in which a PC can access the Internet.

UNIT CONTENTS

This unit contains the following lessons:

Internet Basics

OVERVIEW:
A Growing Influence in Our Lives

By the time it started becoming a household word in the early 1990s, the Internet had existed for more than thirty years. Relatively few people knew what it was, and even fewer had actually used it. By 1994, when people began "surfing the Internet" in large numbers, its potential was only beginning to be understood. Today, the Internet is an inescapable constant in the lives of millions of people around the world, and its reach and usefulness seem almost unlimited.

In fact, the Internet may be one of the most important factors shaping the near future. Its existence has already changed the way many people work, communicate, and do business. The Internet has allowed us to access nearly any kind of information from a PC and has freed us from many kinds of chores. It has given us a new place to shop, study, work, and socialize.

As the "information society" moves forward, an understanding of the Internet may become as important as a college degree, depending on the type of career you want to pursue. Certainly, as a tool for personal communication, research, commerce, and entertainment, the Internet is an indispensable asset you should master. If you use it as a business tool, the Internet will probably be as essential to your job as a word processor, spreadsheet, or any other type of computer application.

This unit introduces you to the basic structure and features of the Internet and shows you how individuals and businesses can connect to the Internet.

OBJECTIVES

- Name the two organizations that created the network now known as the Internet.
- Explain the importance of TCP/IP to the Internet.
- Describe the basic structure of the Internet.
- List the eight major services the Internet provides to its users.

THE INTERNET: THEN AND NOW

The seeds of the Internet were planted in 1969, when the Advanced Research Projects Agency (ARPA) of the U.S. Department of Defense began connecting computers at different universities and defense contractors. The goal of this early project was to create a large computer network with multiple paths—in the form of telephone lines—that could survive a nuclear attack or other disaster. In other words, if one part of the network were destroyed, other parts of the network would remain functional because data could continue to flow through the surviving lines. ARPA also wanted users in remote locations to be able to share scarce computing resources.

Soon after the first links in **ARPANET** (as this early system was called) were in place, the engineers and scientists who had access to this system began exchanging messages and data that were beyond the scope of the Defense Department's original objectives for the project. In addition to exchanging ideas and information related to science and engineering, people also discovered that they could play long-distance games and socialize with other people who shared their interests. The users convinced ARPA that these unofficial uses were helping to test the network's capacity.

At first, ARPANET was basically a wide area network serving only a handful of users, but it expanded rapidly. Initially, the network included four primary host computers. A **host** is like a network server, providing services to other computers that connect to it. ARPANET's host computers (like those on today's Internet) provided file transfer and communications services and gave connected systems access to the network's high-speed data lines. The system grew quickly and spread widely as the number of hosts grew.

The network jumped across the Atlantic to Norway and England in 1973, and it never stopped growing. In the mid-1980s, another federal agency, the National Science Foundation (NSF), joined the project after the Defense Department dropped its funding of the project. NSF established five "supercomputing centers" that were available to anyone who wanted to use them for academic research purposes.

The NSF expected the supercomputers' users to use ARPANET to obtain access but quickly discovered that the existing network could not handle the load. In response, the NSF created a new, higher-capacity network, called **NSFnet,** to complement the older and by then overloaded ARPANET. The link between ARPANET, NSFnet, and other networks was called the **Internet.** The process of connecting separate networks together is called **internetworking.** A collection of "networked networks" is described as being internetworked. This is where the Internet—a worldwide network of networks—gets its name.

NSFnet made Internet connections widely available for academic research, but the NSF did not permit users to conduct private business over the system. Therefore, several private telecommunications companies built their own network backbones that used the same set of networking protocols as NSFnet. Like a tree's trunk or an animal's spine, a network **backbone** is the central structure that connects other elements of the network (see Figure 9.1). These private portions of the Internet were not limited by NSFnet's "appropriate use" restrictions, so it became possible to use the Internet to distribute business and commercial information.

Figure 9.1
At its heart, the Internet uses high-speed data lines, called backbones, to carry huge volumes of traffic. Regional and local networks connect to these backbones, enabling any user on any network to exchange data with any other user on any other network.

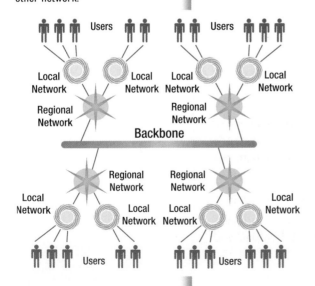

Interconnections (known as gateways) between NSFnet and the private backbones allowed a user on any one of them to exchange data with all the others. Other gateways were created between the Internet and other networks, including some that used different networking protocols.

The original ARPANET was shut down in 1990, and government funding for NSFnet was discontinued in 1995, but the commercial Internet backbone services have easily replaced them. By the early 1990s, interest in the Internet began to expand dramatically. The system that had been created as a tool for surviving a nuclear war found its way into businesses and homes. Now, advertisements for movies are far more common online than collaborations on physics research.

Today, the Internet connects thousands of networks and more than 100 million users around the world. It is a huge, cooperative community with no central ownership. This lack of ownership is an important concept to the Internet, because it means that no single person or group controls the network. Although there are several organizations (such as The Internet Society and the World Wide Web Consortium) that propose standards for Internet-related technologies and guidelines for its appropriate use, these organizations almost universally support the Internet's openness and lack of centralized control.

As a result, the Internet is open to anyone who can access it. If you can use a computer and if the computer is connected to the Internet, you are free not only to use the resources put there by others but to create resources of your own. That is, you can publish documents on the World Wide Web, exchange e-mail messages, and perform many other tasks.

This openness has attracted tens of millions of users to the Internet. As of this writing, it was estimated that more than fifty countries had access and that more than 300 million people will have access to the Internet by the end of 2000. Meantime, the number of actual users continues to climb dramatically, as shown in Figure 9.2.

Figure 9.2
The number of Internet users is expected to continue its dramatic increase for the foreseeable future.

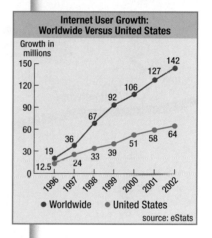

HOW THE INTERNET WORKS

The single most important fact to understand about the Internet is that it can potentially link your computer to any other computer. Anyone with access to the Internet can exchange text, data files, and programs with any other user. For all practical purposes, just about everything that happens across the Internet is a variation of one of these activities. The Internet itself is the pipeline that carries data between computers.

TCP/IP: The Universal Language of the Internet

The Internet works because every computer connected to it uses the same set of rules and procedures (known as protocols) to control timing and data format. The protocols used by the Internet are called **Transmission Control Protocol/Internet Protocol (TCP/IP).**

The TCP/IP protocols include the specifications that identify individual computers and exchange data between computers. They also include rules for several categories of application programs, so programs that run on different kinds of computers can talk to one another. For example, someone using a Macintosh computer can exchange data with a UNIX computer on the Internet.

NORTON
ONLINE

Visit **www.glencoe.com/norton/online/** for more information on **TCP/IP**.

TCP/IP software looks different on different kinds of computers, but it always presents the same appearance to the network. It does not matter if the system at the other end of a connection is a supercomputer, a pocket-size personal communications device, or anything between; as long as it recognizes TCP/IP protocols, it can send and receive data through the Internet.

Routing Traffic Across the Internet

Most computers are not connected directly to the Internet. Rather, they are connected to smaller networks that connect through gateways to the Internet backbone. Figure 9.3 shows a typical Internet connection.

The core of the Internet is the set of backbone connections that tie the local and regional networks together and the routing scheme that controls the way each piece of data finds its destination. In networking diagrams, the Internet backbone is often portrayed as a big cloud because the routing details are less important than the fact that the data passes through the Internet between the origin and the destination.

The basic model for most Internet tools can be described as follows. A client application on a user's computer requests data through the network from a server. As you learned in Unit 2, a server is a powerful computer, generally containing a large hard disk, that acts as a shared storage resource. In addition to containing stored files, a server may also act as a gatekeeper for access to programs or data from other computers. The Internet includes many thousands of servers, each with its own unique address. These servers, in tandem with routers and bridges, do the work of storing and transferring data across the network.

Figure 9.3
In a typical Internet connection, individual computers connect to a local or regional network, which is connected, in turn, to the Internet backbone via a gateway.

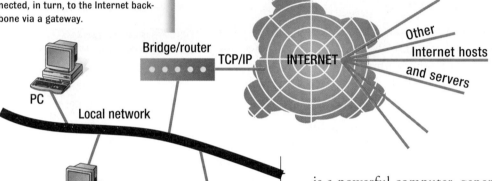

Because the Internet creates a potential connection between any two computers, the data may be forced to take a long, circuitous route to reach its destination. Suppose that you request data from a server in another state:

1. Your request must be broken into packets.

2. The packets are routed through your local network, and possibly through one or more subsequent networks, to the Internet backbone.

3. After leaving the backbone, the packets are then routed through one or more networks until they reach the appropriate server and are reassembled into the complete request.

4. After the destination server receives your request, it begins sending the requested data, which winds its way back to you—possibly over another route.

Along the way between the destination server and your PC, the request and data may travel through several different servers, each helping to forward the packets to their final destination.

Addressing Schemes—IP and DNS Addresses

Internet activity can be defined as computers communicating with one another by using the common "language" of TCP/IP. Examples include the following:

◆ A client system (such as your home computer) communicating with an Internet server

◆ An Internet server computer communicating with a client computer

◆ Two server computers communicating with one another

◆ Two client computers communicating via one or more servers

The computer that originates a transaction must identify its intended destination with a unique address. Every computer on the Internet has a four-part numeric address, called the **Internet protocol address (IP address),** which contains routing information that identifies its location. Each of the four parts is a number between 0 and 255, so an IP address looks like this:

205.46.117.104

Computers have no trouble working with big strings of numbers, but humans are not so skilled. Therefore, most computers on the Internet (except those used exclusively for internal routing and switching) also have an address called a **domain name system (DNS) address**—an address that uses words rather than numbers.

Visit **www.glencoe.com/norton/online/** for more information on **IP addresses** and the **domain name system.**

Domains and Subdomains

DNS addresses have two parts: a host name (a name for a computer connected to the Internet), followed by a **domain** that generally identifies the type of institution that uses the address. This type of domain name is often called a top-level domain. Examples are *.com* for commercial businesses or *.edu* for schools, colleges, and universities. The University of Washington's DNS address is washington.edu; Microsoft's is microsoft.com. This domain is the "dot com" you hear mentioned in advertisements. Many companies now have a DNS address whose first part is the company name, followed by ".com"—hence the now-overused marketing gimmick. Within the United States, the last three letters of the domain usually tell what type of institution owns the computer. Table 9.1 lists the most common types.

Table 9.1	Internet Domains	
Domain	**Type of Organization**	**Example**
.com	Business (commercial)	ibm.com (International Business Machines Corp.)
.edu	Educational	centre.edu (Centre College, Danville, KY)
.gov	Government	whitehouse.gov (The White House)
.mil	Military	navy.mil (The United States Navy)
.net	Gateway or host (or business/commercial)	mindspring.net (Mindspring, a regional Internet service provider)
.org	Other organization (typically nonprofit)	isoc.org (The Internet Society)

Some large institutions and corporations divide their domain addresses into smaller **subdomains.** For example, a business with many branches might have a subdomain for each office—such as boston.widgets.com and newyork.widgets.com. You might also see some subdomains broken into even smaller sub-subdomains, such as evolution.genetics.washington.edu.

Outside the United States (although many institutions and businesses in the United States are starting to use this same address scheme), domains usually identify the country in which the system is located, such as *.ca* for Canada or *.fr* for France. Sometimes, a geographic domain address will also include a subdomain that identifies the district within the larger domain. For example, a business in the Canadian province of British Columbia might have companyname.bc.ca as its DNS address. Some United States institutions such as colleges and elementary schools use the same expanded address scheme. For example, some community colleges include *cc* in their DNS address, whereas some schools include *K12* in their address.

MAJOR FEATURES OF THE INTERNET

The technical details that make the Internet work are only part of the story. The reason that so many people use the Internet has more to do with content than connectivity. For many users, it is a valuable source of news, business communication, entertainment, and technical information.

As a business tool, the Internet has many uses. Electronic mail is an efficient and inexpensive way to send messages and documents around the world. The World Wide Web is both an important advertising medium and a channel for distributing software, documents, and information services. Researchers find that online databases and archives are often more extensive and up-to-date than any library.

To use any of these services, you need a computer that is connected to the Internet in some way. Most individual users connect their computer's modem to a telephone line and set up an account with an **Internet service provider (ISP),** which provides local or regional access to the Internet backbone. Many other users connect to the Internet through a school or business LAN. These methods of connecting to the Internet are discussed later in this unit. The following sections introduce some of the most popular features of the Internet.

The World Wide Web

The **World Wide Web** (the **Web** or **WWW**) was created in 1989 at the European Particle Physics Laboratory in Geneva, Switzerland, as a method for incorporating footnotes, figures, and cross-references into online hypertext documents. A hypertext document is a specially encoded file that uses the **hypertext markup language (HTML).** This language allows a document's author to embed **hypertext links** (also called **hyperlinks** or just **links**) in the document. Hypertext links are the very foundation of the World Wide Web.

As you read a hypertext document—more commonly called a **Web page**—on screen, you can click a word or picture encoded as a hypertext link and immediately jump to another location within the same document or to a different Web page (see Figure 9.4). The second page may be located on the same computer as the original page or anywhere else on the Internet. Because the user does not have to learn separate commands and addresses to jump to a new location, the World Wide Web organizes widely scattered resources into a seamless whole.

NORTON
ONLINE

Visit **www.glencoe.com/norton/online/** for more information on **HTML** and the World Wide Web.

Examples of hyperlinks

When the user clicks the "Business" link, a new Web page opens in the browser window.

A collection of related Web pages is called a **Web site.** Web sites are housed on **Web servers,** Internet host computers that often store thousands of individual pages. When a Web designer copies a page onto a server, the process is called **posting** the page, but it may also be referred to as publishing or uploading. (The term *posting* is also used when other types of documents are placed on Internet host computers, such as posting an article in a newsgroup.)

Popular Web sites (such as those managed by CNN, USA Today, and ESPN) receive millions of **hits** or **page views** every day. When you visit a Web page—that is, download the page from the Web server to your computer for viewing—the action is commonly called "hitting" the Web site. Many Web masters measure their sites' success by the number of hits they receive in a given period of time (see Figure 9.5). A **Web master** is a person or group responsible for designing and maintaining a Web site.

You are visitor Number **139426** to this page!

Web Browsers and HTML Tags

The Web was an interesting but not particularly exciting tool used by scientific researchers—until 1993, when Mosaic, a point-and-click Web browser, was developed at the National Center for Supercomputing Applications (NCSA) at the University of Illinois. A **Web browser** (or **browser**) is a software application designed to find hypertext documents on the Web and then open the documents on the user's computer. A point-and-click browser provides a graphical user interface that allows the user to click graphical objects and hyperlinks. There are also several text-based Web browsers available that are used in non-GUI operating systems, such as certain versions of UNIX. Mosaic and the Web browsers that have evolved from it have changed the way people use the Internet. The most popular browsers are Microsoft's Internet Explorer and Netscape Navigator.

A Web browser displays a Web page as specified by the page's underlying HTML code. The code provides the browser with the following information:

◆ The fonts and font sizes used in the page

◆ Where and how to display graphical images

◆ Whether sound, animation, or other special types of content are included in the page and how to display them

◆ The location of hypertext links and where to go if the user clicks a link

◆ Whether special programming codes, which the browser needs to interpret, are used in the page

When you view a Web page in a browser window, you see only the content as the page's designer intended it to appear. Note, however, that different browser versions may interpret HTML codes differently, so an HTML document may actually look different when displayed in different browsers. For this reason, professional Web designers try to create documents that will look the same in different browsers. The HTML codes are hidden unless you display them in the browser window or in another application. To format a document in HTML, a designer places **HTML tags** throughout the document. The tags, which are enclosed in angle brackets (<>), tell the browser how to display individual elements on the page.

HTML tags are placed around the portions of the document they affect. Most tags, therefore, have a starting tag, such as <H1>, and an ending tag, such as </H1>. A slash indicates an ending tag. If you wanted to format a line of text as a primary heading, you would format it this way:

<H1>My Favorite Links</H1>

The formatting begins with the starting tag and continues to the ending tag. This placement of tags permits precise formatting control within a document. Tags can also be grouped: multiple starting and ending tags can be placed around the same portion of a document.

Figures 9.6 and 9.7 show a simple example of HTML at work with the use of the <strong> tag, which tells browsers to display text in a bold font. In Figure 9.6, the user has created a simple HTML-format file containing one line of text. Because the user surrounded the line with the HTML tags <strong> and </strong>, the browser will display the line in bold text, as shown in Figure 9.7. Even though the tags are part of the document, they do not appear in the browser window.

Figure 9.6
A simple HTML document. The "strong" tag tells the browser to display the enclosed text in a bold font.

Figure 9.7
The document, opened in a Web browser. The text appears in bold.

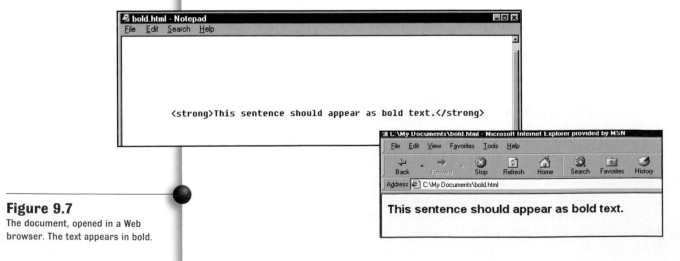

HTTP and URLs

The internal structure of the World Wide Web is built on a set of rules called **Hypertext transfer protocol (HTTP).** HTTP uses Internet addresses in a special format, called a **uniform resource locator (URL).** URLs look like the following:

type://address/path/

In a URL, *type* specifies the type of server in which the file is located, *address* is the address of the server, and *path* is the location within the file structure of the server. The path includes the list of folders (or directories) where the desired file is located. Consider the URL for this book's Web site—http://www.glencoe .com/norton/online/—as shown in Figure 9.8.

If you were looking for a document named *Welcome* at this Web site, its URL might be:

http://www.glencoe.com/norton
/online/welcome.html

Files in other formats may also have URLs. For example, look at the URL for the SunSite FTP archive of PC software at the University of North Carolina:

ftp://sunsite.unc.edu/pub/micro/pc-stuff/

Note that when a URL ends with a folder name rather than a file, the URL includes a final slash character (/).

Because they lead to specific documents on a server's disk, URLs can be long. Regardless, every single document on the World Wide Web has its own unique URL (see Figure 9.9).

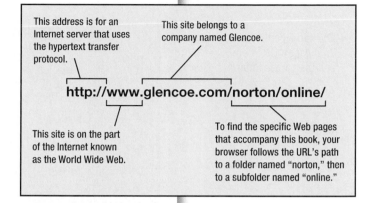

Figure 9.8
Parts of a typical URL.

This address is for an Internet server that uses the hypertext transfer protocol.

This site belongs to a company named Glencoe.

http://www.glencoe.com/norton/online/

This site is on the part of the Internet known as the World Wide Web.

To find the specific Web pages that accompany this book, your browser follows the URL's path to a folder named "norton," then to a subfolder named "online."

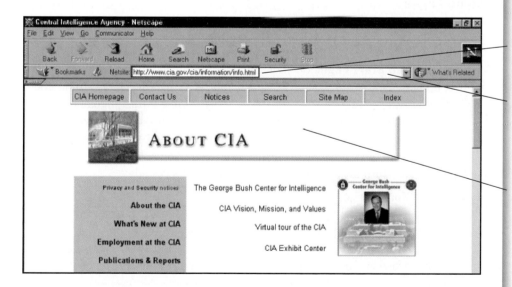

Figure 9.9
Each Web page has its own unique URL, which directs your browser to the document's location.

URL

The browser's address box displays the URL of the current Web page.

Document (Web page being viewed)

As shown in Figure 9.10 on page 192, you use URLs to navigate the Web in two ways:

A. Type the URL for a Web site in the address box of your browser. For example, if you want to visit the Web site of the Internal Revenue Service, click in the browser's address box (to place an insertion point there) and type as follows:

http://www.irs.gov/

Visit **www.glencoe.com/norton/online/** for more information on **HTTP** and **URLs**.

Figure 9.10

You can move from one Web page to another by specifying a URL or clicking a hyperlink. Both navigation methods take you to the same place.

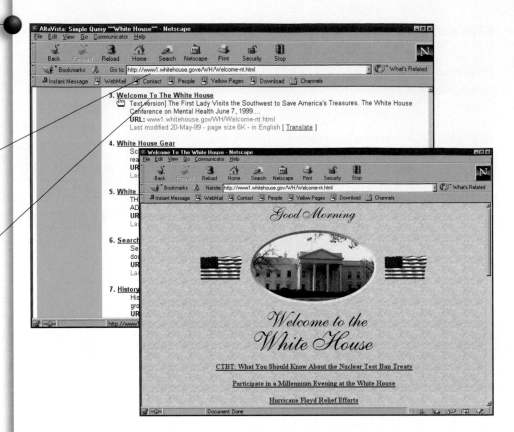

You can type the desired Web page's URL here, and then press Enter.

You can click a hyperlink.

B. Click a hyperlinked word or image, and your browser automatically finds and loads the Web page indicated by the hyperlink. When you point to a hyperlink, the browser's status bar displays the URL to which the link leads.

Home Pages

You have probably heard the term **home page** used to refer to a page named index.htm on a Web site. This term is important, and it has two meanings:

◆ **Personalized Start Page.** On your computer, you can choose a Web page that opens immediately when you launch your Web browser. Use a command in your browser to specify the URL for the desired page. This page is a personalized start page, and it can be on your computer's hard drive or a page from any Web site. For example, if you want to see today's copy of USA Today Online when you launch your browser, you can use the address **http://www.usatoday.com/** as your personalized start page.

◆ **Web Site Home Page.** A Web site's primary page is also called its home page. This page is the first page you see when you enter the site's basic URL in your browser. From this page, you can navigate to other pages on the Web site (and possibly to other sites). For example, if you type the URL **http://www.cnn.com/** into your browser's address box, the CNN home page opens in your browser window.

Helper Applications and Multimedia Content

As versatile as they are, Web browsers alone cannot display every type of content now available on the Web, especially multimedia content. Many Web sites now feature audio and video content, including full-motion animation and movies. These large files require special applications in order to be played in real time across the Web.

Visit **www.glencoe.com/norton/online/** for more information on **helper applications for browsers.**

Because these applications help the browser by being "plugged in" at the right moment, they are called **helper applications** or **plug-in applications.**

Plug-ins are used to support several types of content, including streaming audio and streaming video. Streaming technology works by sending the audio or video content in a continuous stream. The plug-in application receives a portion of the stream and stores it temporarily in a buffer (an area in memory or on disk). After a portion of the stream has been buffered, it is played while the next portion of the stream is stored in the buffer. This buffer-and-play technique is an effective method for playing a large file quickly without waiting for the entire file to download. Multimedia plug-in applications also use file compression to move the process even faster. Even with these techniques, multimedia files can take much longer to download than typical HTML documents.

Figure 9.11
QuickTime Player, RealPlayer, and other multimedia plug-in applications allow you to enjoy streaming audio and video from different sources.

There is a tremendous array of multimedia content available on the Web. For example, sites like broadcast.com, netradio.com, and even Microsoft provide access to radio stations from around the world in addition to Internet-only radio. Television channels such as CNN and The Weather Channel also deliver their audio and video content over the Web. Using plug-in applications such as Microsoft's Windows Media Player, Apple's QuickTime player, or Real Networks' RealPlayer, you can play any of these sources on your desktop (see Figure 9.11).

One of the most commonly used plug-in applications is made by Macromedia, Inc. This tool, called Shockwave, enables Web designers to create high-quality animation or video, complete with audio, that plays directly within the browser window. These types of animation do not require the browser to spawn (launch) an external application for viewing, as is the case with multimedia types displayed in Windows Media Player, QuickTime, and others. The Shockwave player is essential if you want to view many newer Web sites and is available for free from the Macromedia Web site (**www.macromedia.com/**).

Figure 9.12
VRML-enabled Web sites let you move through three-dimensional virtual worlds and interact with animated characters. At this site, you can practice virtual scuba diving.

Another popular type of multimedia content is three-dimensional (3-D) animation. By using a plug-in application to add 3-D viewing capabilities to your browser, you can visit 3-D worlds filled with buildings, landscapes, and animated characters, and navigate them as you would a video game. By using technologies such as **virtual reality modeling language (VRML),** Web designers create virtual worlds for Web users to explore (see Figure 9.12). To visit VRML-enabled Web sites, you need either a VRML browser or (the more common choice) a VRML plug-in application for your standard browser. Several VRML plug-ins, including Live3D, Cosmo Player, and others, are available for free.

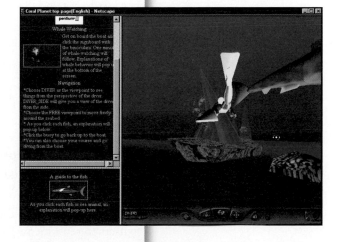

Finding Content With a Search Engine

The Web's greatest advantage is that it provides access to huge quantities of information. But the vastness of its resources is also one of the Web's greatest drawbacks. Without a directory to help you find just the right information or Web site, you could literally spend hours going from one site to another, trying to find what you need.

Fortunately, several specialized Web sites, called **search engines,** have sprung up. These sites use powerful data-searching techniques to discover the type of content available on the Web, where the content is stored, and more. By using a search engine, you can find the right site or information by specifying your topic of interest. For example, if you need to find information on Aristotle, you can visit a search engine site such as Alta Vista or Lycos and type *Aristotle* in the site's Search box. The search engine will provide you with a list of sites that should match your criterion (see Figure 9.13). For more detailed instructions on using search engines, see "Prerequisites" at the front of this textbook.

Figure 9.13
The Alta Vista search engine found more than 92,000 Web pages containing information relating to the term *Aristotle*.

Type a term in the Search For box; then click the Search button.

You can click a category or site to jump to it.

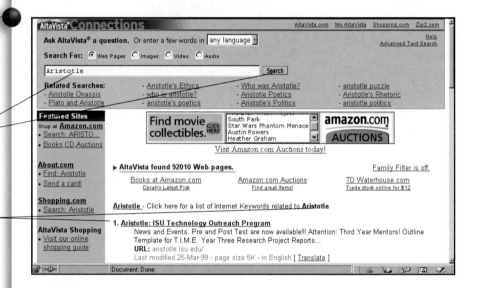

Electronic Mail (E-Mail)

Just as users of a corporate LAN can send e-mail messages to one another, Internet users can exchange e-mail. In fact, the single most common use of the Internet is for the exchange of electronic mail, or e-mail. In 1999 alone, nearly 500 million e-mail messages were transmitted over the Internet. As more people go online, that number will certainly increase.

To create, send, and receive e-mail, you need an **e-mail program** (also called an e-mail client) and an Internet connection through an ISP or LAN. Most e-mail programs permit users to attach data files and program files to messages. For example, you can send a message to a friend and attach a word processing document or some other file to the message. The recipient can then open and use the document on his or her computer. Popular Internet e-mail programs include Eudora, Microsoft Outlook, and Netscape Messenger, among others.

If you have an account with an ISP, or if you are a user on a corporate or school LAN, then you can establish an **e-mail address.** This unique address allows other users to send messages to you and you to send messages to others.

As mentioned earlier, DNS addresses and numeric IP addresses identify individual computers on the Internet. Any single computer might have many separate users, however, and each user must have an account on that computer. A user can set up such an account by specifying a unique **user name.** Some of the largest domains, such as America Online (aol.com) may have millions of different users, each with his or her own user name.

When you send a message to a person rather than a computer, you must include that person's user name in the address. The standard format is the user name first, separated from the DNS address by an "at" symbol (@). For example, suppose you have a friend named John Smith who works (and has an e-mail account) at a company called Widgets, Inc. If the company's DNS address is widgets.com, then John Smith's e-mail address might be

jsmith@widgets.com

You would read this address as "J Smith at widgets dot com." Figure 9.14 shows how addresses are used in e-mail programs.

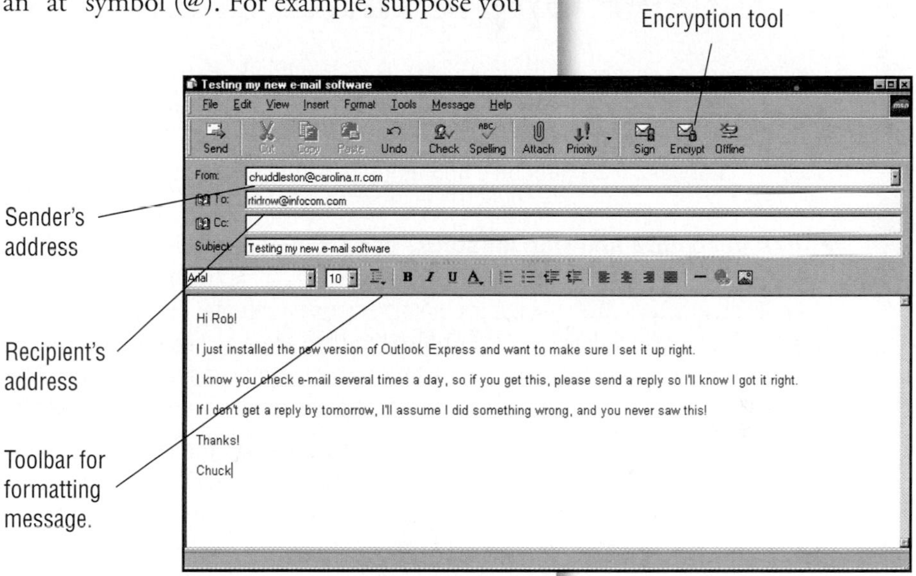

When you send an e-mail message to someone, the message is stored on a server until the recipient can retrieve it. This type of server is called a **mail server.** Many mail servers use the post office protocol and are called POP servers. Nearly all ISPs and corporate LANs maintain one or more mail servers specifically to store and forward e-mail messages.

Figure 9.14

User addresses enable people to send and receive e-mail messages over the Internet. Most e-mail programs provide tools for formatting messages and encoding them for security.

Encryption tool

Sender's address

Recipient's address

Toolbar for formatting message.

Self Check

Answer the following questions by filling in the blank(s).

1. The network that eventually became the Internet was first called

    _____ .

2. Every computer on the Internet has a numeric address called its

    _____ .

3. Hypertext links are more commonly called _____ .

News

In addition to the messages distributed to mailing lists by e-mail, the Internet also supports a form of public bulletin board called **news.** As of this writing, there were more than 45,000 **newsgroups,** each devoted to discussions of a particular topic. Many of the most widely distributed newsgroups are part of a system called **Usenet,** but others are targeted to a particular region or to users connected to a specific network or institution, such as a university or a large corporation.

COMPUTERS
in your career

Career Opportunities and the Internet

Many careers are associated with the Internet, including network administrators, information system professionals, and data communications managers. Aside from careers that focus on architecture and administration of the Internet, many other professions require not only a working knowledge of the Internet but a mastery of the tools used to create and distribute content across it. Here are a few such careers:

◆ **Web Designers and Web Masters.** Corporate Web, intranet, and extranet sites are often developed, designed, and maintained by teams of professionals. At the helm of such teams are experienced designers and Web masters. Web designers bring various traditional design skills to the table—such as experience with graphics, text design, and layout—but they are also skilled with HTML tools and scripting languages. Web masters often provide more technical skills required for high-level network support. One or both of these leaders must also have management skills to direct and coordinate the efforts of a design team.

◆ **Multimedia Developers.** As more people connect to the Internet, companies face increasing competition to provide highly visual, interactive content to capture and retain visitors to their Web sites. This need has already driven up the demand for multimedia developers who can design content for the Internet, particularly the Web. To become marketable in this field, you need a thorough background in multimedia authoring and distribution. These specialists also benefit from programming skills, using languages such as Java, VisualBasic, and others that are widely used on the Internet.

◆ **Programmers.** Programmers are finding all sorts of opportunities in Internet development because Web sites are commonly used to support high-level functions such as interactivity, searches, data mining, and more. To get involved in Internet-related products, these programmers learn a wide variety of languages, including Perl, VisualBasic, Java, C++, and others.

◆ **Writers and Editors.** Just as the Internet has changed the way multimedia content is delivered, it has also changed the way books, periodicals, and other printed media are delivered and viewed by consumers. Most publishing houses and newspapers require their writers and editors to work electronically and to deliver manuscript and articles via the Internet or other network. Many writers must also know how to create content for the Internet and be familiar with HTML. Similarly, editors should know how to work with HTML documents and how to deliver these pages to an Internet site for publication.

Web site design is often done by teams of people, which may include graphic artists, writers and editors, formatters, researchers, programmers, and professionals with expertise in other disciplines.

To participate in a newsgroup, users post **articles** (short messages) about the newsgroup's main topic. As users read and respond to one another's articles, they create a **thread** of linked articles (see Figure 9.15). By reading the articles in a thread, you can see the message that initiated the discussion and all the messages that have been posted in response to it.

Figure 9.15
A series of articles and responses create a thread, or ongoing discussion, in a newsgroup.

rec.scuba.locations - Outlook Express provided by MSN			
File Edit View Tools Message Help			
New Post Reply Group Reply Forward Print Stop Send/Recv Addresses Find Newsgroups			

Subject	From	Sent ▽	Size
Diving in Kaui	Richard Gale	10/05/19...	1KB
Re: Diving in Kaui	PRivas7778	10/06/19...	1KB
Re: Diving in Kaui	Gordon/Carol/...	10/09/19...	1KB
Diving from Cancun ? Getting to Cozumel From Cancun	George Schyver	10/05/1999 ...	1KB
Re: Diving from Cancun ? Getting to Cozumel From Cancun	Rudy Benner	10/05/19...	1KB
Re: Diving from Cancun ? Getting to Cozumel From Cancun	dmilbury	10/05/19...	1KB
Re: Diving from Cancun ? Getting to Cozumel From Cancun	David Souther...	10/06/19...	1KB
Re: Diving from Cancun ? Getting to Cozumel From Cancun	Wade Norton	10/09/19...	2KB
Re: Diving from Cancun ? Getting to Cozumel From Cancun	Gordon/Carol/...	10/09/19...	2KB
Spanish Bay Reef Resort, Grand Cayman	Tigger	10/05/19...	1KB
Re: Spanish Bay Reef Resort, Grand Cayman	David Berry	10/06/19...	3KB
Re: Spanish Bay Reef Resort, Grand Cayman	Rita Daggett	10/07/19...	2KB

These messages form a thread.

A **newsreader** program—the client software—obtains articles from a **news server,** a host computer that exchanges articles with other servers through the Internet. To participate in newsgroups, you must run a newsreader program to log on to a server. Most ISPs provide news access to a news server as part of an Internet account.

To see articles that have been posted about a specific topic, you can **subscribe** to the newsgroup that addresses that topic. Newsgroups are organized into major categories, called domains, and are categorized by individual topics within each domain. Several major domains are part of the Usenet structure, and there are many more alternative domains. Table 9.2 lists the major Usenet domains.

Table 9.2	Common Usenet Domains
Domain	**Description**
comp	Computer-related topics
sci	Science and technology (except computers)
soc	Social issues and politics
news	Topics related to Usenet
rec	Hobbies, arts, and recreational activities
misc	Topics that do not fit into one of the other domains
The most important alternative topics include the following:	
alt	Alternative newsgroups
bionet	Biological sciences
biz	Business topics, including advertisements
clari	News from the Associated Press and Reuters, supplied through a service called Clarinet
k12	Newsgroups for primary and secondary schools

NORTON ONLINE

Visit **www.glencoe.com/norton/online/** for more information on **Internet newsgroups**.

Newsgroup names can be quite long. The name of a newsgroup begins with the domain, followed by one or more words that describe the group's topic, such as alt.food. Some topics include separate newsgroups for related subtopics, such as alt.food.chocolate.

As Figure 9.16 shows, subscribing to a newsgroup is a three-step process. To subscribe, you must download a list of available newsgroups from the server, choose the groups that interest you, and select articles. In most newsreaders, you can choose to reply to an article by posting another article to the newsgroup or by sending a private e-mail message to the person who wrote the original article.

Figure 9.16
Subscribing to a newsgroup.

Step 1: Download list of available newsgroups.

Step 3: Select the article that you want to read.

This is the article.

Step 2: Choose the group that interests you.

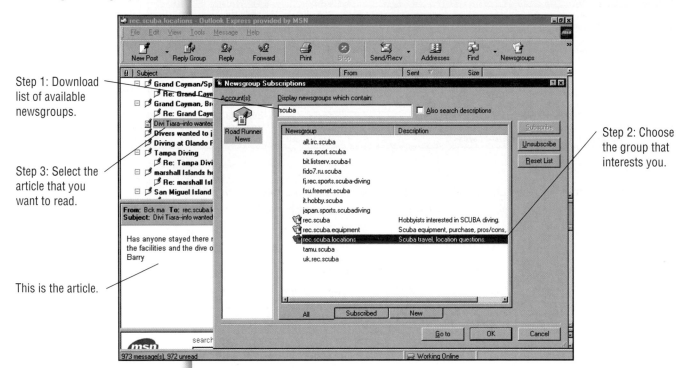

Newsgroups are a relatively fast way to distribute information to potentially interested readers, and they allow people to discuss topics of common interest. They can also be a convenient channel for finding answers to questions. Many questions tend to be asked again and again, so it is always a good idea to read the articles that other people have posted before you jump in with your own questions. Members of many newsgroups post lists of **frequently asked questions (FAQs)** and their answers every month or two.

Remember that, although newsgroups can be a good source of information, there is no fact-checking process for newsgroups. For this reason, newsgroups are also one of the biggest sources of misinformation and rumors on the Internet. Be careful about the information you choose as reliable.

Telnet—Remote Access to Distant Computers

Telnet is the Internet tool for using one computer to access a second computer. With Telnet, you can send commands that run programs and open text or data files. The Telnet program is a transparent window between your own computer and a distant host system—a computer that you are logging on to. Even though the computer is in a different physical place, it is as if you are sitting in front of it

Visit www.glencoe.com/norton/online/
for more information on **Telnet** and FTP.

and operating it. A Telnet connection sends input from your keyboard to the host and displays text from the host on your screen.

Connecting to a Telnet host is easy; enter the address, and the Telnet program sets up a connection. When you see a log-on message from the host, you can send an account name and password to start an operating session. Access to some Telnet hosts is limited to users with permission from the owner of the host, but many other hosts offer access to members of the general Internet public.

Telnet connections are useful for many purposes. For example, Figure 9.17 shows a Telnet connection to a library's online catalog. You can obtain information about books in the library's collection over the Internet as easily as you can from the library's own reference room. Telnet also provides access to online conferences.

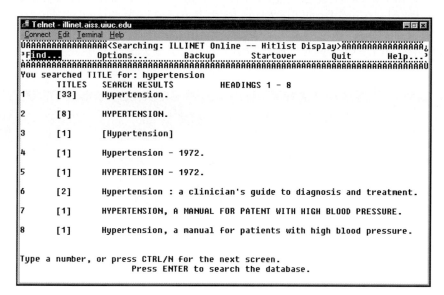

Figure 9.17
A Telnet connection to a library catalog. The user is searching for magazine and journal articles on the subject of hypertension.

FTP

You can use Telnet to operate a distant computer by remote control through the Internet, but sometimes there is no substitute for having your own copy of a program or data file. **File transfer protocol (FTP)** is the Internet tool for copying files from one computer to another.

When a user has accounts on more than one computer, FTP can be used to transfer data or programs between them. Public FTP archives are available and will allow anyone to make copies of their files. These FTP sites are housed on FTP servers—archives often containing thousands of individual programs and files. Anyone can download and use these files with the help of special FTP client software (see Figure 9.18). Because these public archives usually require visitors to use the word *anonymous* as an account name, they are known as **anonymous FTP archives.**

It is not always necessary to use an FTP client to download files from an FTP site.

Figure 9.18
Here is a popular FTP client program named WS_FTP LE. It is being used to transfer a file named assist.exe from Microsoft's anonymous FTP site (the remote site) to the user's computer (the local system).

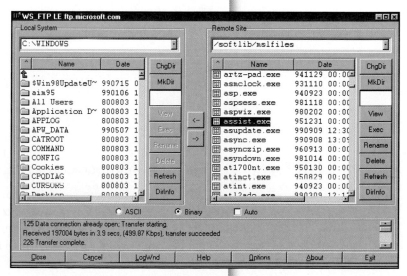

Web browsers also support FTP. In fact, if you visit a Web site such as Microsoft (**www.microsoft.com/**) or Macromedia (**www.macromedia.com/**), you can download programs and data files directly onto your computer through your Web browser. This type of file transfer usually is an FTP operation and is available through many different Web sites.

Although FTP is easy to use, it can be hard to find a file that you want to download. One way to find files is to use **Archie,** the searchable index of FTP archives maintained by McGill University in Montreal. (Archie is a nickname for archives.) The main Archie server at McGill gathers copies of the directories from more than 1000 other public FTP archives every month and distributes copies of those directories to dozens of other servers around the world. When a server receives a request for a keyword search, it returns a list of files that match the search criteria and the location of each file. Many FTP client programs provide Archie search tools, and some Web sites allow you to conduct Archie searches through your Web browser (as shown in Figure 9.19).

Figure 9.19
Web sites like this one allow you to use Archie for a file search on the Internet. Here, the user is searching for files related to the keyword *hypertext*.

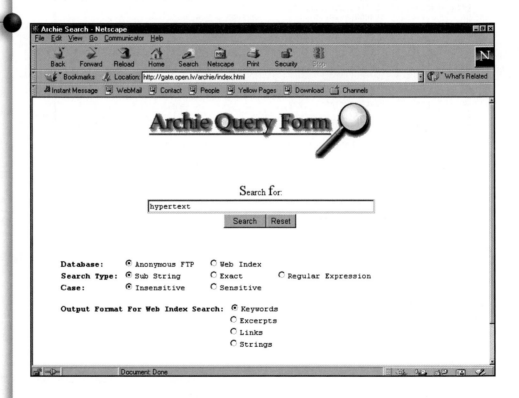

Internet Relay Chat (IRC)

Internet relay chat (IRC), or just **chat,** is a popular way for Internet users to communicate in real-time with other users. Real-time communication means communicating with other users in the present. Unlike e-mail, chat does not require a waiting period between the time you send a message and the time the other person or group of people receives the message. IRC is often referred to as the "CB radio" of the Internet because it enables a few or many people join to a discussion.

IRC is a multi-user system where people join channels to talk publicly or in private. **Channels** are discussion groups where chat users convene to discuss a topic. Chat messages are typed on a user's computer and sent to the IRC channel, whereupon all users who have joined that channel receive the message. Users can then read, reply to, or ignore that message, or create their own message (see Figure 9.20).

Using instant messenger software—like America Online's Instant Messenger, Microsoft's MSN Messenger Service, or Mirabilis' ICQ—you can set up "buddy lists" of people with whom you like to chat. When you and a buddy are online at the same time, you can open a new window on your computer and begin a private chat session. For example, ICQ can notify you when a buddy goes online so that you can begin chatting.

Instant messenger applications are gaining popularity because they give users more control over their chatting environment than traditional IRC channels, which are open to anyone who wants to join. Chat rooms are also an increasingly popular addition to Web sites. Their popularity in this forum makes it possible to participate in chat sessions directly within a Web browser window without installing or running special chat software (see Figure 9.21).

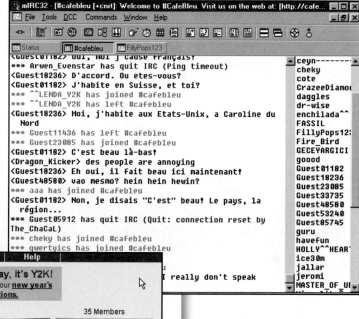

Figure 9.20
A chat in progress. In this chat program (mIRC), the discussions appear in the lefthand pane, and the participants' names appear on the right.

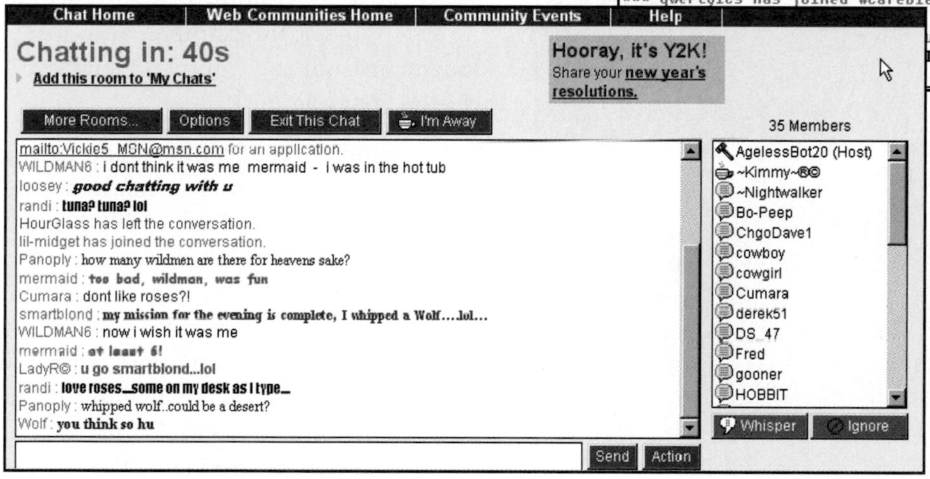

Figure 9.21
Many Web sites, including MSN, CNN, and others, provide chat rooms for visitors. At these sites, you can chat without navigating channels or using special chat software.

ONLINE SERVICES

An **online service** is a company that offers access, generally on a subscription basis, to e-mail, discussion groups, databases on various subjects (such as weather information, stock quotes, newspaper articles, and so on), and other services ranging from electronic banking and investing to online games. Online services also offer access to the Internet, functioning as an ISP to their subscribers. The most popular online services are America Online, CompuServe, and Prodigy.

In addition to Internet access, online services offer other features that typical ISPs do not. For example, America Online has become famous for its casual chat rooms, and CompuServe is probably best known for its discussion forums geared to technically oriented users. These activities do not take place on the Internet, where everyone can access them. Rather, these services are provided only for subscribers to those online services. Discussion groups hosted by online services are often monitored by a **system operator,** or **sysop,** who ensures that participants follow the rules.

INTERNET-RELATED FEATURES IN APPLICATION PROGRAMS

To access most of the services on the Internet, you can use stand-alone applications such as the Web browsers, e-mail clients, and other types of software described so far. However, many popular productivity applications now feature various Internet-related applications. These features enable you to perform two types of tasks:

◆ Retrieve content from the Internet as though it were just another disk on your computer.

◆ Create content for posting on the Web or sending to another person as an e-mail message.

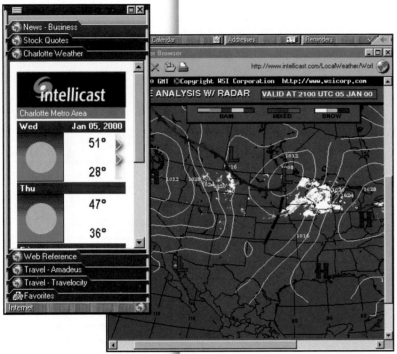

Retrieving Content

By creating Internet-aware applications, software designers try to make the Internet as accessible and useful as your computer's hard disk. These applications allow you to access the Web without manually switching to a browser, for example, or to load a document from the Internet as though it were on your hard disk.

Various products take different approaches to this type of content retrieval. In several parts of Microsoft's Office 2000 suite, for example, a Web toolbar is available. You can use this toolbar to launch your Web browser quickly and visit a specified site. Lotus' SmartSuite features the SmartCenter, which lets you jump from applications directly to Web sites, download files, and more (see Figure 9.22).

Figure 9.22
Accessing the Web through Lotus SmartCenter's custom browser window.

Creating Content

Several types of tools free you from learning to use HTML tags or embedding them manually in documents:

◆ **Save As HTML Command.** By using the program's Save As HTML command, you can convert an existing document into an HTML file, ready to be posted on a Web server. You can then view your HTML page in your browser just like you can view the original document in the word processor.

◆ **Web Templates.** Word processors now provide Web templates, which are predesigned Web pages. You can create entire Web sites from templates, with hyperlinks connecting all the pages in a logical organization.

◆ **Wizards.** A Web-design wizard is a utility that literally walks you through the process of creating a Web page or site. A wizard appears as a series of dialog boxes that ask questions and prompt you to make choices. When you are done, a nearly complete Web page is ready for you to add content.

LESSON QUIZ

True/False

Answer the following questions by circling True or False.

True   False   **1.** Internet is so named because it is a collection of "networked networks."

True   False   **2.** Different types of computers cannot exchange data over the Internet.

True   False   **3.** Examples of subdomains are *.com* and *.edu.*

True   False   **4.** Most individual users connect to the Internet through an ISP.

True   False   **5.** HTML tags are optional components of a Web page.

Multiple Choice

Circle the word or phrase that best completes each sentence.

1. The internal structure of the World Wide Web is based on the _____ .
   A. hypertext markup language   **B.** hypertext transfer protocol   **C.** uniform resource locator

2. Windows Media Player is an example of a(n) _____ .
   A. Web browser   **B.** HTML converter   **C.** helper application

3. To send and receive e-mail messages, you must have a(n) _____ .
   A. e-mail client   **B.** e-mail address   **C.** both A and B

4. In newsgroups, a series of related articles and responses is called a _____ .
   A. newsreader   **B.** Usenet   **C.** thread

5. The _____ is the Internet tool used to copy files from one computer to another.
   A. World Wide Web (WWW)   **B.** file transfer protocol (FTP)   **C.** Usenet

LESSON LABS

Complete the following exercises as directed by your instructor.

1. To determine whether a Web browser is installed on your system, open the Start menu, point to Programs, and search the Programs menu for an application such as Microsoft Internet Explorer or Netscape Navigator. If you find a browser, click its name in the Programs menu to launch the application. Note what happens after you launch the browser and write it down. What appears on the screen?

2. Determine what other types of Internet applications are installed on your system. (You may need your instructor's help.) Check the Programs menu, as you did in Lesson Lab 1. Also, click the Accessories option in the Programs menu; then click Internet Accessories. What other programs are available? An e-mail client or a newsreader? Make a list of the applications and their location in your menu system.

Getting Online, Working Online

OBJECTIVES

- List six ways to connect a computer to the Internet.
- Describe the process of connecting a PC to the Internet through an ISP account.
- Explain why businesses use firewalls.
- Define the terms *intranet* and *extranet*.
- Explain what is meant by "e-commerce."

OVERVIEW:
Joining the Internet Phenomenon

Before you can take advantage of all the services offered by the Internet, you must first be able to connect your computer to the Internet. There are various ways to make this connection, whether the computer is a stand-alone system in a home or is connected to a corporate network. Over time, the process of connecting to the Internet has gotten easier.

As more businesses and people join the Internet community, they are finding that the Internet is enhancing their work lives. Thanks to communications technologies, many businesspeople now work from home instead of commuting to an office or factory each day. The World Wide Web is also used at the corporate level to sell products, provide services, and support business partnerships among companies.

This lesson provides an overview of the options for connecting a computer to the Internet. It shows you how the Internet, intranets, and extranets are affecting the workplace and the way we do business transactions.

ACCESSING THE INTERNET

Because the Internet connects so many computers and networks, there are many ways to obtain access to it. Some methods are appropriate for computers attached to a local area network in a college or corporation, whereas others are better for an isolated computer in a home office or small business.

Direct Connection

In a **direct connection,** Internet programs run on the local computer, which uses the TCP/IP protocols to exchange data with another computer through the Internet. An isolated computer can connect to the Internet through a serial data communications port using either **serial line interface protocol (SLIP)** or **point-to-point protocol (PPP),** two methods for creating a direct connection through a telephone line. This type of connection is an option for a stand-alone computer that does not connect to the Internet through an Internet service provider, as discussed later. However, direct connections are not common.

NORTON
ONLINE

Visit **www.glencoe.com/norton/online/** for more information on **SLIP** and **PPP.**

Remote Terminal Connection

A **remote terminal connection** to the Internet exchanges commands and data in ASCII text format with a host computer that uses UNIX or a similar operating system. The TCP/IP application programs and protocols all run on the host. Because the command set in UNIX is called a shell, this kind of Internet access is known as a **shell account.** Again, this type of connection works for some types of stand-alone computers, but it is not common.

Gateway Connection

Even if a local area network does not use TCP/IP commands and protocols, it may still be able to provide some Internet services, such as e-mail or file transfer. Such networks use gateways that convert commands and data to and from TCP/IP format.

As you learned earlier, many businesses and most individual users obtain access through an Internet service provider (ISP), which supplies the backbone connection. ISPs offer several kinds of Internet service, including inexpensive shell accounts, direct TCP/IP connections using SLIP or PPP accounts, and full-time high-speed access through dedicated data circuits.

Connecting Through a LAN

If a local area network uses TCP/IP protocols for communication within the network, it is a simple matter to connect to the Internet through a router, another computer that stores and forwards data to other computers on the Internet. If the LAN uses a different kind of local protocol, a gateway converts it to and from TCP/IP (see Figure 10.1 on page 206). When a LAN has an Internet connection, that connection extends to every computer on the LAN. This type of connection is commonly used by businesses to provide the LAN's users with Internet access.

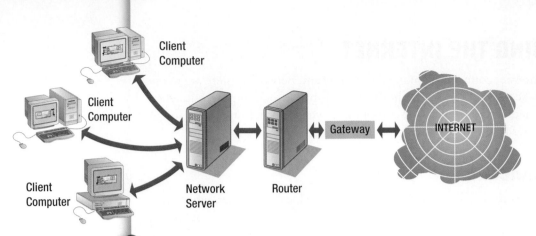

Figure 10.1
If a LAN does not use TCP/IP protocols, it can connect to the Internet through a router and a gateway. However, if a LAN uses TCP/IP protocols, it does not require a gateway to connect to the Internet; just a router is needed.

Figure 10.2
Configuring settings in Windows 98 for an Internet connection through an ISP. When you set up an ISP account, the ISP should provide you with all the instructions and settings you need. A typical account configuration takes only a few minutes using tools in your operating system or provided by the ISP.

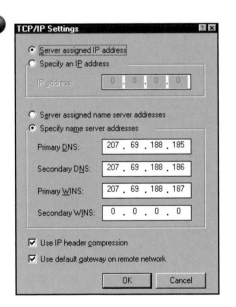

NORTON
ONLINE

Visit www.glencoe.com/norton/online/ for more information on **ISDN service**.

Connecting Through a Modem

If there is no LAN on site, an isolated computer can connect to the Internet through a serial data communications port and a modem by using either a shell account and a terminal emulation program or a direct TCP/IP connection with a SLIP or PPP account. Again, ISPs provide these types of services for home users and businesses who want to connect to the Internet.

Most individual users connect to the Internet by using a telephone line; a 28.8 Kbps, 33.6 Kbps, or 56 Kbps modem; and a SLIP or PPP account. Using settings provided by the ISP, the user can configure the PC's operating system to dial into one of the ISP's server computers, identify itself as the customer's computer, and gain access to Internet services (see Figure 10.2). Depending on the ISP, the customer's computer may be assigned a permanent IP address, or its IP address may change each time it logs on to the ISP's server.

High-Speed Data Links

Modem connections are convenient, but their capacity is limited to the relatively low data-transfer speed of a telephone line. A 56 Kbps modem is fine for text, still images, and low-quality streaming multimedia, but it is really not practical for huge digital audio and video files. Furthermore, when many users are sharing an Internet connection through a LAN, the connection between the bridge or router and the ISP must be adequate to meet the demands of many users at the same time. Fortunately, dedicated high-speed data circuits are available from telephone companies, cable TV services, and other suppliers. Using fiber optics, microwave, and other technologies, it is entirely practical to establish an Internet connection that is at least ten times as fast as a modem link.

ISDN Service

For small businesses and individual users, integrated services digital network (ISDN) is an attractive alternative. ISDN is a digital telephone service that combines voice, data, and control signaling through a single circuit. An ISDN data connection can transfer data at up to 128,000 bits per second. Most telephone companies offer ISDN at a slightly higher cost than the conventional telephone service that it replaces, but costs are coming down.

ISDN service operates on standard telephone lines, but it does require a special modem and telephone service, which add to the cost of the service (see Figure 10.3). Even so, the benefits of ISDN are substantial. For example, you can connect a PC, telephone, and fax into a single ISDN line and use them simultaneously.

Figure 10.3
Many ISDN modems use data compression technologies to double the data transfer rates of a basic ISDN line.

*x*DSL Services

The abbreviation *DSL* stands for digital subscriber line, and several versions of DSL technology are available for home and business use. In fact, the abbreviation often begins with an *x* (*x*DSL) because there are various types of DSL service, each providing a different level of service, speed, bandwidth, and distance.

Cable Modem Service

Many cable companies now use a portion of their network's bandwidth to offer Internet access through existing cable television connections. Cable modem service took some time to become established because it required cable systems to set up local Internet servers (to provide access to the Web, e-mail, and news) and to establish connections to the Internet backbone. As the infrastructure grows, however, cable modem services are springing up in cities around the United States.

Cable television systems send data to users over coaxial cable, which can transmit data as much as 100 times faster than common telephone lines and at a much greater bandwidth. Cable can transmit data and also streaming audio and video simultaneously, at a much higher speed than is possible over standard telephone lines. Because of cable's enhanced bandwidth, Internet data can be transmitted on its own channel, separate from the audio, video, and control signals used for television programming. A user can surf the Internet and watch television at the same time, over the same cable connection, without the two data streams interfering with one another.

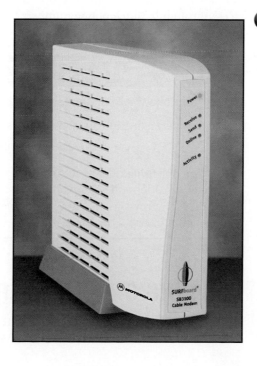

Figure 10.4
Cable modems provide fast data-transfer speeds at costs comparable to a standard ISP account.

To work with a cable modem (see Figure 10.4), the user's PC needs a network interface card and access to a cable television outlet (the kind found in many homes). The cable connection is extended to the modem, which is then connected to the network interface card. As a result, the computer becomes part of a WAN using TCP/IP protocols, whose users share access to the Internet via a dedicated connection.

NORTON ONLINE

Visit **www.glencoe.com/norton/online/** for more information on *x*DSL services and cable modems.

CONNECTING A PC TO THE INTERNET

Connecting a desktop computer to the Internet involves two separate issues: software and the network connection. The industry has developed a standard interface called Windows Sockets, or **Winsock,** that makes it possible to mix and match programs from more than one developer and makes those applications work with any type of network connection. Figure 10.5 shows how applications, the Winsock interface, and network drivers fit together.

Figure 10.5
How Winsock provides an interface between applications and networks.

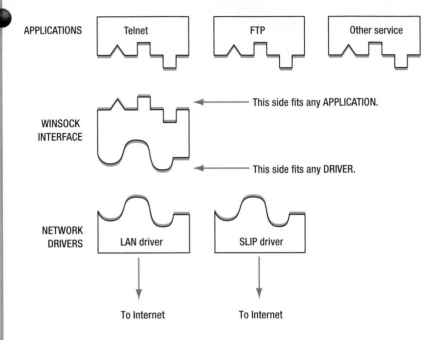

NORTON
ONLINE

Visit **www.glencoe.com/norton/online/**
for more information on **Winsock.**

Many companies offer suites of Internet access tools. These packages usually contain programs for e-mail, Telnet, FTP, a World Wide Web browser, and software for connecting to the Internet. In addition, some packages include sign-up utilities that will work with one or more Internet service providers who offer modem access through local telephone numbers in most major metropolitan areas.

Self Check

Answer the following questions by filling in the blank(s).

1. The serial line interface protocol is one method for creating a(n) _____ over a telephone line.

2. The abbreviation *DSL* stands for _____ .

3. Using a(n) _____ connection, you can surf the Internet and watch television at the same time.

WORKING ON THE INTERNET

The increased use of the Internet and the World Wide Web places networks at even greater risk of undesired intrusion. Many organizations publish information on the Web, whereas others have employees who pass information to the Internet from the company network or download material from the Internet.

Not that long ago, the Internet was the exclusive province of educators, scientists, and researchers. That scenario has changed, and today companies and individuals all over the world are eagerly stampeding into cyberspace. The legal, procedural, and moral infrastructure for this volume of activity simply does not yet exist. Both companies and individuals are taking it one step at a time while the standards are still being defined.

Businesses and Firewalls

With millions of Internet users potentially able to pass information to and take information from the network, the security of business networks is a huge concern. Many businesses set up **firewalls** to control access to their networks by employees and others using the Internet (see Figure 10.6). Firewalls act as barriers to unauthorized entry into a network that is connected to the Internet, allowing outsiders to access public areas but keeping them out of proprietary areas of the network.

A firewall system can be hardware, software, or both. A firewall basically works by inspecting the requests and data that pass between the private network and the Internet. If a request or data does not pass the firewall's security inspection, it is stopped from traveling any further.

Even if a company does not make any portion of its network available to Internet users, it can allow employees to access the network over the Internet. This capability is important for **telecommuters,** or people who work from home or a remote location rather than the office. In these situations, firewalls can ensure that only authorized users access the network over the Internet, while overseeing the activities of internal network users who access the Internet from within the workplace.

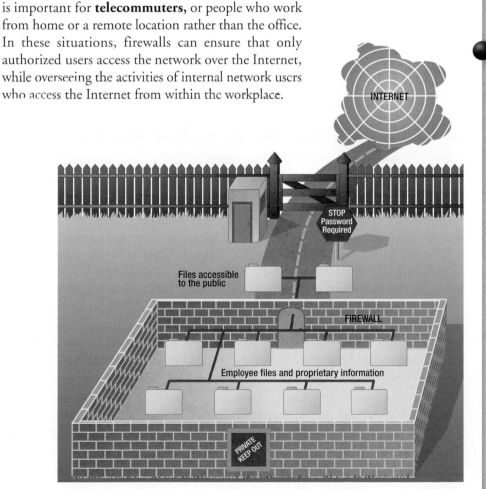

Figure 10.6
Networks connected to the Internet can use a firewall to prevent unauthorized users from accessing private or proprietary information. In many cases, portions of the network are accessible to the public.

Visit **www.glencoe.com/norton/online/** for more information on **firewalls.**

Intranets and Extranets

Corporate and academic networks are being configured more and more often to resemble the Internet. This enables users to work in a Weblike graphical environment, using a Web browser as their interface to corporate data. Two common types of "corporate spin-offs" of the Web are called intranets and extranets.

An **intranet** is a LAN or WAN that uses TCP/IP protocols but that belongs exclusively to a corporation, school, or organization. The intranet is accessible only to the organization's workers. If the intranet is connected to the Internet, then it is secured by a firewall to prevent unauthorized users from gaining access to it.

An **extranet** is an intranet that outside users can access over the Internet. Access to extranets is usually restricted. For example, a corporation may allow external access only by telecommuters and business partners (such as customers or vendors). To gain entrance to the extranet's resources, an external user typically must log on to the network by providing a valid user ID and password. Intranets and extranets are popular for several reasons:

◆ Because they use standard TCP/IP protocols rather than the proprietary protocols used by network operating systems, they are simpler and less expensive to install and configure.

◆ Because they enable users to work in standard (and usually free) Web browsers, they provide a consistent, friendly interface.

◆ Because they function readily with firewalls and other standard Internet security technologies, they provide excellent security against infiltration, viruses, theft, and other problems that arise when unauthorized persons gain access to a corporate network.

While the Web serves a wide variety of purposes, intranets and extranets usually serve only a few general purposes. Most such systems are designed, for example, to support data sharing, scheduling, and workgroup activities within an organization.

Issues for Business Users and Telecommuters

Of course, the technology behind the Internet, intranets, and extranets is only one aspect of doing business online. Whether you use the entire Web in your work or use your company's network via an Internet connection, you need to consider several issues as you work online. Here are just three of those issues:

◆ **Ownership.** Before you start publishing material or downloading material from the Internet, you need to think about what you are doing. Many Internet users assume erroneously that all the data available on it is free and available for use by anyone else. In fact, any piece of text or graphics that you retrieve from the Internet may be covered by trademark or copyright law, making it illegal to reuse it without the owner's consent. This issue is especially important for persons who access the Internet over a corporate network because their employers become involved in cases where copyrights or trademarks are violated.

◆ **Libel.** People are accustomed to voicing their opinions freely in letters and telephone conversations because these are presumably private modes of communication. On the Internet, however, "private" communications (such as e-mail messages) can be quickly forwarded far beyond their intended readership, which amounts to publication. If messages are sent through an employer's network, the employer may become involved if the sender is accused of libel.

Visit **www.glencoe.com/norton/online/** for more information on **intranets** and **extranets**.

Norton Notebook

MINDING YOUR MANNERS ONLINE

Although there is no set of written rules governing behavior on the Internet, the wise user participates in an honor system. On the Internet, appropriate behavior is called netiquette, a combination of *Internet etiquette*. Netiquette is crucial for keeping the Internet a civil place because the Internet is not policed or run by a single person or group. The basic rules of netiquette are as follows:

◆ **Behave As Though You Are Communicating in Person.** When communicating with someone online, act as if you are talking to that person face to face.

◆ **Remember That Your Words Are Open to Interpretation.** If you post jokes, sarcasm, or other attempts at humor, do not be surprised if someone is offended. Word your postings clearly and carefully, and use appropriate language.

◆ **Do Not "Shout" Online.** Typing in ALL CAPITAL LETTERS is like shouting and is considered rude.

◆ **Do Not "Flame" Other Users.** In 'Net-speak, a flame is a posting that contains insults or other derogatory content. Flamers can be shut out of chat rooms, and other users can block a flamer's messages from the e-mail and news accounts.

◆ **Do Not Send Spam.** Spam is the online equivalent of junk mail—uninvited messages, usually of a commercial nature. Most ISPs have strict spam policies. If you are caught distributing uninvited messages to multiple recipients (especially if the messages contain commercial, libelous, or vulgar content), your ISP may cancel your account.

◆ **Do Not Distribute Copyrighted Material.** Usenet newsgroups and many private Web pages are filled with copyrighted and trademarked text and graphics, posted without the owner's permission. Do not be fooled into thinking that text or images are "in the public domain" because you found them on the

Most ISPs provide an appropriate-use policy on their Web site or in their printed documentation. This example is posted on the Web site of Road Runner, an ISP in Charlotte, North Carolina.

TIME WARNER CABLE — CHARLOTTE NORTH CAROLINA

ROAD RUNNER ACCEPTABLE USE POLICY

Road Runner seeks to create and foster an on-line community that can be used and enjoyed by all its members. To further this goal, Road Runner has developed an Acceptable Use Policy with standards for using the service. Although much of what is included here is common sense, Road Runner takes these issues very seriously and will enforce these rules to ensure that an enjoyable environment is provided to all its subscribers.

Road Runner therefore reserves the right to remove any content posted to its system which it deems offensive, inappropriate, or in violation of its policies. Road Runner also reserves the right to suspend or cancel a subscriber's account for engaging in inappropriate conduct. (Subscribers, of course, also remain legally responsible for any such acts). In using Road Runner, subscribers accept these restrictions as well as those set forth in the Subscription Agreement and agree to use the system only for lawful purposes.

In addition, subscribers agree not to use or allow others to use Road Runner:

- to post or transmit hate speech, threats of physical violence, or harassing content;
- to post or transmit material in violation with copyright laws;
- to post or transmit content that is legally obscene or violates child pornography statutes; that contains graphic visual depictions of sexual acts, or visual depictions of sexually explicit conduct involving children, or that contains depictions of children, the primary appeal of which is prurient;
- to post or transmit other sexually oriented material that, in the specific context, is offensive or inappropriate;

Internet. Copyrights still apply; copyright infringement is illegal and can lead to prosecution.

◆ **Do Not Be a Coward.** As a general rule, you should never conceal your identity on the Internet. If you choose to use a screen name, do not hide behind it to misbehave.

Always check the rules when you go online. Nearly all ISPs post an appropriate use policy on their Web site that lists guidelines for acceptable behavior on the Internet. This document may be a simple disclaimer or may take the form of an FAQ. If you violate these guidelines and are reported to the ISP, your account may be dropped. Look for an FAQ before using chat rooms, message boards, newsgroups, and other Internet services, especially moderated ones.

Even though you cannot be seen on the Internet, you can still be identified. Conscientious users of e-mail and newsgroups commonly forward flames or inappropriate postings to the poster's ISP. If an ISP collects complaints about an account holder, it can cancel that person's account. In cases where libel, copyright infringement, or other potential crimes are involved, the ISP may also turn the poster over to the authorities. In one such case (in December 1999), a Florida teenager posted a threatening chat-room message to a Colorado student. Even though the poster had used an alias to hide his identity, federal agents were able to track him down and arrest him.

NORTON ONLINE

Visit **www.glencoe.com/norton/online/** for more information on **netiquette**.

◆ **Appropriate Use.** When using a business network to access the Internet, users must be careful to use network resources appropriately. For example, they should not access recreational newsgroups over the company's Internet connection or download obscene or pornographic images from adult-oriented Web sites.

Why are these issues of concern to business users of the Internet? The answer is simple: If you access the Internet through a corporate network, the network's owner becomes involved if trouble arises from misuse.

Employees also need to protect corporate property—such as trade secrets, telephone lists, personnel records, and product specifications—stored on the network. Suppose, for example, that someone calls you at your office accidentally, meaning to call one of your coworkers. To ensure that this person has the correct telephone number, you agree to e-mail him or her your corporate telephone directory. This simple favor can become a major headache if the caller turns out to be a telemarketer or recruiter who then starts calling everyone on the list.

COMMERCE ON THE WORLD WIDE WEB

As mentioned earlier, the Internet has given us a new place to shop. But more than providing individuals a way to purchase books, CDs, and toys from their PC, the World Wide Web has become a global vehicle for **electronic commerce (e-commerce).** It has created new ways for businesses to interact with one another and their customers.

You have probably heard the term *e-commerce* many times already, especially in television commercials. Although marketers may be overusing the term, e-commerce is a real and important phenomenon that promises to change the way business is done around the world. As evidence, consider that in 1997, an ActivMedia study estimated that more than $24 million in sales were conducted over the World Wide Web. A more recent survey by Goldman, Sachs, & Co. says that $39 billion in e-commerce was done in 1998, with another $114 billion in 1999. Looking forward, the survey predicted that e-commerce sales will total $1.5 trillion by the year 2004.

Figure 10.7
Like many other e-commerce sites that target consumers, amazon.com offers browsing, extensive help systems, secure purchasing, online customer service, and other features.

E-Commerce at the Consumer Level

In simple terms, e-commerce means doing business online. If you have a credit card, a PC, and an Internet connection at home, then you may have already participated in the e-commerce boom by logging on to a site such as amazon.com, eBay, and Buy.com, and ordering a product (see Figure 10.7). There are tens of thousands of Web sites devoted to e-commerce at the consumer level that are ready to give consumers information about products and services, take orders, receive payments, and provide on-the-spot customer service.

Using an e-commerce site is like browsing through an online catalog. More sophisticated sites allow you to search for specific products, look for certain features, and compare prices. They provide an electronic "shopping basket" or "shopping cart," where you can temporarily store information about items you want to buy (see Figure 10.8). You can select an item, store it in the basket, and continue shopping until you are ready to purchase.

When you are ready to make your purchase, you can pay for it in several ways:

◆ **One-Time Credit Card Purchase.** If you do not want to set up an account with the seller, you can provide your personal and credit card information each time you make a purchase.

◆ **Set Up an Online Account.** If you think you will make other purchases from the online vendor, you can set up an account at the Web site (see Figure 10.9). The vendor stores your personal and credit card information on a secure server, then places a special file (called a **cookie**) on your computer's disk. Later, when you access your account again by typing a user ID and password, the site uses information in the cookie to access your account. Online accounts are required at some vendors' Web sites, such as brokerage sites that provide online investing services.

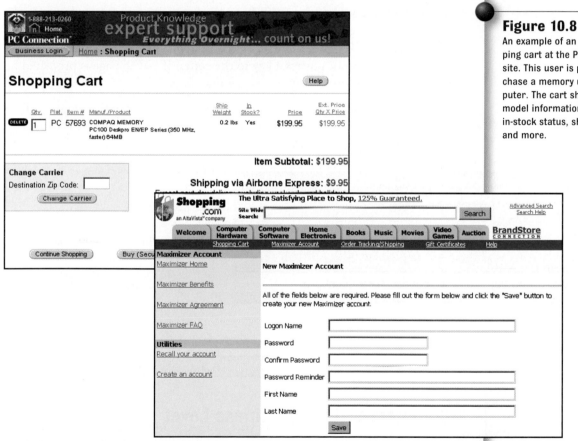

Figure 10.8

An example of an electronic shopping cart at the PC Connection Web site. This user is preparing to purchase a memory upgrade for a computer. The cart shows the product, model information, price, quantity, in-stock status, shipping charges, and more.

Figure 10.9

Setting up an account at an e-commerce Web site.

◆ **Use Electronic Cash.** Electronic cash (also called digital cash) has been available since 1996 but has not yet gained wide public acceptance for online shopping. Electronic cash takes the form of a redeemable electronic certificate, which you can purchase from a bank that provides electronic cash services. Very few e-commerce Web sites accept digital cash.

◆ **Use an Electronic Wallet.** An electronic wallet is a program on your computer that stores credit card information, a digital certificate that verifies your identity, and shipping information. A different version, called a thin wallet, stores the information on a server owned by your credit card company, rather than on your computer.

Security

Reputable e-commerce Web sites use sophisticated measures to ensure that customer information cannot fall into the hands of criminals. One measure is to provide **secure Web pages** where customers enter personal information, credit card and account numbers, passwords, and other information. When using an e-commerce site, you can tell if the current page is secure in two ways (see Figure 10.10):

◆ **Check the URL.** If the Web page's URL begins with *https://* or ends with *shtml,* then the page is secure. In both cases, the letter *s* indicates security measures.

◆ **Check Your Browser's Status Bar.** If you use Microsoft Internet Explorer or Netscape Navigator, a small padlock symbol will appear in the browser's status bar when a secure Web page is open.

Web masters can provide secure Web sites in several ways. One way is to encode pages using **secure sockets layer (SSL)** technology, which encrypts data to make it unusable to anyone who does not have a key to the encryption method. (**Encryption** technology secures data by converting it into a code that is unusable to anyone who does not possess a key to the code.) If a Web page is protected by SSL, its URL will begin with *https://* rather than *http://*.

Another way to protect data sent over the Internet is by using the **secure HTTP (S-HTTP)** protocol. SSL can encode any amount of data; S-HTTP is used to encode individual pieces of data.

Figure 10.10
Verifying a secure Web site.

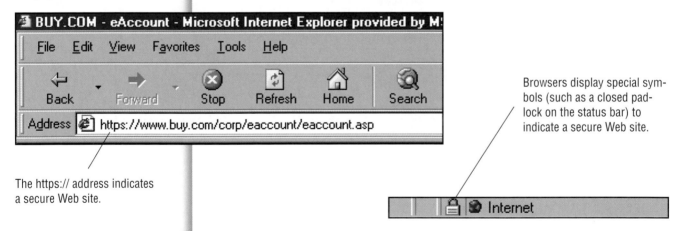

The https:// address indicates a secure Web site.

Browsers display special symbols (such as a closed padlock on the status bar) to indicate a secure Web site.

E-Commerce at the Business Level

When viewed beyond the perspective of individual consumer transactions, e-commerce is an entirely different way for companies to conduct business. Using powerful Web sites and online databases, companies not only sell goods to individual customers, but track inventory, order products, send invoices, and receive payments. Using e-commerce technologies (ranging from LANs to supercomputers), companies are rapidly forming online partnerships to collaborate on product designs, sales and marketing campaigns, and more. Corporate extranets have become an important part of corporate-level e-commerce by giving companies access to vital information on one another's networks.

LESSON QUIZ

True/False

Answer the following questions by circling True or False.

True   False   **1.** Remote terminal connections can be used only with supercomputers.

True   False   **2.** To use ISDN service at home, you must replace your standard telephone lines with special ISDN-only lines.

True   False   **3.** A firewall can control access to a corporate network by someone using the Internet.

True   False   **4.** An intranet can be accessed by anyone over an Internet connection.

True   False   **5.** In simple terms, e-commerce means doing business online.

Multiple Choice

Circle the word or phrase that best completes each sentence.

1. You can set up a direct connection to the Internet over a telephone line by using _____ .
   A. serial line interface protocol   **B.** point to point protocol   **C.** either A or B

2. _____ is one type of high-speed data link.
   A. 56 Kbps   **B.** ISDN   **C.** Winsock

3. To work with a cable modem, your PC needs a(n) _____ .
   A. network interface card   **B.** xDSL connection   **C.** neither A nor B

4. A(n) _____ can be accessed by external users via the Internet.
   A. intranet   **B.** cable modem   **C.** extranet

5. You can pay for online transactions by using a _____ .
   A. credit card   **B.** cookie   **C.** SSL connection

LESSON LABS

Complete the following exercises as directed by your instructor.

1. To determine whether your computer has a modem, click the Start button; then click Settings. When the Settings submenu appears, click Control Panel to open the Control Panel dialog box. If you see a Modems icon, double-click it to open the Modem Properties dialog box. Write down the information about your modem. Then close the Modem Properties dialog box, but leave the Control Panel dialog box open for the next exercise.

2. Use the Control Panel dialog box to see whether your PC has a network interface card installed. Double-click the System icon to open the System Properties dialog box. Click the Device Manager tab; then click the plus sign (+) next to Network adapters. If any adapters are installed, the list expands to show them. Select each adapter in turn; then click Properties to display the Properties dialog box for that adapter. Write down the information for each adapter; then choose Cancel at the bottom of the Properties dialog box.

VISUAL SUMMARY

LESSON 9: Internet Basics

The Internet: Then and Now

■ The Internet was created for the U.S. Department of Defense as a tool for communications. Today, the Internet is a network of inter-connected networks.

■ The Internet carries messages, documents, programs, and data files that contain every imaginable kind of information for businesses, educational institutions, government agencies, and individuals.

How the Internet Works

■ All computers on the Internet use TCP/IP protocols to exchange com-mands and data. Any computer on the Internet can connect to any other computer.

■ Individual computers connect to local and regional networks, which are connected together through the Internet backbone.

■ A computer can connect directly to the Internet, or as a remote terminal on another computer, or through a gateway from a network that does not use TCP/IP.

■ Every computer on the Internet has a unique numeric IP address, and most also have an address that uses the domain name system.

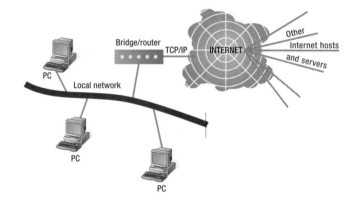

Major Features of the Internet

■ The World Wide Web combines text, illus-trations, and links in hypertext documents.

■ Electronic mail systems enable you to exchange messages with any other user anywhere. You can also attach document or program files to e-mail messages.

■ Telnet allows a user to operate a second computer from his or her machine.

■ FTP is the Internet tool for copying data and program files from one computer to another.

■ Chats are public conferences conducted in real time where people join channels to discuss topics of interest.

Online Services

■ In addition to Internet access, online service companies offer a wide variety of other features such as e-mail, discussion groups, stock quotes, news, and online games.

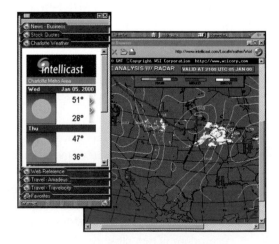

Internet-Related Features in Application Programs

■ Internet tools and services are commonly added to popular application programs such as word processors and spreadsheets. Such features allow you to either create content for the Internet or to access content on the Internet.

LESSON 10: Getting Online, Working Online

Accessing the Internet

■ Users can connect to the Internet through a direct connection, local area networks, high-speed data links, and other means.

■ Individuals and small businesses access the Internet most commonly by setting up an account with an Internet service provider and by using a telephone line and modem.

■ High-speed data links such as ISDN and *x*DSL are more expensive options, but they provide much faster service than standard telephone line connections over a modem.

■ Cable modems are quickly becoming a popular high-speed connection because they use the coaxial cable lines already in many people's homes.

Connecting a PC to the Internet

■ The Winsock standard specifies the Windows interface between TCP/IP applications and network connections. Users can mix and match Winsock-compatible applications and ensure they will work with the user's network connection to access the Internet.

■ Internet application suites are available from many suppliers. They combine a full set of applications and drivers in a single package.

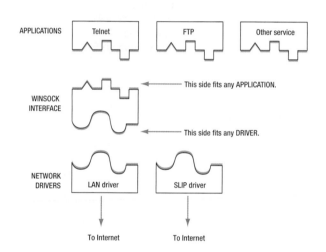

Working on the Internet

■ By connecting their networks to the Internet, companies are creating new ways to conduct business and for employees to work. Telecommuters work from remote locations by connecting to the company network via the Internet.

■ Businesses that connect their networks to the Internet often set up firewalls to prevent unauthorized users from gaining access to proprietary information.

■ Intranets and extranets are internal networks based on TCP/IP, and they support the use of Web browsers.

Commerce on the World Wide Web

■ The act of doing business online is called e-commerce.

■ At the consumer level, it is possible to buy a wide range of goods and services at Web sites. Many such sites maintain a high level of customer service, accept different forms of payment online, and provide a secure environment for transactions.

■ At the corporate level, e-commerce technologies enable companies to form online partnerships, conduct business transactions online, and collaborate on projects.

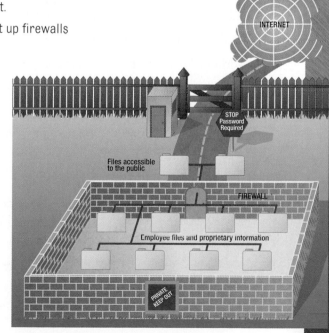

UNIT REVIEW

KEY TERMS

After completing this unit, you should be able to define the following terms.

anonymous FTP archives, *199*
Archie, *200*
ARPANET, *184*
article, *197*
backbone, *184*
browser, *189*
channel, *200*
chat, *200*
cookie, *213*
direct connection, *205*
domain, *187*
domain name system (DNS)
   address, *187*
electronic commerce
   (e-commerce), *212*
e-mail address, *194*
e-mail program, *194*
encryption, *214*
extranet, *210*
file transfer protocol (FTP), *199*
firewalls, *209*
frequently asked questions (FAQs), *198*
helper application, *193*
hit, *189*
home page, *192*
host, *184*
HTML tag, *190*

hyperlink, *188*
hypertext link, *188*
hypertext markup language
   (HTML), *188*
hypertext transfer protocol (HTTP), *191*
Internet, *184*
Internet protocol (IP) address, *187*
Internet relay chat (IRC), *200*
Internet service provider (ISP), *188*
internetworking, *184*
intranet, *210*
link, *188*
mail server, *195*
news, *195*
newsgroup, *195*
newsreader, *197*
news server, *197*
NSFnet, *184*
online service, *201*
page view, *189*
plug-in application, *193*
point-to-point protocol (PPP), *205*
posting, *189*
remote terminal connection, *205*
search engine, *194*
secure HTTP (S-HTTP), *214*
secure sockets layer (SSL), *214*

secure Web page, *214*
serial line interface protocol
   (SLIP), *205*
shell account, *205*
subdomain, *188*
subscribe, *197*
system operator (sysop), *201*
telecommuters, *209*
Telnet, *198*
thread, *197*
Transmission Control
   Protocol/Internet Protocol
   (TCP/IP), *185*
uniform resource locator (URL), *191*
Usenet, *195*
user name, *195*
virtual reality modeling language
   (VRML), *193*
Web browser, *189*
Web master, *189*
Web page, *188*
Web server, *189*
Web site, *189*
Winsock, *208*
World Wide Web (the Web or
   WWW), *188*

KEY TERMS QUIZ

Fill in each blank with one of the terms listed under Key Terms.

1. The process of connecting separate networks is called _____ .

2. In addition to an IP address, most computers on the Internet also have a(n) _____ .

3. A(n) _____ provides local or regional access to the Internet backbone.

4. The term _____ is used when documents are placed on Internet host computers.

5. To format a Web page, the designer places _____ throughout the document.

6. The term _____ can refer to the Web page that opens when you launch your Web browser, or a Web site's primary page.

7. Web sites like Alta Vista are examples of _____ .

8. Some discussion groups hosted by online services are monitored by a(n) _____ .

9. A(n) _____ allows you to view streaming multimedia content from a Web site.

10. Many e-commerce Web sites provide _____ , where customers can enter personal information without fear that it will be stolen.

REVIEW QUESTIONS

In your own words, briefly answer the following questions.

1. What is an Internet host?
2. What is the most popular activity for which people use the Internet?
3. Why is the Internet sometimes described as "a network of networks"?
4. How do most individual computer users connect to the Internet?
5. What is the difference between a Web page and a Web site?
6. Name the parts of a URL.
7. Describe the potential drawback to relying on Internet newsgroups as a source of information.
8. List three technologies people can use to gain high-speed access to the Internet.
9. In basic terms, what does a firewall do?
10. What is the difference between an intranet and an extranet?

DISCUSSION QUESTIONS

As directed by your instructor, discuss the following questions in class or in groups.

1. Despite the promise that the Internet will perhaps one day be as universal as radio and television, how do you feel about the growing commercialization of the Internet? Do you think the motive to use the Internet for profit will affect it negatively as a source of information?
2. Discuss your view of the Internet's value to individual users. How important do you think the Internet is to casual home users? Support your opinion.

 ETHICAL ISSUES Despite all the conveniences it offers to its users, the Internet is filled with pitfalls. With this thought in mind, discuss the following questions in class.

1. People can shop, pay bills, communicate, play, study, and work online. Web designers, Internet marketers, ISPs, and other companies encourage us to use the Internet as much as possible, for any reason. In simple terms, can this use be bad? At what point do we become too dependent on the Internet? At what point does Internet use interfere with normal routines?

2. In the summer of 1999, a large bank fired several workers for using the company network to download pornography from the Web. The workers had also used the company's e-mail system to send copies of the images to one another and to friends outside the company. In your view, was the company too harsh in its punishment? Why? Do you believe the workers did anything illegal or potentially harmful? Support your position.

You and the Computer

Complete the following exercise using a computer in your classroom, lab, or home.

Telnet. Take the following steps to learn about your Telnet software—which is built right into your Windows operating system:

A. Click the Start button to open the Start menu; then click Programs. In the Programs menu, click the MS-DOS Prompt icon. An MS-DOS Prompt window appears on your desktop. A blinking cursor appears in the window, where you can type commands.

B. Type **TELNET** and press Enter. A Telnet window opens on your desktop.

C. Click Help on the menu bar to open the Help menu; then click Contents.

D. In the Telnet Help window, click various help topics and read the information that displays for each one.

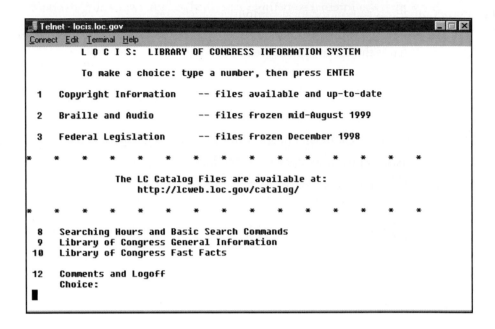

If your computer has an Internet connection, take the following steps to visit a Telnet site. Otherwise, close the Telnet and MS-DOS Prompt windows by clicking the Close buttons on their title bars.

A. On the Telnet menu bar, click Connect to open the Connect menu; then click Remote System. The Connect dialog box opens.

B. In the Host Name box, type one of the following Telnet addresses:

- **locis.loc.gov**—to learn about the Library of Congress.
- **uwmcat.lib.uwm.edu**—to browse the collections at the University of Wisconsin Library.
- **ajb.dni.us**—to search for job listings in the America's Job Bank database.

C. From the Port drop-down list, select *telnet*. From the TermType drop-down list, select *vt100*. (Your instructor may direct you to select different options.)

D. Click Connect. If your connection is successful, the Telnet window will change to display the opening screen of the Telnet site. If not, repeat steps A and B, using a different address.

E. Follow the instructions to log into the site and explore. When you are finished, close the Telnet and MS-DOS Prompt windows by clicking the Close buttons on their title bars. Your Telnet connection will be closed.

Internet Labs

To complete the following exercises, you need a computer with an Internet connection and a Web browser. (For more information on using these tools, see "Prerequisites" at the front of this textbook.)

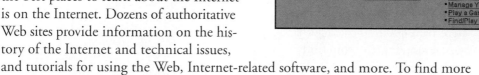

1. **Learn More About the Internet.** One of the best places to learn about the Internet is on the Internet. Dozens of authoritative Web sites provide information on the history of the Internet and technical issues, and tutorials for using the Web, Internet-related software, and more. To find more basic information about the Internet, visit these Web sites:

   - Webmonkey Guides—**http://www.hotwired.com/webmonkey/guides/**
   - An Overview of the Web— **http://www.imaginarylandscape.com/helpweb/www/oneweb.html**
   - NewbieNet—**http://www.newbie.net/**
   - Internet 101—**http://www2.famvid.com/i101/**

2. **Set Up a Free E-Mail Account.** Even if you do not have an ISP account, you can still use e-mail, if you can use a computer with access to the World Wide Web. Visit these sites to learn more about free e-mail accounts. Pick a provider, then follow the directions on that site to set up an account. Remember to write down your user name and password.

   - Hotmail—**http://www.hotmail.com/**
   - Mail.com—**http://www.mail.com/**
   - E-Mail.com—**http://www.email.com/**

IBE Labs

If you have the Interactive Browser Edition (IBE) CD-ROM for this textbook, you may complete the following interactive exercises using the instructions provided in the IBE.

1. **Crossword Puzzle.** Use the clues provided to complete the puzzle.

2. **Labeling.** Create a chart to show how computers access the Internet.

3. **What's Your Recommendation?** Based on the scenarios provided, you must set up domain names for businesses.

4. **Home Network.** This activity focuses on how data flows from one computer to the next via the Internet.

The History of Microcomputers

IN THE BEGINNING

In 1971, Dr. Ted Hoff puts together all the elements of a computer processor on a single silicon chip slightly larger than one square inch. The result of his efforts is the Intel 4004, the world's first commercially available microprocessor. The chip is a 4-bit computer containing 2,300 transistors (invented in 1948) that can perform 60,000 instructions per second. Designed for use in a calculator, it sells for $200. Intel sells more than 100,000 calculators based on the 4004 chip. Almost overnight, the chip finds thousands of applications, paving the way for today's computer-oriented world, and for the mass production of computer chips now containing millions of transistors.

1975

The first commercially available microcomputer, the Altair 880, is the first machine to be called a "personal computer." It has 64 KB of memory and an open 100-line bus structure. Selling for about $400, the Altair 880 comes in a kit to be assembled by the user.

Two young college students, Paul Allen and Bill Gates, unveil the BASIC language interpreter for the Altair computer. During summer vacation, the pair form a company called Microsoft, which eventually grows into the largest software company in the world.

At Bell Labs, Brian Kernighan and Dennis Ritchie develop the C programming language, which quickly becomes the most popular professional application development language.

1976

Steve Wozniak and Steve Jobs build the Apple I computer. It is less powerful than the Altair, but also less expensive and less complicated. Users must connect their own keyboard and video display, and have the option of mounting the

computer's motherboard in any container they choose—whether a metal case, a wooden box, or a briefcase. Jobs and Wozniak form the Apple Computer Company together on April Fool's Day, naming it after their favorite snack food.

1977

The Apple II computer is unveiled. It comes already assembled in a case, with a built-in keyboard. Users must plug in their own TVs for monitors. Fully assembled microcomputers hit the general market, with Radio Shack, Commodore, and Apple all selling models. Sales are slow because neither businesses nor the general public know exactly what to do with these new machines.

Datapoint Corporation announces Attached Resource Computing Network (ARCnet), the first

commercial LAN technology intended for use with micro-computer applications.

1978

Intel releases the 8086 micro-processor, a 16-bit chip that sets a new standard for power, capacity, and speed in microprocessors.

Epson announces the MX-80 dot-matrix printer, coupling high performance with a relatively low price. (Epson from Japan sets up

operations in the U.S. in 1975 as Epson America, Inc. and becomes one of the first of many foreign companies to contribute to the growth of the PC industry. Up until this point, it has been U.S. companies only. According to Epson, they gain 60 percent of the dot printer market with the MX-80.)

1979

Intel introduces the 8088 microprocessor, featuring 16-bit internal architecture and an 8-bit external bus.

Motorola introduces the 68000 chip, used in early Macintosh computers.

Software Arts, Inc. releases VisiCalc, the first commercial spreadsheet program for personal computers. VisiCalc is generally credited as being the program that paved the way for the personal computer in the business world.

Bob Metcalf, the developer of Ethernet, forms 3Com Corp. to develop Ethernet-based net-working products. Ethernet eventually evolves into the world's most widely used network system.

MicroPro International intro-duces WordStar, the first com-mercially successful word processing program for IBM-compatible microcomputers.

1980

IBM chooses Microsoft (co-founded by Bill Gates and Paul Allen) to provide the operating system for its upcoming PC. Microsoft purchases a program developed by Seattle Computer Products called Q-DOS (for Quick and Dirty Operating System), and modifies it to run on IBM hardware.

Bell Laboratories invents the Bellmac-32, the first single-chip microprocessor with 32-bit internal architecture and a 32-bit data bus.

Lotus Development Corporation unveils the Lotus 1-2-3 integrated spreadsheet program combining spreadsheet, graphics, and database features in one package.

1981

IBM introduces the IBM-PC, with a 4.77 MHz Intel 8088 CPU, 16 KB of memory, a keyboard, a monitor, one or two 5.25-inch floppy drives, and a price tag of $2,495.

Hayes Microcomputer Products, Inc., introduces the SmartModem 300, which quickly becomes the industry standard.

Xerox unveils the Xerox Star computer. Its high price eventually dooms the computer to commercial failure, but its features inspire a whole new direction in computer design. Its little box on wheels (the first mouse) can execute commands on screen (the first graphical user interface).

1982

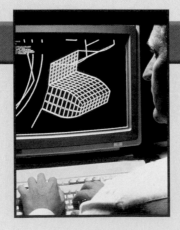

Intel releases the 80286, a 16-bit microprocessor.

AutoCAD, a program for designing 2-D and 3-D objects, is released. AutoCAD will go on to revolutionize the architecture and engineering industries.

Work begins on the development of TCP/IP. The term *Internet* is used for the first time to describe the worldwide network of networks that is emerging from the ARPANET.

1983

Time magazine features the computer as the 1982 "Machine of the Year," acknowledging the computer's new role in society.

Apple introduces the Lisa, the first commercial computer with a purely graphical operating system and a mouse. The industry is excited, but Lisa's $10,000 price tag discourages buyers.

IBM unveils the IBM-PC XT, essentially a PC with a hard disk and more memory. The XT can store programs and data on its built-in 10 MB hard disk.

The first version of C++ programming language is developed, allowing programs to be written in reusable, independent pieces called objects.

The Compaq Portable is released, the first successful 100 percent PC-compatible clone. Despite its hefty 28 pounds, it becomes one of the first computers to be lugged through airports.

1984

Adobe Systems releases its PostScript system, allowing printers to produce crisp print in a number of typefaces, as well as elaborate graphic images.

Apple introduces the "user-friendly" Macintosh microcomputer.

IBM ships the IBM-PC AT, a 6 MHz computer using the Intel 80286 processor, which sets the standard for personal computers running DOS.

IBM introduces its Token Ring networking system. Reliable and redundant, it can send packets at 4 Mbps; several years later it speeds up to 16 Mbps.

Satellite Software International introduces the WordPerfect word processing program.

1985

Intel releases the 80386 processor (also called the 386), a 32-bit processor that can address more than 4 billion bytes of memory, and performs ten times faster than the 80286.

Aldus releases PageMaker for the Macintosh, the first desktop publishing software for microcomputers. Coupled with Apple's LaserWriter printer and Adobe's PostScript system, PageMaker ushers in the era of desktop publishing.

Microsoft announces the Windows 1.0 operating environment, featuring the first graphical user interface for PCs.

Hewlett-Packard introduces the Laser Jet laser printer, featuring 300 dpi resolution.

1986

IBM delivers the PC convertible, IBM's first laptop computer and the first Intel-based computer with a 3.5-inch floppy disk drive.

Microsoft sells its first public stock for $21 per share, raising $61 million in the initial public offering.

The First International Conference on CD-ROM technology is held in Seattle, hosted by Microsoft. Compact disks are seen as the storage medium of the future for computer users.

1987

IBM unveils the new PS/2 line of computers, featuring a 20-MHz 80386 processor at its top end. This product line includes the MicroChannel bus, but is not a great success because consumers do not want to replace industry standard peripherals. To compete with IBM's MicroChannel architecture, a group of other computer makers introduces the EISA (Extended Industry Standard Architecture) bus.

IBM introduces its Video Graphics Array (VGA) monitor offering 256 colors at 320 × 200 resolution, and 16 colors at 640 × 480.

The Macintosh II computer, aimed at the desktop publishing market, is introduced by Apple Computer. It features an SVGA monitor. Apple Computer introduced HyperCard, a programming language for the Macintosh, which used the metaphor of a stack of index cards to represent a program—a kind of visual programming language.

Motorola unveils its 68030 microprocessor.

Novell introduces its network operating system, called NetWare.

1988

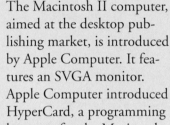

IBM and Microsoft ship OS/2 1.0, the first multi-tasking desktop operating system. High price, a steep learning curve, and incompatibility with existing PCs contribute to its lack of market share.

Apple Computer files the single biggest lawsuit in the computer industry against Microsoft and Hewlett-Packard, claiming copyright infringement of its operating system and graphical user interface. Ashton-Tate sues Fox Software and The Santa Cruz Operation, alleging copyright infringement of dBase.

Hewlett-Packard introduces the first popular ink jet printer, the HP Deskjet.

Steve Jobs' new company, NeXT, Inc., unveils the NeXT computer featuring a 25-MHz Motorola 68030 processor. The NeXT is the first computer to use object-oriented programming in its operating system and an optical drive rather than a floppy drive.

Apple introduces the Apple CD SC, a CD-ROM storage device allowing access to up to 650 MB of data.

A virus called the "Internet Worm" is released on the Internet, disabling about ten percent of all Internet host computers.

1989

Intel releases the 80486 chip (also called the 486), the world's first one-million-transistor microprocessor. The 486 integrates a 386 CPU and math coprocessor onto the same chip.

Tim Berners-Lee develops software around the hypertext concept, enabling users to click on a word or phrase in a document and jump either to another location within the document or to another file. This software provides the foundation for the development of the World Wide Web, and is the basis for the first Web browsers.

The World Wide Web is created at CERN, the European Particle Physics Laboratory in Geneva,

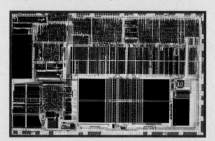

Switzerland for use by scientific researchers.

Microsoft's Word for Windows introduction begins the "Microsoft Office" suite adoption by millions of users. Word for DOS had been the second-highest-selling word processing package behind Word Perfect.

1990

Microsoft releases Windows 3.0, shipping 1 million copies in four months.

A multimedia PC specification setting the minimum hardware requirements for sound and graphics components of a PC is announced at the Microsoft Multimedia Developers' Conference.

The National Science Foundation Network (NSFNET) replaces ARPANET as the backbone of the Internet.

Motorola announces its 32-bit microprocessor, the 68040, incorporating 1.2 million transistors.

1991

Apple Computer launches the PowerBook series of battery-powered portable computers.

Apple, IBM, and Motorola sign a cooperative agreement to design and produce RISC-based chips, integrate the Mac OS into IBM's enterprise systems, produce a new object-oriented operating system, and develop common multimedia standards. The result is the PowerPC microprocessor.

1992

With an estimated 25 million users, the Internet becomes the world's largest electronic mail network.

In Apple Computer's five-year copyright infringement lawsuit, Judge Vaughn Walker rules in favor of defendants Microsoft and Hewlett-Packard, finding that the graphical user interface in dispute is not covered under Apple's copyrights.

Microsoft ships the Windows 3.1 operating environment, including improved memory management and TrueType fonts.

IBM introduces its ThinkPad laptop computer.

1993

Mosaic, a point-and-click graphical Web browser is developed at the National Center for Supercomputing Applications (NCSA), making the Internet accessible to those outside the scientific community.

Intel, mixing elements of its 486 design with new processes, features, and technology, delivers the long-awaited Pentium processor. It offers a 64-bit data path and more than 3.1 million transistors.

Apple Computer expands its entire product line, adding the Macintosh Color Classic, Macintosh LC III, Macintosh Centris 610 and 650, Macintosh Quadra 800, and the Powerbooks 165c and 180c.

Apple introduces the Newton MessagePad at the Macworld convention, selling 50,000 units in the first ten weeks.

Microsoft ships the Windows NT operating system.

IBM ships its first RISC-based RS/6000 workstation, featuring the PowerPC 601 chip developed jointly by Motorola, Apple, and IBM.

1994

Apple introduces the Power Macintosh line of microcomputers based on the PowerPC chip. This line introduces RISC to the desktop market. RISC was previously available only on high-end workstations.

Netscape Communications releases the Netscape Navigator program, a World Wide Web browser based on the Mosaic standard, but with more advanced features.

Online service providers Compu-Serve, America Online, and Prodigy add Internet access to their services.

After two million Pentium-based PCs hit the market, a flaw in the chip's floating-point unit is found by Dr. Thomas Nicely. His report is made public on CompuServe.

Linus Torvalds releases Linux, a freeware version of UNIX created by a worldwide collaboration of programmers who shared their work over the Internet.

1995

Intel releases the Pentium Pro microprocessor.

Motorola releases the PowerPC 604 chip, developed jointly with Apple and IBM.

Microsoft releases its Windows 95 operating system with a massive marketing campaign, including prime-time TV commercials. Seven million copies are sold the first month, with sales reaching 26 million by year's end.

Netscape Communications captures more than 80 percent of the World Wide Web browser market, going from a start-up company to a $2.9 billion company in one year.

A group of developers at Sun Microsystems create the Java development language. Because it enables programmers to develop applications that will run on any platform, Java is seen as the future of operating systems, applications, and the World Wide Web.

Power Computing ships the first-ever Macintosh clones, the Power 100 series with a PowerPC 601 processor.

1996

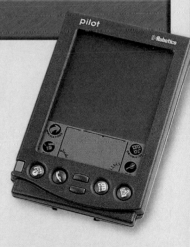

Intel announces the 200 MHz Pentium processor.

U.S. Robotics releases the PalmPilot, a personal digital assistant that quickly gains enormous popularity because of its rich features and ease of use.

Microsoft adds Internet connection capability to its Windows 95 operating system.

Several vendors introduce Virtual Reality Modeling Language (VRML) authoring tools that provide simple interfaces and drag-and-drop editing features to create three-dimensional worlds with color, texture, motion video, and sound on the Web.

The U.S. Congress enacts the Communications Decency Act as part of the Telecommunications Act of 1996. The act mandates fines of up to $100,000 and prison terms for transmission of any "comment, request, suggestion, proposal, image or other communication which is obscene, lewd, lascivious, filthy, or indecent" over the Internet. The day the law is passed, millions of Web page backgrounds turn black in protest. The law is immediately challenged on Constitutional grounds, ultimately deemed unconstitutional, and repealed.

1997

Intel announces MMX technology, which increases the multimedia capabilities of a micro-processor. Also, Intel announces the Pentium II microprocessor. It has speeds of up to 333 MHz and introduces a new design in packaging, the Single Edge Contact (SEC) cartridge. It has more than 7.5 million transistors.

AMD and Cyrix step up efforts to compete with Intel for the $1000-and-less PC market. Their competing processors are used by PC makers such as Dell, Compaq, Gateway, and even IBM.

The U.S. Justice Department charges Microsoft with an antitrust lawsuit, claiming Microsoft was practicing anticompetitive behavior by forcing PC makers to bundle its Internet Explorer Web browser with Windows 95.

Netscape Communications and Microsoft release new versions of their Web browser. Netscape's Communicator 4 and Microsoft's Internet Explorer 4 provide a full suite of Internet tools, including Web browser, newsreader, HTML editor, conferencing program, and e-mail application.

Digital Video/Versatile Disk (DVD) technology is introduced. Capable of storing computer, audio, and video data, a single DVD disk can hold an entire movie. DVD is seen as the storage technology for the future, ultimately replacing standard CD-ROM technology in PC and home entertainment systems.

1998

Microsoft releases the Windows 98 operating system. Seen mainly as an upgrade to Windows 95, Windows 98 is more reliable and less susceptible to crashes. It also offers improved Internet-related features, including a built-in copy of the Internet Explorer Web browser.

The Department of Justice expands its actions against Microsoft, attempting to block the release of Windows 98 unless Microsoft agrees to remove the Internet Explorer browser from the operating system. Microsoft fights back and a lengthy trial begins in federal court, as the government attempts to prove that Microsoft is trying to hold back competitors such as Netscape.

Intel releases two new versions of its popular Pentium II chip. The Pentium II Celeron offers slower performance than the standard PII, but is aimed at the $1,000-and-less PC market, which quickly embraces this chip. At the high end, the Pentium II Xeon is designed for use in high-performance workstations and server systems, and is priced accordingly. Both chips boost Intel's market share, reaching deeper into more vertical markets.

Apple Computer releases the colorful iMac, an all-in-one system geared to a youthful market. The small, lightweight system features the new G3 processor, which outperforms Pentium II–based PCs in many respects. The iMac uses only USB connections, forcing many users to purchase adapters for system peripherals, and the computer does not include a floppy disk drive.

1999

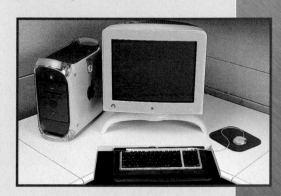

Intel unveils the Pentium III processor, which features 9.5 million transistors. Although the Pentium III's performance is not vastly superior to the Pentium II, it features enhancements that take greater advantage of graphically rich applications and Web sites. A more powerful version of the chip (named Xeon) is also released, for use in higher-end workstations and network server systems.

With its Athlon microprocessor, Advanced Micro Devices finally releases a Pentium-class chip that outperforms the Pentium III processor. The advance is seen as a boon for the lower-price computer market, which relies heavily on chips from Intel's competitors.

Apple Computer introduces updated versions of its popular iMac computer, including a laptop version, as well as the new G4 system, with performance rated at 1 gigaflop, meaning the system can perform more than one billion floating point operations per second.

The world braces for January 1, 2000, as fears of the "Millenium Bug" come to a head. As airlines, government agencies, financial institutions, utilities, and PC owners scramble to make their systems "Y2K-compliant," some people panic, afraid that basic services will cease operation when the year changes from 1999 to 2000.

2000

Shortly after the New Year, computer experts and government officials around the world announce that no major damage resulted from the "millennium date change," when computer clocks rolled over from 1999 to 2000. Immediately, a global debate began to rage: had the entire "Y2K bug" been a hoax created by the computer industry, as a way to reap huge profits from people's fears? Industry leaders defended their approach to the Y2K issue, stating that years of planning and preventive measures had helped the world avoid a global computer-driven catastrophe, which could have brought the planet's economy to a stand-still.

Microsoft introduces Windows 2000 on Feb. 17. It is the biggest commercial software project ever attempted and one of the largest engineering projects of the century, involving 5345 full-time participants, over half of them engineers. The final product includes almost 30 million lines of code.

On March 6, Advanced Micro Devices (AMD) announces the shipment of a 1 GHz version of the Athlon processor, which will be used in PCs manufactured by Compaq and Gateway. It is the first 1 GHz processor to be commercially available to the consumer PC market. Within days, Intel Corp. announces the release of a 1 GHz version of the Pentium III processor.

In April, U.S. District Judge Thomas Penfield Jackson rules that Microsoft is guilty of taking advantage of its monopoly in operating systems to hurt competitors and leverage better deals with its business partners. Soon after the finding, the Department of Justice recommends that the judge break Microsoft into two separate companies: one focused solely on operating systems, the other focused solely on application development. Microsoft quickly counters by offering to change a number of its business practices. The judge rules to divide the software giant into two companies. As of this writing, Microsoft is appealing the ruling.

Using Web-Based Search Tools

It is not always easy to find what you want on the Web. That is because there are tens of millions of unique Web sites, which include hundreds of millions of unique pages! This appendix explains the basics of Web search tools and their use. However, there are many more specific search tools available than can be listed here. To search the Web successfully, you should use this appendix as a starting point; then spend some time experimenting with a variety of search tools.

The exercises in this appendix assume your computer is connected to the Internet and you can launch and use a Web browser to navigate the World Wide Web. For more information, consult your instructor, or read "Prerequisites: What You Should Know Before Using This Book," and Unit 5, "The Internet and Online Resources."

SEARCH TOOLS

The two most basic and commonly used Web-based search tools are:

◆ **Directories.** A directory enables you to search for information by selecting categories of subject matter. The directory separates subjects into general categories (such as "companies"), which are broken into increasingly specific subcategories (such as "companies—construction—contractors—builders and designers"). After you select a category or subcategory, the directory displays a list of Web sites that provide content related to that subject.

◆ **Search Engines.** A search engine lets you search for information by typing one or more words. The engine then displays a list of Web pages that contain information related to your words. (This type of look-up is called a keyword search.)

Any search engine lets you conduct a search based on a single word. Most also let you search for multiple words, such as "scanner AND printer." A growing number of engines also let you use "plain English" phrases or questions as the basis for your search, such as "movies starring Cary Grant" or "How do cells divide?"

Note that both types of search tools are commonly called search engines. While this is not technically correct, the differences between the two are blurring. This is because most Web-based search tools provide both directories and keyword search engines.

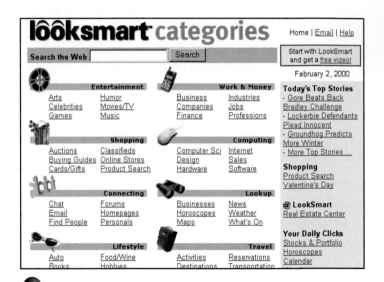

The LookSmart home page. You can use the site's directory to search for Web sites relating to many topics.

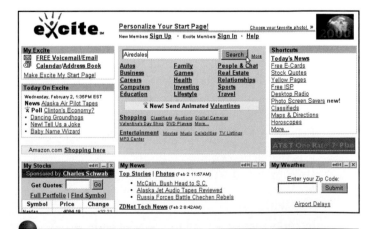

Excite is one of the older search engines on the Web, and keeps expanding its offerings. Using the Excite search engine, you can search for information by using one or more words, a phrase, or a question.

USING A DIRECTORY

Suppose you want to find some Web sites that provide information about the latest digital cameras. Perhaps you want to buy a camera, or just want to read about the technology before deciding whether to buy one. In the following exercise, you will use the LookSmart directory to find Web sites that provide "buyers guide" information.

1. Launch your Web browser.

2. In the Location/Address bar, type **www.looksmart.com/** and press Enter. The LookSmart home page opens in your browser window.

3. Under Computing, click the Hardware category. A new page appears, displaying a list of subcategories under the Hardware category.

4. Click the Peripherals subcategory; then click Digital Camera/Video; then click Buyers Guides. After you click the last subcategory (Buyers Guides), a new page appears listing sites that provide information about buying digital cameras.

5. Browse through the list of Web sites, and click one. The new site opens in your browser window. After reviewing it, you can use your browser's Back button to navigate back to the list of buyers guides to choose another.

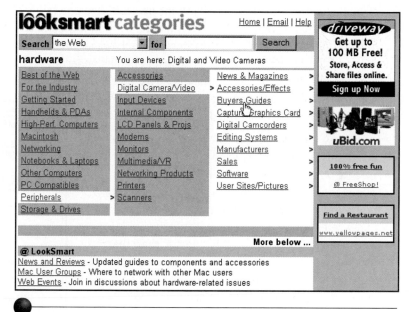

Selecting categories and subcategories of topics in the LookSmart directory.

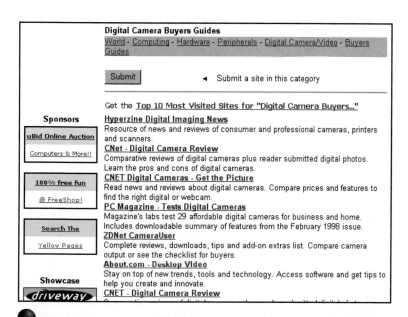

After you select the final subcategory, LookSmart displays a list of Web sites that provide information related to your topic.

Sites listed in a directory will generally provide valuable, relevant information. This is because, before adding a site to its list, a directory reviews the site's content. Sites that offer poor content may not be included in the list. For this reason, Web sites listed in a directory are considered to be "pre-screened." Also, because the list of suggested sites has already been reviewed, you are unlikely to find a site listed multiple times within the same topic category. This is a big advantage over search engines, which are notorious for listing the same sites multiple times.

USING A SEARCH ENGINE

Suppose you want to find some information about ink jet printers. You know there are many different types of printers, available at a wide range of prices. You also know you are interested in a color printer rather than a black-and-white one. In the following exercise, you will use a search engine to help you find the information you need.

1. Launch your Web browser.

2. In the Location/Address bar, type **www.lycos.com/** and press Enter. The Lycos home page opens in your browser window.

3. In the Search For text box, type **"ink jet printer"** (include the quotation marks) and click the Go Get It! button. A new page appears, listing Web pages that contain information relating to ink jet printers. Note, however, that the list includes thousands of pages! Unlike most directories, search engines generally do not "screen" other Web sites for quality of content. Rather, they assume a Web site is relevant to your needs if it contains terms that match the keywords you provide.

4. To narrow the search results, you must provide more specific search criteria. Click in the Search For text box, and type **"color ink jet printer"** (again, including the quotation marks); then click the Go Get It! button. Another page appears, listing a new selection of Web sites that match your keywords. Note that this list is shorter than the original one, by several thousand matches. Still, you want to continue narrowing your search, so you decide to provide more criteria.

5. Click in the Search For text box, and type **"color ink jet printer reviews"** (with quotation marks); then click the Go Get It! button. The list of matching Web sites has shrunk even further, but is still quite long.

The Lycos home page.

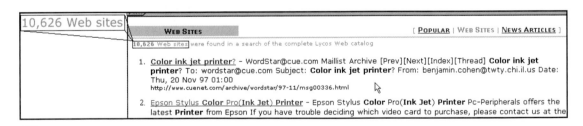

Search engines commonly produce thousands (even hundreds of thousands) of matches, depending on your search criteria. To narrow your list of results, you need to provide more specific keywords.

Scroll through the list, and notice if it contains any duplicate entries. How many of the suggested pages actually seem irrelevant to your search criteria? Duplicate and useless entries are two significant problems users encounter when working with search engines.

Further, in addition to listing Web pages, search engines frequently also list articles posted to Internet newsgroups and messages posted in chat rooms or in Web-based discussion groups. Sometimes you may find such results helpful, but other times they may only interfere with your search.

Fortunately, most search engines provide other tools to help you search more accurately, finding Web pages that are more relevant to your interests. These include Boolean operators and advanced search tools, which are discussed in the following sections.

Using Boolean Operators in Your Searches

Most search engines allow you to use special words, called Boolean operators, to modify your search criteria. Boolean operators are named after George Boole, a 19th century British mathematician.

There are three basic Boolean operators you can use in searching: AND, OR, and NOT. To use an operator, simply include it in the text box where you type your keywords. The following table shows simple examples of keyword searches that include the operators, and explains how the operator affects each search.

Operator	Search Criteria	Effect
AND	printer AND color	The search engine looks only for pages that include both terms, and ignores pages that include only one of them.
OR	printer OR color	The search engine looks for pages that include either or both of the terms.
NOT	printer NOT color	The search engine looks for pages that include the term *printer*, which do not also include the term *color*. The engine ignores any pages that include both terms.

Some search engines also support a fourth operator, NEAR. This operator determines the proximity, or closeness, of your specified keywords. For example, you may specify "printer NEAR color," with a closeness of 10 words. This tells the search engine to look for pages that include both terms, where the terms are no more than 10 words apart.

A good way to determine whether you need to use operators is to phrase your interest in the form of a sentence, and then use the important parts of the sentence as your keywords along with the appropriate operators. Here are some examples:

Interest	Search
I need information about cancer in children.	cancer AND children
I need information about dogs.	dog OR canine
I need information about acoustic guitars, but not electric guitars.	guitar NOT electric

A few (but not all) search engines will let you use multiple operators and set the order in which they are used. Suppose, for example, that you want to want to find information about cancer in dogs. You might set up your search criteria like this:

```
(dog OR canine) AND cancer
```

This tells the engine to look for pages that include either "dog," "canine," or both, and then to search those pages for ones that also include "cancer."

A few search engines accept symbols to represent operators. For example, you may be able to use a plus sign (+) to represent the AND operator, and a minus sign (−) to represent NOT.

Many search engines use implied Boolean logic by default, meaning you may not need to include an operator in some searches. For example, if you type this search criteria:

dog canine

Some search engines will assume that you want to find pages that include either term (using the OR operator by default), and others will assume you want pages that include both terms (using the AND operator by default).

When dealing with implied logic, remember that each search engine operates in a slightly different way. For example, in some engines, you should use quotation marks when searching for a phrase or when you want all words to be included, as in:

"ink jet printer"

Without the quotation marks, some engines will return pages that include the word "ink," others that include "jet," and others that include "printer," as well as pages that include all three.

The best way to determine how any search engine works is to study its Help-related pages. The Help section will tell you whether or how you can use operators with that particular engine.

Using Advanced Search Options

To overcome the problems of duplicate and irrelevant results, nearly all search engines provide a set of advanced search options, sometimes called advanced tools. It is important to remember that each engine's advanced tool set is somewhat different from the others', but they all have the same goal of helping you refine your search criteria to get the best results.

In some engines, advanced search options include support for phrase-based searching or Boolean operators, as already discussed. In other engines, an advanced search provides you with customized tools. At Excite, for example, if you select the Advanced Search link, you can work in a special form to structure your search criteria. The form lets you specify multiple words and phrases, and decide whether each one "must," "must not," or "should

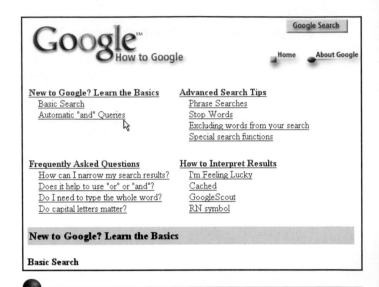

The Help links at the Google search engine site. This Help section provides a basic overview of Google and how it conducts searches. You also can find information about Google's support for Boolean operators, basic and advanced search techniques, and more. The Help section is the best place to start when working with a search engine for the first time.

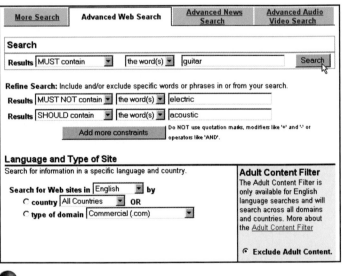

Setting up an advanced search in Excite.

be" included in the results. The form also provides tools that let you filter adult-oriented content (such as pornographic Web sites) from your results, and search for information in a different language or from a given country.

When using some advanced tool sets, such as those provided by Excite, you should not use operators in the text boxes. This is because the form itself is based on Boolean logic, and is designed to help you create complex Boolean-based searches without deciding which operators to use, or where to use them.

As mentioned earlier, the best way to learn about a specific search engine's advanced options is to study its Help section, and then to practice using the tools. After you learn to use an engine's advance options, you may never want to conduct a search without them.

METASEARCH ENGINES

In addition to the tools described in the preceding sections, a new breed of Web-based search engines is also gaining popularity. These sites, called metasearch engines, use multiple search engines simultaneously to look up sites that match your keywords, phrase, or question.

Examples of metasearch engines include Dogpile (**www.dogpile.com/**), Mamma (**www.mamma.com/**), and The BigHub (**www.thebighub.com/**). Metasearch engines are helpful if you are not certain which keywords to use, or if you want to get a very long list of Web sites that meet your search criteria.

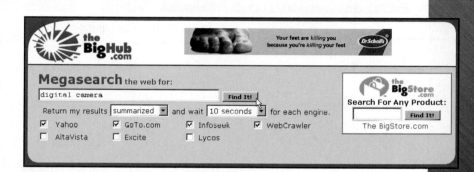

The BigHub is an example of a metasearch engine. This site enables you to specify terms for a keyword search, and to select the search engines you want to use. When you click the Find It! button, all the selected engines conduct simultaneous searches. The BigHub compiles all the results into a single list.

SITE-SPECIFIC SEARCH TOOLS

Many high-volume Web sites feature built-in search tools of their own, meaning you do not have to navigate to a different site in order to conduct a search. Sites such as Microsoft Corporation (**www.microsoft.com/**), CNN Interactive (**www.cnn.com/**), Netscape Communications (**www.netscape.com/**), and many others feature such tools. Generally, these site-specific search tools enable you to look for information on the Web site you are currently visiting.

Suppose, for example, you are visiting the Microsoft Web site and want to find information about Flight Simulator, a popular Microsoft game. Instead of jumping from one page to another looking for information, you can click in the Search box, type the words *Flight Simulator* and click the Go button. The site's search engine displays a list of pages on the Microsoft site that are related to Flight Simulator.

Some site-specific search tools also let you search outside that particular site. At ZDNet's site (**www.zdnet.com/**), for example, you can type one or more keywords in the Search box, then decide whether you want to search only the ZDNet site or the entire Web for related information before clicking the Go button.

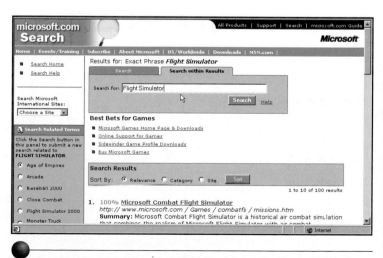

Searching for information about Flight Simulator at the Microsoft Web site.

APPENDIX C

Self Check
Answers

UNIT 1

Lesson 1, page 11
1. computer
2. memory
3. disk drive

Lesson 2, page 29
1. pointer
2. magnetic coil
3. viewing angle

UNIT 2

Lesson 3, page 55
1. binary
2. Registers
3. architecture

Lesson 4, page 75
1. network server
2. Electronic mail (e-mail)
3. peer-to-peer network

UNIT 3

Lesson 5, page 104
1. GUIs
2. Macintosh computer
3. operating environment

Lesson 6, page 119
1. insertion point (or cursor)
2. label
3. arguments

UNIT 4

Lesson 7, page 149
1. bitmap
2. file format
3. Electronic photographs

Lesson 8, page 165
1. interactivity
2. convergence
3. Hypermedia

UNIT 5

Lesson 9, page 195
1. ARPANET
2. Internet Protocol (IP) address
3. hyperlinks (or links)

Lesson 10, page 208
1. direct connection
2. digital subscriber line
3. cable modem

Current Issues in Computing

Health, privacy, and ethical issues face individual computer users every day. It is true that these concerns affect many individuals, but they have an impact on large segments of society and therefore are being addressed as societal problems. Chief among these problems are ergonomic and health issues, computer-related crimes, and environmental damage caused by the improper disposal of computer hardware and software. This appendix introduces you to some of the personal and societal problems that stem from our reliance on—and misuse of—computer systems.

HEALTH ISSUES

Much is being done to make computers easier, safer, and more comfortable to use. Ergonomics, the study of the physical relationship between people and their tools—such as their computers—addresses these issues. The term *ergonomically correct* means that a product has been designed to work properly with the human body, reducing the risk of strain, stress, or other types of injuries.

Repetitive Stress Injuries and Eyestrain

The field of ergonomics did not receive much attention until repetitive stress injuries (RSIs)—a group of ailments caused by using the body continuously in ways it was not designed to work—began appearing among clerical workers who spend most of their time entering data on computer keyboards. Carpal tunnel syndrome is the best-known repetitive stress injury—a wrist or hand injury caused by extended periods of keyboarding.

Ergonomically designed chairs.

If you routinely use a computer, you can avoid fatigue and strain by choosing the proper furniture for your workplace. Perhaps the most important piece of computer furniture is a comfortable, ergonomically designed chair.

Another important factor in avoiding keyboard-related RSIs is the keyboard itself. A few years ago, keyboard designers realized that a flat keyboard is not well suited to the shape of our hands. Ergonomic keyboards allow the user's hands to rest in a more natural position than traditional flat keyboards. Many ergonomic keyboards are made so that the user's hands must remain in one position; other designs break the keyboard into two or more separate parts that the user can adjust for a customized fit.

Ergonomically designed keyboards are available in several shapes and sizes and offer various features that make them more comfortable to use than standard keyboards. On this model, the keyboard is divided into two sections, allowing the hands to remain in a more natural position. It also features a built-in wrist pad.

Another area of concern is protecting people's vision. Staring at a computer screen for long periods can strain or even injure the eyes. In fact, eyestrain is the most frequently reported health problem associated with computers. Antiglare screens cut down on light reflecting off the surface of the monitor. They are useful in bright offices or in cases where a window faces the monitor.

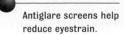
Antiglare screens help reduce eyestrain.

Electromagnetic Fields

Electromagnetic fields (EMFs) are created during the generation, transmission, and use of low-frequency electrical power. These fields exist near power lines, electrical appliances, and any piece of equipment that has an electric motor. A debate has continued for years whether EMFs can be linked to cancer. There is enough data, however, to raise suspicion. Given the pervasiveness of EMFs in our homes and workplaces, the issue cannot be ignored. Populations deemed to be at greatest risk include children, pregnant women, and anyone who spends many working hours near a piece of electrical equipment.

EMFs are composed of electrical and magnetic components. The magnetic field is the one that raises the health concern. Electrical fields lose strength when they come in contact with barriers such as clothing and skin. A magnetic field, however, will penetrate most materials, even concrete or lead. Magnetic fields attenuate—lose strength rapidly—with distance. Options to reduce your risk from EMFs include the following:

◆ Taking frequent breaks away from the computer

◆ Sitting at arm's length away from the system unit and monitor

◆ Using a flat-panel display, which does not radiate EMFs

Tips for Healthy Computing

If you use a computer frequently, you can avoid health issues by adopting good habits such as the following:

◆ **Choose a Good Chair and Computer Desk.** Look for a chair that provides back support, armrests, and adjustable height. Your computer desk should hold the keyboard level with or slightly below your hands. Your forearms should be held parallel to the floor. The desk should allow you to change the keyboard's height. You should not have to reach up, forward, or down to touch the keyboard.

◆ **Position Your Monitor Correctly.** Place your monitor directly in front of you, about 2 to 2½ feet away, and a little below eye level. Tilt the monitor's face upward about 10 degrees. This angle will enable you to view the monitor comfortably without bending your neck. If you have vision problems that require corrective lenses, consult an optometrist about the best way to position your monitor.

◆ **Sit Up Straight.** Do not slouch as you type, and keep your feet flat on the floor in front of you. Do not cross your legs in front of you or under your chair for long periods.

◆ **Keep Your Wrists Straight.** Your hands should be in a straight line with your forearms as you type and when viewed either from above or from the side. If you keep your wrists bent in either direction, you can cause muscle fatigue and increase your risk of injuries.

A properly designed computer desk features a built-in shelf or tray to hold the keyboard and mouse.

- ◆ **Do Not Rest Your Wrists on Anything as You Type.** If you have a wrist support, use it only when you are resting your hands, not when you are actually typing. Resting the wrist while typing disables the forearms from moving the hands and puts undue strain on the hands and fingers.

- ◆ **Be Gentle.** Avoid pounding the keys or gripping the mouse too tightly.

- ◆ **Learn to Type.** You will use the keyboard more efficiently and naturally if you learn how to type. The "hunt and peck" technique not only hurts productivity but leads to fatigue and stiffness.

- ◆ **Rest Your Eyes Occasionally.** Eyestrain develops from staring at a fixed distance for too long. Even if you cannot get up, look around you and focus on different objects at various distances. Also, try closing your eyes for a minute or so and letting them relax.

- ◆ **Set Your Monitor for Healthy Viewing.** Even if your monitor can operate at high resolution, it is not necessarily the best setting for your eyes. At higher resolutions, text and icons appear smaller on the screen, which can lead to squinting and eyestrain.

- ◆ **Take Frequent Breaks.** Occasionally get up, move around, and stretch.

PRIVACY ISSUES

As people use their computers, they generally assume that their activities are private and their personal information is safe. Unfortunately, this is not always true. For example, commercial Web sites often collect information from visitors. Many companies then sell this information, sometimes against the wishes of the individual. Privacy advocates view this practice as an invasion of the individual's privacy because it involves trading a person's private information. But this practice is not against the law; there is no explicit constitutional right to privacy. However, such protection may soon be necessary, given the computer's power to collect, organize, and sort data about people, and the power it gives people to contact one another.

Junk Faxes and Junk E-Mail

Junk faxes—unsolicited and unwanted facsimile messages received from unnamed senders—usually invite the recipient to purchase a product or service, to call a salesperson, or to consider a get-rich-quick scheme. Junk faxes tie up the recipient's resources, including paper, ink, and online time. Senders of junk faxes frequently program their machines to send the faxes during business hours and to not transmit the sender's identity or fax number. These tactics interfere with the normal business use of many busy fax machines and leave the recipient helpless to identify or respond to the sender. For these reasons, Congress passed an "anti-junk fax" law in 1991, which prohibits anyone from sending a fax without including an identifier and return phone number. Efforts are also under way in most states to toughen state and local anti-junk fax laws.

Junk e-mail is a lot like old-fashioned junk mail; that is, you open your electronic mailbox and find that it contains unwanted messages from various senders. Like traditional junk mail, junk e-mail usually includes solicitations to purchase a product or service or invitations to participate in get-rich-quick schemes. Some junk e-mail messages, however, are filled with lewd—even obscene—material.

 Although it is now illegal to send unsolicited junk faxes without the sender's identification, junk fax messages are still common. These messages waste time, money, and resources.

The debate continues about whether junk e-mail should be outlawed. Like junk faxes, junk e-mail ties up resources for both the recipient and the Internet service provider. Many people complain that they spend too much time downloading and sorting through junk e-mail, creating a loss of productivity. Currently, there is no comprehensive national law regulating spam (a few state laws are now in effect, and their effectiveness is being tested), but experts agree that federal laws should be in place within the next few years.

Protecting Your Online Privacy

Information about our private lives is available to a degree unimaginable just a few years ago. With the Internet's explosion in popularity, people are revealing more about themselves than ever before. You can take measures to prevent too many people from getting that information and to reduce the number of unwanted or unsolicited e-mail messages:

◆ **Avoid Being Added to Mailing Lists.** When you fill out a warranty, subscription, or registration form—either on paper or online—make sure it includes an option that prevents your information from being added to a mailing list. If the option is available, check it; if it is not, do not return the form. If there is any doubt, contact the organization and learn its policies regarding mailing lists.

◆ **Make Online Purchases Only Through Secure Web Sites.** Before you purchase anything over the Internet, make sure that the transaction is secure. First, if you use a current browser, such as Internet Explorer 5.0 or Netscape Navigator 5.0, the browser can tell you whether the server is secure. Check your browser's security settings before proceeding with a transaction. Second, check the vendor's Web site to see whether you have the option to switch to a secure server before making the transaction. If this option is available, take it.

◆ **Never Assume That Your E-Mail Is Private.** Watch what you say, especially when using your company's or school's e-mail system. Never respond to an unsolicited e-mail message, especially if you do not recognize the sender. Be careful when giving out your e-mail address.

◆ **Be Careful When Posting to Newsgroups.** Many Internet newsgroups and chat rooms are unsupervised. If you post a message to a group, your e-mail address and interests can make you easy prey for pranksters. Before posting a message to any group, watch the group for a few days to determine whether its users are trustworthy. Try to determine whether the group is supervised by a system operator and get that person's address, if possible.

◆ **Contact Your Internet Service Provider.** Most Internet service providers do not tolerate the use of their e-mail servers for the distribution of unsolicited e-mail. They typically reserve the right to terminate service to anyone who knowingly violates their appropriate use policies.

◆ **Use Filters In Your E-Mail Program.** You may be able to use filters in your e-mail program to block out junk e-mail. (A filter is a software tool used to establish conditions for selecting/rejecting data that meets those criteria.) Microsoft Outlook, Netscape Messenger, Eudora Pro, and other e-mail programs provide simple filtering tools.

◆ **Make Use of Online Services.** Several commercial Web-based services can also help you minimize junk e-mail. Services such as NoThankYou (**www.nothankyou.com/**) allow you to register your e-mail address and, for a fee, will notify known junk e-mailers that you want to be removed from their mailing lists. Services like Zero Junk Mail (**www.zerojunkmail.com/**) provide specialized filtering software to help you prevent junk e-mail from reaching your computer.

Privacy Issues Facing Corporate Computer Users

Another threat to privacy can occur between a company and its employees. Electronic communications systems such as e-mail and voice mail are controlled by corporate computer systems. The company has access to the contents of communications, even if employees intend their messages to be private. In fact, many companies routinely monitor their employees' communications for the following reasons:

◆ To protect trade secrets

◆ To prevent the distribution of libelous or slanderous messages

◆ To prevent the system's users from downloading or copying data that is illegal, pornographic, or infected by computer viruses

◆ To ensure that organizational resources are not being wasted or abused

In the workplace, always remember that the computer systems—and the data stored on them, even your e-mail messages—is considered the company's property.

Although some people contend that businesses have no right to monitor their employees' use of communications systems, the opposite is true. In a business setting, the computers, network, communications equipment, and software are usually the property of the company. By extension, all information contained on the system or carried by the system is also the property of the company.

COMPUTER CRIME

Although the types of computer-related crimes are numerous and widespread, a few categories of online criminal activity continue to attract the most attention and affect the most people. Those activities include the illegal copying of software, infiltrating private computer systems, and stealing hardware or data.

Software Piracy

The biggest legal issue affecting the computer industry is software piracy, which is the illegal copying of programs. Piracy is a huge problem because it is so easy to do. In most cases, it is no more difficult to steal a program than it is to copy a music CD that you have borrowed from a friend. Software pirates give up the right to receive upgrades and technical support, but they gain the use of the program without paying for it.

In most cases, when you purchase commercial software you are not actually buying the software itself. Instead, you are paying for a license to use the software. Although software licensing agreements can vary in their terms, they usually place restrictions on the user, such as allowing the user to make only one archive (backup) copy of the program for safekeeping. These licenses generally prohibit the user from making multiple copies of the software, installing it on more than one machine at a time, or giving copies of the program to someone else.

Software is pirated in many ways. The simplest method is to copy the software from its original floppy disk or compact disk. Users on a network can copy certain types of software directly from the server or even exchange programs over their organization's e-mail system. The Internet has become the biggest hotbed of piracy, however, because pirates distribute programs by e-mail, across rogue sites on the Web, and in newsgroups.

Software Forgeries

Blatant software forgery with the intent to sell is similar to selling clothes or leather goods as designer labels when they are really cheap imitations. Copying software, however, is far easier than copying designer clothing. Although aggressive new treaties are forcing some countries to ensure more protection against pirating and forging of software, forgery is big business in some parts of the world. For example, in the mid- to late 1990s, as the Windows 95 and Windows 98 operating systems were being developed and tested for commercial release, black marketers in Asia were busily making illegal duplicates of the beta software (software in the developmental stage and not ready for release to the public) and selling the copies to anyone who would purchase them.

Computer Viruses

In general, a virus is a parasitic program that infects another, legitimate program, which is sometimes called the host. To infect the host program, the virus modifies the host so that it contains a copy of the virus. However, e-mail viruses do not necessarily require a host program to infect a computer. While some e-mail viruses can be transmitted as an infected document file, others can be carried within the body of certain types of e-mail messages. Viruses can be programmed to do many things including the following:

◆ Copy themselves to other programs or areas of a disk. (Most viruses exhibit this feature, which does little or no other damage.)

◆ Display information on the screen

◆ Destroy data files

◆ Erase the contents of an entire disk

◆ Stay dormant for a specified time or until a given condition is met before becoming active

Here are some common ways to pick up a virus:

◆ From an infected disk (a diskette, a CD created by someone with a CD-R system, a removable hard disk, and so on) received from another user. In this case, the virus could be in the boot sector of the disk or in an executable file (a program) on the disk.

◆ By downloading an infected executable file to your computer across a network, an online service, or the Internet.

◆ By copying to your disk a document file that is infected with a macro virus. An infected document might be copied from another disk or received as an attachment to an e-mail message.

To help prevent virus infections, take the following precautions:

◆ Install a reputable antivirus program, run it frequently, and keep its virus definitions up to date. Some experts suggest using two different antivirus programs and running them on an alternating schedule. Some popular antivirus programs include *Norton Antivirus, Symantec Antivirus for the Macintosh, IBM AntiVirus, McAfee VirusScan,* and *Virex.*

◆ Do not open e-mail attachments from people you do not know.

◆ Check your Web browser, e-mail program, and newsreader and make sure that their security settings are set to the highest possible level. In addition, you may want to set your e-mail program not to accept messages delivered in HTML format.

◆ Be alert to new developments in viruses by periodically checking virus-related sites on the Web. These informational sites are hosted by the makers of antivirus programs, universities, and security experts.

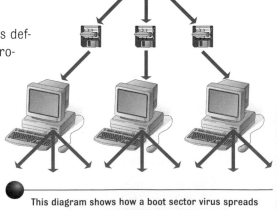

This diagram shows how a boot sector virus spreads from a single computer to many computers via an infected floppy disk. Viruses can also be spread from one machine to another across corporate computer networks or the Internet.

Hardware, Software, and Data Theft

Although hardware theft has been going on for many years, the problem was not particularly serious until the introduction of the microcomputer in the 1970s made valuable equipment much easier to move. The problem skyrocketed with the popularity of small portable computers. Many organizations now secure their computer equipment with steel cables. Even relatively inexpensive items such as keyboards are often locked to the desk or to the rest of the computer.

In some facilities, especially businesses, expensive software can be found stored on bookshelves or in workers' cubicles or offices, within easy reach. When stored in the open, such software is easy to steal. Many corporations maintain secure software "libraries," where valuable software is kept under lock and key. In these settings, if an employee needs to install a piece of software, he or she notifies the company's Information System's (IS) department. Then an IS worker installs the software on the employee's machine or gives the employee the user rights needed to access the software from the company's network server. Either way, the software cannot be duplicated from its original disks.

Steel cables, similar to those used to secure bicycles, are used to lock computers to desks at many schools, libraries, and businesses.

In businesses and government, the theft of data can be far more serious than the theft of hardware or software programs, which can be replaced fairly easily. Most companies and government agencies use security measures to limit access to their computer systems. One common method is to provide user identification codes and passwords to authorized employees. Before an employee can log on, or access a computer's files, the employee must enter a user ID or user name that identifies that person to the system. Usually, employees also need to enter a password, a word or symbol usually chosen by the user, that verifies the user's identity. If a user's identification code or password does not match the records in the computer's security software, the user is locked out of the system.

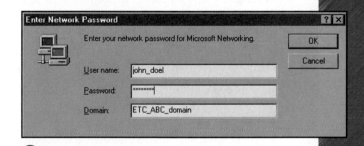

A network log-on screen. Before accessing any disks or data on the network, the user must provide his or her identification and a password and specify the portion of the network to be accessed.

Perhaps the most effective form of security is encryption, which is a method of encoding and decoding data. Encryption is used most often in messaging systems such as electronic mail. One common encryption method, known as the DES (Data Encryption Standard), can encode a message in more than 72 quadrillion ways. Because a special software key is used to decode the message, unauthorized interception of the message is less of a threat. In many messaging systems, DES encryption takes place without users even knowing it.

COMPUTERS AND THE ENVIRONMENT

A computer system bought today will be obsolete in, at most, two to three years. During that time, you may need to upgrade several parts of the machine. Every time that software is updated, the disks and other materials from the previous release are discarded. The introduction of new operating systems has had a particularly noticeable impact on the volume of discarded hardware and software.

Reducing the environmental impact is easier with software than with hardware. Much software is already available online, and documentation is commonly provided on disk rather than in printed form. In the coming years, you may download almost all new applications from the Internet rather than buying them (and their packaging) in a store.

Getting rid of old hardware is a little trickier. You should not throw old computers into the trash, because many of them contain nickel-cadmium (nicad) batteries, and cadmium is a toxic heavy metal. To address this problem, some hardware manufacturers have begun programs to collect and properly dispose of old computers. Some companies now donate their old computers to nonprofit organizations, which can use them because they often do not need the latest technological advances to stay competitive.

Another environmental concern relating to computers is a direct result of how we use them. If you visit a typical office, you will find many computers running but not being used. If you come back to the same office at night, you might find all the computers still turned on. In some cases, leaving computers running is justified because employees use modems to access their systems at night, and some automatic backup systems are used only at night. In other cases, the problem is old-fashioned thinking that it is cheaper and less damaging to leave the computer running than to turn it on and off every day.

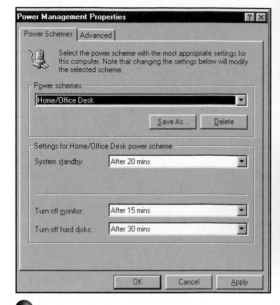

Hardware and software manufacturers have taken steps to reduce the amount of power used by computer systems. Most newer computer systems feature energy-saving options—some are hardware-specific; others are provided by the operating system. For example, the user can set the system to "go to sleep" after a specified period of nonuse. In sleep mode, the computer's hard disk may stop spinning and the monitor may turn off. To "wake up" the system, the user needs only to move the mouse or press a key on the keyboard.

Modern operating systems, such as Windows 98, provide users with some control over the power use of their systems.

ETHICS IN COMPUTING

Advances in computer and communications technologies have placed tremendous new capabilities in the hands of everyday people. We can use information, sounds, and images that once could be used only by specially trained professionals using highly sophisticated tools. With these new capabilities, however, comes a set of responsibilities. Until a set of laws establishes guidelines for ethical computer use, personal ethics and common sense must guide us in our daily work and play, both online and offline. A sample code of conduct suggested by the Computer Ethics Institute is listed below:

◆ Do not use a computer to harm other people.

◆ Do not interfere with other people's computer work.

◆ Do not snoop around in other people's computer files.

◆ Do not use a computer to steal.

◆ Do not use a computer to bear false witness.

◆ Do not copy or use proprietary software for which you have not paid.

◆ Do not use other people's computer resources without authorization or proper compensation.

◆ Do not appropriate other people's intellectual output.

◆ Always think about the social consequences of the program you are writing or the system you are designing.

◆ Always use a computer in ways that ensure consideration and respect for your fellow humans.

NUMERALS

3-D modeling software Graphics software used to create electronic models of three-dimensional objects. Types of 3-D modeling software include surface, solid, polygonal, and spline-based modelers.

A

absolute cell reference In a spreadsheet program, a cell reference that does not change when copied to a new cell.

activate (1) To initiate a command or load a program into memory and begin using it. (2) To choose; for example, you can activate a resource by choosing its icon, toolbar button, or file name.

active matrix LCD A liquid crystal display (LCD) technology that assigns a transistor to each pixel in a flat-panel monitor, improving display quality and eliminating the "submarining" effect produced by some types of flat-panel monitors. Also called a *thin-film transistor display*.

active window On the computer screen, the window in which the user's next action will occur. The active window's title bar is highlighted, while the title bars of inactive windows appear dimmed.

address bus A set of wires connecting the computer's CPU and RAM, across which memory addresses are transmitted. The number of wires in the bus determines the amount of memory that can be addressed at any one time.

alphanumeric keys On a computer keyboard, the keys that include the letters of the alphabet, numerals, and commonly used symbols.

annotation In presentation programs, a feature that enables the user to embed notes in individual slides. The notes can be made visible only to the presenter, or they can be printed out for distribution to the audience.

anonymous FTP archives FTP sites with files available to the general public. So called because the user types the word "anonymous" as the account name.

application software Any computer program used to create or process data, such as text documents, spreadsheets, graphics, and so on. Examples include database management software, desktop publishing programs, presentation programs, spreadsheet programs, and word processing programs.

Archie A catalog of file names maintained by McGill University in Montreal. Internet users can search and locate a file among thousands of directories listed on this service.

argument (1) In a spreadsheet, the values or cell references within a formula on which the function performs its operation. (2) In programming, an item of information needed by a function or subroutine to carry out its instructions. Also called a *parameter*.

arithmetic logic unit (ALU) The component of the CPU that handles arithmetic and logic functions. Instructions are passed from memory to the ALU.

ARPANET Acronym for *Advanced Research Projects Agency Network*. An early network developed by the Department of Defense to connect computers at universities and defense contractors. This network eventually became part of the Internet.

B

article A message posted to an Internet newsgroup. A series of related articles and responses is called a *thread*.

ASCII An 8-bit binary code developed by the American National Standards Institute (ANSI) to represent symbolic, numeric, and alphanumeric characters. The ASCII character set is the most commonly used character set in PCs.

backbone The central structure of a network, which connects other elements of the network and handles the major traffic.

back up To create a duplicate set of program or data files in case the originals become damaged. (A duplicate file made for this purpose is called a *backup* file.) Files can be backed up individually, by entire folders, and by entire drives. Backups can be made to many types of storage media, such as diskettes, optical disks, or tape. The term is correctly used as two words as a verb ("I am going to *back up* the files on the server.") and as one word as a noun or adjective ("He used a *backup* utility to make a backup of that file.")

bandwidth The amount of data that can be transmitted over a network at any given time. Bandwidth may be measured in bits per second (bps) or in hertz (Hz).

bar code reader An input device that converts a pattern of printed bars (called a *bar code*) into a number that a computer can read. A beam of light reflected off the bar code into a light-sensitive detector identifies the bar code and converts the bar patterns into numeric digits, which can be transferred to a computer. Bar code readers are commonly used in retail stores.

binary field A database field that stores binary objects (such as clip art, photographs, screen images, formatted text, sound objects, and video clips) or OLE objects (such as graphs or worksheets created with a spreadsheet or word processor).

binary large object (BLOB) (1) A graphic image file, such as clip art, a photograph, a screen image, formatted text, a sound object, or a video clip. (2) An OLE object, such as a graph or worksheet created with a spreadsheet or word processor; frequently used with object-oriented databases.

binary number system A system for representing the two possible states of electrical switches, which are on and off (also known as *base 2*). The binary number system gets its name from the fact that it includes only two numbers: 0 and 1. In computer storage and memory systems, the numeral 0 represents off, and a 1 represents on.

bit The smallest unit of data that can be used by a computer.

bitmap A binary representation of an image in which each part of the image, such as a pixel, is represented by one or more bits in a coordinate system. Also called a *raster*.

block A contiguous series of characters, words, sentences, or paragraphs in a word processing document. This term is also sometimes used to describe a range of cells in a spreadsheet. Once a block of text or cells has been selected, the user can perform many different actions on it, such as moving, formatting, or deleting.

booting Starting a computer. The term comes from the expression "pulling oneself up by one's own bootstraps."

bridge A device that connects two LANs and controls data flow between them.

browser See *Web browser*.

bus The path between components of a computer or nodes of a network. The bus's width determines the speed at which data is transmitted. When used alone, the term commonly refers to a computer's data bus.

bus network A network topology in which all network nodes and peripheral devices are attached to a single conduit.

button In graphical user interfaces, a symbol that simulates a push button. The user clicks a button to initiate an action.

byte The amount of memory required to store a single character. A byte is comprised of eight bits.

C

cache memory High-speed memory that resides between the CPU and RAM in a computer. Cache memory stores data and instructions that the CPU is likely to need next. The CPU can retrieve data or instructions more quickly from cache than it can from RAM or a disk.

cathode ray tube (CRT) A type of monitor or TV screen that uses a vacuum tube as a display screen. CRTs are most commonly used with desktop computers.

CD-Recordable (CD-R) drive A peripheral device that enables the user to create customized CD-ROM disks. Once data has been written to a CD-R disk, that data cannot be changed (overwritten). CD-R disks can be read by any CD-ROM drive. CD-R drives are commonly used to create backup copies of program or data files, or to create duplicates of existing compact disks.

CD-ReWritable (CD-RW) drive A peripheral device that enables the user to create customized CD-ROM disks. Unlike a CD-R disk, a CD-RW disk's data can be overwritten, meaning the data can be updated after it has been placed on the disk. CD-RW disks can be read by any CD-ROM drive.

CD-ROM drive A specialized type of disk drive, which enables a computer to read data from a compact disk. Using a standard CD-ROM drive and compact disk, the computer can only read data from the disk and cannot write data to the disk.

cell In a spreadsheet or database table, the intersection of a row and column, forming a box into which the user enters numbers, formulas, or text. The term also is used to refer to the individual blocks in a table created in a word processing program.

cell address In a spreadsheet, an identifier that indicates the location of a cell in a worksheet. The address is composed of the cell's row and column locations. For example, if the cell is located at the intersection of column B and row 3, then its cell address is B3.

cell pointer A square enclosing one cell of a spreadsheet, identifying that cell as the active cell. The user positions the cell pointer in a worksheet by clicking the mouse on the cell or by using the cursor movement keys on the keyboard.

cell reference The address of a spreadsheet cell used in a formula.

central processing unit (CPU) The computer's primary processing hardware, which interprets and executes program instructions and manages the functions of input, output, and storage devices. In personal computers, the CPU is composed of a control unit, an ALU, built-in memory, and supporting circuitry such as a dedicated math processor. The CPU may reside on a single chip on the computer's motherboard, or on a larger card inserted into a special slot on the motherboard. In larger computers, the CPU may reside on several circuit boards.

channel A discussion group where chat users convene to discuss a topic.

character formatting In a word processor, settings that control the attributes of individual text characters, such as font, type size, type style, and color.

characters per second (cps) A measure of the speed of impact printers, such as dot matrix printers.

chat See *Internet Relay Chat (IRC)*.

choose See *activate*.

circuit board A rigid rectangular card—consisting of chips and electronic circuitry—that ties the processor to other hardware. In a personal computer, the primary circuit board (to which all components are attached) is called the *motherboard*.

clicking Selecting an object or command on the computer screen (for example, from a menu, toolbar, or dialog box) by pointing to the object and pressing and releasing the primary mouse button once.

client/server A hierarchical network strategy in which the processing is shared by a server and numerous clients. In this type of network, clients provide the user interface, run applications, and request services from the server. The server contributes storage, printing, and some or all processing services.

clip art Predrawn or photographed graphic images, which are available for use by anyone. Some clip art is available through licensing, some through purchase, and some for free.

Clipboard A holding area maintained by the operating system in memory. The Clipboard is used for storing text, graphics, sound, video or other data that has been copied or cut from a document. After data has been placed in the Clipboard, it can be inserted from the Clipboard into other documents, in the same application or a different application.

cluster On a magnetic disk (such as a hard disk) a group of sectors that are treated as a single data-storage unit. The number of sectors per disk can vary, depending on the type of disk and the manner in which it is formatted.

coaxial (coax) cable A cable composed of a single conductive wire wrapped in a conductive wire mesh shield with an insulator in between.

command-line interface A user interface that enables the user to interact with the software by typing strings of characters at a prompt. MS-DOS is an example of a command-line interface.

communications device An input/output device used to connect one computer to another to share hardware and information. This family of devices includes modems and network interface cards.

compact disk (CD) A type of optical storage device, identical to audio CDs, which can store about 650 MB of data, or about 450 times as much as a diskette. The type of CD used in computers is called Compact Disk Read-Only Memory (CD-ROM). As the device's name implies, you cannot change the information on the disk, just as you cannot record over an audio CD.

compact disk read-only memory (CD-ROM) The most common type of optical storage medium. In CD-ROM, data is written in a series of lands and pits on the surface of a compact disk (CD), which can be read by a laser in a CD-ROM drive. A standard CD stores approximately 650 MB, but data on a standard compact disk cannot be altered.

compatible Describes the capability of one type of hardware, software, or data file to work with another.

complex instruction set computing (CISC) Describes a type of processor designed to handle large and comprehensive instruction sets. CISC processors are commonly used in IBM-compatible PCs and Macintosh computers.

computer An electronic device used to process data, converting the data into information that is useful to people.

computer-aided design (CAD) The use of computers to create complex two- or three-dimensional models of buildings and products, including architectural, engineering, and mechanical designs.

computer-generated imagery (CGI) The process of using powerful computers and special graphics, animation, and compositing software to create digital special effects or unique images. CGI is frequently used in filmmaking, game design, animation, and multimedia design.

computer system A four-part system that consists of hardware, software, data, and a user.

context menu In the Windows 95 and Windows 98 operating systems, a brief menu that appears when the user right-clicks on certain items. The menu contains commands that apply specifically to the item that was right-clicked. Also called a *shortcut menu*.

control unit The component of the CPU that contains the instruction set. The control unit directs the flow of data throughout the computer system.

cookie A special file that stores personal information, such as credit card data. Web sites create cookies and store them on the user's computer. Later visits to the site read the cookie to access your account.

Copy An application command that makes a duplicate of data selected from a document and stores it in the Clipboard without removing the data from the original document. The data then can be used in other documents and other applications.

counter field A database field that stores a unique incrementing numeric value (such as an invoice number) that the DBMS automatically assigns to each new record. Also called *autonumber field*.

cursor A graphic symbol on screen that indicates where the next keystroke or command will appear when entered. Representations include a blinking vertical line or underline, a box, an arrow, and an I-beam pointer. Also called the *insertion point*.

cursor-movement keys On a computer keyboard, the keys that direct the movement of the on-screen cursor or insertion point, including the up, down, left, and right arrows, and the Home, End, Page Up, and Page Down keys.

Cut An application command that removes data selected from a document and stores it in the Clipboard. The data is no longer a part of the original document. While in the Clipboard, the data can be used in other documents or applications.

cylinder A vertical stack of tracks, one track on each side of each platter of a hard disk.

D

data Raw facts, numbers, letters, or symbols that the computer processes into meaningful information.

data area The part of the disk that remains free to store information after the logical formatting process has created the boot sector, FAT, and root folder.

data bus An electrical path composed of parallel wires that connect the CPU, memory, and other hardware on the motherboard. The number of wires determines the amount of data that can be transferred at one time.

data communications The electronic transfer of data between computers.

database A collection of related data organized with a specific structure.

database management system (DBMS) A computer program used to manage the storage, organization, processing, and retrieval of data in a database; also called *data management software*.

date field A database field that stores a date.

decimal number system The system that uses 10 digits to represent numbers; also called *base 10*.

decoding During file compression, the process of reinserting bits stripped away during encoding, performed at the receiving end.

density A measure of the quality of a magnetic disk's surface. The higher a disk's density, the more closely the iron oxide particles are packed and the more data the disk can store.

deselect The opposite of *select*. In many applications, the user can select, or highlight, blocks of text or objects for editing. By clicking the mouse in a different location or pressing a cursor-movement key, the user removes the highlighting and the text or objects are no longer selected.

desktop In a computer operating system, a graphical workspace in which all of the computer's available resources (such as files, programs, printers, Internet tools, and utilities) can be easily accessed by the user. In such systems, the desktop is a colored background on which the user sees small pictures, called icons. The user accesses various resources by choosing icons on the desktop.

device Any electronic component attached to or part of a computer; hardware.

dialog box A special-purpose window that appears when the user issues certain commands in a program or graphical operating system. A dialog box gets its name from the "dialog" it conducts with the user as the program seeks the information it needs to perform a task.

digital The use of the numerals 1 and 0 (digits) to express data in a computer. The computer recognizes the numeral 1 as an "on" state of a transistor, whereas a 0 represents an "off" state.

digital camera A video camera that converts light intensities into digital data. Digital cameras are used to record images that can be viewed and edited on a computer.

digital convergence The process of combining multiple digital media types (such as text, graphics, video, and sound) into a single multimedia product.

digital versatile disk or **digital video disk (DVD)** A high-density optical medium capable of storing a full-length movie on a single disk the size of a standard compact disk (CD). Unlike a standard CD, which stores data on only one side, a DVD-format disk stores data on both sides. Using compression technologies and very fine data areas on the disk's surface, newer-generation DVDs can store several gigabytes of data.

digitizing Converting an image or a sound into a series of binary numbers (1s and 0s), which can be stored in a computer.

direct connection A permanent connection between your computer system and the Internet. Sometimes called a *dedicated line*.

directory A tool for organizing a disk. A directory contains a list of files and other directories stored on the disk. A disk can hold many directories, which can in turn store many files and other directories. Also called a *folder*.

disk drive A storage device that holds, spins, reads data from, and writes data to disks.

diskette A removable magnetic disk, encased in a plastic sleeve. The most common diskette size is 3.5 inches; older 5.25-inches diskettes are less commonly used. Also called a *floppy disk* or a *floppy*.

diskette drive A device that holds a removable floppy disk when in use; read/write heads read and write data to the diskette.

document A computer file consisting of a compilation of one or more kinds of data. There are many different types of documents, including text documents, spreadsheets, graphics files, and so on. A document, which a user can open and use, is different from a program file, which is required by a software program to operate.

document area In many software applications, the portion of the program's interface in which the active document appears. In this part of the interface, the user can work directly with the document and its contents. Also called the *document window*.

document formats In productivity applications, settings that affect the appearance of the entire document, such as page size, page orientation, and the presence of headers or footers.

document window See *document area*.

domain A name given to a computer and its peripherals connected to the Internet, which identifies the type of organization using the computer. Examples of domain names are *.com* for commercial enterprises and *.edu* for schools. Also called a *top-level domain*.

domain name system (DNS) A naming system used for computers on the Internet. This system provides an individual name (representing the organization using the computer) and a domain name, which classifies the type of organization. DNS converts an e-mail address into a numeric Internet Protocol (IP) address for transmission.

dot matrix printer A type of impact printer that creates characters on a page by using small pins to strike an inked ribbon, pressing ink onto the paper. The arrangement of pins in the print head creates a matrix of dots—hence the device's name.

dot pitch The distance between phosphor dots on a monitor. The highest-resolution monitors have the smallest dot pitch.

dots per inch (dpi) A measure of resolution commonly applied to printers, scanners, and other devices that input or output text or images. The more dots per inch, the higher the resolution. For example, a printer with a resolution of 600 dpi, it can print 600 dots across and 600 down in a one-inch square, for a total of 360,000 dots in one square inch.

double-clicking Selecting an object or activating a command on the screen by pointing to an object (such as an icon) and pressing and releasing the mouse button twice in quick succession.

dragging Moving an object on the screen by pointing to the object, pressing the primary mouse button, and holding down the button while dragging the object to a new location.

drag and drop Moving text or graphics from one part of the document to another by selecting the desired information, pressing and holding down the primary mouse button, dragging the selection to a new location, and releasing the mouse button. Also called *drag-and-drop editing*.

draw program A graphics program that uses vectors to create an image. Mathematical equations describe each line, shape, and pattern, allowing the user to manipulate all elements of the graphic separately.

driver A small program that accepts requests for action from the operating system and causes a device, such as a printer, to execute the requests.

dual-scan LCD An improved passive matrix technology for flat-panel monitors in which pixels are scanned twice as often, reducing the effects of submarining and blurry graphics.

E

EBCDIC Acronym for *Extended Binary Coded Decimal Interchange Code*. An 8-bit binary code developed by IBM to represent symbols and numeric and alphanumeric characters; most commonly used on IBM mainframe computers.

edit To make modifications to an existing document file.

electronic commerce The practice of conducting business transactions online, such as selling products from a World Wide Web site. The process often involves the customer's providing personal or credit card information online, presenting special security concerns. Also called *e-commerce*.

electronic mail A system for exchanging written, voice, and video messages through a computer network. Also called *e-mail*.

e-mail address An address that identifies an individual user of an electronic mail system, enabling the person to send and receive e-mail messages. The e-mail address consists of a user name, the "at" symbol (@), and the DNS.

e-mail program (or **e-mail client**) Software that lets you create, send, and receive e-mail.

encoding The process of stripping away unneeded bits of digital source material, resulting in the transmission of smaller files.

encryption The process of encoding and decoding data, making it useless to any system that cannot decode (decrypt) it.

Ethernet The most common network protocol.

execute To load and carry out a program or a specific set of instructions. Executing is also called *running*.

expansion board A device that enables the user to configure or customize a computer to perform specific tasks or to enhance performance. An expansion board—also called a *card, adapter, or board*—contains a special set of chips and circuitry that add functionality to the computer. An expansion board may be installed to add fax/modem capabilities to the computer, for example, or to provide sound or video-editing capabilities.

expansion slot The area of the motherboard into which *expansion boards* are inserted, connecting them to the PC's bus.

extranet A network connection that enables external users to access a portion of an organization's internal network, usually via an Internet connection. External users have access to specific parts of the internal network but are forbidden to access other areas, which are protected by firewalls.

F

Fast Ethernet A networking technology, also known as *100Base-T*, that uses the same network cabling scheme as Ethernet but uses different network interface cards to achieve data transfer speeds of up to 100 Mbps.

feedback loop In interactive multimedia products, the interaction that occurs between the user and the program. As the user responds to the program by making choices and the program responds to the user by changing its behavior, a two-way "loop" of interaction takes place.

fiber-optic cable A thin strand of glass wrapped in a protective coating. Fiber-optic cable transfers data by means of pulsating beams of light.

field The smallest unit of data in a database, used to group each piece or item of data into a specific category. Fields are arranged in a column and titled by the user.

file A set of related computer data (used by a person) or program instructions (used by an application or operating system) that has been given a name.

file-allocation table (FAT) In a diskette or hard disk, a log created during the logical formatting process that records the location of each file and the status of each sector on the disk.

file format A standardized method of encoding data for storage.

file server The central computer of a network, used for shared storage. A server may store software applications, databases, and data files for the network's users. Depending on the way a server is used, it may also be called a *network server*, *application server*, or just *server*.

file server network A hierarchical network strategy in which the server is used to store and forward files to the nodes. Each node runs its own applications.

file transfer protocol (FTP) A set of rules that dictates the format in which data is sent from one computer to another.

filter A DBMS tool that enables the user to establish conditions for selecting and displaying a subset of records that meet those criteria.

firewall An antipiracy method for protecting networks. A network node acts as a gateway, permitting access to public sections of the network while protecting proprietary areas.

FireWire The version of the IEEE 1394 expansion bus standard used in Macintosh computers.

flat-file database A database file consisting of a single data table, which is not linked to any other tables.

flat-panel display A thin, lightweight monitor used in laptop and notebook computers. Most flat-panel displays use LCD technology.

floppy disk See *diskette*.

folder See *directory*.

font A family of alphanumeric characters, symbols, and punctuation marks that share the same design. Modern applications provide many different fonts and enable users to use different fonts in the same document. Also called a *typeface*.

form A custom screen created in a database management system (DBMS) for displaying and entering data related to a single database record.

formatting (1) The process of magnetically mapping a disk with a series of tracks and sectors where data will be stored. Also called *initializing*. (2) The process of applying formatting options (such as character or paragraph formats) to a document.

formula A mathematical equation within a cell of a spreadsheet. To identify it and distinguish it from other spreadsheet entries, a formula begins with a special symbol, such as a plus sign or an equal sign.

formula bar In spreadsheet programs, a special text box that displays the active cell's address and the formula or data entered in that cell. The user may be able to enter or edit data or formulas in this box.

frame (1) In networking, a small block of data to be transmitted over a network. A frame includes an identifying header and the actual data to be sent. Also called a *packet*. (2) In animation, a single still image that, when viewed with many other images in rapid succession, creates the illusion of motion. (3) In many software applications, a special tool that enables the user to place an object—such as a text box or an image from a separate file—in a document. The frame surrounds the object in the document, enabling the user to position and resize the object as needed.

frequently asked questions (FAQ) A document routinely developed by a news group, which lists questions most commonly asked in the news group, along with their answers. FAQs help a news group's members avoid the repeated posting of the same information to the group.

function (1) In a spreadsheet, a part of a formula used to perform complex operations, such as adding the contents of a range or finding the absolute value of a cell's contents. (2) In programming, a block of statements designed to perform a specific routine or task.

function keys The part of the keyboard that can be used to quickly activate commands, designated F1, F2, and so on.

G

game controller A specialized type of input device, which enables the user to interact with computer games. Two popular types of game controllers are *game pads* and *joysticks*.

game pad A type of game controller that usually provides two sets of controls—one for each hand. These devices are extremely flexible and are used to control a wide variety of game systems.

gateway A computer system that can translate one network protocol into another so that data can be transmitted between two dissimilar networks.

gigabyte (GB) Equivalent to approximately one billion bytes; a typical measurement of data storage.

goal seeking A data-analysis process that begins with a conclusion and calculates the values that will lead to the desired outcome, such as figuring a mortgage amount based on an affordable monthly payment.

graphical user interface (GUI) A user interface in which actions are initiated when the user selects an icon, a toolbar button, or an option from a pull-down menu with the mouse or other pointing device. GUIs also represent documents, programs, and devices on screen as graphical elements, which the user can use by clicking or dragging.

H

H/PC See *handheld personal computer*.

handheld personal computer (H/PC) (or **palmtop**) A personal computer that is small enough to be held in one hand.

handle In many productivity applications, a specialized portion of a *frame*, which enables the user to drag the frame to resize it.

hard disk A nonremovable magnetic storage device included in most PCs. A stack of aluminum or glass platters, each coated with iron oxide, enclosed in a hard disk drive.

hard disk drive (or **hard drive**) A device that consists of the hard disk platters, a spindle on which the platters spin, a read/write head for each side of each platter, and a sealed chamber that encloses the disks and spindle. Many hard disk drives also include the drive controller, although the controller is a separate unit on some hard disk drives.

hardware The physical components of a computer, including processor and memory chips, input/output devices, tapes, disks, modems, and cables.

helper application (or **plug-in application**) A program that must be added to your browser in order to play special content files, especially those with multimedia content, in real time.

hertz (Hz) The frequency of electrical vibrations, or cycles, per second.

highlight To select a block of text or cells for editing. Selected text is highlighted—displayed in a different color from the remaining text in a document.

hit A visit to a Web site. Also called a *page view*.

home page An organization's principal Web page, which provides pointers to other Web pages with additional information.

host A computer that provides services to other computers that connect to it. Host computers provide file transfer, communications services, and access to the Internet's high-speed data lines.

HTML See *Hypertext Markup Language*.

HTML tag A code used to format documents in Hypertext Markup Language (HTML) format.

hyperlink See *hypertext link*.

hypermedia Text, graphics, video, and sound linked and accessible in a hypertext format.

hypertext link (**hyperlink** or **link**) A word, icon, or other object that when clicked jumps to another location on the document or another Web page.

hypertext markup language (HTML) A page-description language used on the World Wide Web that defines the hypertext links between documents.

hypertext transfer protocol (HTTP) A set of file transfer rules used on the World Wide Web that control the way information is shared.

I

icon A graphical screen element that executes one or more commands when chosen with a mouse or other pointing device.

IEEE 1394 A new expansion bus technology that supports data-transfer rates of up to 400 Mbps. Called *FireWire* in Macintosh computers.

image scanner An input device that digitizes printed images. Sensors determine the intensity of light reflected from the page, and the light intensities are converted to digital data that can be viewed and manipulated by the computer. Sometimes called simply a *scanner*.

impact printer A type of printer that creates images by striking an inked ribbon, pressing ink from the ribbon onto a piece of paper. Examples of impact printers are dot-matrix printers and line printers.

incompatible The opposite of *compatible*. Describes the inability of one type of hardware, software, or data file to work with another.

initializing See *formatting*.

ink jet printer A type of nonimpact printer that produces images by spraying ink onto the page.

input device Computer hardware that accepts data and instructions from the user. Input devices include the keyboard, mouse, joystick, pen, trackball, scanner, bar code reader, microphone, and touch screen, as well as other types of hardware.

input/output device A device that performs both input and output functions. Modems and network interface cards are examples of input/output devices.

insertion point See *cursor*.

instruction set Machine language instructions that define all the operations a CPU can perform.

integrated pointing device A pointing device built into the computer's keyboard, consisting of a small joystick positioned near the middle of the keyboard, typically between the *g* and *h* keys. The joystick is controlled with either forefinger. Two buttons that perform the same function as mouse buttons are just beneath the spacebar and are pressed with the thumb. Also called a *TrackPoint*.

interactive Refers to software products that can react and respond to commands issued by the user or choices the user makes.

interactive media A software product that reacts and responds to user input.

interactivity In multimedia, a system in which the user and program respond to one another. The program gives the user choices, which the user selects to direct the program.

Internet Originally, a link between ARPANET, NSFnet, and other networks. Today, a worldwide network of networks.

Internet protocol (IP) address A unique four-part numeric address assigned to each computer on the Internet, containing routing information to identify its location. Each of the four parts is a number between 0 and 255.

Internet relay chat (IRC) A multiuser system made up of channels, which people join to exchange messages either publicly or privately. Messages are exchanged in real-time, meaning they are transmitted to other users on the channel as they are typed in.

Internet service provider (ISP) An intermediary service between the Internet backbone and the user, providing easy and relatively inexpensive access to shell accounts, direct TCP/IP connections, and high-speed access through dedicated data circuits.

internetworking The process of connecting separate networks together.

intranet An internal network whose interface and accessibility are modeled after an Internet-based Web site. Only internal users are allowed to access information or resources on the intranet; if connected to an external network or the Internet, the intranet's resources are protected from outside access by firewalls.

J

joystick An input device used to control the movement of on-screen components; typically used in video games.

JPEG A bitmap file format commonly used to display photographic images. Stands for *Joint Photographic Experts Group*.

K

keyboard The most common input device, used to enter letters, numbers, symbols, punctuation, and commands into the computer. Computer keyboards typically include numeric, alphanumeric, cursor-movement, modifier, and function keys, as well as other special keys.

kilobyte (KB) Equivalent to 1,024 bytes; a common measure of data storage.

L

label Descriptive text used in a spreadsheet cell to describe the data in a column or row.

laptop computer See *notebook PC*.

laser printer A quiet, fast printer that produces high-quality output. A laser beam focused on an electrostatic drum creates an image to which powdered toner adheres, and that image is transferred to paper.

link See *hypertext link*.

Linux A freely available version of the UNIX operating system. Developed by a worldwide cooperative of programmers in the 1990s, Linux is a feature-rich, 32-bit, multi-user, multiprocessor operating system that runs on virtually any hardware platform.

liquid crystal display (LCD) monitor A flat-panel monitor on which an image is created when the liquid crystal becomes charged; used primarily in notebook and laptop computers.

local area network (LAN) A system of PCs located relatively near to one another and connected by wire or a wireless link. A LAN permits simultaneous access to data and resources, enhances personal communication, and simplifies backup procedures.

logical field A database field that stores only one of two values: yes or no, true or false, on or off, and so on. Also called a *Boolean field*.

logical formatting An operating system function in which tracks and sectors are mapped on the surface of a disk. This mapping creates the master boot record, FAT, root folder (also called the root directory), and the data area. Also called *soft formatting* and *low-level formatting*.

M

Macintosh operating system (Mac OS) The operating system that runs on PCs built by Apple Computer. The Mac OS was the first commercially available operating system to use a graphical user interface, to utilize Plug and Play hardware compatibility, to feature built-in networking, and to support common user access.

magnetic disk A round, flat disk covered with a magnetic material (such as iron oxide), the most commonly used storage medium. Data is written magnetically on the disk and can be recorded over and over. The magnetic disk is the basic component of the diskette and hard disk.

mail merge The process of combining a text document, such as a letter, with the contents of a database, such as an address list; commonly used to produce form letters.

mail server In an e-mail system, the server on which messages received from the post office server are stored until the recipients access their mailbox and retrieve the messages.

mainframe computer A large, multiuser computer system designed to handle massive amounts of input, output, and storage. A mainframe is usually composed of one or more powerful CPUs connected to many input/output devices, called *terminals*, or to personal computers. Mainframe systems are typically used in businesses requiring the maintenance of huge databases or simultaneous processing of multiple complex tasks.

master boot record A small program that runs when a computer is started. This program determines whether the disk contains the basic components of an operating system necessary to run successfully. If the boot record determines that the required files are present and the disk has a valid format, it transfers control to one of the operating system programs, which continues the process of starting up.

megabyte (MB) Equivalent to approximately one million bytes. A common measure of data storage capacity.

megahertz (MHz) Equivalent to millions of cycles per second; a common measure of clock speed.

memo field A database field that stores text information of variable length. Also called *description field*.

memory A collection of chips on the motherboard or on a circuit board attached to the motherboard, where all computer processing and program instructions are stored while in use. The computer's memory enables the CPU to retrieve data quickly for processing.

memory address A number used by the CPU to locate each piece of data in memory.

menu A list of commands or functions displayed on screen for selection by the user.

menu bar A graphical screen element—located above the document area of an application window—displaying a list of the types of commands available to the user. When the user selects an option from the menu bar, a list appears, displaying the commands related to that menu option.

microcomputer See *personal computer (PC)*.

microphone An input device used to digitally record audio data, such as the human voice. Many productivity applications also can accept input via a microphone, enabling the user to dictate text or issue commands orally.

microprocessor An integrated circuit on a single chip that makes up the computer's CPU. Microprocessors are composed of silicon or other material etched with many tiny electronic circuits.

minicomputer A midsize, multiuser computer capable of handling more input and output than a PC but with less processing power and storage than a mainframe. Also called a *midrange computer*.

model A three-dimensional image that represents a real or imagined object or character; created using special computer software programs, including surface modelers, solid modelers, spline-based modelers, and others.

modifier keys Keyboard keys that are used in conjunction with other keys to execute a command. The IBM-PC keyboard includes Shift, Ctrl, and Alt keys; the Macintosh keyboard also has the Command and Option keys.

monitor A display screen used to provide computer output to the user. Examples include the cathode ray tube (CRT) monitor, color monitor, monochrome monitor, flat-panel monitor, and liquid crystal display (LCD).

motherboard The main circuit board of the computer, which contains the CPU, memory, expansion slots, bus, and video controller. Also called the *system board*.

mouse An input device operated by rolling across a flat surface. The mouse is used to control the on-screen pointer by pointing and clicking, double-clicking, or dragging objects on the screen.

MPEG A multimedia data compression standard used to compress full-motion video. Stands for *Moving Pictures Experts Group*.

MS-DOS Acronym for *Microsoft-Disk Operating System*. The command-line interface operating system developed by Microsoft for PCs. IBM selected DOS as the standard for early IBM and IBM-compatible machines.

multimedia Elements of text, graphics, animation, video, and sound combined for presentation to the consumer.

multimedia authoring An application that enables the user to combine text, graphics, animation, video, and sound documents developed with other software packages to create a multimedia product.

multimedia PC A PC capable of producing high-quality text, graphics, animation, video, and sound. A multimedia PC may include a CD-ROM or DVD drive, a microphone, speakers, a high-quality video controller, and a sound card.

multitasking The capability of an operating system to load multiple programs into memory at one time and to perform two or more processes concurrently, such as printing a document while editing another.

Musical Instrument Digital Interface (MIDI) A specialized category of input/output devices used in the creation, recording, editing, and performance of music.

navigation The process of moving through a software program, a multimedia product, or a Web site.

network (1) A system of interconnected computers that communicate with one another and share applications, data, and hardware components. (2) To connect computers together, in order to permit the transfer of data and programs between users.

network computer (NC) A specialized computer that provides basic input/output capabilities to a user on a network. Some types of NCs provide storage and processing capabilities, but other types include only a keyboard, mouse, and monitor. The latter category of network computer utilizes the network server for processing and storage.

network interface card (NIC) A circuit board that controls the exchange of data over a network.

network operating system (NOS) A group of programs that manage the resources on a network.

network server See *file server*.

network version An application program especially designed to work within a network environment. Users access the software from a shared storage device.

new media A term encompassing all types of interactive multimedia technologies.

news A public bulletin board service on the Internet, organized into discussion groups representing specific topics of interest.

news server A host computer that exchanges articles with other Internet servers.

newsgroup An electronic storage space where users can post messages to other users, carry on extended conversations, and trade information.

newsreader A software program that enables the user to post and read articles in an Internet news group.

node An individual computer that is connected to a network.

non-impact printer A type of printer that creates images on paper without striking the page in any way. Two common examples are ink jet printers, which spray tiny droplets of ink onto the page, and laser printers, which use heat to adhere particles of toner to specific points on the page.

nonvolatile The tendency for memory to retain data even when the computer is turned off (as is the case with ROM).

notebook computer A small, portable computer with an attached flat screen, typically battery or AC powered and weighing less than 10 pounds. Notebook computers commonly provide most of the same features found in full-size desktop computers, including a color monitor, a fast processor, a modem, and adequate RAM and storage for business-class software applications. Also called a *laptop computer*.

NSFnet Acronym for *National Science Foundation Network*. A network developed by the National Science Foundation (NSF) to accommodate the many users attempting to access the five academic research centers created by the NSF.

numeric field A database field that stores numeric characters.

numeric keypad The part of a keyboard that looks and works like a calculator keypad, with 10 digits and mathematical operators.

O

Object Linking and Embedding (OLE) A Windows feature that combines object embedding and linking functions. OLE allows the user to construct a document containing data from a single point in time or one in which the data is constantly updated.

online service A telecommunications service that supplies e-mail and information search tools.

operating environment An intuitive graphical user interface that overlays the operating system but does not replace it. Microsoft Windows 3.x is an example.

operating system (OS) The master control program that provides an interface for a user to communicate with the computer, manages hardware devices, manages and maintains disk file systems, and supports application programs.

OS/2 Warp A single-user, multitasking operating system with a point-and-click interface developed by IBM and Microsoft to take advantage of the multitasking capabilities of post-8086 computers.

output device A hardware component, such as a monitor or printer, that returns processed data to the user.

P

packet A small block of data transmitted over a network, which includes an identifying header and the actual data to be sent. Also called a *frame*.

page view See *hit*.

pages per minute (ppm) A common measure for printer output speed. Consumer-grade laser printers, for example, typically can print from 6 to 10 pages per minute depending on whether text or graphics are being printed.

paint program A graphics program that creates images as bitmaps, or a mosaic of pixels.

paragraph A series of letters, words, or sentences followed by a hard return.

paragraph format A setting that affects the appearance of one or more entire paragraphs, such as line spacing, paragraph spacing, indents, alignment, tab stops, borders, and shading.

parallel interface A channel through which eight or more data bits can flow simultaneously, such as a computer bus. A parallel interface is commonly used to connect printers to the computer; also called a *parallel port*.

parallel processing The use of multiple processors to run a program. By harnessing multiple processors, which share the processing workload, the system can handle a much greater flow of data, complete more tasks in a shorter period of time, and deal with the demands of many input and output devices. Also called *multiprocessing (MP)* or *symmetric multiprocessing (SMP)*.

passive matrix LCD Liquid crystal display technology, used for flat-panel monitors, that relies on a grid of transistors arranged by rows and columns. In a passive matrix LCD, the color displayed by each pixel is determined by the electricity coming from the transistors at the end of the row and the top of the column.

Paste An application command that copies data from the Clipboard and places it in the document at the position of the insertion point. Data in the Clipboard can be pasted into multiple places in one document, multiple documents, and documents in different applications.

PC Card A specialized expansion card the size of a credit card, which fits into a computer and is used to connect new components.

PC video camera A small video camera, which connects to a special video card on a PC. When used with videoconferencing software, a PC video camera enables users to capture full-motion video images, save them to disk, edit them, and transmit them to other users across a network or the Internet.

PC-to-TV converter A hardware device that converts a computer's digital video signals into analog signals for display on a standard television screen.

peer-to-peer network A network environment in which all nodes on the network have equal access to at least some of the resources on all other nodes.

personal computer (PC) The most common type of computer found in an office, classroom, or home. The PC is designed to fit on a desk and be used by one person at a time; also called a *microcomputer*.

photo-manipulation program A multimedia software tool used to modify scanned photographic images, including adjusting contrast and sharpness.

photorealistic Describes computer-generated images that are lifelike in appearance and not obviously models.

pixel Contraction of *picture element*. One or more dots that express a portion of an image on a computer screen.

Plug and Play An operating system feature that enables the user to add hardware devices to the computer without performing technically difficult connection procedures.

plug-in application See *helper application*.

point-to-point protocol (PPP) A communications protocol used for linking a computer directly to the Internet. PPP features include the ability to establish or terminate a session, to hang up and redial, and to use password protection.

pointer An on-screen object, usually an arrow, used to select text; access menus; move files; and interact with programs, files, or data represented graphically on the screen.

pointing device A device that enables the user to freely move an on-screen pointer and to select text, menu options, icons, and other on-screen objects. Two popular types of pointing devices are mice and trackballs.

posting Publishing a document on the Internet, using one of its services, such as news, FTP, or the World Wide Web.

presentation program Software that enables the user to create professional-quality images, called *slides*, which can be shown as part of a presentation. Slides can be presented in any number of ways, but are typically displayed on a large screen or video monitor while the presenter speaks to the audience.

printer An output device that produces a hard copy on paper.

print head In impact printers, a device that strikes an inked ribbon, pressing ink onto the paper to create characters or graphics.

processing A complex procedure by which a computer transforms raw data into useful information.

processor See *central processing unit (CPU)*.

program (1) A set of instructions or code executed by the CPU, designed to help users solve problems or perform tasks. Also called *software*. (2) To create a computer program. The process of computer programming is also called *software development*.

prompt In a command-line interface, the onscreen location where the user types commands. A prompt usually provides a blinking cursor to indicate where commands can be typed. Also called a *command prompt*.

protocol A set of rules and procedures that determine how a computer system receives and transmits data.

query In a database management system (DBMS), a search question that instructs the program to locate records that meet specific criteria.

QuickTime A multimedia playback standard, developed for use with Macintosh computers, which enables the user to play high-quality audio and video content on the desktop.

QuickTime VR A "virtual reality" version of the QuickTime file format, which enables multimedia developers to create virtual-reality-like environments from flat, two-dimensional images.

random access memory (RAM) A computer's volatile or temporary memory, which exists as chips on the motherboard near the CPU. RAM stores data and programs while they are being used and requires a power source to maintain its integrity.

range In a spreadsheet, a rectangular group of contiguous cells.

read-only memory (ROM) A permanent, or nonvolatile, memory chip used to store instructions and data, including the computer's startup instructions.

read/write head The magnetic device within the disk drive that reads, records, and erases data on the disk's surface. A read/write head contains an electromagnet that alters the polarity of magnetic particles on the storage medium. Most disk drives have one read/write head for each side of each disk in the drive.

RealAudio A program that plays streaming audio broadcast over the Internet.

RealPlayer The standard for playing streaming audio and video content downloaded from Web servers.

RealVideo A program that plays streaming video broadcast over the Internet.

record A database row composed of related fields; a collection of records makes up the database.

reduced instruction set computing (RISC) Refers to a type of microprocessor design that uses a simplified instruction set, using fewer instructions of constant size, each of which can be executed in one machine cycle.

refresh rate The number of times per second that each pixel on the computer screen is scanned; measured in hertz (Hz).

register High-speed memory locations built directly into the ALU and used to hold instructions and data currently being processed.

relational database A database structure capable of linking tables; a collection of files that share at least one common field.

relative cell reference A spreadsheet cell reference that changes with respect to its relative position on the spreadsheet when copied to a new location.

remote terminal connection An Internet connection in which the TCP/IP programs and protocols run on a UNIX host computer. The local computer exchanges data and commands in ASCII format.

report A database product designed by the user that displays data satisfying a specific set of search criteria presented in a predefined layout.

resolution The degree of sharpness of an image, determined by the number of pixels on a screen, expressed as a matrix.

right-click When using a two-button mouse, to use the right mouse button to select an object or command on the screen.

ring topology A network topology in which network nodes are connected in a circular configuration. Each node examines the data sent through the ring and passes on data not addressed to it.

root directory See *root folder*.

root folder The top-level folder on a disk. This primary folder contains all other folders and subfolders stored on the disk. Also called a root *directory*, or sometimes just the *root*.

router A computer device that stores the addressing information of each computer on each LAN or WAN and uses this information to transfer data along the most efficient path between nodes of a LAN or WAN.

ruler An on-screen tool in a word processor's document window. The ruler shows the position of lines, tab stops, margins, and other parts of the document.

run See *execute*.

scanner An input device used to copy a printed page into the computer's memory and transform the image into digital data. Various scanners can read text, images, or bar codes. Sometimes called an *image scanner*.

scroll bar A vertical or horizontal bar displayed along the side or bottom of a document window, which enables the user to scroll horizontally or vertically through a document by clicking an arrow or dragging a box within the scroll bar.

search engine A Web site that uses powerful data-searching techniques to help the user locate Web sites containing specific types of content or information.

sector A segment or division of a track on a disk.

secure HTTP (S-HTTP) An Internet protocol used to encrypt individual pieces of data transmitted between a user's computer and a Web server, making the data unusable to anyone who does not have a key to the encryption method.

secure sockets layer (SSL) An Internet protocol that can be used to encrypt any amount of data sent over the Internet between a client computer and a host computer.

secure Web page A Web page that uses one or more encyption technologies to encode data received from and sent to the user.

select (1) To highlight a block of text (in a word processor) or range (in a spreadsheet), so the user can perform one or more editing operations on it. (2) To click once on an icon.

serial interface A channel through which a single data bit can flow at one time. Serial interfaces are used primarily to connect a mouse or a communications device to the computer. Also called a *serial port*.

serial line interface protocol (SLIP) A method for linking a computer directly to the Internet by using a phone line connected to a serial communications port.

server See *file server*.

shell account A type of Internet access used by remote terminal connections, which operates from a host computer running UNIX or a similar operating system.

Shockwave A plug-in application that allows interactive animations and audio to play directly in a Web browser window.

shortcut menu See *context menu*.

site license An agreement in which an organization purchases the right to use a program on a limited number of machines. The total cost is less than would be required if individual copies of the software were purchased for all users.

slide An individual graphic that is part of a presentation. Slides are created and edited in presentation programs.

Small Computer System Interface (SCSI) A high-speed interface that extends the bus outside the computer, permitting the addition of more peripheral devices than normally could be connected using the available expansion slots.

software See *program*.

solid model A 3-D model created in a solid modeling program, and which appears to be a solid object rather than a frame or polygon-based object.

sort To arrange database records in a particular order—such as alphabetical, numerical, or chronological order—according to the contents of one or more fields

sound card An expansion card that records and plays back sound by translating the analog signal from a microphone into a digitized form that the computer can store and process and then translating the modified data back into analog signals or sound.

spreadsheet A grid of columns and rows used for recording and evaluating numbers. Spreadsheets are used primarily for financial analysis, record keeping, and management, and to create reports and presentations.

star network A network topology in which network nodes connect to a central hub through which all data is routed.

Start button A Windows 95/98/2000/NT screen element, found on the taskbar, that displays the Start menu when selected.

Start menu A menu in the Windows 95/98/2000/NT operating systems, which the user can open by clicking the Start button. The Start menu provides tools to locate documents, find help, change system settings, and run programs.

status bar An on-screen element that appears at the bottom of an application window and displays the current status of various parts of the current document or application, such as page number, text entry mode, and so on.

storage The portion of the computer that holds data or programs while they are not being used. Storage media include magnetic or optical disks, tape, and cartridges.

storyboard A production tool that consists of sketches of scenes and actions that map a sequence of events; helps the author to edit and improve the presentation.

subdomain A division of a domain name system (DNS) address that specifies a particular level or area of an organization, such as a department or a branch office.

subscribe To select a news group so the user can regularly participate in its discussions. After subscribing to a news group in a newsreader program, the program automatically downloads an updated list of articles when it is launched.

supercomputer The largest, fastest, and most powerful type of computer. Supercomputers are often used for scientific and engineering applications and processing complex models using very large data sets.

Super VGA (SVGA) An IBM video display standard capable of displaying resolutions up to 1024 × 768 pixels, with 16 million colors.

swap in To load essential parts of a program into memory as required for use.

swap out To unload, or remove, nonessential parts of a program from memory to make room for needed functions.

system call A feature built into an application program that requests a service from the operating system, as when a word processing program requests the use of the printer to print a document.

system clock The computer's internal clock, used to time processing operations. The clock's time intervals are based on the constant, unchanging vibrations of molecules in a quartz crystal, and currently measured in megahertz (MHz).

system operator (sysop) In an online discussion group, the person who monitors the discussion.

system software A computer program that controls the system hardware and interacts with application software. The designation includes the operating system and the network operating system.

T

table A grid of data, set up in rows and columns.

task switching The process of moving from one open window to another.

taskbar A Windows 95/98/2000/NT screen element, displayed on the desktop, which includes the Start button and lists the programs currently running on the computer.

telecommuter A person who works at home or on the road and requires access to a work computer via telecommunications equipment, such as modems and fax machines.

teleconference A live, real-time communications session involving two or more people in different locations, using computers and telecommunications equipment.

Telnet An Internet service that provides a transparent window between the user's computer and a distant host system.

template A preformatted document used to quickly create a standard document, such as a memo or report.

terabyte (TB) Equivalent to one trillion bytes of data. A measure of storage capacity.

terminal An input/output device connected to a multiuser computer, such as a mainframe.

text box In word processing and desktop publishing software, a special frame that enables the user to contain text in a rectangular area. The user can size and position the text box like a frame, by dragging the box or one of its handles. Also see *frame*.

text code A standard system in which numbers represent the letters of the alphabet, punctuation marks, and other symbols. A text code enables programmers to use combinations of numbers to represent individual pieces of data. EBCDIC, ASCII, and Unicode are examples of text code systems.

text field A database field that stores a string of alphanumeric characters. Also called *alphanumeric field* or *character field*.

thread A series of related articles and responses about a specific subject, posted in a newsgroup.

time field A database field that stores a time.

title bar An on-screen element displayed at the top of every window that identifies the window contents. Dragging the title bar changes the position of the window on the screen.

Token Ring IBM's network protocol, based on a ring topology in which linked computers pass an electronic token containing addressing information to facilitate data transfer.

toolbar In application software, an on-screen element appearing just below the menu bar. The toolbar contains multiple tools, which are graphic icons (called *buttons*) representing specific actions the user can perform. To initiate an action, the user clicks the appropriate button.

topology The physical layout of wires that connect the computers in a network; includes bus, star, ring, and mesh.

touch pad See *trackpad*.

touch screen An input/output device that accepts input directly from the monitor. The user touches words, graphical icons, or symbols displayed on screen to activate commands.

track An area used for storing data on a formatted disk. During the disk-formatting process, the operating system creates a set of magnetic concentric circles on the disk: these are the tracks. These tracks are then divided into sectors, with each sector able to hold a given amount of data. By using this system to store data, the operating system can quickly determine where data is located on the disk. Different types of disks can hold different numbers of tracks.

trackball An input device that functions like an upside-down mouse, consisting of a stationary casing containing a movable ball that is operated by hand. Trackballs are used frequently with laptop computers.

trackpad A stationary pointing device that the user operates by moving a finger across a small, touch-sensitive surface. Trackpads are often built into portable computers. Also called a *touchpad*.

TrackPoint See *integrated pointing device*.

transistor An electronic switch within the CPU that exists in two states, conductive (on) or nonconductive (off). The resulting combinations are used to create the binary code that is the basis for machine language.

transition In a presentation program, an animation-like effect applied when switching from one slide to the next in a presentation.

Transmission Control Protocol/Internet Protocol (TCP/IP) The set of commands and timing specifications used by the Internet to connect dissimilar systems and control the flow of information.

twisted-pair cable Cable used in network connections. Twisted-pair cable consists of copper strands, individually shrouded in plastic, twisted around each other in pairs and bound together in a layer of plastic insulation; also called *unshielded twisted-pair (UTP) wire*. Twisted-pair wire encased in a metal sheath is called *shielded twisted-pair (STP) wire*.

U

Unicode A character set that provides 16 bits to represent each symbol, resulting in 65,536 different characters or symbols, enough for all the languages in the world.

uniform resource locator (URL) An Internet address used with HTTP in the format type://address/path.

Universal Serial Bus (USB) A new expansion bus technology that currently enables the user to connect 127 different devices into a single port. USB is relatively fast, supporting data-transfer rates of 12 Mbps.

UNIX A 32-bit, fully multitasking, multithreading operating system developed by Bell Labs in the 1970s. A powerful, highly scalable operating system, UNIX (and variants of it) is used to operate supercomputers, mainframes, minicomputers, and powerful PCs and workstations. UNIX generally features a command-line interface, although some variants of UNIX feature a graphical operating environment, as well.

Usenet A popular system of news groups accessible on the Internet and maintained by volunteers.

user The person who inputs and analyzes data using a computer.

user interface The on-screen elements that enable the user to interact with the software.

user name A code that identifies the user to the system; often the user's full name, a shortened version of the user's name, or the user's e-mail name. Also called a *user ID*.

V

value A numerical entry in a spreadsheet—representing currency, a percentage, a date, a time, a fraction, and so on—which can be used in formulas.

vector A mathematical equation that describes the position of a line.

Video Graphics Array (VGA) An IBM video display standard capable of displaying resolutions of 640 × 480, with 16 colors.

video controller A circuit board attached to the motherboard that contains the memory and other circuitry necessary to send information to the monitor for display on screen. This controller determines the refresh rate, resolution, and number of colors that can be displayed. Also called the *display adapter*.

Video for Windows An audio/visual standard developed by Microsoft as a way to store and display compressed audio and video information.

video RAM (VRAM) Memory on the video controller (sometimes called *dual-ported memory*), which can send a screen of data to the monitor while receiving the next data set.

videoconference A live, real-time video communications session involving two or more people using computers, video cameras, telecommunications and videoconferencing software.

virtual reality modeling language (VRML) A special programming language that enables designers to create 3-D virtual environments (such as furnished rooms, shopping centers, and so on) for use in World Wide Web pages. Users with VRML-enabled browsers can navigate through these environments with a great deal of freedom, entering and exiting rooms, interacting with objects, looking through windows, and so on.

volatile The tendency for memory to lose data when the computer is turned off, as is the case with RAM.

W

Web browser A program that enables the user to view Web pages, navigate Web sites, and move from one Web site to another.

Web master A person or group responsible for designing and maintaining a Web site.

Web page A document developed using HTTP and found on the World Wide Web. Web pages contain information about a particular subject with links to related Web pages and other resources.

Web server An Internet host computer that may store thousands of Web sites.

Web site A collection of related Web pages.

what-if analysis A data analysis process used to test how alternative scenarios affect numeric results.

wide area network (WAN) A computer network that spans a wide geographical area.

window An area on the computer screen in which an application or document is viewed and accessed.

Windows A family of operating system products developed and produced by Microsoft Corp. The vast majority of personal computers run Windows, whose versions include Windows 3.*x*, 95, 98, NT, and 2000. Windows versions 3.*x* and earlier were actually operating environments—graphical interfaces that ran on top of the DOS operating system. In versions 95 and later, Windows is a full-fledged operating system.

Windows 2000 An operating system that provides the file system, networking, power, and stability of Windows NT with the user-friendly interface and features of Windows 98.

Windows 3.*x* A term used to refer to the Windows 3.0, 3.1, and 3.11 family.

Windows 95 A 32-bit operating system developed by Microsoft and released in 1995. Windows 95 features preemptive multitasking, plug and play capabilities, built-in networking, and the ability to access 16- and 32-bit applications.

Windows 98 An upgrade to Windows 95, Windows 98 includes a number of enhancements, including a built-in Web browser and Internet-related tools, online upgradability, and other features.

Windows NT A 32-bit operating system developed by Microsoft and released in 1993; designed for powerful workstations and restricted to running 32-bit applications; supports peer-to-peer networking, preemptive multitasking, and multiprocessing. The NT stands for "new technology."

Windows NT Server Version of Windows NT incorporating all of the features of Windows NT Workstation with additional functions to support network servers.

Windows NT Workstation A version of Windows NT designed to look like consumer versions of Windows with an underlying OS almost completely different. Windows NT Workstation runs a wide variety of CPUs, is designed for a stand-alone PC, has good security features, and is more fault-tolerant than other Microsoft operating systems.

Winsock *Windows Sockets*, a standard network interface that makes it possible to mix and match application programs from more than one developer to communicate across the Internet.

wireframe model A CAD tool that represents 3-D shapes by displaying their outlines and edges.

wireless communication Communication via computers that relies on infrared signals, microwaves, or radio waves to transmit data.

word processing software Software used to create and edit text documents such as letters, memos, reports, and publications. Also called a *word processor*.

word processor See *word processing software*.

word size The size of the registers in the CPU, which determines the amount of data the computer can work with at any given time. Larger word sizes lead to faster processing; common word sizes include 16 bits, 32 bits, and 64 bits.

word wrap A word processing feature that computes the length of each line of text as the text is entered.

workbook A data file created with spreadsheet software, containing multiple worksheets.

worksheet The data file created with spreadsheet software.

workstation A fast, powerful microcomputer used for scientific applications, graphics, CAD, CAE, and other complex applications. Workstations are usually based on RISC technology and operated by some version of UNIX, although an increasing number of Intel/Windows NT-based workstations are coming into popular use.

World Wide Web (the Web or WWW) An Internet service developed to incorporate footnotes, figures, and cross-references into online hypertext documents.

WYSIWYG Acronym for *What You See Is What You Get*. A display mode that shows a document as it will appear when printed.

INDEX

All Table of Contents and lesson opener illustrations created by Tom White.

Photos

Abbreviation Key: IBM = Courtesy International Business Machines Corp. Unauthorized use not permitted.

Feature Article Headers: *Computers in Your Career* Comstock; *Productivity Tip* PhotoDisc; *Techview* Richard Laird/FPG.

Cover Guy Crittendon; **iv** (t)The Stock Market, (b)Aaron Haupt; **v** (left, t to b)Aaron Haupt, SuperStock, U.S. Department of Defense Camera Combat Center, Liaison Agency, (right, t to b)©1999 Dan Abrams, Dan Nelken/Liaison Agency, NASA/Roger Ressmeyer/CORBIS; **xiii xxiv xxvi** Aaron Haupt; **5 6 7** Kreber Studios; **8** IBM; **9** (t)Amanita Pictures, (b)Tom McCarthy/SKA; **10** Mark Burnett; **14** (tl cl)IBM, (tr)SGI, (cr)Hewlett Packard, (b)Aaron Haupt; **15** (t cl)Sun Microsytems, (cr)Compaq, (b)Hewlett Packard; **16** H. Shrikumar; **20** Aaron Haupt; **21** (t)IBM, (bl br)Aaron Haupt; **22** (t)Aaron Haupt, (b)Compaq; **23** IBM; **24** (t)Aaron Haupt, (cl)Bob Daemmrich/The Image Works, (cr)Jose L. Peleaz/The Stock Market, (b)IBM; **25** (t)The Stock Market, (c)B. Busco/The Image Bank, (b)Sony; **26** (l)SGI, (c r)IBM; **28** (t)IBM, (b)Applied Optical Company; **30** (l)Compaq, (r)SGI; **31** Kreber Studios; **36** (t)Amanita Pictures, (b)Compaq; **37** (tl tr)Aaron Haupt, (tc)Sony, (bc)Compaq, (b)SGI; **48** Newer Technology; **51** Mark Burnett; **52** Aaron Haupt; **53** (t)Mark Burnett, (b)3Com; **54** (bl br)Advanced Micro Devices, Inc., (others)Intel; **56** Cyrix; **57** (t)Aaron Haupt, (b)Compaq; **69** Chuck Keeler/Stone; **76** Tom McCarthy/SKA; **77** IBM; **79** (t)Property of AT&T Archives. Reprinted with permission of AT&T, (b)D. Sarraute/ The Image Bank; **84** (t)Newer Technology, (b)Intel; **85** Property of AT&T. Reprinted with permission of AT&T; **88 125** Mark Burnett; **134** Charles Gupton/The Stock Market; **137** Mark Burnett; **144** (t)Mark Burnett, (c)©1997 Disney/MPTV, (bl)Universal Photo/MPTV, (br)©1998 Touchstone/MPTV; **145** Larry Hamill; **147** (t)Amanita Pictures, (b)Hewlett Packard; **148** Courtesy Noritsu Koki, Ltd.; **150** Larry Hamill; **151** Glencoe photo; **155** ©1997 Universal Photo by David James/MPTV; **156** Mark Burnett; **161** (l)LWA-DANN Tardif/The Stock Market, (r)Aaron Haupt; **166** Larry Hamill; **167** Used with permission of n-vision, inc.; **174** Mark Burnett; **175** Amanita Pictures; **176** (t)Hewlett Packard, (b)Larry Hamill; **196** Kreber Studios; **207** Motorola; **222** (t)Intel, (c b)The Computer Museum, Boston; **223** (tl)Datapoint Corp., (tr)Apple Corp., (c br)Intel, (bl)VisiCalc; **224** (tl)Microsoft Corp., (tc)Used with permission of Lotus Development Corp., (tr)Bell Laboratories, (cl)IBM, (cr)Apple Corp., (hl)Hewlett Packard, (br)Intel; **225** (t)Compaq, (cl)Apple Corp., (cr)IBM, (bl)Microsoft Corp., (bc)Intel, (br)Hewlett Packard; **226** (tl)IBM, (tr)courtesy PhotoDisc. All rights reserved, (cl)IBM, (cr)Apple Corp., (bl)Shahn Kermani/ Liaison Agency, (br)Motorola; **227** (tl)Intel, (tr)Donna Covent/ MIT News Office, (c)IBM, (b)Apple Corp.; **228** (tl)Microsoft Corp., (tr)IBM, (cl)Intel, (cr)Motorola, (b)Apple Corp.; **229** (tl)Microsoft Corp., (tc)Intel, (tr)Motorola, (c)Power Computing, (b)Amanita Pictures; **230** (tl)Intel, (tr)Amanita Pictures, (bl br)Aaron Haupt; **231** (tl)Intel, (tr)Aaron Haupt, (c)Amanita Pictures, (b)Advanced Micro Devices, Inc.; **239** (t)BodyBilt Seating, (b)Doug Martin; **240** (t)Fellowes, (b)Aaron Haupt; **242** Amanita Pictures; **243** Kit Kittle/CORBIS; **246** Kensington Microware.

Screen Captures

Abbreviation Key: AV = Reproduced with the permission of AltaVista. Alta Vista and the AltaVista logo are trademarks of AltaVista Company. **COREL** = Screen shots are copyright ©Corel Corporation and Corel Corporation Limited. All rights reserved. Corel, WordPerfect, Quattro, Presentations, and Paradox are trademarks or registered trademarks of Corel Corporation or Corel Corporation Limited. Reprinted by permission. **IBM** = Courtesy International Business Machines Corporation. Unauthorized use not permitted. **LOTUS** = Screen Captures ©2001 Lotus Development Corporation. Used with permission of Lotus Development Corporation. **MS** = Screen shot reprinted by permission from Microsoft Corporation. **NET** = Netscape Communicator browser window ©1999 Netscape Communications Corporation. Used with permission. **REAL** = ©RealNetworks and/or its licensors, 1995–1999, All rights reserved. RealNetworks, RealAudio, RealPlayer, WebActive, and the RN logo are registered trademarks of RealNetworks.

xiv MS; **xvii** (t)MS, (c b)NET; **xviii** (t)MS & ©2000 USA TODAY, a division of Gannett Co. Inc., (b)NET & ©2000 sgi; **xix xx** NET; **20** Adobe; **40** MS; **41** (t)NET & ©2000 footmouse.com. All rights reserved, (b)NET & ©1999 NEC Technologies, Inc. All rights reserved; **59 61** MS; **66** MS & @Backup, SkyFiler, SmartClone, and @Backup WorkGroup Edition are all trademarked services of the SkyDesk Corporation; **71** NET; **81** MS; **82** (t)MS, (b)courtesy Apple Inc.; **88** NET & permission of Synectics Business Solutions, Inc.; **89** MS & ©1999 Artisoft Inc.; **92 93** MS; **94** LOTUS; **95** NET & COREL; **96** COREL; **97** ©2000 Inbit Incorporated. All rights reserved; **99** MS; **100** UNIX; **101** IBM; **102** MS; **103** (t)MS, (b)©2000 Falcon Networking; **105** MS; **106** (t) COREL, (b)MS; **109** COREL; **110** MS; **112** ©2000 footmouse.com. All rights reserved; **113** (t)MS, (b)LOTUS; **114** COREL; **115 116** MS; **117** (t)LOTUS, (c b)MS; **118** LOTUS; **120** MS; **121** (t)MS, (b)COREL; **122** (tl tr)COREL, (bl)MS, (br)LOTUS; **123 124** MS; **128** (t)LOTUS, (b)MS; **130** (t)COREL, (b)MS; **131** COREL; **132 133** LOTUS; **136** MS; **148** MS, **157** (tl tr)MS & ©2000 Internal Revenue Service. All rights reserved, (bl br) MS & ©2000 The White House. All rights reserved; **158** MS & © 2000 The White House. All rights reserved; **164** file photo; **165** NET & REAL; **168** ©1996–2000 PowerProduction Software Inc. All rights reserved; **169** (l)MS, (r)file photo; **170** (l)REAL, (r)MS; **171** (t)courtesy MTV, (b)MS & ©2000 Virtually VancouVR. All rights reserved; **172** (t)©2000 Cable News Network. All rights reserved & REAL, (b)MS; **174** NET; **177** Courtesy MTV; **180 181** MS; **189** (t c)NET & ©2000 ABC News Internet Ventures, (b)NS; **190** MS; **192** (l)NET & AV, (r)NET & ©2000 The White House. All rights reserved; **193** (t)REAL, (c)file photo, (b)NET; **194** AV; **198** MS; **199** MS; **200** NET; **201** MS; **202** MS & LOTUS; **211** MS & ©1999 Time Warner Cable, Inc. All rights reserved; **212** MS & Amazon.com is a registered trademark or trademark of Amazon.com, Inc. in the U.S. and/or other countries. ©2000 Amazon.com; **213** (l)MS & PC Connection and MacConnection are divisions and registered trademarks, (r)NET & AV; **214** MS & ©1999–2000 BUY.COM Inc. All rights reserved; **216** MS & LOTUS; **221** (t)WebMonkey is a registered service mark and/or trademark of Wired Ventures, Inc., a Lycos company. All rights reserved, (b)NET & ©1997–2000 Snap and its content providers. All rights reserved; **226** Novell; **228** MS; **229** ©Jeff Harrington; **232** (t)MS & ©LookSmart Ltd. Reproduced with permission of LookSmart, (b)NET& ©2000 Excite. All rights reserved; **233** MS & ©LookSmart Ltd. Reproduced with permission of LookSmart; **234** NET & Lycos® is a registered trademark of Carnegie Mellon University, licensed to Lycos, Inc.; **236** (t)MS & Used with permission of Google Inc., (b)MS & ©2000 Excite. All rights reserved; **237** (t)NET & ©2000 The Big Hub.com. All rights reserved, (b)MS; **247 248** MS.